Dan De Quille,
The Washoe Giant

Western Literature Series

Western Trails: A Collection of Short Stories by Mary Austin
selected & edited by Melody Graulich

Cactus Thorn
by Mary Austin
with foreword and afterword by Melody Graulich

Dan De Quille, the Washoe Giant: A Biography and Anthology
prepared by Richard A. Dwyer and Richard E. Lingenfelter

Western Literature Series

Dan De Quille
1829–1898

Dan De Quille, The Washoe Giant

A Biography and Anthology

prepared by

Richard A. Dwyer

and

Richard E. Lingenfelter

UNIVERSITY OF NEVADA PRESS

RENO & LAS VEGAS

University of Nevada Press, Reno, Nevada 89557 USA
Copyright © 1990 Richard A. Dwyer and Richard E. Lingenfelter
All rights reserved
Designed by David Comstock
Printed in the United States of America

Library of Congress Cataloging-in-Publication Data

Dwyer, Richard A.
Dan De Quille, the Washoe giant : a biography and
anthology /
prepared by Richard A. Dwyer and Richard E. Lingenfelter.
p.   cm.—(Western literature series)
Bibliography: p.
ISBN 0-87417-152-0 (alk. paper)
1. De Quille, Dan, 1829–1898.   2. Authors, American—19th
century—
Biography.   I. Lingenfelter, Richard E.   II. De Quille, Dan,
1829–1898.   III. Title.   IV. Series.
PS1525.D35D8 1990
818'.409—dc20   89-16584
                                    CIP

Now, if the men of my age of the world—the Comstock age—were so much inferior in stature to our first parents, was there anything strange in my appearing a giant in the eyes of people living on the earth a thousand years later than the Comstock period? I thought not.

—*Petrified! Or the Stewed Chicken Monster*

Contents

Preface

$\mathcal{D}$AN DE QUILLE (WILLIAM WRIGHT, 1829–98) was Nevada's most popular writer in the nineteenth century. A prolific and versatile storyteller and journalist, he captured for posterity much of the spirit of the western mines. His talent quickly won him the local editorship of the Virginia City *Territorial Enterprise,* which he held off and on for thirty years. But he aspired to much more and eventually gained something of a national reputation with his lively book *The Big Bonanza* and colorful sketches in magazines and Sunday supplements. In all, he left a literary legacy of well over a million words.

The Big Bonanza was reprinted by Alfred A. Knopf in 1947, and more recently by others, and chance pieces have been resurrected from time to time. Most notably, Grant Loomis and Richard Lillard revived some of De Quille's tall tales in the *California Folklore Quarterly* and the *Pacific Historical Review* in the 1940s; Duncan Emrich anthologized a few of his stories in *Comstock Bonanza* published by Vanguard in 1950; Glen Dawson reprinted *Snowshoe Thompson* in a limited edition in 1954; Westernlore Press printed his book-length *Washoe Rambles* in 1963; and the Book Club of California recently published in a limited edition an odd batch of manuscripts, found in the California Historical Society collection, as *Dan De Quille of the Big*

Bonanza (1980). Now, Lawrence I. Berkove has issued one of the manuscripts in Berkeley's Bancroft Library.

Despite these efforts, much of De Quille's best writing still lies nearly forgotten in the pages of scattered newspapers and magazines, all but lost to readers today.

To right this wrong to William Wright, we have assayed the wealth of his writing in the files of the *Golden Era,* the *Territorial Enterprise,* and many other papers and magazines, as well as his own extensive collection of clippings and manuscripts in the Bancroft Library. From this bonanza we have extracted rich nuggets of his best and most entertaining work for a new generation of readers. We include his tall tales and hoaxes, such as "Silver Man" and "Solar Armor," outrageous tales such as "The New Rock of Horeb," personal adventures, comic sketches, ghostly mysteries, and romantic stories. To give some perspective on these works, as well as the man and his times, we have added a biographical sketch, based on his letters and other new findings, and some discussion of Wright's works. We have also undertaken, perhaps vainly, to compile a checklist of all his imaginative writings, to which we anticipate many additions will be made.

For their generous aid in gathering these materials and for granting permission to reproduce them, we thank the Bancroft Library of the University of California, and especially Irene Moran, the California Historical Society, Lee Mortensen of the Nevada Historical Society, and Robert Blesse of Getchell Library at the University of Nevada-Reno.

The Washoe Giant

PICTURE THIS. ON A WINDY STREET CORNER in Virginia City, Nevada, in the early 1860s, flamboyant Mark Twain stands bathed in sunlight and, lagging a bit behind and definitely in his shadow, is genial Dan De Quille. Such an image is readily conjurable to most of those who have even heard of De Quille, whose fairly constant fortune it has been to be compared with America's greatest humorist. But De Quille and his work are well worth looking at in their own right. In what follows we explore both man and work, and we find sharp contrasts between the writer who considered himself the Washoe Giant and his current pale image. But first we trace the evolution of that picture.

The earliest images of De Quille are, in fact, at odds with the prevailing consensus. The comparison of Twain and De Quille used to go the other way, as Albert Bigelow Paine found in the course of assembling *Mark Twain: A Biography*. He corresponded with Twain's former boss on the Virginia City *Territorial Enterprise,* Joseph T. Goodman, about the first flush days of the Comstock mining excitement. Paine was especially interested in the relationship between Twain and his senior partner in local reporting, Dan De Quille. Goodman was frank:

> If I had been asked to prophesy which of the two men, Dan De
> Quille or Sam, would become distinguished, I should have said De

3

Quille. Dan was talented, industrious, and, for that time and place, brilliant. Of course, I recognized the unusualness of Sam's gifts, but he was eccentric and seemed to lack industry; it is not likely that I should have prophesied fame for him then.   (v. I, p. 216)

Goodman's judgment was echoed by that of Judge C. C. Goodwin, another early associate of both Twain and De Quille. He wrote: When "Mark Twain was a reporter with Dan De Quille, the latter had much more power than Twain and was of vast service to him, for in those days Mark was unseasoned in newspaper work and more or less uncouth" (Lura Wright's manuscript, p. 3, Bancroft Library, Box 3).

These contemporaries, Joe Goodman and Judge Goodwin, along with Wells Drury and a couple of others, are responsible for developing this initial contrast in expectation into something like the fable of the ant and the grasshopper: steady, pedestrian De Quille versus the prodigal Twain. Subsequent commentary has evolved toward the current consensus of faint praise for De Quille. The present state of the fable is probably best presented by Paul Fatout, who concludes that De Quille

> was a man of mild disposition and placid temper that made him a stabilizer, a sort of presiding genius or mentor of the whole unruly crew. A model craftsman, he practiced methodical work habits and exercised a meticulous care for accuracy. Because he was shy, gentle, loath to offend, his humorous pieces, which he called "quaints," were droll, whimsical, puckish, sometimes mildly sentimental. At the same time he was the best known, best liked, and most promising writer on the paper, having published many sketches in the *Golden Era* and attracted the attention of the New York *Knickerbocker Magazine*. Nevertheless, he made no effort to seek a national audience; contented with his berth in Virginia, he remained there until the *Enterprise* died in 1893.
>
> (*Mark Twain in Virginia City*, p. 33)

This image, however, stands in sharp contradiction to contemporary accounts of the man: that shy, gentle Quaker seems to have gotten into a number of barroom fights; that steady, contented worker was fired repeatedly because he got too drunk to write a word; that honest, incorruptible mining reporter took gifts of stock for favorable publicity and wrote not a word about the frauds, mismanagement, and manipulation of the major mining stocks; that solid citizen and sensitive spirit all but abandoned his wife and family for the better part of forty years. The contradictions abound and challenge the easy contrasts of the legend. There is much to unravel.

One place to begin is with a look at what the legend of Dan De Quille does *not* include. He is pictured almost wholly within the framework of Virginia City and his career on the *Territorial Enterprise*. That is, little is said about the other three significant periods of his life—his youth in Ohio and early maturity in Iowa, for instance, during which he married and fathered five children. It was in this first life, amid his extended family and lasting till he was nearly thirty, that he received the literary and religious schooling and acquired the habits of work and self-discipline upon which his later life was founded. Here, too, he first felt those constraints against which he later struggled at great personal cost. The legend also says little about the adventurous life he led in the West from his overland trek in 1857 until he went to work for Joe Goodman in 1862. But this period of great expectations, both in prospecting and in writing, set the stage for those glowing estimates by his contemporaries about his future. Only after these two formative periods did he settle into full-time newspaper work. Only then did he encounter Mark Twain and his effortless charm. And only then did De Quille begin to drink heavily, get into fights, and otherwise strain against his fate. Finally, after more than twenty years in journalistic harness, Dan De Quille entered the last period of his life unexamined in the legend—the extensive episodes of rustication from the *Enterprise* during which, with some of his family once more about him, he wrote prodigiously on topics as remote from the Comstock as he could imagine.

In the biographical sketch that follows, we will focus on those portions of his life, early and late, spent outside of the shadow of Twain, trying to fathom Dan De Quille's struggle for contentment with his toil through the waning years of Nevada's silver age.

Firm Foundation

I have Quaker uncles and I am proud of them. I have Quaker aunts and I glory in them. I have Quaker cousins and I—love them; especially the demure, rosy-cheeked little Quakeresses.

My father was a Quaker; my grandfather was a Quaker; my great grandfather was a Quaker; and my great great grandfather was a Quaker and came over and settled, did old Anthony, with Penn in Pennsylvania.

After the division in the Society of Friends, which took place in 1827, my people were Hicksites, that is, followers of the doctrine of Elias Hicks, who, while he professed the religion of Fox, adopted the theology of William Penn.

Penn's *Sandy Foundation Shaken,* in its black, time-worn cover, is one of the first books of which I have any recollection. It was to be found in the libraries of all my uncles on my father's side of the house.   (GE, July 31, 1864)

Thus William Wright fondly recalled the association of family, discipline, and books that later sustained him throughout a long, productive, and often turbulent life as a journalist on Nevada's Comstock Lode, a world away from these foundations.

Knox County lies in central Ohio along the Kokosing River, and it was there that the Wright family emigrated when the region was still a wilderness. On Will's mother's side, the Presbyterian Markleys settled in Knox County as well, after leaving the north of Ireland and living for a time in Philadelphia. Of the nine children of Paxton and Lucy Wright, William was the first, born on May 9, 1829. He spent his first eighteen years in Knox County and later characterized the region and its religion with both affection and tension in a story called "Eloping with a Quakeress." Wright recalled the old brick church that stood on the edge of the back woods, two miles north of Fredericktown—how the profound silence of the meditation periods wrestled with his boyish restlessness:

I used often to wonder what would be my fate if I should happen for a moment to forget myself and give a sudden yell. I would think on this till it seemed as though I must yell in spite of myself; the more I tried to keep from thinking of it, the more I would think, and at last would be forced to put my hand over my mouth for fear I should shout inspite of all my exertions to remain silent—so oppressive was the profound stillness."   (GE, November 6, 1864)

Wright also recalled his childhood introduction to literature in a later letter to his sister Lou:

Just here I desire to tell you something which will delight you. I have a very distinct recollection of sitting with my hands resting upon the knees of our father, long before you were born, in the old cabin home in Ohio, listening to him as he read aloud *Sketches by Boz,* as they came to us week after week in the old Philadelphia *Atheneum,* a literary weekly newspaper. This was when Dickens was only known as 'Boz.' Father had a keen appreciation of the humorous and was delighted with the sketches. He was also much pleased with the sketches of Major Jack Downing, a satirical political humorist, now out of date, somewhat after the Nasby style. Our one novel, the only one we possessed at that time was James Fenimore Cooper's second sea tale, the *Red Rover,* published in 1827. It was a much-borrowed and much-abused book. It was always going among the neighbors—it was indeed a 'rover.' It at last became necessary to give it new backs of country-tanned calf-skin. Then the leaves began to go. At last we became quite 'short' on Red Rover, but still what then was left of it was in brisk demand. I think some of its readers must have literally devoured it. It used to travel miles away and be gone six or eight months coming home at last terribly worried, but the very next day some-one would come to the house to know—"has your *Red Rover* got home yet?" I am thus particular about this book because it was the only novel that the family possessed in its early history.

(William Wright, letter to his sister Lou, June 14, 1874)

In 1847, when Will Wright was eighteen, his family pulled up stakes and moved west—to Iowa. They settled in Muscatine County near West Liberty, on the overland trail about fifteen miles east of Iowa City. At that time the village consisted of five houses and the Eagle Hotel, about a mile east of Wapinoenoc Creek. Will's father died soon after the move, and the duties of the head of the household fell on him. In 1853, at the age of twenty-four, he married Caroline Coleman and took up residence nearby on a farm given him by an uncle. Over the next four years they had five children, two of whom died in infancy. But Will's son Paxton and daughters Mell and Lura survived him.

Looking back on those Iowa days from Washoe four years later, Will rhapsodized:

Put the western man upon the arid wastes and rugged, barren hills of Washoe, with the fierce heat of the meridian sun beating upon his head, and the blaze of its refracted rays flashing and darting into his face, and his thoughts turn on—*corn.* Don't laugh. He don't think of corn cakes, or ripe fields of corn, but of the green, waving, dense acres of the unripe plant—before the tassles have dropped their golden showers of fructifying pollen. Often, when toiling over some rocky, burning mountain, or traversing some fiery desert, have I mentioned to my companions the cornfields of

the West; asking—"How would you like to be there?" "Oh! that I were there—Oh! that I could crawl underneath the green awning of arched rows and stretch myself on the cool ground, breathing again the fresh, delicious perfume, so well remembered and more grateful than the odors wafted on the breezes from the Western Isles!" All this may appear very far-fetched to my home-abiding readers. They may be unable to discern or appreciate any great degree of the beauty, and, perhaps, none of the poetry of—corn! Indeed, I fear they may consider what I have said above as being merely intended as "a big thing on Snyder." But let these *hombres* pass one year on these sterile plains and hills, and we shall hear them sigh, if not for the mush-pot, for the cornfields of the West.
(Letter from Dan De Quille, CFG, September 13, 1861)

While in Iowa, Will Wright began to develop some sort of literary ambitions. His daughter Lura says his first writing was done for the county school lyceum and that later he wrote letters and sketches for the local Iowa papers. In a note in one of his scrapbooks, Will says of a clipping, "I wrote this item in 1856 in Iowa, found it in 1868 going around California." The attached clipping reads:

An indian requested an agent in Northern Iowa to furnish him with whiskey for a young warrior who had been bitten by a rattlesnake, intimating that four quarts would be necessary. "Four quarts!" repeated the agent with surprise, "much as that?" "Yes," replied the indian, "four quarts—snake very big."
(William Wright Papers scrapbook, folder 120)

Wright is also said to have sent a piece to Charles Godfrey Leland, editor of *Graham's Illustrated Magazine,* and received encouragement. But the West was in the air in the dozen years between the discovery of gold in California and the coming of the Civil War. Thousands of perfectly dutiful family men bid what they thought would be a temporary good-bye to their loved ones and headed west to rough it in search of fortune and adventure. Leaving his own stakes firmly in place, Will Wright and his brother Hank went a'roving. It would be forty years before the rover would get home again for good.

Great Expectations

Will Wright arrived late in the gold regions of California. Over the previous decade the world had rushed in, roiled about, and settled down to large-scale placer and hard-rock mining, interspersed with colonies of serious Chinese gleaners. The major excitement of 1857 was the "East Belt" rush around Tuolumne, somewhat similar in structure to the Mother Lode ten miles west. Wright seems to have looked this scene over before moving up to the northern mines and the region around the South Yuba River in Nevada County.

Not far below the headwaters of the South Yuba, Scotchman Creek joins it. Facing each other on its banks were the camps of Alpha and Omega, the latter originally called Delirium Tremens. From the base of Omega, Wright toured and prospected on his own and in the company of several small groups in the northern mines, the Mother Lode, and as far south as the Mono Lake region on the eastern slope of the Sierra. It was also from this base that he and his brother Hank embarked on hunting expeditions to the Sacramento Delta in the winter of 1857–58. Wright saved memories of the hunting trips for reminiscences not to be published until the nineties, but he reported immediately on the prospecting tour in a letter to his brother-in-law, Dr. J. M. Benjamin, in January of 1860:

> We are still stopping at this sweet-scented little place but are not making much over 'grub.' R. M. Cameron is here cabining with us—he is not particularly in love with the country and don't think of marrying here. He talks a good deal of what Old Ben would say to this and that thing. Bob has got so fat that he looks the very picture of "a middle aged gentleman in easy circumstances." He is heavy on boiled cabbage. You should have seen the amount of that succulent vegetable he mowed away for dinner today. Hank, also, is fattening up, but as for me—think of the fattest alderman you ever read of, cheeks hanging over his shoulders, stomach resting on his knees, legs like an elephant and an arm like a joint of stovepipe, and even then you can't begin to imagine how fat I am. I have to sleep in two beds and then am nearly froze.

Having indulged in self-caricature, De Quille goes on to spoof the genre of romantic travelers' tales:

> I have been running about some this last fall. I traveled about a thousand miles on foot through the Southern Mines and over the mountains into Utah. We had a pony to carry our blankets and camping utensils while we took it on foot and 'driv the hoss.' I can assure you it was *highly romantic* to see five lusty hombres straggling through the country after a little old crowbait of a pony, packed with bags, bundles, frying-pans and blankets till nothing

but [the] end of his nose and the tip of his tail was visible. Then part of the time the mud was knee deep and the rain would pour down for a week straight ahead, then snow and rain and rain and hail. The ravines and small creeks would rise and these we would have to haul off our boots and wade—the water so cold it cut like a knife. Then "how romantic" to camp out on such nights and bake bread and get supper. Then after getting to bed and just when the rain was coming down by pailfulls and the wind blowing a hurricane, over goes the tent and we rush out to set it up—get it nearly up and a puff takes it from us, some of the pegs pull up and some of the ropes break and away the ——d thing goes, fluttering and pitching down the hill with five half naked and distracted hombres in full chase. I know it sounds "very romantic" to hear men tell how they done their own washing and mending, baked their own bread and slapjacks and all that kind of thing, but the fun of it is all in your eye after the first week.

But things were not always bad, and De Quille goes overboard in the opposite direction of glamorizing the West:

On going down we had good weather and enjoyed our trip as well as men could under the circumstances. We started early or late in the morning, just as we felt like doing, went as far as we pleased and stopped where we pleased—went into all the peach orchards we found, and stuffed ourselves at the vineyards to the degree that we were unable to travel more than eight to ten miles per day, and sometimes when the peaches were *very* good, only two miles of an afternoon. Then we had to stop and jaw all the Diggers we saw and put off jokes on the John Chinamen. We went to see everything worth seeing which we could hear of—saw the Big Trees, the great cave in Calaveras Co., the Bower cave in Tuolumne Co., Sutter's "Old Mill" (or the placer where it was, as there is nothing left of it now) at Coloma, where the first gold was found—had a peep at Yo Semite falls, crossed the summit of the Sierra Nevada mountains and slept on it in a snow-storm without a tent or other covering than blanket, and our softest lullabye was the growl of a grizzly or the rush of an avalanche. We floated on the waters of that "Dead Sea" called Mono Lake and went down the Mono Pass, where jack-mules are lowered from rock to rock by the tail, with a rope or windlass—but notwithstanding Cedar Falls is not a bad place—much wano por Melican man—aqui poco tempo! mucha malo, me no caree.

Finally, De Quille shifts into imaginative high gear and starts telling whoppers:

> You have heard, no doubt, of the *Big Trees*—but you can form no idea of their size without visiting them. Why, Ben if one of the smallest of them was standing in the street in front of Bishop's drug store, and it should be cut down, the butt of it would be lying on the ground so long as to be *perfectly rotten* before the top got to the ground. A large tree, called the "Father of the Forest," from its immense size is supposed to have been blown up by the roots about the time of the big blow on the Cedar Falls & Minnesota R.R. and the top of it lacked about four feet of being on the ground when we got there. Then there is a hollow one—called the "Horseback Ride"—from the fact that people are in the habit of riding through it on horseback. I saw a man start to ride through it on a horse thirty-seven hands high, on the keen lope, and he would have gone through slick enough if his horse had not scared at some men, who were about the middle of the log, raising a liberty pole with an American flag on the top, and jumped out at a knot hole. These stories may look large to folks back there, but I can't help it. They were not near so big when I first wrote them, but this infernal climate is so moist I see they have swelled a good deal since.

Wright's adventures in camping out over four successive seasons from 1858 to 1861 led him from the Sacramento Delta to Yosemite and the eastern slope of the Sierra, to the western portion of the Utah (later Nevada) Territory and the sinks of the Carson and Humboldt rivers. These hunting, prospecting, and sightseeing expeditions gave him material for more than casual letters home, though these reveal a knack for anecdote and humorous exaggeration. Will Wright also began to submit more polished pieces to both hometown and western papers under the pseudonym *Dan De Quille*. In picking this monicker, he was not only punning on his real name and chosen profession, he was bidding to compete with such other American humorists who called themselves Petroleum V. Nasby, Artemus Ward, and Orpheus C. Kerr among others.

In his literary prospecting, De Quille struck pay dirt with the *Golden Era*. The editors and proprietors of this San Francisco weekly, Joseph E. Lawrence and James Brooks, maintained a stable of about forty steady contributors. Of them all, Dan De Quille came to enjoy their greatest favor. By the fall of 1860 they were publishing one of his letters or literary pieces almost every week and they continued doing so through the spring of 1862 when he went to work for the *Enterprise*.

Early in June of 1860, after the Paiute War was concluded in favor of the growing white population, De Quille joined the rush to Washoe and became the *Golden Era*'s regular correspondent from the new mines. His letters contained not only the highlights of the local news, but vivid, often comic, sketches of life in the mines that still make lively reading today, as the samples presented later show. In addition to his correspondence, he occasionally sent along more intentionally literary pieces, of which "Another Strike" and "No Wife nor Mother's Care" withstand best the test of time. From Washoe, Dan also set out on prospecting expeditions to outlying districts. One trip to the east across the Carson Sink and up to a camp called Silver Hill in the summer of 1861 provided him with enough material for a book-length series of articles entitled "Washoe Rambles," which has been suggested as a model for Mark Twain's *Roughing It*.

In these early writings, De Quille was blazing a trail, amounting to an apprenticeship, that took him from letters to newsletters, news articles, and features, to sketches and more elaborate fiction. Although his progress was uneven and some of his sketches, such as his archaic portraits of "Ye California Miner," "Ye Chinaman," and others, are hard reading today, they were well received at the time. Indeed, by the fall of 1861, the *Golden Era* editors wrote:

> During more than a year past, the columns of the *Golden Era* have given constant proof of the genial, generous and noble qualities which distinguish our correspondent, "Dan De Quille." His contributions are always of the most acceptable order. They are characterized by a fresh, vigorous and unaffected style, an unfailing fund of humor, a fertile fancy, and a comprehensive knowledge of human nature, acquired in a life of varied experience and adventurous self-reliance. His comic sketches are widely copied and entitle the author to rank among the cleverest wits of the day. More agreeable or entertaining sketches of travel than the "Washoe Rambles" would be difficult to mention. In the realm of romance also, Dan De Quille is equally at home. His characteristics as a writer, *eminently western and Californian,* are already impressed upon the literature of the Pacific coast. (GE, September 15, 1861)

De Quille was also working hard to enlarge that impression, and half a year later the *Era* editors proudly noted:

> Far and wide are Dan De Quille's stories and sketches, his notes of travel, quaint conceptions and sober suggestions, copied, commended, and spread abroad through the land. In the generosity of his literary dispensations, our long-time faithful and cherished contributor presents himself regularly in the columns of the principal paper published in Nevada Territory—his principal place of residence—while his letters find their way every week to the Cedar Falls *Gazette,* printed in his former home—in Iowa—out West.
>
> Nor do these journals fill up the field over which his labors are so liberally extended, for in the New York *Knickerbocker,* of January, 1862, a cordial greeting and prominent place in the "Editor's Table," are given to Dan De Quille's "Knick and Mace in Washoe," a delightful article, richly worthy of type-life in that old established and widely known periodical.   (GE, March 9, 1862)

The *Knickerbocker Magazine* promoted a national literature, mingling the contributions of established writers with those of the rising generation. For it, Dan wrote a fantasy in which he drops in at the Book and Periodical Depot, Silver City, and runs into the personification of the magazine, Old Knick in his bright coat, and holds a friendly conversation with the journal. He tells about his current life in Washoe and then reveals a bit about his earlier pseudonyms:

> I once was "M.S. (Milton Shakespeare) Dobbs," once "Picaroon Pax," once "Ebenezer Queerkut," and once—but enough! I blush to look at this formidable list of aliases. It really does look suspicious and might go far to convict the most innocent person that ever paced this mundane sphere, let alone one who has murdered—both old poetry and prose. Thank Heaven, I can look Knick in the face. He knows nothing of Dobbs, or Pax, or "Aitch See Kay."

The *Knickerbocker* editor responded in the same issue with some flattering banter of his own and concluded with this invitation:

> We incline to you De Quille and know you, O man of many names, for one who hath wit into him and a heart. Come again from foreign lands, O thou Master Trougemone, to whom full seventy lands are known, man who playest on 'coyotes' and 'can-

13

ons' and 'gulches' and all the other musical instruments peculiar to California, and sing us thy songs.   (K, January 1862)

A couple of other contributions to the *Golden Era* in this period show the direction in which De Quille might have gone as a writer had not a fortunate fate soon drawn him to the *Enterprise.* These were serialized romances. The first, "Tom Bently, or Love, Art and Gold," started out as a comedy in pseudo-Irish dialect and moved toward sentimentality and didacticism. The other, "Orthon, the Familiar spirit, or, the Invisible Bride," set in medieval France, seems truly awful stuff today. But *Era* readers loved them both. The editors even printed a fan's mash note to Dan in response to the first:

> Now Dan De Quille, you are the man,
>   You are the man, dear Quille;
> Your image is before me, Dan,
>   You've made my bosom thrill.
>
> I've read your story, Dan, my boy,
>   You well describe each hill;
> You never say a word too coy—,
>   You do not, Mister Quille.
>
> You tell of love, as well you can,
>   Of gold, quartz rock and mill;
> Of panning out the dirt, dear Dan,
>   And writing with your quill.
>
> Your tale I think of, night and day,
>   It is a theme which fills
> My heart and soul with spirits gay;
>   You're a dear one, Mister Quille.
>
>   (GE, May 4, 1862)

The affection was mutual, as Dan himself responded: "Not a day, friend Era, but I think of you or some of your numerous and agreeable family, many of whom gave their first timid chirp in the world of letters from under the generous shelter of your broad, protecting wings. Yes, I think I love you all" (GE, April 13, 1862). What De Quille's Comstock companions, including Twain, would think of such stuff we will consider later in this discussion.

The other literary event that helps us see De Quille's self-conception at this time concerns the publication in *Harper's* from December 1860 to February 1861 of J. Ross Browne's "A Peep at Washoe." Although Dan affects never to have heard of him, Browne was a well-known world traveler and humorist. As both a writer and a resident of the Comstock, De Quille objected to Browne's breezy sketch of the region:

> The impression left on the mind of the reader of Browne's "Peep" is that there may be a few tons of good silver ore in the Comstock, but owing to the poisonous nature of the water, the terrible storms of wind, rain and snow, the fact that there is nothing to live on but brandy and gin, and the general meanness of the country, that it would be impossible for human beings to exist in Washoe, and the reader is ready to conclude that when J. Ross Browne left, everybody that could get away followed suit, and, in fact, had there been none here with better 'grit' than J. R. B. possessed, the chatter of eight quartz mills would not be singing in my ears at the present moment. But Ross is now wandering in Germany writing letters for the Sacramento *Union* and I will say to him and his "Peep"— *adios!*

But Browne stuck in his mind, and, after reporting further on mining matters to readers of the *Gazette,* De Quille was moved to comment on his own literary ambitions:

> I wish it to be understood that in these letters I do not aim at penetrating to a depth exceeding six miles into any particular subject, nor do I endeavor to rival the elegance, correctness, and brilliancy of literary stars of the first magnitude. I am content to glimmer in a dusky corner of the literary firmament, somewhere between Dickens and Thackeray, and would not desire to blaze alongside of such transcendant lights as Sylvanus Snobb or Bub Nedline.   (CFG, May 17, 1861)

Although this passage was written with tongue firmly in cheek, it seems important that Dan here comes down on the side of literature as opposed to the mere popularity of such bestsellers as Sylvanus Cobb and Ned Buntline (Edward Judson), who had started out as a contributor to the *Knickerbocker* and wound up producing over two hundred dime novels.

Thus, in these years of 1860, '61, and '62, Dan De Quille made a number of strokes toward a self-portrait as a western man of letters. The great volume of his writing and its variety, the high level of journals to which he contributed, and the interest he expressed in the profession of writing and the careers of other writers all suggest that he saw himself as a contender, in the running for the role of author, albeit in the rocky hills of Washoe.

Salad Days

While Dan De Quille was busy shipping off manuscripts by weekly stages east and west—letters to the *Gazette* and sketches to the *Golden Era*—he was also inching his way toward Virginia City. But just as he had arrived too late in California for the gold rush, he dawdled as well on his way to the great Comstock silver excitement. He seems to have lingered at Johntown at the foot of the Virginia Range and moved successively uphill to Silver City and then Gold Hill, where he worked for a while in the Yellow Jacket mine. This kind of regular employment put food on the table, but he was contributing in earnest to such papers as the *Washoe Times,* in whose opener he appeared (March 16, 1861), and the *Silver Age,* published at the time in Carson City until its proprietors also moved with the crowd up to Virginia the following year to start the *Daily Union.*

The quality of De Quille's writing, particularly in the *Golden Era,* caught the eye of the owners of the daily *Territorial Enterprise,* Joseph T. Goodman and Denis McCarthy, and their editor, Rollin M. Daggett, who invited him aboard in June of 1862. As well as being able to use steady work, he seems to have thought he could use his columns of local reporting as a kind of notebook to nourish more formal publication in the magazines and eventual books. He did not foresee that the job would use him up over the next thirty years.

Just six months after he landed his job on the *Enterprise,* he took off for Iowa on a visit that lasted eight months. He had been planning the visit even before he got the job, however, and these plans may have prompted the paper's owners to offer a similar job to Samuel Clemens, who had been sending in correspondence from Aurora and vainly angling for a post with the Sacramento *Union.* By August anyway, the two of them were making the rounds and knocking out both real and fictitious copy.

The story of their intimate association, off and on for the next two years, is amusingly told in De Quille's sketches and reminiscences in the selections. Their association has also been studied by Albert Bigelow Paine, Edgar Branch, and a number of later scholars. We will confine ourselves here to interpreting it from a different perspective. The first part of their companionship, before Dan actually did leave

Nevada for a visit home, has been seen as that between mentor and pupil in the consensus view. But in the following send-off by Clemens, there is much patronizing lurking amid the affectionate rhetoric:

> Old Dan is gone, that good old soul, we ne'er shall see him more—for some time. He left for Carson yesterday, to be duly stamped and shipped to America, by way of the United States Overland Mail. As the stage was on the point of weighing anchor, the senior editor dashed wildly into Wasserman's and captured a national flag, which he cast about Dan's person to the tune of three rousing cheers from the bystanders. So, with the gorgeous drapery floating behind him, our kind and genial hero passed from sight; and if fervent prayers from us, who seldom pray, can avail, his journey will be as safe and happy as though ministering angels watched over him. Dan has gone to the States for his health, and his family. He worked himself down in creating big strikes in the mines and keeping all the mills in this district going, whether their owners were willing or not. These herculean labors gradually undermined his health, but he went bravely on, and we are proud to say that as far as these things were concerned, he never gave up—the miners never did, and never could have conquered him. He fell under a scarcity of pack-trains and haywagons. These had been the bulwark of the local column; his confidence in them was like unto that which men have in four aces; murders, robberies, fires, distinguished arrivals were creatures of chance, which might or might not occur at any moment; but the pack-trains and the haywagons were certain, predestined, immutable! When these failed last week, he said *"Et tu Brute,"* and gave us his pen. His constitution suddenly warped, split and went under, and Daniel succumbed. We have a saving hope, though, that his trip across the Plains, through eighteen hundred miles of cheerful haystacks, will so restore our loved and lost to his ancient health and energy, that when he returns next fall he will be able to run our five hundred mills as easily as he used to keep five score moving. Dan is gone, but he departed in a blaze of glory, the like of which hath hardly been seen upon this earth since the blameless Elijah went up in his fiery chariot.   (TE, December 28, 1862)

De Quille's trip, in fact, had more of a literary touch than Clemens allowed. It took him by way of Salt Lake City where he stayed with Thomas and Fanny Stenhouse, both writers and critics of Mormon life who were to stay in contact with Dan in later years. De Quille spent about six months in Iowa visiting family and friends he had not seen in six years and quickly discovering that he had become "in some degree a stranger." Soon he was complaining about how "exceedingly dull" the old place was and turned to writing occasional pieces for the local papers to while away the days. By the time summer came he had had his fill of home and set out for New York, and from there in early August he sailed on the *North Star* to take the Panama route back west. He reached San Francisco later that month and went straight to the *Golden Era* office to reestablish himself as the "Washoe Giant" in a delightful fantasy called "Petrified, or the Stewed Chicken Monster," which he had cooked up enroute.

While De Quille was away, Clemens, who had begun to write under the name of Mark Twain, not only filled in as local reporter on the *Enterprise,* he began to develop San Francisco connections as well. In the company of Clement "The Unreliable" Rice of the rival *Union,* Twain took extended visits to the Bay and started submitting letters to the *Morning Call* and the *Golden Era.* De Quille returned to Virginia City on September 5, and a lively rivalry began with Mark Twain in the *Enterprise* the very next day, when the following locals appeared:

> "Dan De Quille"—This gentleman arrived yesterday from San Francisco, looking in due health and spirits. After recovering from the fatigue of the journey he will resume his labors on the columns of this paper. His host of friends will be pleased to hear of his return.
>
> Mark Twain.—This individual started for San Francisco yesterday. During his absence the moral tone of this column will be much improved. It could not be otherwise.

The *Golden Era* editors took their stand two weeks later, putting a piece by De Quille on the first page and one by Twain on the last— but that would soon change. Sharing a room in Daggett and Myers's boardinghouse only heightened the rivalry between the two men, and De Quille soon made their high jinks the subject of a piece for the *Golden Era* entitled "No Head nor Tail."

At the same time, De Quille was caught up in a somewhat schizophrenic internal struggle as he tried to combine writing for the genteel tastes of the San Francisco literati with working among drunks, blowhards, and practical jokers. All these tensions and differences between the two men, their lifestyles and their associated writing styles, climaxed in the birth of the *Occidental*—Washoe's aspiring literary journal. Only a couple of selections survive from it (and an account of a collective writing scheme), but these are enough to show the antithetical directions in which Dan was being pulled. One of his own contributions was a rapturously lyrical piece called "Lost in the Sierras." A sample: "Dull is the boom of the snow falling from the tops of the lofty pines; a lonely grouse is startled and flies across to an opposite mountain, with a din that echoes far up and down the canyon. Now all is still: where is he who is lost so high up the mountain? Ominous, sad, is the stillness. See, he lies with his face on his arms—his breast against the snow" (GE, March 27, 1864). At the other extreme is the version of the original romantic novel on which the novelists were to collaborate as hilariously told in Twain's *Roughing It.* There is probably enough poetic truth in his mockery of the "feeble, struggling, stupid journal" to convict its disputatious makers.

The other direction in which Dan was being pulled was anything but literary. Unfortunately, his local reporting during the early 1860s is known mainly from reprints in other papers, only scattered issues of the *Enterprise* having survived from that period. But there are some samples of the kind of raillery, banter, and tasteless comedy in which the whole troupe of Washoe newsmen habitually engaged. As a classic example, here is De Quille's half of his contest with Twain in providing readers of the *Enterprise* with hair-raising accounts of fictitious calamities:

We may have said some harsh things of Mark Twain, but now we take them all back. We feel like weeping for him—yea, we would fall on his breast and mingle our tears with his'n. But those manly shirt front of his air now a bloody one, and his nose is swollen to such an extent that to fall on his breast would be an utter impossibility. Yesterday, he brought back all our things and promised us that he intended hereafter to lead a virtuous life. This was in the forenoon; in the afternoon he commenced the career of virtue he had marked out for himself and took a first lesson in boxing. Once he had the big gloves on, he imagined that he weighed a ton and could whip his weight in Greek-fire. He waded into a professor of the 'manly art' like one of Howlan's rotary batteries, and the professor, in a playful way he has when he wants to take the conceit out of forward pupils, let one fly straight out from the shoulder and busted Mr. Twain in the snoot, sending him reeling—not exactly to grass, but across a bench—with two bountiful streams of claret spouting from his nostrils. At first his nose was smashed out till it covered nearly the whole of his face and looked like a large piece of tripe, but it was finally scraped into some resemblance of a nose, when he rushed away for surgical advice. Pools of gore covered the floor of the Club Room where he fought, and he left a bloody trail for half a mile through the city. It is estimated that he lost several hogsheads of blood in all. He procured a lot of sugar of lead and other cooling lotions and spent the balance of the day in applying them with towels and sponges. After dark, he ventured forth with his nose swollen to the size of several junk bottles—a vast, inflamed and pulpy old snoot—to get advice about having it amputated. None of his friends recognize him now, and he spends his time in solitude, contemplating his ponderous vermillion smeller in a two bit mirror, which he bought for that purpose. We cannot comfort him, for we know his nose will never be a nose again. It was always somewhat lopsided; now it is a perfect lump of blubber. Since the above was in type, the doctors have decided to amputate poor Mark's smeller. A new one is to be made for him of a quarter of veal. (GE, May 1, 1864)

Horseplay though this is, people do not generally wish such mutilation on each other without drawing on some underlying tensions. For Twain, this rage for overdoing it was not long in coming to a head. He first got into trouble with his audience for his account of the "Sanitary Ball," intimating that its proceeds would be sent to foster interracial marriage in the East. And the climax of his brief Comstock career came with his notorious "Massacre at Dutch Nick's," in which the clues to the hoax were overwhelmed by the tasteless details of blood and guts. In the end, the best solution was simply to blow town and head for the Bay. This time, the Gold Hill *News* wrote the send-off, echoing the collective groans of the other Washoe papers:

Those groans were not for the *Enterprise* in the abstract, but for the *Enterprise* as the vehicle of Mark Twain's abominations. He has vamosed, cut stick, absquatulated; and among the pine forests of the Sierras, or amid the purlieus of the city of earthquakes, he will tarry awhile, and the office of the *Enterprise* will become purified, and by the united efforts of Goodman and Dan De Quille once more merit the sweet smiles of the ladies of Carson.

(GHN, May 30, 1864)

The problem with this prediction seems to have been that contact with the bonny Twain, as well as the local thirst for copy in "the horrible style," rendered Dan less fit to continue cultivating those sweet smiles. His production of saccharine romances dropped off as he concentrated on delivering the local reports, spiced with the occasional hoaxes and tall tales for which he is now best remembered. The earliest and one of his best, "The Wonder of the Age—A Silver Man," written several months after Twain left, is reprinted among our selections. "Traveling Stones," written a few years later and one of his most widely copied hoaxes, shows the narrow path he trod in that genre:

A gentleman from the southern part of Pahranagat, who passed through this city a day or two since on his way to Sacramento, Cal., showed us a half a dozen or so of very curious pebbles—not curious in appearance, but rather curious in action. They were almost perfectly round, the majority of them nearly as large as a black walnut, and appeared to be of an irony nature. About the only remarkable thing about these pebbles—and it struck us as rather remarkable—was that when distributed about upon a floor, table or other level surface, within two or three feet of each other, they immediately began traveling toward a common centre and there huddled up in a bunch like a lot of eggs in a nest. A single stone, removed to the distance of three and a half feet, upon being released at once started off with wonderful and somewhat comical celerity to rejoin its fellows; taken away four or five feet it remained motionless. Mr. Hart, the gentleman in whose possession we saw these rolling stones, says they are found in a region of country that, although comparatively level, is nothing but bare rock. Scattered over this barren region are little basins, from a few feet to a rod or two in diameter, and it is in the bottom of these that the rolling stones are found. They are from the size of a pea to five and six inches in diameter. The cause of these stones rolling together is doubtless to be found in the material of which they are composed, which appears to be loadstone or magnetic iron ore.

(TE, October 26, 1867)

This slight piece was copied by papers far and wide and brought a deluge of letters requesting some of the curious stones. It is said even the great P. T. Barnum wrote to offer $10,000 if they could be made to perform under a circus tent. Dan retold the tale in print himself a number of times and eventually included it in his *Big Bonanza*. That brought a new onslaught of inquiry and he finally confessed in feigned disgust:

The story of the little traveling stones seemed to supply a want that had long been felt—to fit exactly and fill a certain vacant nook in the minds of men—and they traveled through all the newspapers of the world. This we did not so much mind, nor were we much worried by letters of inquiry at first, but it has now been some years since we ceased to enjoy them. First and last, we must have had bushels of letters asking about these stones. Letter after letter have we opened from foreign parts in the expectation of hearing something to our advantage—that half a million had been left us somewhere or that somebody was anxious to pay us four bits a column for sketches about the mountains and the mines—and have only found some other man wanting to know all about those traveling stones.

So it has gone on all these fifteen years. Our last is from Tiffin, Ohio, dated Nov. 3, and received yesterday. His name is Haines, and he wants to know all about those stones, could he obtain several and how? Not long since we had a letter from a man in one of the New England States who informed us that there was big money in the traveling stones. We were to send him a carload, when he would exhibit and sell them, dividing the spoils with us. We have stood this thing about fifteen years, and it is becoming a little monotonous. We are now growing old, and we want peace. We desire to throw up the sponge and acknowledge the corn; therefore we solemnly affirm that we never saw or heard of any such diabolical cobbles as the traveling stones of Pahranagat— though we still think there ought to be something of the kind somewhere in the world. If this candid confession shall carry a pang to the heart of any true believer we shall be glad of it, as the true believers have panged it to us, right and left, quite long enough. (TE, November 11, 1879)

This kind of story represents a more authentic response to the peculiarities of life on the Comstock than the "attractive but academic and timorous genteelism" of the fiction of the "Feminine Fifties" and its periodical perpetuators. The detached narrator—developed by Twain, De Quille, and the Washoe newspaper fraternity—coolly mediating between the formalities of the pretentious East and the barbarities of the Wild West, is a true voice. But it is not that of a man of letters.

On Twain's departure, De Quille took up with Alf Doten as a boon companion. The same age as Dan, Alf was a native of Massachusetts who had come to California in 1849 and headed for the goldfields. He arrived in Nevada in 1863 and, in standard fashion, his letters to the papers brought him an invitation to serve as the "local" on the Virginia City *Union* the following year. He also served on the *Enterprise* before moving to a long association with the Gold Hill *News*. His extensive *Journals* have been edited by Walter Van Tilburg Clark, and they meticulously record a long and curious fellowship with Dan De Quille. The two were drinking partners, frequently cruising until daybreak, and Alf regularly records Dan's disabilities, hangovers, bouts of delirium, fistfights, and hospital sojourns. Doten comes off, then, as both an intimate accomplice and an objective witness to De Quille's alcoholism, demoralization, and debasement.

The great expectation of 1865 was the rush to the Meadow Lake District in the High Sierra, about sixty miles west of Virginia. The *Enterprise* and the *Union* sent De Quille and Doten to Summit City to cover the excitement, which they did and got caught up in it as well. In addition to speculating in "feet" on the lodes, they partied. Doten's letters, which alone survive, record their discovery of the local drink, Ho, Joe, which "cannot be mistaken either in smell, taste or its effects. Why, the very first drink of it makes a man's finger ends tingle and the roots of his hair pull . . . and he shouts 'Ho, Joe!' at once. A second drink makes him see stars. The third . . . will make him forget to pay for his liquor. At the fourth . . . he commences to tell lies about his best friend. The fifth drink completely demoralizes him; he does not recognize his creditors when he sees them . . . and finds it impossible to tell the truth" (VC *Union,* September 17, 1865). Doten, in fact, created a persona for De Quille as an imbiber and renewed it the following year when Dan returned to the district on a social visit: "Dan is now engaged with Brier and Parker who have organized a club for the destruction of a 'Ho, Joe.' At last accounts they were all very busy, and from appearances, have been at work quite diligently" (VC *Union,* July 28, 1866).

Doten had quit the *Union* and joined the *Enterprise* on October 22, 1865, and records in his diary a number of occasions when he had to fill in for De Quille, who was "too demoralized" to do the locals. In late April 1866, Alf became local editor in chief, noting that "Dan will assist me somewhat but he is going to attend to his own business outside for a while and then go home to the states." Dan didn't get back to the states, but in July he did go back to Meadow Lake to work on Ho, Joe again, and from there in the fall he went to Downieville, where he dried out during the winter. When he finally returned to the Comstock in February 1867, he promptly got his job back, and Doten was laid off.

Back in the harness again, De Quille was soon straining at all the demands upon him. Yet he still found occasional humor in his situation:

> People in general have very little patience with the shortcomings of a local editor and consider it a solemn duty they owe themselves and the community to rate him soundly and "eye him over" at every opportunity. That their opportunities are not more frequent is not their fault. So terribly do they cut him up that often he is thrown into such an awful state of nervous trepidation that he does not recover his usual self-complacent serenity of mind and demeanor for hours and hours; and perhaps through the inattention consequent upon such a state loses several opportunities to participate with congenial spirits in those social delights which arise from a free circulation of the flowing bowl . . .

A FEW OF HIS DAILY DUTIES.

> The "local" must know to the minute when every meeting of all the religious societies, all the secret societies, gymnastic clubs, political clubs, fire companies, military companies and every other kind of company, club or society takes place. He must know the hours when the several Courts will be in session—what they have done and what they intend doing; must attend the meeting of the city authorities and report their proceedings; must find out the names of all the passengers who arrive and depart by the public conveyances; must see all the dog, man, and cock fights—all the runaway teams, fires, funerals, foot races, festivals, picnics, parades, balls and public exhibitions and a thousand other things; for if he should miss seeing any of these things he is obliged to write twice as much about them—in order to make folks believe he saw them—as though he had actually been present. He must not forget while doing all these things to keep a sharp look out for the arrival of Hon. Polliwog Smith and at the same time keep well posted in regard to the movements of Hon. Augustus Bump and Rev. So-and-so and Professor This-and-that—all great men and each worthy of a neat little "Personal."   (TE, June 28, 1868)

More often, however, Dan relieved the strain by going on a binge again. On April 4, 1867, Doten records that De Quille "got into a muss while drunk at Wood's Bank Exchange about 4 o'clock this morning in the course of which he called Billy Gregory a 'son of a bitch'—Billy struck him with his fist full on the right cheek, laying it open some and blacking his right eye, swelling his nose, & darkening his left eye a little—I had to localize for him this evening & will for 3 or 4 days till he gets once more presentable." But within ten days, De Quille and Doten "went to Chinatown & all the white whore houses in that direction." On April 24, "Dan was drunk yesterday & got up a poor local—Drunk this morning & down at 'Bow Windows' [Jenny Tyler's bordello] abed—slept about all day." Doten did the local for him again. In November 1867 Doten got on as associate editor of the Gold Hill *News* but continued to record his cruising episodes with De Quille. On December 16, Doten says De Quille got a black eye from Louis La Page. By April 1868, Dan was on the verge of getting "his walking ticket" from Goodman once again, so he tried joining the Good Templars to sober up. "He has been on a big spree for a very long time," Doten noted, "and was now forced to do better or else lose his place on the *Enterprise*." But sure enough, he fell off the wagon again and on July 5, 1869, after a big Independence Day, "Dan De Quille got discharged this morning by Joe Goodman—He had been very dissipated of late, and got up a dissipated local—Joe will do the local now, commencing with today—He will send Dan out in the country to sober up, as he can't do it here." De Quille left on July 8, but was back on the eighteenth because Joe Goodman was going to Yosemite and needed him to localize.

Doten continues this dreary chronicle of De Quille's sprees and binges, job troubles and illnesses with loving interest. On April 7, 1870, "Dan has been in station house with the delirium tremens the last 2 or 3 days—[Policeman George] Downey took him to the County Hospital this morning—got it bad." And so on and on it went as Dan was laid off for drunkenness for a couple more months starting in March of 1871, and for six months in August of 1872. By then it is doubtful that even De Quille could any longer see the humor in his failings, which he had described so lightheartedly in a self-caricature several years before:

> We went up to the California Wine depot, corner of C and Smith, or thereabout, and made the acquaintance of a mixture of Angelica and White Wine—something known as "half-and-half." We

rather like our new acquaintance and we saw all of him we could. He is smooth as a maiden's cheek and strong as a wild Spanish steer. He made us believe that we ought to call on a lady friend. "Zert-ly," said we—and we called. Said the lady—"How do you do, sir!" "Eszactly," said we, "zem's our sent-muns! Our cause id it just; zurvive it must!" "I don't see the point of your remark, sir." "You don' see ze point? If you understood the radiations of zee intangible emanations of two souls that beat as one, progressing eternally towarz that perfec-zion of commun-ca-zion which con-stitu-ze the—" "That is enough, sir. It is very evident that you have been communing with spirits." "Yez, um! Half-an'-half." "Good day, sir. Call again." "Call again—*call* again! but ain't I calling now? Don' ye see I ain't done a-calling yet? I'me in for—for ze war! I ain't ready to be muzzard out!" "But I am really very busy." "Busy—busy! don't you know—'Haste makes waste' and that pro-cras-zinazion is 'er thief time? Don't ye know that—Alwas takin' out of the meal tub and never puttin' in, soon come er bottom? and that 'There are as good fish in the sea as ever was caught?' Good-bye unappreziative monster—aducks, unsociable iceberg! Henceforth I'm a outcast and a wandering hermit!" The door closed and we shook the dust from our feet and departed. At a street corner we met a woman carrying a large basket. We pitied the woman and resolved to carry the basket for her. Very politely we told her of our good intentions and took hold of the basket. "Sir," said she, "you are too kind." "Not at all, mum, but within er bounds of reason, I may say I'm kinder—kinder—" "Kinder weak in the knees," says she, and away she went. Seeing there was no use in giving chase, we cried—"Farewell, most self-reliant of women. If a time should come when I can bleed in your cause, I'll die or persist in the attempt." Shortly after this about a yard square of sidewalk hit us square in the forehead. On getting up we saw a policeman nearby and concluding he had thrown it at us we took him by the arm and led him to the Station-house. Here there was something said about twenty dollars, and we told the fellow that we didn't want to be hard on him and lock him up just because we happened to be busted, so we lent him what he required. So ended our first friendly meeting with our smooth acquaintance "Half-and-Half."   (GE, October 15, 1865)

Thus went the salad days on the Comstock with De Quille and Twain and Doten before the discovery of the big bonanza.

The Big Bonanza

In March of 1873, a crew working at the 1,167-foot level of the Consolidated Virginia mine, on a drift run in from the Gould and Curry, encountered a modest body of ore that attracted the attention of John Mackay and the other owners. At that time the main shaft was down to about 710 feet and descending about 3 feet a day. By October the main shaft had reached the 1,167-foot level, and a drift was run a couple of hundred feet to the southeast, where it struck a very large ore body indeed—the top of the Big Bonanza. De Quille sketches the occasion:

> Although all this wealth was in sight in the mine, the people of the town, walking over and around the mine, knew nothing of it. What was in the mine was known only to those at work there and to the officers of the company. I had the satisfaction of being the first 'outsider' to descend into the mine and inspect the deposit, in regard to which—the mine being closed to visitors—there had been a thousand surmises, favorable and unfavorable. I took samples from all parts of the ore-body and had them assayed. The highest assay obtained was $623.63 per ton, and the lowest $93.67, seven samples being tested. Thus it will be seen that even the top of the bonanza was wonderfully rich.   (*The Big Bonanza*, p. 365)

The event marked the begining of a wonderfully rich period in the life of Dan De Quille as well. Over the next decade, from his early forties to fifties, De Quille would write his big book and hundreds of thousands of words of other copy, from fillers to lengthy fiction, as he worked the bonanza of his own creativity.

Even before the advent of the bonanza, Dan seems to have pulled himself together. Alf Doten reports that on January 27, 1873, "Dan left me and went on the *Enterprise* today, because they wanted him and he has got all right and straight once more—Has been off the *Enterprise* about 6 months, by reason of dissipation." By October Doten was married and, thus, one major temptation to spree was withdrawn. As De Quille put it in the margin of a letter to his sister Lou, "I am now on good terms with all the ghosts in my old castle" (June 14, 1874).

These letters, in fact, are not the least valuable body of his writing from this era. About twenty of them survive, and they reveal De Quille's strong and continuous links with his family, the progress of his writing career, his entanglements in Comstock business and politics, and his revived relationship with Mark Twain. We will start with the business and politics.

Perhaps too much has been made of De Quille's incorruptability. Here is a recent sample: "The most dramatic illustration of De Quille's total incorruptability came in the mid-1870s when Flood, Fair, Mackay and O'Brien gave De Quille and the *Enterprise* the exclusive story of the tremendous new discoveries at the Consolidated Virginia. Throughout all the ensuing excitement of the Bonanza, De Quille scrupulously avoided taking special advantage of his priviliged information" (*Dan De Quille of the Big Bonanza,* p. 14).

As Dan's letters will show, this is not quite right. It is true that he does not seem to have been interested in money per se, and he certainly did not die rich. But he was in the direct employ of very powerful men who were obsessed with money and who did die very rich. They knew the power of an apparently disinterested press and they used it to further their schemes. In this case, De Quille seems to have been flattered at being chosen: "Tonight came an order from Wm. Sharon to admit me to the mines—Ophir and the rest, now shut down to most people—whenever I see fit to go into them; also some hints of what he wants me to do for him in the way of writing descriptions. Sharon the millionaire and Senator-elect! Hold your breath! Tis he the mighty Comstock King who thus proffers his requests to your humble brother! Oh!" (William Wright, letter to his sister Lou, December 10, 1874).

Of course, the owners of the Bonanza firm accepted his quite accurate estimate of the value of the lode and then capitalized the corporation at just that value—leaving little room for future profits for the public stockholders.

Among those many ever-hopeful stockholders was Dan De Quille. Here is what he had to reveal to Lou in a letter dated December 17, 1874: "Stocks are keeping up well. I think of buying some Overman stock in a few days if it remains at $70 per share till I can get it. I shall buy 20 shares and pay half down when the broker will carry the whole, and I get all profit by paying him the interest on $700. This is called buying on a margin. Of course I get all it sells for above $70, even though it should bring $150 the next day—merely paying my broker the interest and a small commission. The Overman is sure to go up soon. Goodnight."

On January 6, 1875, at the high point of general speculation on the shares of Comstock mines, which Dan helped create and in which he indulged, he wrote:

Dear Lou—My article in the San Francisco *Chronicle* appeared there yesterday and here today. It is highly spoken of by our people here. The *Chronicle* wrote a 'leader' on it and complimented me by name, giving my name and *nom de plume*. The diagrams are finely engraved.

I will make at least $10,000 on my California and Consolidated Virginia. I yesterday invested $300 of my $1,000 in Mexican stock and today have already—just in one day—made $500 on it. My Phil Sheridan—which cost me nothing—is $7 per share and I have 50 shares. They are getting it *richer* every day in the California and Consolidated Virginia. I am sure to make a *house* and maybe half a dozen houses. I drop you these lines in great haste.

If there was ever a self-portrait of a man being set up for a fall, this was it. De Quille and a host of other petty speculators did not have long to wait. Within a few weeks, stock prices tumbled, creating problems as well for William C. Ralston's Bank of California. In the aftermath, the Bonanza firm of Mackay, Fair, Flood and O'Brien prospered, Ralston committed suicide, and William Sharon picked up his estate and reorganized the bank. He also bought the newspaper, forming the Enterprise Publishing Company, and became Dan De Quille's boss. In a rambling, midnight letter to Lou, Dan relates how he came to switch his hopes from stocks to books.

I fear from the general tenor of your last letter that I have given you a too exalted idea of what I am likely to make in stocks. How I may come out time alone can tell. At the time I wrote, everything went up just as I told you and I was far ahead. Now all stocks have dropped and I am the humblest of the humble. Today all stocks were lower than since I first wrote you. The first day after I bought Mexican stock I could have sold at $500 advance—today I am but $65 ahead on it. In all I am but $895 ahead on California, Con. Va. and Mexican, not more than $2,000 ahead on everything. It is a long story to tell, but I expect everything to go up next week. The 24 shares of Mexican bought for me by my friend Captain Curtis at $70 per share has never been so high since and closed yesterday at $57, as you will see by the report of sales yesterday which I enclose. But I have faith in the mine and will hold on. The beauty of the whole thing is that I am risking no money out of my earnings. I am steadily sending home the usual amount and more. If by mixing myself up in this wild stock speculation head and ears, any money should stick to me, well and good. I must no more excite you unnecessarily. At the time I wrote, things were as I said. The next day all might be changed. I forgot to warn you against this. I still think I shall be better off in the end than if I had not mixed in this business. I had nothing to lose. Talk, and the best talk to be got, was what was and is wanted.

Our millionaires, shrewd as they are in business, are no writers. I could say what they were trying to say, therefore I stand in the light of their champion—but they deliver over their dollars with a poor grace, and sometimes I have half a notion to show them the terrible damage I could do them in a single paragraph. But too many of my old friends would be hurt. Those who are trying to put stocks down would give thousands of dollars to know what I could tell them in three lines, yet they have never thought of it. I could knock the California stock down $100 dollars per share tomorrow by asking a single question, which is: "What effect will Six-Mile Canyon have on the orebody of the California, the canyon named, as we all know, passing through about the center of the claim?" Then to add—"The disturbing influence of ravines and canyons is proverbial," would cause the knees of 500,000 persons to tremble. But this thing I will not do here. All this about mines must bewilder and bother you. I shall say no more about mines.

I sent you a paper puffing me away up as a prophet and enclose you more of the same kind of stuff. I let it all go because it may be the means of putting money in my pocket. I am now after money and my *own folks* for friends. My own and a *very few* others. All others are liars and the truth is not in them. I publish in todays *Enterprise* "Pilot Wylie." In one sense there is nothing in it, yet in another there is still something. It will be copied. I sent it—as I think I told you—to the N. Y. Sunday *Mercury*. Seeing nothing of it, I sent to ask about it. Today I got it back with word that it was unsuited to their "Table Talk"—a fact which I knew but was willing to have allowed it to go in some other part of their paper. The fact is that they were afraid of getting into trouble about it on account of the real names of Sam Clemens (Mark Twain), Capt. Sam Bowers and Old Wylie being used in it. I don't care the snap of my finger for Mark Twain nor in what way I make use of his name, and as for the others, I never saw them nor expect to. The *Mercury* folks want me to write some sort of cogitations for their "Table Talk", but I don't think I will humor them. In the East they are too much afraid of our off-hand and irreverent way of mentioning men of note and standing. Here we don't care a d——, excuse the pen, whether a man is worth $5 or $5,000,000. We speak of him as we find him. There they fear a libel suit if any real name is mentioned.

The matter of my book is pushed and crowded upon me every day. All I have to do to make money if all else fails is to turn clown and publish a book. I can get all the money I want. Many men with their pockets overflowing would almost turn their wrongside out for the sake of having a paragraph in the book about themselves, when, if I were sick and destitute and not likely to print a book, would not give me a single dollar.

I am beginning to receive short histories of what this man and what that man did on certain trying occasions, for it is thought that my book will give all that has ever happened on the Pacific Coast. Yesterday I received an account from the mad man of Wells, Fargo & Co. and this coast of how he crossed the mountains in some big storm. I have not read it yet, but I have no doubt I might make a hero of him and not half try. Before trying, however, I think I should get his check for about $500 worth of the books, which is a good way of securing the success of a "work of merit" in these degenerate days.

In case I start in on a book, I shall go after the rich men of this coast for enough to make me safe and then shall make them print the book and give me all of the profits of it. There is no use of doing things by halves. If they are bound to have a book, I will give them a book—red hot. I want to be in a position to snap my fingers at the critics who are sure to go after me and my book and to have money to hire newspapers to let me give the critics as good as they send. (William Wright, letter to his sister Lou, January 24, 1875)

How revealing this is of what might be called the local conception of his role and scope. Behind the bluster is a distinct sense of having been used and abused. As the *house* he hoped to make came tumbling down, De Quille felt that old Quaker meeting urge to shout. But the petty revenges contemplated here would ultimately give way to a worthier conception of a book about the big bonanza.

Part of the force behind this other idea for a book may have come from his sister. Lou Wright Benjamin's inclinations were literary. She seems to have followed the career of Mark Twain after the publication of *Roughing It* in 1872, asking her brother for any papers he might have kept over the preceding decade. De Quille responded by sending her a couple of envelopes with notes that he had carried about in his jacket until they were worn out, an invitation to Twain's wedding, and his own account of some adventures with Twain and the Fitches in the Virginia rooming house. He wittily concludes by throwing in a bonus:

> I send you two letters written by Marks, the would-be murder and suicide. They were his last literary efforts and precious on that account. As you seem to have a taste for the curiosities of literature, you doubtless will treasure them. It will be quite a study for you to trace the workings of the fellow's brain after it was filled with thoughts of murder and self-destruction. You may give them to the religious women who torment you as choice bits of unpublished literature. (William Wright, letter to his sister Lou, May 17, 1874)

And in the margin Dan snipes once more: "One of these is a specimen of the writing of "Mark Twain," Saml. L. Clemens, the other of [Joseph] Marks, a would-be murderer and an actual suicide who now lies under the sod. You will probably be able to distinguish between the two." Little love lost there.

Lou persisted, couching her requests in chat about Mary Shelley and Dickens, to which Dan responded:

> I think I have read *Frankenstein* but am not certain. I remember to have read of someone having created an unpleasant party by the use of chemicals; it may have been your Frankenstein monster. I will look up the book. I can doubtless find it in one of our public libraries. I like something in all of Dickens' novels; can hardly say which I prefer, but think *David Copperfield* and the *Posthumous Papers of the Pickwick Club* . . . Mark Twain has been republishing some of his sketches in pamphlet form; 32 pages, price two-bits— "Jumping Frog," etc. He keeps grinding these things over and over as long as he thinks there is a cent in them. I have his last batch and will send you the pamphlet as soon as I have glanced it over. I never could see much in the "Jumping Frog," yet that yarn was the one which first brought Mark into notice. The story was told him by an old chap who still lives in his cabin in Amador County, California. Gillis, our news editor, knows the old fellow well and was with Mark when he told him the yarn. The only funny thing about it is the idea of loading a frog with shot.

Besides taking these potshots at his sister's favorites, De Quille tries to make his own case with her:

I see the West Liberty *Enterprise* publishes my "Tarantula of Cal-averas." It has also been published by the New York *Sun* and will now go the rounds. The *Sun,* you must know, has the largest number of subscribers of any paper in the United States. The managing editor, Mr. [Amos] Cummings, took a great notion to me when he was on this coast about a year ago. He told the *Enterprise* folks that all he saw about their office that he wanted was "Dan" and he was bound to get me to New York somehow. Before leaving he told me that if I ever found it necessary to leave here, he wanted me to come to them, and if I ever got out of health to come to New York and he would go with me to Florida— where he has been and where there is a chance to pick up many curious yarns. Mr. Jones—Senator [John P.] Jones of Nevada—is now hand-in-glove with the President. If I were of an office-seeking turn of mind, what a chance I would have now! as Jones is a great friend of mine—as are all the family.

(William Wright, letter to his sister Lou, June 14, 1874)

Lou seems to have taken the hint—her letters have not survived— and encouraged Dan to write about his own writing. He complies:

My story of the man who was frozen to death by a solar armor of his own invention was illustrated in one of the Eastern pictorials. It was not well done, however. The artist made a terrible-looking beast of your Woodhouse. The *Scientific American* thought enough of that sell to copy it, it being somewhat in their line.

I have my head full of yarns, but get no time to write them out. On Sundays I am generally too tired. I have a horrible yarn about completed. The nub of the thing is that a party of men who are perishing on the Plains tap an old man who is traveling with them and who is swollen as big as a hogshead with the dropsy. By this plan (a doctor being of their party) they save their lives—getting a whole keg of water. The old fellow who was tapped after a time straddles the keg with cocked revolver, keeps the others away, swearing that the water is all his own. [in margin] I am a little afraid this will prove too disgusting, but I can make the thing quite funny. (William Wright, letter to his sister Lou, August 23, 1874)

This classic piece, which he called "The New Rock of Horeb, or the Physician's Miracle," (p. 59) was finally published in November, and he wrote Lou:

My story of "The New Rock of Horeb" has been a great success here—in one respect; it has made everybody sick. The day it was published it spoiled the breakfast and dinner of all who read it. Common writers only aim to influence the mind, but a man of genius goes clear down to the stomach—he at once assails the citadel of man! Through the stomach, the brain and all the great nervous centres are affected—get into a man's stomach and you have got him. Make him lose a meal and he will never forget you or your work. Hereafter I shall leave ordinary scriblers to fool around with the brain, while I shall make a direct attack upon the stomach—take my man right "where he lives!"

(Letter dated November 29, 1874)

His other efforts, however, were being praised highly, although he was still anxious about his sister's reaction to them, as well as that of a wider audience:

I don't know how you will like "Buttermouth Bill." It is merely a sketch of character, but it is quite a faithful picture of the ways of a certain class in this country—the "sports"—though Bill is a peculiar specimen of that class. There are but few among the "sports" who are quite so *oleaginous* as Bill. I have been complimented on the sketch by at least 50 persons here, among others some of the editors of rival papers and also by the District Judge of this county—Hon. Richard Rising. He said it was a very true sketch of "sport" life and characteristic of the country. He said—"You must give us more of your sketches. I told you long ago to keep at it," said he. Our newly elected District Attorney, Judge Campbell, who a few days since was at the point of death from pneumonia, had the sketch read to him as he lay in bed. Mr. Daggett, our chief editor, says the sketch ought to travel. I fear that outside of this state it will not be understood. (Letter dated November 10, 1874)

At the same time, Dan was trying to encourage his sister to write professionally. Whether he did this in the spirit of therapy for the recent death of her husband, or in recognition of her latent talents, it would pay off three decades later when she published a book of her own in 1905.

Last Sunday I sent you a picture of our Coroner with a sketch of an exploit he was supposed to have performed. All there was about it was that he and two or three others did go out into the hills and collect the remains of a skeleton. Now, I want you to take the outlines of the sketch I sent you and write it up in your style, finishing up the story more particularly from first to last. When you have done this, send it to me and I will go over it and add what may occur to me. I think we may thus get up one of the most ludicrous and horrible sketches of the day. What a subject for illustration! Fancy a spiritual engraving on wood representing the old fellow on the full gallop with the skull bouncing at his back on the string; the big spine and a few ribs at the saddle-bow; the ends of the ribs peeping from his pockets, and, raised aloft in his right hand, a skeleton arm, with the bony fingers spread wide as the impromptu whip is brandished in the air!—mane and tail of steed streaming in the wind and eyes of both horse and rider starting from their sockets! Whoop-la! (Letter dated November 1, 1874)

Two letters later, Dan chastises Lou for not taking up "our" wild story, gives further encouragement, sketches their future as a writing family:

You can write well enough if you will—you do so in every letter I get from you—then, why not help me a little? By starting in with me you will get over your *infernal* modesty and in the course of time we will have a new writer in the family with a *nom de plume* of "Lou De Quille" then we will have a "Mell De Quille"—Dan, Lou and Mell—just think of it! sweeping the whole continent! crossing the ocean and taking Europe by storm.
(Letter dated November 29, 1874)

Meanwhile De Quille was moving ahead with plans for a book—or better yet, two books—in order to satisfy both his commercial and his literary ambitions:

I have written to Mark Twain about a publisher for my book and about the whole business. I expect an answer shortly. Meantime, A. L. Bancroft & Co. of San Francisco are anxious to either publish the book or to have the management of its sale on this coast. I shall give them no answer till after hearing from Mark. Mr. Goodman thinks the book would take better than anything that has been published for a long time. He is at San Francisco and has volunteered to copy any sketches I may want from the *Golden Era* . . .

I have not yet finished a single sketch for the book, though I am getting the material together and doing what I can toward it when I can spare time from the book I am now engaged upon. Two books and the local columns of the paper is a big job to have on hand at one and the same time. . . . I have yet to write a description of the 'bonanza mines' and an account of the discovery and early history of the Comstock, with something of the present appearance of Virginia City etc. We expect to print 10,000 the first edition. It will be a big help toward selling the second book—the sketches—as I put in a little something pleasant whenever I can, dry as is the subject. I think I should call it *The Big Bonanza*. . . . I am of the opinion that this book will give me a start that will enable me to get out others about rambles and things I have seen—sketchy narratives. I shall have it copyrighted and expect to keep the thing going, like a directory, giving the changes in the leading mines in each new edition and adding a few short mining sketches, little humorous things about the mines, and perhaps some statistics. Thus it will eventually become quite a book.

(Letter dated March 28, 1875)

The story of how this two-book (or more) project came to be compromised into the single volume *Big Bonanza* was well told by Oscar Lewis about forty years ago. It needs only brief summary here. The decisive factor was Mark Twain. He had a timely brainstorm that there should be a best-seller about the revived Comstock and that De Quille should write it, just at the moment that De Quille was sending his letter to Twain asking for advice in making such a book. Twain threw himself into the project with characteristic gusto, fired off a telegram and a dazzling 21-page letter to De Quille full of crafty schemes for composition and marketing. Along with this went an invitation to join Twain in Hartford, where they might both work and socialize.

Twain's confident imperatives to throw everything into one book—anecdotes, statistics, biographies, illustrations—presented De Quille with a genuine dilemma. Joe Goodman's advice had been exactly the opposite—write the promotional guidebook the owners wanted and do it in Virginia, using the proceeds to finance the leisure needed for a more literary effort. Twain wanted it all and right away, organic unity and generic decorum be damned, as in the brilliant patchworks of his own *Innocents Abroad* and *Roughing It*.

In the end, De Quille took Twain's advice, shipping his extensive files of clippings and notebooks east for a five-month sojourn in New England. After reading the first thousand of De Quille's manuscript pages, Twain seems to have gotten bored with the book. But he continued to promote it after De Quille had returned west. In November, Twain wrote to his publisher, Elisha Bliss, saying, "I think you had better rush Dan's book into print, by New Year's if possible, and give *Tom Sawyer* the early Spring market. I don't want to publish in the Summer—don't want to wait till Fall—shall have a bigger book by then" (*Mark Twain's Letters to his Publishers*, p. 92).

Paradoxically, De Quille's acceptance of Twain's advice may have been both the more literary course and the best local strategy as well. He never found time in Virginia to write the volume of sketches, and the disappointing local sales of *The Big Bonanza* probably reflect the more general decline of the Comstock after the big fire of October 1875—with which the book ends—and the pinching out of the bonanza ore just a few years later. The most beneficial consequence of his return to "literary" activity was the motivation it gave him. "I am grinding out a sketch or little story every week," he wrote Lou in February 1876. "I want to keep my name before the people." The editors of the *Enterprise* also encouraged him by giving him a weekly features section—"Sunday Frivolities"—in which to place his longer efforts. Despite Dan's tone, the pieces that he was "grinding out" at this time were in fact among his finest, including "The Goblin Frog," a fantasy about the discovery of the Comstock, a misogynous libel in "Torture Unutterable," ghost stories like "A Musical Coffin," and tales of mountain men like "Elam Storm" and "The Reverend Olympus Jump."

But it was a hard grind, and when the publication of *The Big Bonanza* failed to bring all the success that De Quille had hoped for, he fell back on the bottle again in the winter of 1876 77, lost his job, and was laid up in the county hospital for two months before he was able to get back in harness once more.

After that relapse, his older daughter, Mell, then in her twenties, forgiving all those years of separation, came out from Iowa to help her father stay sober. It was a trying ordeal for her, though not particularly because of him, as she revealed in a letter to her aunt Lou in March 1878:

> I have just scribbled a few lines to Lue [her sister Lura] in answer to her letter received this evening, and it is now with trembling pen that I address you, for well I know that by my long silence I have incurred your displeasure and with such a temper as you possess, is it any wonder I shrink and tremble? . . . I intended writing to you the night I wrote to Lue, but unfortunately commenced shedding tears before I had finished her letter, and you know when the fountain is unsealed, there is no power on earth will stop it—so I lay down on the lounge and cried myself to sleep. Of course I

dreamed. Dreamed of going home and finding you all at a festival. Lue was the only one who seemed glad to see me; not seeing Ma, I asked Lue to go with me to find her. We found her sitting outdoors on a rustic chair—she was larger and fatter than Ellen Elliott, and her features were fixed and her eyes white and stoney—she did not look at all like Ma, but I pretended not to notice how changed she was and spoke to her and kissed her, but she did not know me till Lue said, "Don't you see it is Mell?" Then she said, "Oh, yes, but where is the anchor you always wore in your hair?" I said, "I never wore one." "Oh yes, you always did and you left your watch and chain in the lumber yard and it was stolen." Then she laughed a horrible laugh and commenced telling me about the sawmill. She said—"It chops and chops and chops and chops and chops" and kept saying it over and over about fifty times; finally I said—"Yes I know all about it, but aren't you glad to see me?"

Then she said—"Yes I will be when Jimmie comes home." By this time I was crying and thought she must be insane and was just turning to Lue to ask how long Ma had been so strange, when Pa came home and I was heartily glad, for ridiculous as it seemed after I wakened, it was fearfully real in my sleep, and for several days I could not get that horrible object that Lue said was Ma out of my mind. And now don't you think I am sufficiently punished for not writing?

Mrs. Putnam came up yesterday to tell me that she and Mrs. Cohen were coming to call the first of the week and wanted to know about what time would be most convenient for me to have them come. I told her between three and four and she said they would perhaps call today—so I hurried and got my work done and my toilet made, darkened the room a little so that the spots on my dress would not show quite so much and sat in pleasant expectancy for half an hour, but they did not come, and to think that I shall have that performance to go through with every day till they come makes me almost too happy.

I have never returned any of the calls that I have received. Pa speaks to me about it nearly every week, but I am not courageous enough to start out making fashionable calls, with that old grey shawl and my dilapidated old straw hat. I prefer that people should think that I do not care to cultivate the acquaintance of Virginia people as some of them do.

The people out here are very sensitive as to what people from the east think of them. At the same time considering themselves a little better and a good deal smarter than eastern people. Still it is not a bad place to live if you have plenty of money. Money is everything. No matter what one has been, if they can become possessed of a few thousands, their passed [*sic*] is forgotten and they are now the delightful Mr. and Mrs. So-and-so, and it is useless to hint they have ever been anything else; no one would believe it. Perhaps though it is the same all over the world.

You seem to have been reading quite extensively this winter. Since I have been cooking upstairs, I have had time to read but very little. Pa got some scientific pamphlets yesterday. He brought one up and told me I must read it tonight. It treats of the geology of the stars and looks quite readable, but as there are 278 pages of it, hardly think I shall devour it tonight. The other pamphlets treat of bugs and grub worms. I believe when I have finished the happy little grub worm will send him to you.

I haven't finished reading the Bible yet, some way do not get wildly interested in it, though I think there are some excellent things in it. However, I do not think it any more the word of God than is Shakespear. Though I have not read Ingersoll's "Oration on the Gods," I have read several of his lectures and am convinced that he knows no more about our Creator or the hereafter than do we ourselves. He argues well, for it is his trade and it is by so doing that he earns his bread. But even he acknowledges an unknown power; he calls it Nature. It doesn't matter, it is all powerful, and though they call it by any name they please, in my belief it is God, and that there is a hereafter I haven't the least doubt.

But I must not begin to discuss religion, for it is almost time for Pa to come and I must make haste or I will not finish this tonight. . . . You see I am getting sleepy. It is almost two o'clock.
(Mell Wright, letter to her aunt Lou, March 26, 1878)

Whatever the emotional costs to her, Mell's presence in Virginia seems to have been very beneficial to her father—perhaps even essential, as he became prolific again. In addition to the voluminous news and feature writing that he was doing for the *Enterprise* at this time, De Quille also pursued other literary projects. He published several pieces in the San Francisco *Argonaut*, as well as four stories in the *Nevada Monthly* during its short life in 1880. In 1878 he even got out a little tourist booklet for the trains entitled *The Wonders of Nevada, Where They Are and How to Get to Them. A Guide for Tourists to the Great Silver Mines, the Lakes, the Towns, and the Mountains,* a 32-page paperback in an edition of 10,000. But he did so anonymously, as

Robert Armstrong has recently shown. Hoping to cash in on the commercial demand without jeopardizing his literary pretentions, he let the typesetter, William Sutherland, copyright it.

In 1881, Thompson and West published Myron Angel's massive *History of Nevada*—part bottomless archive of data on every aspect of the state, part "mug-book" flattering the subscribing notables. It includes among its many treasures an account of journalism in Nevada, partly written by De Quille, which in turn contains one of the sharpest perceptions of the origin and shape of Dan's peculiar situation. With it we end this section.

> The daily newspaper is remorseless in its demands upon the time and brains of its editors, particularly in the smaller cities where the editorial corps is limited and a few individuals make the paper, whose columns, as the skeleton forms lie upon the stone, sometimes, to the tired writers, yawn like the chasm of Yosemite, and few opportunities are offered for studied literary efforts. In this harness of toil and drudgery true genius at times is recognized and is rescued from its fate by some good fortune, but generally the brightest are subdued under the dark routine of labor, the demands of earning a livelihood and the narrow groove in which business and politics force the mind. In this harness Mr. Wright has toiled and with all its disadvantages has won a name.
>
> (*History of Nevada*, p. 319)

The Limbo of Myth and Fiction

The Thompson and West *History of Nevada* contains a biographical sketch of Dan De Quille that is an intriguing mixture of fact and error. It states that the year 1860 "found him in the region of the Comstock, where he has since resided, where he has happily married and where a son and two daughters bless his honored home" (p. 318). We know, of course, that De Quille was married in Iowa and that all his children were born there before he left for the West in 1857. But it may be that they were all living with him in Virginia City for a time when this was written in 1880, although the census taker didn't find them.

His son, Paxton, however, was certainly with him in 1882. Most important, his wife Caroline and daughters Mell and Lura were there in 1885 when he really needed them to help sustain him after he had been fired from the *Enterprise* the previous fall with no apparent hope of being rehired again. Alf Doten, who got De Quille's job a few months later, gave no reason for De Quille's firing in his diary. But it was most likely his chronic drunkenness or it may have been a falling out with the managing editor Henry Shaw. Whatever the cause, the loss of his job again, this time for over two years, finally had a powerful sobering effect upon him, and he threw himself into free-lancing to try to make enough to live on.

In 1885 he also lost his brother Hank, with whom he had first gone roving, and his reflections in this last letter to his sister Lou mirror his own fate as well as a growing sense of mortality.

I was glad to get a letter from you, but sorry to hear the news it brought. This news, however, was not altogether unexpected. Through several letters from Iowa, I had heard that Henry was still scouting out through the mountains and wilds of Colorado, Idaho and Montana. It is no business for an old man to engage in. A young man may sleep night after night in the open air and may rough it in all manner of ways, but as the years begin to pile their snows on his head, he must be on his guard against chills in his lungs and cold and aches in his bones. The young man finds his colds and aches only temporary, but to the old man they come to stay. Henry should never have gone out on his last chase for "phantom fortune." It would have been better for him to have acted as clerk or assistant salesman for one of the other boys or to have started a little shop or stand of some kind of his own out of which he could have made a living.

I think it strange that none of the Stuart boys wrote in regard to his sickness and death; but they are big cattlemen, are often out scouting for and shooting stock-thieves and probably did not hear of what had happened for some time and then may have thought that Henry had other friends or acquaintances who had written. In these wild new places people are apt to be very careless about these things. Once a man is dead and put under the ground they think no more about him. It may yet turn out that the man who died at Deer Lodge was another Henry Wright, but in all my reading of exchanges from those counties I have never met with the name. I somehow feel it in my heart that the man who died at Deer Lodge was our brother Henry. Once a man becomes thoroughly infatuated in the chase for mines and saturated with the spirit of prospecting, he will rove on as long as life is left him. On this coast we frequently meet with old men tottering on the verge of the grave who are still prospecting—still hoping to hit upon something that will make them rich in a day. However, we see men pursue every kind of business until the hand of death is laid upon them. When you hear from the Stuarts let me know what they say. Granville is the one that would be most likely to write. He was of a literary turn and the best of the lot.

De Quille, by then with his wife and daughters at his side, was busy chasing his own "phantom fortune," dashing off prospective pieces to papers all across the country. As he added in the same letter to Lou:

> You ask what papers I am writing for. Well, at present I am writing for the New York *Sun,* the New York *Weekly,* the Carson *Free Lance,* from two to three columns a week for the Salt Lake *Tribune* (the "Gruene Ganse," Green Goose, papers) and an occasional article for the Virginia *Chronicle* and one or another of the San Francisco papers. I should have answered your letter sooner, but I had to write a story for the New York *Weekly.* It is entitled "Bendix Biargo" and is in five chapters. The N.Y. *Weekly* is a story paper. Generally you are obliged to read about six months in it to get to a single marriage. Now in my story I have a marriage in every chapter, which I think is a big improvement upon the stories that most of the young ladies are writing. Bob Burdette, Ned Buntline, Josh Billings, among others not unknown to fame, write stories and sketches for the *Weekly.* I wrote my story in one day and two nights, working one night until 3 a.m. and until 2-1/2 a.m. the next. Last Saturday I sent three sketches to the *Sun* and today sent my usual contribution to the Salt Lake *Tribune.* . . . Mell has been down at San Francisco for over two weeks. We expected her to return tomorrow, but as yet have had no letter from her saying what day she would start back. She went to visit the studios of the several artists at the "Bay" to see what is being done in the art world of the Pacific Coast and to pick up any new ideas for new things of any kind that may fall in her way.
>
> Caroline is reading the N.Y. *Sun.* I had an article in the one that came today, nearly two columns in length, descriptive of the Combination shaft and deep shafts and bore holes in all parts of the world. The shaft here is the second deepest vertical shaft in the world, being over 3100 feet in depth. Lou [Lura] is playing the piano and "Nig" the cat, who brings up the rear of the family procession with much gravity, is posing as a perfect piece of feline propriety. Pax, you know, is in Nebraska. He is painting portraits, landscapes and other pictures as a business, but when he wants a bit

of recreation sets to work upon the side of a house, barn or fence, or paints a wagon or a sign. It is pretty much my old business.

I should think you would try your hand on a story, or at least on some character sketches. I believe you would succeed. I occasionally see little sketches in the West Liberty *Enterprise* that I attribute to you.

Caroline and Lura send their love to you and Roy and to all others of our tribe whom you may see. Mell may be back tomorrow before I mail this. At all events, I shall remind her that she owes you a letter, but I believe she thinks it is the other way. I shall have space here for a word tomorrow before mailing this.

Well, Mell got home today. Her health was improved by the trip. She had a good visit with her friends and feels repaid for her outlay of time and money. Mr. Hamilton, an artist, assures her that she can easily average $5 a day in San Francisco teaching oil painting and crayon, but her pupils here have been anxiously awaiting her return. I send you a N.Y. *Weekly* containing a little sketch—"A Marital Lesson." Love to Roy and all others of the "Clan." As ever your loving brother, Will.

(Letter dated August 31, 1885)

De Quille's unflagging efforts found their reward particularly among the publishers of the burgeoning periodical syndicates who bought many of his pieces. These included not only Amos Cummings of the New York *Sun* but also S. S. McClure, who founded a literary syndicate in 1884, Irving Bacheller, who established the New York Press Syndicate the same year and introduced Kipling and Doyle to American audiences, and John Brisben Walker, who bought that syndicate and later published *Cosmopolitan* and paid Dan the most he ever received for a story—$100.00. He usually got only $10.00 to $20.00 for his pieces, earning about $.005 a word, plus Goodwin paid him $5.00 each for a weekly Nevada news column for the Salt Lake *Tribune*. Dan's efforts also won him the praise of his Nevada colleagues, such as Sam Davis of the Carson *Appeal,* who wrote:

Since Dan De Quille retired from the *Enterprise* his pen has been busier than ever. There is an immense amount of literary vitality in Dan and although he is becoming personally something like Don Quixote, he is still weaving his stories and sketches out of his tireless imagination, and his wit is as spritely and his powers of description as vigorous as ever. One can hardly pick up a paper of any note that some good thing from Dan is not found therein. Dan is no 'chestnut' gatherer, but brimming as of old with originality. He now writes regularly for the New York *Sun,* New York *Weekly,* Salt Lake *Tribune,* Sacramento *Bee,* San Francisco *Maverick,* Carson *Free Lance* and a lot of other papers of which we have forgotten the names. Whenever a paper wants a new story on short notice it telegraphs to Dan, and grabbing a few quires of paper and a pencil, he starts at work so as to have the story ready to catch the next mail. How he manages to write so much and keep it up so long and do it all so well, is a mystery to his oldest friends. People have been watching Dan for thirty years, expecting him to give out, but he keeps on running like an artesian well.

(*Appeal,* January 25, 1886)

In reprinting this appreciation, the San Francisco *Maverick* added that "Dan De Quille, notwithstanding the praise poured upon Mark Twain and Bill Nye by friendly journalists, is the leading humorist of the past and present on this coast. . . . Joaquin Miller may wear long hair, Bill Nye 'store clothes,' Bret Harte foreign honors and Mark Twain diamonds and the Grant memoirs, but Dan De Quille always wears a smile."

Along with writing much fresh material, Dan was extensively re-working his own tailings. About ten years earlier, for example, he had written a piece on Snowshoe Thompson for the *Enterprise.* Now, in November of 1885, he wrote a much-expanded account for the Sacramento *Record-Union,* then refined it the following year for the *Overland Monthly,* and extracted from that another sketch for the Genoa *Courier* a few months later. De Quille's practice of sending out as new work previously published pieces, often with little or no re-working, got him at least one rebuke from his longtime friend Amos Cummings of the New York *Sun* in the summer of 1886 when a cat story he had sent in was found to be already in print. Resorting to his clipping files for material also got De Quille accused of claim jumping early the following year when he sent Cummings a pioneer reminiscence titled "The Green Dragon of the Plains." Shortly after it appeared in print, someone sent to Cummings a clipping from the Philadelphia journal *Saturday Night,* dated May 3, 1879, containing a feature by one Geoffrey Randolph titled "The Green Dragon of the Plains." Cummings passed the clipping along to Dan with the following note:

44

New York, Feb 25, 1887

Dear Dan:

Here's a nice sucker! I send it to you so as to enable you to form an estimate of the number of shitasses in the universe. Josh Billings will be accused of plagiarizing Shakespeare next. Go right on. Everything is all right here, old man. The world progresses if men do not, and God is good to those who do good work—sometimes!

The world was indeed progressing, but without the Comstock. After the big one, there would be no more bonanzas. Down in the mines of the Comstock, the veins pinched out and the lower levels were invaded by ever-rising hot waters. But although the declining productivity of the mines brought with it a steady depopulation of Virginia City, it had no effect on the steady growth in output on the part of Dan De Quille. And for a while, there was not much change in his subject matter.

The articles and features that De Quille reworked and composed anew for the San Francisco papers and the eastern syndicates continued to focus on Washoe and the Sierra. He wrote a series called "Die Gruene Ganse" about a "Dutch" bierstube beloved by the miners, for the Salt Lake City *Tribune*, run by his old friend Judge Goodwin. He also catered to the contemporary taste for ghost stories, often introduced as visions produced by another sort of spirits.

Even after he was finally hired back on the *Enterprise* at the end of February 1887, "by orders" of John Mackay, he kept on freelancing. In 1889 he also brought out a new, greatly expanded version of his paperback tourist guide. Renamed *A History of the Comstock Silver Lode and Mines, Nevada and the Great Basin Region, Lake Tahoe and the High Sierras,* it ran to 158 pages and finally bore his name as author. But he allowed his fancy very little range here, although he did take some potshots, like this one against the former nemesis of Mackay and the other bonanza kings:

Sutro is a town laid off at the mouth of the Sutro Tunnel by Adolph Sutro. Mr. Sutro claimed that his town would kill Virginia City, as all reduction works would be located there, and all the miners would reside there, passing to and from their work through the tunnel. As there would no longer be any need of anyone remaining in Virginia, the place would be given up to bats and owls—coyotes would sit upon the peak of Mount Davidson and "bay the moon." Believing Mr. Sutro to have got hold of the mantle of some ancient financial prophet, many persons were induced to flee the "wrath to come" (bats, owls and coyotes), and settle down at the mouth of the tunnel. There was quite a brisk little town there for a few years, but when the tunnel was completed and the miners discharged, Sutro's "bats and owls" came home to roost—they found no rest for the soles of their feet at Virginia. Once the men who had been engaged in driving the tunnel went away, there was nothing more to make or keep up a town than at any other point along the edge of the valley; for the big reduction works promised by Mr. Sutro were never built.

(pp. 104–105)

De Quille's new *History,* however, was not a commercial success. Tourists would not come in great numbers to the Comstock until much later, prophetic though Dan was about the attractions of the region. Instead, Washoe continued to decline, and with it the *Enterprise,* which temporarily folded in January of 1893. The San Francisco *Examiner* promptly held a wake in the form of a collection of five tributes to the paper and its staff, published on January 24, just eight days after the suspension of the *Enterprise.* Leading off was De Quille's own "Story of the *Enterprise,*" followed by Rollin M. Daggett's "*Enterprise* Men and Events," Sam Davis's "The *Enterprise* Poets," Wells Drury's "Dan De Quille, Presiding Genius of the *Enterprise,*" and concluding with Arthur McEwen's "Heroic Days on the Comstock." It is a remarkable gathering for its silences as well as its assertions, for its mythologizing of the Comstock, and for its casting the legend of Mark Twain and Dan De Quille. Here is Dan's initial cool characterization of his co-worker:

It was here that Mark Twain first became connected with the paper as 'local.' We then called him 'Josh,' a *nom de plume* he adopted while in Aurora, from which place he sent communications to the *Enterprise.* 'Josh' and 'Dan' were then the local team. In December, 1862, I left for the 'States' by the overland route, and was all winter on the plains, stopping at Salt Lake, Denver and other places, and reaching the Mississippi February 8th. I was absent nine months, and when I returned 'Josh' was Mark Twain. He said he had become 'sick of the Josh business' and had invented a *nom de plume* that had 'some sense in it,' at the same time explaining the meaning as it has often been explained since.

("Story of the *Enterprise*," January 24, 1893)

Then there is Daggett's opinion: "Twain was abnormally lazy and made Dan, who was almost his peer in humor, do nearly all the work, but the two made a magnificent team and the paper sparkled with humor while they wrote for it" (*"Enterprise* Men and Events," January 24, 1893). Next there is Wells Drury's curiously distorted celebration of the presiding genius:

He was a miner before he began to write for the press, and it was by sending accounts of mining developments in outside camps that he first attracted the attention of the *Enterprise* editors. Through all the years of his reportorial work he never shed his character as a miner. A miner he started out, and a miner he is today—in spirit if not in deed. Whatever other changes were made in the staff of the paper, Dan remained through good years and bad years, through barasca and bonanza, and his conscience never swerved from the firm conviction that the true calling of a first-class newspaper is to publish items concerning prospects, locations, mines and mills, shafts, tunnels, drifts, ore developments, stopes, assays and bullion outputs. All other matters to him appeared inconsequential and of no material interest. If there was a murder, a sensational society episode or a political contest, any one of them was welcome to space after his mining notes were provided for. If they interfered with what he considered the real mining news of the day they had to be condensed or left over till some more convenient season. Dan was right, judging from his standpoint. He was a miner in a mining country writing for miners, who had a livelier interest in the latest mineral developments of the Julia, the Ophir, the Lady Bryan or the Belcher, than in learning the result of a presidential election. Dan's hope was and is undying. He has never lost faith in the Comstock, and he was one of the first outsiders to solve the existence of the huge 'plum' of the big bonanza in the Con. Virginia and California mines. One day he startled John Mackay and Jim Fair by pointing out the exact position of the ore body that their diamond drills had revealed to them, but which had not then been uncovered to the vulgar gaze. Dan had worked out the problem from his knowledge of ore developments on both sides of that wonderful deposit.

It must not be thought, however, that Dan can write nothing but mining items. He has a fund of quaint humor, and when his attention is not distracted by quartz or placers, produces some of the most readable sketches that have ever been written on the Coast. ("Dan De Quille, Presiding Genius of the *Enterprise*," January 24, 1893)

Drury worked only briefly on the *Enterprise* and, of course, never saw Dan's letters to his sister agonizing over his literary career, but it is interesting to see mythmaking at work. Finally, there is the best piece, Arthur McEwen's. In the mid-1870s, he was on the rival Virginia City *Evening Chronicle* and later worked for W. R. Hearst in San Francisco. He claimed no one had ever written truly about the Comstock, though Mark Twain came closest in spirit. "It was there that Mark got his point of view—that shrewd, graceless, good-humored, cynical way of looking at things as they in fact are—unbullied by authority and indifferent to traditions—which has made the world laugh." He adds, "Clemens was sloth-like in movement, had an intolerable drawl, and punished those who offended him by long-drawn sneering speech."

McEwen further freezes the Twain-De Quille legend:

> The local department of the *Enterprise*, for which Mark Twain and Dan De Quille were responsible, was as unlike the local department of a city newspaper of the present as the town and the time were unlike the San Francisco of today. The indifference to 'news' was noble—none the less so because it was so blissfully unconscious. Either Mark or Dan would dismiss a murder with a couple of inches, and sit down and fill up a column with a fancy sketch. They were about equally good in the sort of invention required for such efforts, and Dan very often did the better work. But the one had reach and ambition; the other lived for the moment. Dan De Quille remains still on the old lode, outlasting the *Enterprise*. He is not soured at his fate, and no man has heard him utter a word of envy of his more fortunate coworker of the past. Indeed, no man ever knew Dan De Quille to say or do a mean thing. A bright-minded, sweet-spirited, loyal and unaffected old philosopher he, with a love for the lode and a faith in it that neither years nor disappointment can quench.
>
> ("Heroic Days on the Comstock," January 24, 1893)

Perhaps inspired by this collective interpretation of his past and present relationship with Mark Twain, Dan De Quille submitted a long article entitled "Salad Days of Mark Twain" which was published in the *Examiner* on March 19, 1893, some six weeks after the group tribute. He elaborated further in "Reporting with Mark Twain" in the *Californian Illustrated Magazine* in July, and in that same magazine in August, he published "Artemus Ward in Nevada." He even wrote some notes for a piece on Bret Harte that remains in manuscript. In contrast to his earlier guarded remarks about himself and Twain, in these later pieces ("Salad Days" in *The Life and Times of the Virginia City Territorial Enterprise,* 1971) Dan throws himself into the spirit of self-mythologizing: "Improvements of all kinds, new discoveries in the mines, accidents, cutting and shooting affrays, fires and all manner of exciting events crowded themselves upon us. However, we went merrily along, joking and laughing, and never feeling the weight of the work we were doing in the whirl and excitement of the times."

De Quille wasn't rehired by the new lessees when the *Enterprise* was revived early in December 1893. He was left to support himself piecemeal for the rest of his days. Though crippled with rheumatism and his health failing, he still doggedly stayed on the Comstock and wrote feverishly. But his efforts didn't all pay and the unpublished manuscripts began to accumulate. He had some success reworking the lode one last time in a string of articles for the *Engineering and Mining Journal* in New York and the *Mining and Scientific Press* in San Francisco. He also turned to mining his earlier experiences in the California gold fields and delving even deeper into his youth in the Midwest. When those veins too were nearly exhausted he let his imagination take him even farther afield. For the American Press Association, he wrote a 16-column novelette with a New England setting, "Importing an Ancestor"; and for the *Californian Illustrated Magazine,* he wrote "Peter Crow Among the Witches" set in Kentucky in slavery times. The most lucrative, however, was a 10,000-word tale set in Mexico, called "An Indian Story of the Sierra Madre." He sold it to *Cosmopolitan* in 1895 for $100, and it was published with illustrations by Frederic Remington. He also wrote pieces about the Aleutians and even, in "A Combat with Tigers," about India. But like his earlier romantic pieces, these later inventions lacked the freshness of perspective and detail that only personal experience could provide.

De Quille wrote some very odd things too. For Judge Goodwin's Salt Lake City *Tribune,* he wrote an intemperate series of articles attacking the demonetization of silver, striking an uncharacteristic low note in a Christmas Eve, 1893, piece called "The Shylock Curse of the World." He also penned his longest work which was unpublished in his lifetime, a 227-page manuscript entitled "Dives and Lazarus: Their Wandering and Adventures in the Infernal Regions." It has only recently been brought out in an edition by Lawrence I. Berkove. In an unaddressed cover letter, meant perhaps for Goodwin, Dan describes the work:

> Very many personages, places and subjects are introduced of which no hint is given in the headings of chapters. I have been careful to say nothing to offend people of any religion. The menagerie contains the whale that swallowed Jonah, Balaam's ass, etc.; the museum, the jawbone used by Samson, Moses' rod, etc. These places are outside of the Celestial City in a park. Although Lazarus passes St. Peter's gate, he does not enter the city of Jehovah itself, owing to an accident which brings him back to earth. Therefore I have not profaned the Heavenly City by entering it and describing the things thereof.
>
> The reason why I have thought of sending you the series of sketches of the adventures of Dives and Lazarus for use in your Sunday paper is because of your being strongly on the side of Lazarus—the people—in the fight for silver. No Eastern paper would touch such sketches, but they would please the miners everywhere on the Pacific Coast. I have spoken to some of our miners about the adventures and found they at once caught the idea of "Dives and Lazarus." Properly illustrated, the sketches would make a small book that would sell well among miners and silver men—indeed among all opposed to the plutocracy.
>
> (Unaddressed letter, n.d.)

As Dan's health came to deteriorate badly, it was a member of that plutocracy, John W. Mackay, who came forward with the funds to get him home to Iowa and maintain him till death. We have our choice of final images of Dan De Quille. Alf Doten gives us a parting glimpse of him leaving Virginia City on the train with his wife and daughter in July of 1897, "so terribly broken down with rheumatism and used up generally that he cannot live long anyway . . . back humped up double and . . . merely animated skin and bone, almost helpless." Wells Drury, on the other hand, sensed more life left in Dan, to whom he wrote this letter:

I wish that I were able to help you on in your efforts to sell some of your stories. The first article was published and I read it, which is the highest compliment I can pay to any person; but what became of the second? Did they print it? If so it escaped my attention.

Let me make a suggestion to you, Dan, that may be of value. The *Examiner* is paying handsomely for those short stories and jokes that you will see in their colored Sunday supplement. Take a look at the stuff. It is just in your line, and I feel confident that you can grind out a lot of the kind of matter they want. It sells better than long stories, considering the amount of work involved.

What did you do with all your old mss that you used to have piled away? I should think some of that might be furbished up so that it would bring some ducats. If any of the stuff that you sold me in times past for the Sacramento *News* can be worked over, you are heartily welcome to go ahead so far as I am concerned, and if I don't complain no one else has a right to do so. What the *Examiner* wants is light verse and skittish stuff of the very lightest and latest kind. You can turn it out by the ton if you are feeling anything like your old self.

A long time ago you promised that I should edit your memoirs or stories. What's the matter with having me try some of them while they might do you some good. If you have any mss that you think might be sold here, I would take pleasure in trying to help you find a purchaser. Do you still hold any interest in the copyright of your book, *The Big Bonanza?* If you do, that might be sold for something. I make these suggestions for the reason that you may have overlooked them in your survey of available matters in your escritoire.

Anyhow, Dan, when you have no more use for your collection of your own stories, you know you have consented that I shall have the pleasure of looking them over, and if there are any that you think are not worthy to be kept as specimens of your pencraft, they shall be disposed of according to your wish.

Good bye, dear Dan, I hope this letter may cheer you and possibly may put you in the way of pulling a few, if not a great many, dollars from the journalistic tread-mill.

Your true friend, Wells Drury.
                    (Wells Drury letter to Dan De Quille, n.d.)

In his book, *An Editor on the Comstock Lode* (1936), Drury quotes a last letter written to him by Dan De Quille from Iowa in 1898: "I am living like a fighting-cock and don't do a thing but swing in a hammock under a shade-tree, surrounded by my children and grandchildren. My hardest work is to nurse my rheumatism while I drink milk punch (which the doctor kindly prescribes) and listen to the singing of the birds. It's all mighty smooth and nice, but I often yearn to be back in old Storey County, where there is some snap and vigor in the air, even in summer. Next winter I'm going to visit the plantation of a Kentucky friend who has promised me a banquet of baked 'possum and sweet potatoes." Although he didn't live to see Kentucky—dying in West Liberty on March 16, 1898—it is clear how we should finally picture De Quille. Of these two views, Doten's and Drury's, of the tireless worker who rolled before us the magical stones of Pahranagat, the choice is easy. As Camus said of Sisyphus, we must imagine him happy.

Epilogue

Here lies the famous Dan De Quille
He lied on earth; he now lies still.
His f-lying soul somewhere did soar,
There to lie forevermore.

(VDU, December 2, 1864)

Alf Doten penned this doggerel just after he met De Quille. But it must stand as Dan's best epitaph. His more lasting monument, of course, has been *The Big Bonanza*—still in print after more than a hundred years. But De Quille never completed the other legacy he hoped to leave—a book of his best sketches and stories. We offer this volume as a facsimile of what Dan might have made it.

Before he died, De Quille sent Wells Drury a "sheaf of his humorous sketches" to be placed in the San Francisco papers. But despite Drury's hopes, Dan's unmarried daughter Lura kept her father's treasure trove of manuscripts and clippings after his death. And after her mother's death, she took them with her when she went to live with her aunt Lou in Oregon. By then Lou had remarried and she also finally worked herself up to the status of author, as Dan had so long encouraged. Under the pseudonym "Katharine," she published a delightful collection of *Letters from an Oregon Ranch,* with McClurg & Company of Chicago in 1905.

But neither Lura nor Lou ever succeeded in doing anything with Dan's accumulated works. In 1914–15 George Wharton James wrote to Lura offering to edit and publish a selection of her father's sketches, but nothing came of that either. Years later De Quille's vast collection of manuscripts, clippings, and letters unexpectedly turned up in an old trunk bought from a San Francisco book dealer by Harry L. Day, a retired Coeur d'Alene mine owner and western history buff. A decade after his death, his son Henry, a Berkeley graduate, finally gave the collection to the Bancroft Library in 1953. There they repose, the source of much of this volume and, we would hope, others to come. The smaller collection in the California Historical Society Library in San Francisco, of uncertain provenance, may represent the "sheaf of sketches" sent to Drury.

In addition to this material legacy, there is that mythical image of Dan that pervades not only the extensive body of historical writing on the Comstock, but a growing shelf of fiction. Of more than a dozen novels set on the Comstock, none has done more to dramatize Dan De Quille than Vardis Fisher's *City of Illusions* (1941). There Fisher re-creates De Quille in the character of Steve Gilpin, who, in one episode concerning the disappearance of Sam Clemens's pipe, provokes this long-drawn, sneering speech from his excitable friend:

> "Steve Gilpin," he roared, "spends his life on fatuous and feeble nondescripture that he calls quaints! A lazar among intellectuals, a piddling and paltry philogynist, a hobsnobbing litteratourist among dull books and spiritual megrims! His idea of a jest, a prank, a witticism is to hide a man's pipe!"
>
> After another long moment of searching he let out an awful howl. "The damned sterile curse of a man!—who can find no worthier test of his inventive faculties than to hide a pipe! A molehill and fleabite of a fellow, pitiable, contemptible, fribbling and niggardly, with a catchpenny mind and a trinket for a soul; a dawdling sluggard sunk in his own stupor, sired by a comma and foaled by a trance! A hackneyed purveyor of logomachy, designed to intrigue all the dolts and tomfools in a land where chuckleheads run for office and lackbrains make the laws! And he calls it wit!"
>
> Slowly he searched as if half-paralyzed with wrath. "This master of mystagogy, this narcotic fetus of an intellect, descending to the despicable and bedridden practice of hiding pipes—"
>
> Unexpectedly he found his pipe and marched back quietly to his desk. (pp. 208–209)

Leaving the real Dan De Quille, for the rest of this volume, to speak for himself.

Sketches
From the Comstock

Hard Traveling

The New Rock of Horeb

*The Physician's Miracle. A Remarkable
Adventure in a Nevada Desert—
The Perils of the Old-Time Cut-Offs.*

---

*I*n rummaging among the archives of the Pacific Coast Pioneers a short time since, we came upon an account of a rather singular adventure out in one of our eastward-lying deserts, where so many emigrants perished in the early days while struggling to reach the gold-fields of California. The manuscript is supposed to have been written by old Paul Latson, but whether or not he was one of the party whose adventure is related is not known. It is enclosed in a large unsealed envelope, on which is written nothing but the name "Paul Latson." The secretary of the Society of Pacific Coast Pioneers informs us that it is his impression that the manuscript was placed in his hands by Governor Roop, now dead, to be given to the old man Latson when he should next visit the hall of the society. Old Paul has been dead some years, and the manuscript still remains, as we have said, among the archives of the Pacific Coast Pioneers, where are also to be seen

---

Subtitled "The Physician's Miracle," this fantasy in "the horrible style" is presented as a recently discovered manuscript. From the *Territorial Enterprise,* November 22, 1874. See De Quille's letter to his sister Lou, November 29, p. 33 above. Discussed in Stephen Fender's *Plotting the Golden West* (Cambridge, 1981), p. 150. In this and the selections that follow, we on occasion have silently emended the mechanics of the texts for better readability.

many other curious things. The localities mentioned in the narrative are all correctly given, but we have no means of ascertaining the truth of the story in other respects—further than that an old member of the Pioneers informs us that he was acquainted with Dr. Curtis Corbin and thinks he heard him relate something of the kind some years ago, when living at Downieville, California. The only introduction to the story is this:

"Hearing that Old Amos Skinner—who is now alive and well, and who is running a brewery at Mud Springs—has been for years reporting that myself and some others most shamefully treated him, and finally attempted to murder him on the Plains in the fall of 1852, I have here written out a full account of the affair, which I think will show that under the circumstances we could not well have done otherwise than as we did."

Then at once begins the following story, which we give as in the manuscript, except that in places we have omitted some unimportant particulars.

The Start and the Party

"In the spring of 1852 a party consisting of myself and five others started across the Plains for California. We got together by chance, as it were, at Council Bluffs, Iowa, where we fell in with one Amos Skinner, as disagreeable an old fellow as ever breathed the breath of life. He had rigged up a six-horse team and was willing to take a few passengers for California, provided he could get them on his own terms. He was a hard, miserly old devil. Most of us paid him about all the money we had and agreed to work for him a certain length of time after getting through to the gold mines. One man—Dr. Curtis Corbin—got much better terms than the rest of us. Old Skinner—we all called him Old Skinner, though he was not above forty-five years of age—was dropsical and wanted the doctor along as his medical adviser. Indeed, as we afterward learned, Old Amos was undertaking the trip as a sort of kill-or-cure experiment.

"The members of our party were Zeb Debold, an honest little Dutchman; Gustave Venard, a young Frenchman from St. Louis, Missouri; Jack Austin, a good-hearted, devil-may-care young Missourian; the doctor, Old Amos, and myself.

"We left Council Bluffs with a train of about thirty wagons, and, having a good team, got along as well as any party in the train. Beside the six horses worked to the wagon, we had a riding animal—a stout Canadian horse, tough as a rhinoceros, called Canadian Bill—which we rode by turns or led behind the wagon. Save a few growls, we got along very well together—we passengers—but nobody could get along with Old Amos Skinner. His plan seemed to be to wait till he had found out what we all wanted to do, when he would order just the contrary. But that he had got hold of about all of our money, we would have left him to his own devices and scattered among the other wagons of the train.

"As we traveled on, his dropsy and ill nature seemed to increase. At last he rode in the wagon all the time, being unable to mount the riding animal.

"At the City of Rocks we left Lander's Cutoff, taking the road leading to Humboldt Wells. Before reaching the Wells—at Thousand-spring Valley, I think it was—we fell in with an old Rocky Mountain trapper named Charles Manton, but who was known as Mountain Charley. This man was anxious to get through to California. He pretended to know all about the country and seemed to us to be a great blowhard. However, he some way got into the good graces of Old Skinner at once. Amos appeared to be delighted to take him into our party, without money and without price. By secretly advising with Mountain Charley, the old fellow could issue orders that looked very sharp, and he gave them with great firmness and grace, as being original. With his aide-de-camp, the wonderful Mountain Charley, to lean upon, he could now be as contrary as he pleased.

More Trouble With Amos

"Old Amos at last grew so bad that we could but pity him. He was swollen up as big as a hogshead, and had to be assisted in and out of the wagon at camping places. He had taken a dislike to Dr. Corbin, and refused to take the medicine the doctor prepared for him—was all the time chewing some herb that Mountain Charley got for him. This a good deal distressed the doctor, who was as gentle and kindhearted as a woman. He would often say to us that if Mr. Skinner— he always spoke respectfully of Old Skinner—would only take his medicines, they would afford him great relief.

61

Amos Issues a Proclamation

"Leaving the Wells, we passed on down to Gravelly Ford, on the Humboldt River. Here, to the astonishment and dismay of all hands—all but Mountain Charley, who said nothing—Old Amos crawled up, and holding by the dashboard of the wagon, declared that we were here to leave the train with which we had been traveling and take a cutoff to the southward, by the way of Fish Creek Mountains, to Humboldt Lake. He swore it was all nonsense to make a great circuit by way of the bend of the river to the northward. Wagons had been through by the cutoff and he was going that way. This announcement brought about a great storm. The whole train halted and there was a great powwow. Zeb Debold swore in Dutch, Gustave Venard in French, Jack Austin poured forth 'Pike County' profanity, and there was the devil to pay. Old Amos was firm. He swore he would travel the cutoff if not a man save Mountain Charley remained with him."

Here we leave out two or three whole pages of the manuscript. Through the representations of the doctor, all were induced to remain with the wagon. When the doctor had declared that he would go with the sick man, all concluded to go—they, it seems, loving him as a brother.

They Take the Cutoff

"It was sad [thus continues the story] to part with the train and with those with whom we had traveled so many weeks. As the long line of wagons passed on out of sight, more than one of us felt a choking sensation in the throat. Looking at our lone wagon standing on the bank of the river, about to be driven out into the unknown cutoff, we felt like putting a bullet through Old Skinner's head and turning the team in the direction of the train.

"Finally, after a long speech from the doctor about duty and humanity—a new road—plenty of grass and water and the like, we moved away on the new route feeling very lonely indeed.

"At length we reached Fish Creek Mountains and finally were camped on Fish Creek itself. Thus far the route had proven a very good one, there being an abundance of both water and grass. Old Skinner was in better humor than we had ever seen him, and even resumed taking his medicine. Leaving our camp on Fish Creek, we traveled all day through a region which gradually grew more sterile, and at night found ourselves in a place where there was neither water nor grass.

"The next morning we continued our course, hoping to find either a creek or a spring. Gradually the few wagon tracks visible scattered and finally all disappeared. The water we had brought from Fish Creek was now gone—not a drop in the keg—and we were beginning to suffer from thirst. Old Skinner would crawl up to the front of the wagon and lay his course, asserting positively that in going less than ten miles we should find plenty of water and grass. On and on we toiled, but no oasis met our eager gaze.

Lost

"That night we again camped in the midst of a dreary alkali desert. Mountain Charley, who during the afternoon had begun to look wild and uneasy, now acknowledged that he did not know where we were. Old Skinner caved utterly; began to abuse Mountain Charley for the first time, and turned to us, whom formerly he had so abused, for comfort. Little comfort could we give.

"That night we slept but little. We were disturbed by the constant neighing of the poor horses and distressed by dreams of lakes and rivers, when we drank oceans of water, yet were not satisfied.

"Slowly, stiffly, and wearily we began our weary march the third morning. The sun beat down upon us from a cloudless sky, and his piercing rays, reflected upward from the glittering salt and alkali of the plain, well nigh blinded us. Our poor animals began to lag and halt. All except Old Amos were on foot, toiling on by the side of the wagon, and sometimes pushing at the wheels. At last we began to throw out the heavier articles of our load and before night all was gone except a small quantity of provisions, guns, and ammunition— all went. Jack Austin and Old Skinner did hang onto their revolvers, but these were the only weapons left in the party.

Their Sufferings Begin

"At last we began to see lakes, with grass and groves of trees upon their borders, and drove on and on only to find them constantly receding. Finally the doctor bethought himself and explained to us that these were only seeming lakes—mirages—yet we could hardly

63

believe that they were not real, for we saw reflected in them rocks and knolls, as we had often seen in real lakes. As the sun descended, these tantalizing illusions departed and we saw only the dreary desert waste spread before us. By the setting sun we laid our course westward. But we made next to no progress. Our animals were stopping every moment, and at last one of them began to lie down occasionally. Water! water! was all we thought of or talked about. We were tortured with thirst till we were well-nigh insane.

"All day we had been nearing what seemed to be a long range of mountains on the northwestern side of the desert, and late at night we reached a range of black, rocky hills. Luckily, as it seemed to us, we found before us the mouth of a big dry ravine. We urged our exhausted horses on, a rod at a time, till we were a hundred yards or more up this ravine, when they could be forced no further. Groaning in an almost human tone, the horses fell down in the sand, strewing the bottom of the ravine, and refusing to move. Even when unhitched from the wagon they refused to rise, and soon two of them were dead. Canadian Bill was the only animal that seemed to have any life left and he, too, after rambling and sniffing about for a time, passed down the ravine and stretched himself upon the sand.

"As with the horses, so in a lesser degree with the men—Mountain Charley was as bad as the rest of us. We all lay about on the sand, with tongues swollen and throats parched, suffering the tortures of the damned. Jack Austin, who seemed stronger than the rest of us, finally wandered off up the ravine in search of water, but in half an hour came back and reported it as dry above as where we were halted. Remarking that the horses seemed very quiet—not a moan being heard from them—Jack went to where they lay and in a moment after cried out in a tone of surprise: 'Why, every last hoss is dead and as stiff and cold as a mackerel!'

"'My God!' cried I, 'why didn't we think of it sooner and cut their throats and get their blood! It would have saved all our lives. Try them yet, Jack!' continued I, and crawling out to where the animals lay we cut and slashed at their throats, but not a drop of blood would flow. The doctor gave a scientific explanation of this sudden stiffening after death, which was very plausible, but what we wanted just then was blood. We went in search of Canadian Bill, with the benevolent intention of cutting his throat, but the restless beast had risen from where we saw him lie down and was nowhere to be found.

The Doctor Makes a Startling Announcement

"An occasional groan was heard from Old Amos as he lay in the wagon, and the doctor, who went to ask how he felt, got from him only some muttered curses about Mountain Charley and the cutoff. Coming back to where we were lying about on the sand near a scant fire of sagebrush and greasewood—hot as were the days, the nights were cold and a fire was a comfort—the doctor sat for a long time musing, his head resting between his hands. At last he aroused himself and said, in a voice which thrilled and startled us all, weary and desperate as we were: 'Friends, you have seen those horses die; soon, one by one, we shall drop off in the same way. All that can save our lives is water. This you all know, but you will be astonished when I tell you that at this very moment there is water within your reach— water enough to save all of our lives! You sit and stare at me, but I am telling you the truth!'

"All had been aroused by these earnestly spoken words from the doctor, whose perfect truthfulness not one of us for a moment doubted.

"'Where, Doctor, where?' cried all in a breath, as each man rose upon his elbows.

"'Why, here—here, near us all—here, within our reach is water enough to save all of our lives!' answered the doctor.

"The men gazed about upon the dreary rocks, lifeless shrubs, and parched earth in a bewildered way, and there was silence till Zeb Debold whispered: 'Der poor, goot doctor! Ah, Gott! he is been gone out fon his hedt. He sees der vater all apout in effery places!'

"'I be ver' sorry, Doctaire, to impart to you zee information,' said Gustave, 'but vat you see be nossing but zee sagebrush and zee sand. No vattaire, Doctaire—no vattaire!'

"'I am not looking at the sand, nor am I thinking of the sand,' said the doctor. 'I am thinking of the water—water which we may obtain.'

"'Mine Gott!' whispered Zeb. 'Der poor doctor! He will pe der first to go. He already got visions of his prain!'

"'He rave all zee time of zee vattaire,' said Gustave.

"'For God's sake, Doctor!' said Mountain Charley, 'if you know where there is a single drop of water, tell me. I'll go get it. If it's only a drop of dew on a leaf, or a drop of sweat on a stone, I'll look for it!'

"'It is more than that; there are gallons of it. Yes,' musingly, 'four or five, maybe six gallons—enough to fill our water keg. There is no other way. I've thought it all over—we must have it. It will save our lives!'

"Here Mountain Charley lost his suddenly awakened interest and again stretched himself upon the ground.

"'Poor yendleman,' said Zeb, 'he dieder first.'

"'What he talk,' said Gustave, 'appear to me to have one signification mysterieux. He exclaim zat we shall obtain fife, seex gallon vattaire immediatement. Diable! c'est impossible! He have mirage of zee prain!' Then turning to the doctor, as to a sick child, he said: 'Oui, certes, we all see zee vattaire, chere enfant!'

"'You all see it?' said the doctor, in some surprise. 'Impossible! I have not yet told you how we may get it.'

"'Dat vas all right, Doctor,' said Zeb, in a soothing tone, 'pooty soon you pring der wasser; den we all dake a trink.'

"'What is the doctor driving at?' whispered Jack Austin in my ear. 'He means something—something he don't like to come square out about. He is no more out of his head nor what the rest of us is. You jist pump him a little.'

"Although inclined to believe, with the Frenchman, that the doctor had 'mirages of zee prain,' I said: 'Doctor, why all these mysterious hints? If you think you can find water, why not speak out at once?'

Old Amos Fears Desertion

"'Oh! water! water!' cried Old Amos from the wagon; 'if you have water there, for the love of God give me some!'

"Being assured that we had no water, the old fellow disappeared from the front of the wagon, to which he had crawled, and stretched himself, moaning, in its bottom.

"'We cannot discuss this matter here,' said the doctor, nodding his head toward the wagon.'Let us withdraw some distance up the ravine, when I will explain all.'

"We had no more than started when Old Amos, who was all ears, crawled to the front of the wagon and wanted to know where we were going. 'Going up the ravine a short distance to look for Canadian Bill,' said I.

"'No, you ain't!' cried Amos in a tone of alarm—'no, you ain't! You are going to desert me. You are going to leave me here to die!

You can't carry me and you don't want to kill me, so you are going to leave me here to perish! I see it all. Oh, God! Oh, God! Doctor Corbin! Oh, God! Doctor Corbin! don't you desert me. Don't—for heaven's sake—don't leave me here to die! Get them to come back and put me on Canadian Bill; he is still strong and can carry me. Take me with you—save my life—and not a man shall work a day for me when we get through to California!'

"All this was uttered in a terribly rapid and earnest manner and at times in a tone almost rising to a shriek. What was to be done? The doctor said we could not go near the wagon to talk; Amos objected to having Mountain Charley remain with him and wanted us all to come back. Finally, however, he said: 'Leave Jack Austin with me and you may go.' So Austin was sent back.

A Horrible Proposition

"After toiling to some distance up the ravine the doctor requested us all to be seated, when he at once began: 'My friends, I have told you of water accessible to us in quantity sufficient to save all of our lives. I have told you no lie. But what you will say when I tell you how it is to be obtained, I cannot even conjecture.'

"'This is the way you have been talking all the time,' said Mountain Charley, roughly; 'tell us how we are to get it!'

"'Yes' said Gustave, 'we all perish for zee vattaire; will Doctaire Corbin have zee goodness to tell us how it is to be obtain?'

"'My friends,' said the doctor, speaking in a hurried and desperate manner, 'the water of which I have been hinting is contained in the body of Mr. Skinner. We must tap him and draw it off!'

"'Oh, mon Dieu! mon Dieu!' cried Gustave; 'Zee vattaire vich is to safe our life repose in zee body of Meestaire Skinnaire! Ugh! ugh! Zee reflection is to me ver disagreeable!'

"'Mine Gott!' cried Zeb, 'was fur trink makes der wasser ous der pelly of der oldt man?'

"'I have thought it all over and it is our only salvation,' said the doctor. He then continued. 'If we had only thought sooner of killing the horses and drinking their blood; if we had only thought of it before they stiffened, it would have been some relief. We must now assuage our thirst as I propose.'

"'I've knowed men as have been obliged to drink wuss nor that,' said Mountain Charley, 'much wuss! A dozen times today I've looked at the d——d old growler and thought how comfortable he must be layin' thar with all that water a sloshin' about in him. I think the doctor is right; let's have it out of him! I ain't one that wants to die.'

"'Doctor, you surely are not in earnest in what your propose?' said I.

"'Never more in earnest in all my life. It must be done or we all die. I have my instruments yet; it will not hurt Mr. Skinner—indeed, it will be a great relief to him. To tap is not my usual practice, but it is not a dangerous operation. Shall it be done, or will we all die together?'

"'I likes not to die,' whined Zeb, 'but mine Gott, das wasser ous der oldt man!'

"'C'est horrible!' muttered Gustave, spitting, 'I shall nevaire compose me my stomach to retain him!'

"'It is disgusting to think of,' said I; 'besides, who knows but it may give us all the disease?'

"'Disease be d——d!' cried the doctor, more fiercely and excitedly than I had ever before heard him speak; 'we are all dead men as we stand, unless we do this thing.'

The Doctor's Convincing Lecture

"We all remained silent, when the doctor proceeded to deliver a sort of lecture on the peculiar water. 'When we come to the point,' said he, 'dropsy is not a disease of itself, but a symptom of some other disease; perhaps disease of the liver. Now, from the peculiarity of the hepatic circulation, when cirrhosis of the liver exists, the veinous system of all the abdominal viscera becomes congested, and that congestion finally relieves itself by an effusion of serum into the sac of the peritoneum. What is this serum—this serous fluid which collects in the closed cavities of the body, and in the cellular tissues? It is merely the liquid portion of the blood—a liquid resembling in appearance the whey of milk—and its principal ingredient is albumen. Now, albumen is the nourishing matter found in all manner of animal and vegetable food, and in the white of eggs we have it in a nearly pure state. Thus you see that what I propose to extract from the body of Mr. Skinner is both food and drink.'

"'Vat you say, Doctaire, sound ver well, but still I have not zee stomache,' said Gustave.

"'Nonsense!' said the doctor, and he enthusiastically continued: 'No doubt you have all heard of perishing travelers on the great

African deserts saving their lives by killing a camel and drinking the water from its false stomach; but what about this same water from the stomach of the camel—what is the truth about it? The truth is, according to Captain George Francis Lyon—the most truthful of all African explorers—that the fifth or false stomach of the camel, which contains the water, also contains undigested food, must be strained, and then is very bitter to the taste. Now, how much better to quaff the water I propose to extract from the body of Mr. Skinner—a nice old gentleman with whom you are all well acquainted—than to guzzle the dirty fluid that is strained from the paunch of a hideous humpbacked camel!'

"'Bah!' cried Gustave, 'to le diable wis zee acquaintance. Give to me zee nasty paunch of zee dirty camaile!'

"Again the doctor talked long and earnestly, while the men mutely stood and listened, trying to be convinced.

"Finally Mountain Charley said: 'I've eat dead mule when I wasn't sufferin' half what I am now—I'm with the doctor!'

"'Certainment zee doctaire know best,' said Gustave.

"'Vell, den,' said Zeb, 'if we don't gone to die, let us hold no more cosnolidations of de matter, but go and done der yob!'

The Rod Smites the Rock of Horeb

"It was agreed that the doctor should break the news to Old Amos, when we all stole back to the campfire. All of the arguments of the doctor were lost on Old Amos, but this had been thought of and arranged for. The doctor got his instruments ready and, turning to us quietly, said, 'Bring the old man out!' We knew what this meant and at once laid hold of him.

"Again our water cask was full and old Amos again lay groaning in the wagon. Zeb remarked, 'De old yendleman comed out like one pig hogsheads and he goed pack like one little empdy parrels!' Nobody else said a single word. Jack Austin, who would have nothing to do with the operation, lay with his face turned to the ground, and the rest of us were huddled about the fire. Half an hour after Mountain Charley said: 'Well, Doctor, the water is here!' The doctor answered never a word. He sat with his head in his hands, rocking himself to and fro and sighing heavily occasionally. He knew that all were awaiting his example.

"Another half hour passed, when he hastily arose and went to the keg. Coming back to the fire, he threw himself upon the ground, heaving a great sigh of relief; not a word was spoken by anyone.

"Mountain Charley was the next to arise and go to the cask. When he came back and stretched himself before the fire, Zeb said to him: 'Vas der wasser a little schlippery?'

"'H——l no!' said Charley. 'There is nothing bad about it!'

"Zeb went next; then the Frenchman, and, finally, I——. Well, Jack Austin was the only one that refrained.

"Old Amos soon began to growl from the wagon that he was dying of thirst, so we went and relieved him. All that he said as he drank was that he was 'getting back his own.'

"In about an hour, the dose was more liberally repeated by all hands. Old Amos then swore that we were becoming too extravagant, and that, 'the way things were going,' we should all soon be as badly off as ever. He was bound to have the keg placed alongside of him in the wagon so that he could 'have an eye on it,' as he said. In order to pacify him, we finally complied with his request.

Old Amos Asserts His Rights

"What we had drank so far relieved our torture that in a short time after we lay down we were all sound asleep. When we awoke in the morning the sun was shining down fiercely upon us. Jack Austin was nowhere to be seen, nor could we—though we looked in all directions—see our last horse, Canadian Bill, whose throat we would have cut without mercy could we have found him. Nobody seemed to care about Jack being gone—we hardly spoke of it. What was any life but our own to us?

"Mountain Charley began to look wistfully toward the wagon, and presently arose and went staggering up to it for that which would assuage his thirst. As he approached we heard Old Amos cry out sharply, 'Stand back or you are a dead man! I will see,' continued he, 'that I am not robbed and left to perish!'

"Approaching the wagon, to our astonishment we saw Old Amos seated astride the keg, holding his six-shooter cocked in his hand. 'This water is all my own,' cried he; 'every drop of it! You got the start of me last night, when you most treacherously and villainously tapped me. You all guzzled your fill then; but Jack Austin is gone and I have the only pistol in the crowd and will have my way for awhile.

You are all well and strong and may pack off on foot as soon as you please; not a gill of this water do you get!'

were thunderstruck. Without a word we withdrew to a safe

ion.' Old Amos evi-
ringing him to terms.
in with the heat of a
re almost insane with
xed and begged Old
l with loathing during
I write of it—was life
of any ordinary death.
our lips, but whenever
ed up and, straddling
r, swearing he would
e water,' said he, 'is all
I will be able to travel;
oner you pack off the
ers and bacon, but no
own!'
we hit upon a plan for
to put it into execution.
of the wagon and began
iled for the purpose had
t fire to its light cover of
is pistol at one and an-
that the whole cover of
ring a howl of rage, he

tumbled out over the front of the wagon, dropping his pistol, which fell upon the tongue of the vehicle and was discharged. Instantly the Frenchman seized the weapon and, cocking it, thrust it down at Old Skinner's head and fired. Undoubtedly the old man's brains would have spattered the sand had not the doctor pushed the weapon aside just as the trigger was pulled.

The Rescue

"In a moment we had pulled the keg out of the burning wagon and were just proceeding to satisfy our thirst, when the report of a pistol near at hand caused us to look about in astonishment, yet with some faint gleams of hope lighting our faces.

"'Fire off our pistol!' cried old Amos, raising to a sitting position on the sand.

"'Bang!' went the pistol, and the instant after it was answered by the shrill whoops of half a dozen mounted men, who at the moment turned into the mouth of the ravine, some two hundred yards below. Seeing our wagon in flames, the men put spurs to their horses and dashed forward on a full gallop. 'Put out the fire first!' shouted one of them as they dashed up and hurriedly dismounted. The remnant of the burning cover was quickly torn from the wagon, but some of the woodwork still blazed.

"'If we only had some water to spare!' said one of the strangers.

"'There's the stuff in the keg that the man who came into the station told us about! Take the hammer out of the wagon, knock in the head of the keg and throw the d——d stuff on the fire!'

"'No you don't!' cried Old Amos, throwing himself across the keg, 'no you don't; it's all mine! all mine!'

"'Fool!' cried one of the men, taking Old Amos by the coat collar and tumbling him over in the sand. "We've brought you water fit for Christians to drink, several canteens of it!' With this he knocked the head out of the keg, and with its contents soon extinguished what fire remained.

"As soon as all had received a small quantity of the water brought by the strangers, we were told that we were within three miles of Rock Springs Station and at no great distance from the Sink of the Humboldt. At this point was camped a train of about forty wagons. The station was at the next large ravine below the one in which we had unhappily landed. In his determination to die traveling, Jack Austin had crawled along down toward the station, not knowing where he was going. About a mile out he came up with Canadian Bill, the pony, and, getting hold of his tail, the pair traveled on, the sagacious animal evidently smelling the water while it was yet over two miles away. Jack's story brought the party of emigrants to our assistance. That evening we were all safe at Rock Springs Station."

Snowshoe Thompson

*T*he most remarkable and most fearless of all our Pacific Coast
mountaineers was John A. Thompson, popularly known as "Snowshoe Thompson." For over twenty years he braved the winter storms,
as both by day and by night he traversed the high Sierra. His name
was the synonym of endurance and daring everywhere in the mountains, where he was well known, and famous in all the camps and
settlements. He was seldom seen in the valleys, or any of the large
towns except Sacramento, as he only went when business called him.
Notwithstanding that he seldom left his mountain home, there are but
few persons of middle age on this side of the continent who have not
heard of Snowshoe Thompson, or who have not in times past read an
occasional paragraph in regard to some one of his many wonderful
exploits. Before the completion of the Central Pacific Railroad, when
he was regularly crossing the Sierra Nevadas during the winter
months, with the mails strapped upon his back, more was heard of
him through the newspapers and otherwise than during the last few
years of his life; yet every winter up to the last he lived, he was

---

De Quille's best piece of straightforward historical reporting. Concerns the
career of pioneer skier John A. Thompson, 1827–76. From the *Overland
Monthly,* 8 (October 1886), pp. 419–35.

constantly performing feats that excited the wonder and admiration even of his neighbors and friends, though for years they had been familiar with his powers of endurance and his undaunted courage.

These feats would have been heralded far and wide had they been performed in a more accessible or populous region. He, however, thought lightly of the daring and difficult things he did. They were nearly all done in the course of his regular business pursuits. It was very seldom that he went out of his way to do a thing merely to excite astonishment or elicit applause.

John A. Thompson was a most industrious, energetic, public-spirited, and deserving man. The early settlers on both sides of the Sierra Nevada Mountains were much indebted to him, as for months during the winter season there would have been no communication between the eastern and western slopes, or between California and the older states by overland mail, but for his enterprise and daring. It is strange that no connected and extended notice of his life, labors, and achievements has thus far been written. Nearly ten years have elapsed since his death, and about all that can be learned in regard to the career of Snowshoe Thompson is from paragraphs published from year to year in times past, and scattered through all the newspapers of the Pacific Coast. His exploits and experiences in the mountains, which would fill a volume, are liable to pass into oblivion in a few years more. The experiences were nearly all lost when he ceased to live, as he alone could properly relate them; and the exploits, for the most part, live only in the memories of his old friends and companions in the mountains. Among these death is busy, while some have removed to distant regions, and dates and details have faded from the minds of the few that yet remain and are able to give some account of the main features of the old mountaineer's achievements.

In the following sketch I have presented all that I have been able to collect through letters written to those mountain men who knew Thompson; also all that I can recollect of his adventures as related to me by himself only two or three months before his death, when I had a long talk with him—a talk which was, at the time, supposed to be but preliminary to many talks, when he would more particularly enter into the story of his "disastrous chances, moving accidents," and "hair-breadth 'scapes." There are, doubtless, still many matters of interest in regard to the life and labors of Snowshoe Thompson that might be gathered by a personal visit to the field of those labors, and to the people among whom his busiest years were spent; but it is worthwhile to preserve thus much of his achievements amid the snows and storms of the wilds of the Sierra.

John A. Thompson, the man to whom the people of the Pacific Coast gave the name of "Snowshoe Thompson," was born at Upper Tins, Prestijeld, Norway, April 30, 1827; and died at his ranch in Diamond Valley, at the head of Carson Valley, thirty miles south of Carson City, Nevada, May 15, 1876, after an illness of but a few days.

Mr. Thompson was a man of splendid physique, standing six feet in his stockings, and weighing 180 pounds. His features were large, but regular and handsome. He had the blonde hair and beard, and fair skin and blue eyes of his Scandinavian ancestors; and looked a true descendant of the sea-roving northmen of old. Although he spoke English as well as a native-born American, one would not have been much surprised to have heard him break forth in the old Norse. Had he lived in the days when his ancestors were carrying terror to all the coasts of Europe, he would have been a leader, if not a king, among them. On the sea he would have been what he was in the mountains—a man most adventurous, fearless, and unconquerable.

At the age of forty-nine years, he seemed in the very prime of life. His eye was bright as that of a hawk, his cheeks were ruddy, his frame muscular, and his *tout ensemble* that of a hardy mountaineer, ready to take the field and face the dangers of the wilderness and the elements at a moment's notice. His face wore that look of repose and he had that calmness of manner which are the result of perfect self-reliance and a feeling of confidence in the possession of the powers to conquer. He was a man who seemed out of place in the valleys. Next to the "sæterdale" and "fjelle" of his native land, his true home was where he selected it, amid the grand rocks, peaks, and pines of the Sierra.

In the year 1837, when ten years of age, Thompson left his native land, and with his father and family came to the United States. The family made Illinois their first halting place, but in 1838 they left that state and went to Missouri. In 1841, the family left Missouri and went to Iowa, where they remained until 1845, when they returned to Illinois.

In 1851, Mr. Thompson, then twenty-four years of age, was smitten with the "gold fever," and came across the plains to California. The trip was no more to him than it would have been to a young Indian.

While living in the western states, his spare time had always been spent in hunting deer and other game on the prairies, and in trapping quail, prairie chickens, and wild turkeys; therefore, he was thoroughly inured to a frontier life, and about all that troubled him on the plains was the tediousness of the journey.

He landed at Hangtown, now known as Placerville, and for a time mined at Coon Hollow and Kelsey's Diggings. He presently became dissatisfied with the life and luck of a miner, and concluded to try the valleys. He went to Putah Creek, Sacramento Valley, and set up as a ranchman. He lived on his ranch during the years 1854–1855, but his eyes were constantly turned eastward toward the mountains—toward where the snowy peaks glittered against the deep blue sky. He did not feel at home in the valleys; he did not like mining; and for a time he was undecided in what direction to turn.

Early in the winter of 1856, while still at work on his Putah Creek ranch, Mr. Thompson read in the papers of the trouble experienced in getting the mails across the snowy summit of the Sierra Nevada Mountains. At the time he was engaged in cutting wood on his ranch. What he heard and read of the difficulties encountered in the mountains, on account of the great depth of the snow, set him to thinking. When he was a boy in Norway, snowshoes were objects as familiar to him as ordinary shoes are to the children of other lands. He determined to make a pair of snowshoes out of the oak timber he was engaged in splitting. Although he was but ten years of age at the time he left his native land, his recollections of the shoes he had seen there were in the main correct. Nevertheless, the shoes he then made were such as would at the present day be considered much too heavy and somewhat clumsy. They were ten feet in length, were four inches in width behind the part on which the feet rest, and in front were four inches and a quarter wide.

Having completed his snowshoes to the best of his knowledge, Thompson at once set out for Placerville, in order to make experiments with them. Placerville was not only his old mining camp, but was also the principal mountain town on the Old Emigrant Road— the road over which the mails were then carried. Being made out of green oak, Thompson's first shoes were very heavy. When he reached Placerville, he put them upon a pair of scales, and found that they weighed twenty-five pounds. They were ponderous affairs, but their owner was a man of giant strength, and he was too eager to be up and doing to lose time in making another pair out of lighter wood.

Stealing away to retired places near the town, Thompson spent several days in practicing on his snowshoes. His whole soul was in the business, and he soon became so expert that he did not fear letting himself be seen in public on his snowshoes. He was so much at home on them that he felt he should do no discredit to his native land.

When he made his first public appearance, he was already able to perform such feats as astonished all who beheld them. His were the first Norwegian snowshoes ever seen in California. At that time, the only snowshoes known were those of the Canadian pattern. Mounted upon his shoes—which were not unlike thin sled runners in appearance—and with his long balance pole in his hands, he dashed down the sides of the mountains at such a fearful rate of speed as to cause many to characterize the performance as foolhardy. Not a few of his old friends among the miners begged him to desist, swearing roundly that he would dash his brains out against a tree, or plunge over some precipice and break his neck. But Thompson only laughed at their fears. With his feet firmly braced and his balance pole in his hands, he flew down the mountain slopes, as much at home as the eagle soaring and circling above the neighboring peaks.

Snowshoe Thompson did not ride astride his guide pole, nor trail it by his side in the snow, as is the practice of other snowshoers when descending a steep mountain, but held it horizontally before him, after the manner of a tightrope walker. His appearance was most graceful when seen darting down the face of a steep mountain, sway-ing his long balance pole now to this side and now to that, as a soaring eagle moves its wings.

Having satisfied himself in regard to what he could do on his snowshoes, Thompson declared himself ready to undertake to trans-port the mails across the mountains. His first trip was made in Janu-ary, 1856. He went from Placerville to Carson Valley, a distance of ninety miles. With the mail bags strapped upon his back, he glided over fields of snow that were in places from thirty to fifty feet in depth, his long Norwegian shoes bearing him safely and swiftly along upon the surface of the great drifts.

Having successfully made the trip to Carson Valley and back to Placerville, Snowshoe Thompson became a necessity, and was soon a fixed institution of the mountains. He went right ahead and carried the mails between the two points all that winter. Through him was kept up the only land communication there was between the Atlantic States and California. All then depended upon Snowshoe Thompson, and he never failed. No matter how wild the storms that raged in the mountains, he always came through, and generally on time.

He fearlessly set forth into the swaying and roaring pine forests, pushed across the snow-buried valleys, and faced the towering mountains at times when other men would not have ventured a mile from their homes. At that time, the passes through the Sierras were little known. Even those who knew something about them and the wagon road in summer would have failed to recognize any landmarks in winter, under the disguise of a depth of snow so great that in some of the deep valleys the tops of tall pine trees were almost buried. Often and often was it predicted, when Thompson set out, that he would not be seen again until his body was found on the melting away of the snow the next summer. He, however, had no fear. The storms that rocked the pines did but stir his Norwegian blood—the blood of the old Vikings—and aroused in him a spirit of defiance, a desire to sally forth and battle with the genii of the tempest.

The loads that Snowshoe Thompson carried strapped upon his back would have broken down an ordinary man, though wearing common shoes and traveling on solid ground. The weight of the bags he carried was ordinarily from sixty to eighty pounds; but one winter when he carried the mails for Chorpenning his load often weighed over one hundred pounds.

In going from Placerville to Carson Valley, owing to the great amount of uphill traveling, three days were consumed; whereas, he was able to go from Carson Valley to Placerville in two days, making forty-five miles a day. Not a house was then found in all that distance. Between the two points all was a wilderness. It was a Siberia of snow. In wildness and dreariness, if not in severity, it was the equal of that northern portion of Snowshoe's native country in which dwell the Lapons and Qvaens; while Sulitelma, Sneehaeten, Skagotoels and Galdhoeppigen, the highest mountains of Norway, are mere pigmies in comparison with the principal peaks of the Sierra.

While traveling in the mountains, Snowshoe Thompson never carried blankets, nor did he even wear an overcoat. The weight and bulk of such articles would have encumbered and discommoded him. Exercise kept him warm while traveling, and when encamped he always built a fire. He carried as little as possible besides the bags containing the mail. During the first year or two after he went into the business, he carried a revolver. Finding, however, that he had no use for such a weapon, and it being of the first importance to travel as light as possible, he presently concluded to leave his pistol at home.

All that he carried in the way of provisions was a small quantity of jerked beef, or dried sausage, and a few crackers or biscuits. He never carried provisions that required to be cooked. The food that he took into the mountains was all of a kind that could be eaten as he ran. For drink he caught up a handful of snow, or lay down for a moment and quaffed the water of some brook or spring. He never took with him brandy, whisky, or liquor of any kind. He was a man that seldom tasted liquor.

Snowshoe never stopped for storms. He always set out on the day appointed, without regard to the weather, and he traveled by night as well as in the daytime. He pursued no regular path—in a trackless waste of snow there was no path to follow—but kept to a general route or course. By day he was guided by the trees and rocks, and by night looked to the stars, as does a mariner to his compass. With the places of many stars he was as familiar as ever was Hansteen, the great astronomer of the land of his birth.

At the time Thompson began snowshoeing in the Sierras, nothing was known of the mysteries of "dope"—a preparation of pitch, tallow, and other ingredients which, being applied to the bottom of the shoes, enables the wearer to lightly glide over snow softened by the rays of the sun. Dope appears to have been a California discovery. It is made of different qualities and different degrees of hardness and softness. Each California snowshoe runner has his "dope secret," or his "pet" dope, and some are so nice in this respect as to carry with them dope for different hours of the day, using one quality in the morning when the snow is frozen, and others later on as the snow becomes soft. As Thompson used no dope, soft snow stuck to and so clogged his shoes that it was sometimes impossible for him to travel over it. Thus, it frequently happened that he was obliged to halt for several hours during the day and resume his journey at night, when a crust was frozen on the snow.

Snowshoe's night camps—whenever the night was such as prevented him from pursuing his journey, or when it was necessary for him to obtain sleep—were generally made wherever he happened to be at the moment. He did not push forward to reach particular points, as springs or brooks. He was always able to substitute snow for water without feeling any bad effect. He always tried, however, to find the stump of a dead pine at which to make his camp. After setting fire to the dry stump, he collected a quantity of fir or spruce boughs, with which he constructed a sort of rude couch or platform on the snow. Stretched upon his bed of boughs, with his feet to his fire and his head resting upon one of Uncle Sam's mail bags, he slept as soundly as if occupying the best bed ever made, though perhaps beneath his couch there was a depth of from ten to thirty feet of snow.

Occasionally, his slumbers were interrupted by either disagreeable or startling accidents. Sometimes his fire, burning downward toward the roots of the stub or stump beside which he was camped, melted the snow underneath his platform of boughs to such an extent that it was undermined, and he suddenly found himself sliding down into a deep pit—a pit filled with fire.

When unable to find a dry stump, he looked for a dead pine tree. He always selected a tree that had to it a decided lean. If he could avoid it, he never made his camp beside a tree that was perfectly straight. For this there was a good reason. It very often happened that the tree set on fire in the evening was burned through and fell to the ground before morning. When he had a leaning tree at the foot of which to encamp, he was able to make his bed on the safe side; but when the tree stood perfectly erect, he knew not on which side of it to build his couch. It not infrequently happened that he was aroused from sleep in the morning hours by the loud cracking of the tree at the foot of which he was reposing, and he was then obliged to do some fast as well as judicious running, in order to save his life. This was a bit of excitement that he did not crave when wearied with a hard day's travel, and he never made his camp by a decidedly straight tree when it was possible for him to do better.

However, he did not always camp by trees and stumps. He sometimes crawled under shelving rocks and there made his bed of boughs, building a small fire on the bare ground in front of it. At a place called Cottage Rock, six miles below Strawberry Valley, he had a small, dry cavern in the shape of an oven in which he was in the habit of housing as often as he could make it convenient to do so. There his bed of boughs was always ready for him. Curled up in his cavern—which was but little larger than an ordinary baker's oven—with a fire of blazing logs in front, he slept in comfort and safety.

This cavern was the one palatial hotel on his route. When he could reach it, he was perfectly at ease and happy. It then seemed to him that there was nothing to care for. He could give himself up to the soundest sleep, with no fear of being awakened by the crack of a falling tree or the pawing of a grizzly. He only camped when he felt the necessity of obtaining sleep, and when sufficiently refreshed by his slumbers was in the habit of arising and pursuing his journey, whatever the hour of the day or night, provided that a blinding snowstorm and utter darkness did not prevail.

When Snowshoe Thompson was carrying the mail from Genoa, Nevada, to Murphy's Camp, California, in 1862, he traveled by way of Woodford's, Markleyville, Hermit Valley, and the Big Trees. At Hermit Valley were some deserted houses, and occasionally he found it convenient to lodge for a night in one of these. The snow was frequently so deep in that elevated region that it was a difficult matter to find the houses, so completely were they buried beneath the great drifts. He was obliged to prospect for the buildings by probing the snow with his balance pole. Even after a house was found, all difficulties were not ended. The trouble then was to get into it. When he had found a house, Thompson used to begin taking possession of it by collecting dry branches from the surrounding trees, which he threw down the chimney. Then he would dig down into the snow, tear some boards from the gable end, and so let himself in.

At first, Thompson tried to take possession of the buildings by crawling down the chimneys, but his bulk made all such attempts ridiculous and exasperating failures. On one occasion he got stuck in a chimney when nearly down to the fireplace. For a time he could get neither up nor down. He felt himself swelling up, and for a few minutes was more frightened than he had ever been at the sight of a wild beast or by the sharp cracking of a falling tree.

In talking with Thompson about his mountain experiences, I once asked him if he ever lost his way in the wilds. "No," said he, "I was never lost—I can't be lost! I can go anywhere in the mountains, day or night, storm or shine. I can't be lost," repeated he, tapping his forehead with his forefinger. "I've got something in here that keeps

81

me right. I have found many persons who were lost—dozens of men, first and last—but I have never been lost myself. There is no danger of getting lost in a narrow range of mountains like the Sierras, if a man has his wits about him."

Mr. Thompson then proceeded to explain that he was always able to keep his course and know his whereabouts by observing the trees and rocks and the configuration of the ground. Keilhan, the great Norwegian geologist, was not a closer observer of rocks than was Thompson, so far as they concerned his business of finding his way through the mountains. Few mountain men give much attention to rocks, yet they are as good as guideposts when understood. The central axis and crest of the Sierra range are formed of granitic rocks. These rocks, and the slates and other rocks lying in regular order below, will always tell a man who understands them just how far down the slope of the range he has gone. They will also tell him—by the moss and lichens growing on them—the points of the compass. An observant man may always tell whether he is on the north or the south side of the hill by the trees. There are trees growing on the south side of hills that are seldom seen on the north side. A difference in the growth of moss and in the thickness of the bark on the north and the south sides of trees will also be noted. When a man is lost in the mountains, he must not wander uphill and downhill at random. As soon as he becomes aware that he has lost his reckoning, he must constantly travel downhill. If he starts from a slope, this will lead him to a ravine, the ravine to a cañon, and the cañon to a creek or river. By traveling down the river, he will soon come out below the snow line on the one side or the other of the range. He need never be out long enough to starve to death.

"Yes," said Thompson, "I have found a great many lost men, and have rescued some men when they were at death's door. I once found a man who had been four days in Lake Valley, unable to find his way out. Every day the man set out, and every night he found himself back at the little shanty from which he set forth in the morning. He knew nothing about the course of the prevailing winds, about trees and rocks, or about the stars in the heavens, not to speak of the formation and configuration of the mountains.

"One day the lost man got out of Lake and into Hope Valley; yet at night he was again back in his shanty. The fellow would have starved to death up there in the mountains had it not happened that there had been a lot of potatoes left in the shanty. He was living on these potatoes when I found him, but they would have lasted only a day or two longer.

"I said to the man: 'When you were in the valley you describe—Hope Valley—didn't you see a river going down out of the mountains?' 'Yes,' said he, 'I saw a river.' 'Well,' said I, 'that was the main branch of the Carson River. Six miles down that would have taken you into Carson Valley.' 'Why, I thought it was the American River on the other side of the mountains,' said the fellow, staring at me as if he could hardly believe I was telling him the truth.'"

About Christmas, in the year 1856, Snowshoe Thompson saved the life of James Sisson, who had been lying in an old deserted cabin in Lake Valley twelve days, with his feet frozen. There was some flour in the cabin, and on this Sisson had subsisted. He was in the cabin four days without a fire. During this time he ate the flour raw, just as it came from the sack. On the fifth day, while rummaging about the shanty, he had the good fortune to find some matches. These were where no one would have thought of looking for matches, as they were scattered about under some hay that lay on the floor.

After finding the matches, Sisson made a fire and thawed out his boots, when he was able to get them off. For four days he had lain in the cabin with his boots frozen to his feet. When found by Mr. Thompson eight days later, Sisson's legs were purple to the knees. Sisson was confident from the appearance of his legs that mortification had set in. He knew that unless his legs were amputated, he must soon die. As he could expect no assistance from the outside world, he had concluded to himself undertake to perform the required operation. There was an ax in the cabin, and with this he had determined to cut off his frozen legs. But for the opportune arrival of Thompson, Sisson would the next day have attempted to disjoint his legs at the knees, for that was the day he had fixed upon for undertaking the operation.

At the time he found Sisson, Thompson was on his way from Placerville to Carson Valley. It was in the night, and on coming to the log house—which was occupied in the summer as a trading post—Thompson halted for a moment and was knocking the snow off his shoes by striking them against the cabin when he heard someone cry out. Going inside, he found Sisson situated as related above. A considerable amount of provisions had been left in the cabin in the fall, but all except the flour had been stolen by the Indians.

Thompson chopped a supply of wood for the unfortunate man, and making him as comfortable as was possible with the means at hand, left for Genoa to obtain assistance. While Thompson was cutting the wood, Sisson called out to him and begged him not to dull the ax—the place being full of rocks—as he might yet want it for the purpose of taking off his legs. Sisson was firmly of the opinion that when Thompson left him he would never see him again. He thought Thompson would never be able to get down out of the mountains, and was of the opinion that in case he did succeed in reaching the valley, he would not attempt to return to the cabin.

Mr. Thompson told Sisson he would surely return and take him away, and advised him not to think of attempting to amputate his legs, as on cutting the arteries he would bleed to death. But Sisson had thought of that. He intended to make a sort of compress or tourniquet of some pieces of baling-rope, which he would twist round his legs with a stick, in such a way that a bit of rock would be pressed upon the arteries. Then with firebrands he would sear the ends of the arteries and the raw flesh of the stumps of his legs. Sisson's mind was so much occupied with his plans for the amputation of his legs that Thompson was almost afraid to leave the ax where he could get hold of it; he did so only upon receiving from Sisson a solemn promise that he would wait three days before attempting to use it on his knees.

On leaving the cabin, Thompson traveled all night, and early next morning arrived at Genoa. He there raised a party of six men—W. B. Wade, Harris, Jacobs, and other old settlers—to return with him and bring Sisson down to the valley. By Thompson's advice the party carried with them a few tools for use in making a sled. Snowshoes were also hastily constructed for the men composing the relief party. As none of these men had ever done much traveling on snowshoes, they furnished Thompson not a little amusement during the journey by their mishaps and involuntary antics.

After much hard work, the party arrived at the lone cabin late in the evening, to the great joy of Sisson, who at sight of so many men felt that he was saved.

That night they constructed a hand sled on which to carry the frozen man down to Carson Valley. In the morning they awoke to find that nearly two feet of new snow had fallen; there was a depth of eight feet before. The new snow made it very hard to get along with the hand sled. Under Sisson's weight it plowed deeply along, and at times was buried almost out of sight.

The first day the party got no farther than to Hope Valley, where they encamped. Sisson was made as comfortable as possible on a bed of boughs. As they had expected to reach Genoa in one day, they had taken along with them no blanket and but few other comforts for the frozen man.

The second day they reached Genoa, and at once procured the medical assistance which Sisson's case so urgently demanded. The doctors found that it would be necessary to amputate both of Sisson's feet. Before the operation could be performed, however, the physician said he must have some chloroform. As Snowshoe Thompson never did things by halves, he at once set out, crossed the Sierra, and traveled all the way to Sacramento in order to get the required drug. Finally, the long-delayed operation was performed. Sisson survived it, and at last accounts was living somewhere in the Atlantic states.

Although Snowshoe Thompson carried no weapons when in the mountains, he always carried matches. He kept them safely stowed away in a tight tin box, or securely wrapped in a piece of oiled silk.

"One night," said he to the writer, "I lost my matches in a creek at which I stopped to drink. That night I lay out on the snow without fire. It was very uncomfortable and I did not sleep much, but I had no fear of freezing. When awakened by the cold, I got up, exercised a little, and after that took another nap. So I put in the night.

"I never was cold when traveling. I never had my feet, or even my fingers or ears frozen. I was always more troubled with too great warmth than with cold. I would perspire freely at midnight on the coldest nights that ever blew. The heavy pack on my back and my vigorous exercise kept me warm."

At times, when traveling at night, Thompson was overtaken by blizzards, when the air would be so filled with snow and the darkness so great that he could not see to proceed. On such occasions, he would get on top of some big rock which the winds kept clear of snow, and there dance until daylight appeared; the lateness of the hour and the blinding storm preventing his making one of his usual camps. A certain notch or pass in the mountains was much addicted to blizzards, and at that point was a big, flat rock on which Thompson danced many a midnight jig.

In 1861–1862, Snowshoe Thompson carried the United States mail on the Big Tree route. "There," said he, "I once undertook to make a shortcut from Woodford's to Hermit Valley by way of Markleyville—or where that town now stands—when I got into trouble. In the summer I had gone out to look up this cutoff. I looked through one pass, and found it would not do. Then I found another, which I looked through and saw that it was on a direct line—a straight shoot—toward Hermit Valley; but I only looked through the pass—did not go through it to see what was on the other side. I took it for granted that it was all right.

"When I made my first trip for the winter—in November, 1861—I struck out for my new pass. I went through it flying, but after getting through I butted up against perpendicular precipices for a whole day. These were the walls of a big cañon through which passes one of the tributaries of the Carson River. I would rather have crossed the Snaebraen or the Folgonfondon, the biggest glaciers in Norway, than to have faced this great wall of perpendicular rock. Snowshoes were of no use against it. Finally, about night on the second day of the trip, I found a way through the cliffs, crawled up to the opposite side of the cañon and sat down on a rock, pretty nearly tired out; for I had on my back all this time a load of mail weighing over eighty pounds.

"That night I did not look far for a sleeping place. I made my camp at the foot of a big pine tree, near the spot where I escaped out of the cañon. The tree I selected was one from about the roots of which the wind had blown away nearly all the snow, leaving a deep pit, such as is often seen in the winter about trees in the mountains. Down into this pit I descended, after throwing into it a supply of fuel and boughs for a bed. The surrounding wall of snow was so high that I could not see out.

"After taking possession of the pit, I set to work and dug a hole in the wall of snow, making a place like an oven. I spread spruce boughs on the floor, making a good bed. Then I built a fire against the side of the tree. The heat of the fire was thrown back on me, and I slept comfortably all night. Two feet of new snow fell during the night, but I knew nothing of it till morning. I then awoke and found the mouth of my den closed. At first I hardly knew what was the matter; but I presently pushed my way through the snow that blocked the door of my house, and rose through it to the full light of day. By a change of wind the snow had been lodged in the pit, had put out my fire, and had almost filled the hole to a level with the surrounding snow. In my little den I had lain as snug and warm as if I had been in the best house in the country. After that I often made such camps.

"The third day, at four o'clock in the evening, I reached Hermit Valley, thirty-six miles from the Big Trees. All this time I had lived on two biscuits that I put into my pocket for a lunch when I left Woodford's. You see, I did not doubt that I should reach Hermit Valley in the evening of the first day. When I set out I thought my new cutoff all right; but, like most cutoffs, it turned out all wrong."

In Norway the frugal peasantry make a species of bread or cake of the inner bark of the pine, in years when there is a scarcity of grain. Doubtless Thompson would have gone to the pine trees for food had he been out two or three days longer.

Although Snowshoe Thompson traveled through the wilds of the Sierra for more than twenty winters, he never in all that time encountered a grizzly bear, nor even saw a bear of any kind. Hundreds of times, however, he saw their tracks in the snow, and also in the mud about springs and brooks. Sometimes the tracks he saw had been so recently made that the water from the oozy ground was still running into and had not filled them. At times he was so close upon them that he imagined their odor still lingered in the air. Not unfrequently he came to places where a number of bears had been traveling together. He once saw where a troop of eight had passed along. He several times saw the track of the huge grizzly with a clubfoot, known to mountain men and hunters as "Old Brin," a name given the beast on account of his being of a peculiar brindle color. When he had a clear field, Thompson did not fear the bears; he could easily run away from them on his snowshoes.

Said Thompson to the writer, when speaking of wild animals:

"I was never frightened but once during all my travels in the mountains. That was in the winter of 1857. I was crossing Hope Valley, when I came to a place where six great wolves—big timber wolves—were at work in the snow, digging out the carcass of some animal. Now, in my childhood in Norway I had heard so many stories about the ferocity of wolves that I feared them more than any other wild animal. To my eyes, those before me looked to have hair on them a foot long. They were great, gaunt, shaggy fellows. My course lay near them. I knew I must show a bold front. All my life I had heard that the wolf—savage and cruel as he is—seldom has the courage to attack anything that does not run at his approach. I might easily run away from bears, but these were customers of a different kind. There was nothing of them but bones, sinews, and hair. They could skim over the snow like birds.

"As I approached, the wolves left the carcass, and in single file came out a distance of about twenty-five yards toward my line of march. The leader of the pack then wheeled about and sat down on his haunches. When the next one came up he did the same, and so on, until all were seated in a line. They acted just like trained soldiers. I pledge you my word, I thought the devil was in them! There they sat, every eye and every sharp nose turned toward me as I approached. In the old country I had heard of man-wolves, and these acted as if of that supernatural kind. To look at them gave me cold chills, and I had a queer feeling about the roots of my hair. What most frightened me was the confidence they displayed, and the regular order in which they moved. But I dared not show the least sign of fear, so on I went.

"Just when I was opposite them, and but twenty-five or thirty yards away, the leader of the pack threw back his head, and uttered a loud and prolonged howl. All the others of the pack did the same. 'Ya-hoo-oo! ya-oo, woo-oo!' cried all together. A more doleful and terrific sound I never heard. I thought it meant my death. The awful cry rang across the silent valley, was echoed by the hills, and reechoed far away among the surrounding mountains.

"Every moment I expected to see the whole pack dash at me. I would just then have given all I possessed to have had my revolver in my hand. However, I did not alter my gait nor change my line of march. I passed the file of wolves as a general moves along in front of his soldiers. The ugly brutes uttered but their first fearful howl. When they saw that their war cry did not cause me to alter my course nor make me run, they feared to come after me, so they let me pass.

"They sat still and watched me hungrily for some time, but when I was far away I saw them all turn about and go back to the carcass. Had I turned back, or tried to run away when they marched out to meet me, I am confident the whole pack would have been upon me in a moment. They all looked it. My *show* of courage intimidated them and kept them back."

Snowshoe Thompson was out in the war which the people of

Nevada had with the Piutes, in May, 1860, and was in the battle fought at Pyramid Lake, May 12, when the whites were routed with great slaughter. Of the 105 men who went into the fight, 76 were killed and several wounded. Thompson was in the thick of the fight. He was near Major Ormsby, of Carson City, when he fell. His own horse was shot from under him, and for a time he was face to face with several Indians. When the retreat began—which was general and most disastrous—he struck out on foot for the Truckee River. In speaking of this race for life, Thompson said: "I pledge you my word that more than once I wished that all the valley was buried in snow, and I was mounted on my snowshoes."

As he ran toward the river, a horse ran after him. The frightened animal kept close at his back, as if seeking his protection. A man cried out to him: "Why don't you get on that horse which is following behind you?" At this Thompson wheeled about, and as he did so his elbow struck against the animal's nose. It was a horse all saddled and bridled, whose owner had fallen in the fight. Thompson mounted and thus got away. He always said he believed the Lord sent him that horse. But for the horse, he would doubtless have been slain. The Indians followed the volunteers for nearly twenty miles, killing all they came up with.

In the early days, before the discovery of silver, Snowshoe Thompson carried letters from California to the miners who were at work in the placer diggings on Gold Cañon, at and about Chinatown (now Dayton), and at Johntown, at that time the mining metropolis of Nevada—then western Utah. He also carried letters and papers to the miners working on Six-mile Cañon, at the head of which Virginia City now stands. He saw the hole in which Peter O'Reilley and Pat McLaughlin struck the first silver ore, a short time before the strike was made, and was told by them that they were getting "very fair prospects" in gold.

In June, 1859, O'Reilley and McLaughlin got into a sort of heavy, blue material filled with gold, which they did not understand. They could get nothing out of it but gold, yet it was so heavy that they thought it must be the ore of some metal. Thompson took a sample of this stuff, wrapped it in a piece of ordinary check shirting, and carried it to Placerville. There he showed it to Professor W. Frank Stewart, the well-known geologist and mining expert, who was then editing the Placerville *Weekly Observer,* and to whom Snowshoe was wont to bring items of news from Gold Cañon and the Plains, even as far east as Salt Lake City. Mr. Stewart at once pronounced the blue stuff to be silver ore of the richest kind. The sample was carried to Sacramento and assayed, where it was found to be black sulphuret of silver, and so rich that the assayer could hardly believe his figures. About the same time, a sample of the ore was assayed at Nevada City, California, with the same astonishing result. Then at once broke out a grand excitement over the news of the wonderful silver discovery that had been made east of the Sierras, in Washoe, as the Comstock mining region was then called.

Snowshoe Thompson always asserted that to Mrs. L. S. Bowers— better known as the "Washoe Seeress," on account of her many predictions in regard to mining and other matters—belonged the credit of the discovery of the Comstock. He said that in 1858, when Mrs. Bowers (then the widow Cowan) was keeping a boardinghouse in Johntown, she one day said to him: "Thompson, I wish you'd see if you can't get me a peep-stone the next time you go down to Sacramento."

"What is a peep-stone?" asked Thompson.

"It is a ball of glass shaped like an egg," said Mrs. Bowers, "and to be a good one, it should be perfectly transparent. I have one, but it is old and has become cloudy. I want you to find me one that is perfectly clear."

"What use do you make of it? What is it good for?" asked Thompson.

"I can find out all manner of things with it," said the seeress. "If anything is stolen, I can find the thief and the article stolen. By looking into the peep-stone I can see the faces of the dead; can trace persons that are missing; can see hidden treasure; and can see rich ore lying deep in the ground. What I now want a good peep-stone for is to find a mine that I have seen through my old one. It is the richest mine in the world. It is at no great distance from here, but I can't exactly make out its surroundings."

Speaking of this, Thompson said: "I promised to try to find what Mrs. Bowers wanted. When I next went down to Sacramento, I visited all the stores in the city in search of a peep-stone. They laughed at me in a good many places. When I told them what a peep-stone was like, and how it was used, some laughed until tears ran down their cheeks. I had to laugh myself, yet I was determined to find a peep-stone, if there was such a thing in the place. I went to all the hardware stores, to the jewelry stores, and to every store that kept any kind of glassware. I then thought I might find what I was in search of in some out-of-the-way little shops. So I went about everywhere inquiring for a peep-stone, and nearly everywhere was laughed at. No peep-stone was to be had in all Sacramento."

Thompson then went on to say: "My wife, who is an English woman, told me that she had seen peep-stones in England and in Scotland when she was a girl. I think Mrs. Bowers brought her old peep-stone from Scotland." Thompson appeared to be a believer in the virtues of the peep-stone. Superstitions of many kinds prevail in the land of his birth. In the "sæter," or huts of the mountaineers, wild legends of witches and enchanters, and their doings in the days before the reign of Olaf I, are still related. Even to this day some of the peasantry believe, with the Laplanders, that certain witches keep the wind tied up in leathern bags, letting it out for good or evil, as may suit their purposes.

Thompson said Mrs. Bowers was greatly disappointed when he returned to Johntown and told her that in all the great city of Sacramento no such thing as a peep-stone was to be found. No doubt that city fell many degrees in her good opinion when she found that one could not go there and at once get such an ordinary and necessary little article as a peep-stone.

Not being able to procure a bright, new peep-stone, Mrs. Bowers fell back upon her old one. In using it, Thompson said she looked through it endwise. In this way she asserted that she could see at a certain point an immense deposit of ore. Tracing the ore upward she could see the surface ground; but was not sure that she saw the rocks, soil, and surrounding hills distinctly. Some of the cloudy spots in the peep-stone appeared to fall in the way, and mingle with the various features of the landscape.

In the spring of 1859, Thompson went up to Six-mile Cañon to deliver letters and papers to the miners at work in the placers at that point. While he was in the cañon, one of the miners pointed up the hill to where a hole was visible just above the head of the ravine, and said to him: "Do you see that little cut up there on the hillside?"

Thompson answered in the affirmative, when the miners said: "Well, that is the place that Mrs. Bowers saw in her peep-stone. She has never been up here—has never seen the spot herself—but the place where that work is being done agrees in every particular with what she told the boys to look for. They may yet find the big mine Mrs. Bowers describes, for they sometimes get as high as ten cents to the pan up there."

Thompson had almost forgotten the peep-stone. When that miraculous pebble was thus recalled, he gazed up the hill at the little excavation and its surroundings with renewed interest. The prospects the men were then getting at the point were such as induced them to go to a sawmill, of which Thompson for a time had charge, and get a lot of narrow lumber (batting), from which they made a V-shaped flume and carried upon the ground a small stream of water. The men who put in this flume worked in and about the cut on the hillside, but finding they could not make much more than grub, they gave up the diggings and went away.

Peter O'Reilley was a spiritualist, and also a firm believer in the powers of the Washoe Seeress and her peep-stone. Therefore, taking Pat McLaughlin with him as a partner, he went to work in the deserted hole. He and Pat worked a long time without getting better pay than had been found by the former owners, and were about to give up and go to the placers at Dogtown, on the Walker River, when they had the good fortune to cut into a mass of decomposed black sulphuret of silver, filled with glittering spangles of free gold. The grand mining discovery of the age was that moment made—the great Comstock silver lode was found!

Thompson informed me that he saw the pit from which they were taking out the silver and gold, on the ground of the Ophir Mining Company, and it was at the point where the first hole was dug, in accordance with the directions given by Mrs. Bowers, and the same that was pointed out to him by the miners on Six-mile Cañon while the first owners were still at work. Mr. Thompson always asserted, and doubtless firmly believed, that to Mrs. Bowers alone was due the credit of the discovery of the Comstock lode.

Snowshoe Thompson's account of the virtues of the peep-stone is borne out by what is related of it by Lyman Jones, an old-timer on Gold Cañon and the man who built the first house in Virginia City;

whose wife was the first white woman who lived in that town and whose daughter Ella was the first white child seen in the place. Mr. Jones says he remembers to have seen the peep-stone used by Mrs. Bowers when she was living at Johntown. He says that on one occasion her peep-stone was the means of procuring a Mexican a "most unmerciful" whipping, and of the recovery of a lot of stolen gold dust.

Joe Webb, a miner then working on Gold Cañon—and a man well known to all old-time Nevadans—had a sack of gold dust stolen. The Washoe Seeress was consulted, and in turn she consulted her peep-stone. After looking into the stone for a time, she said she could see the thief. She named a certain Mexican working on the cañon as the man who had stolen the gold.

The "boys"—a lot of agreeable, good-natured six-footers—made a social call on the Mexican named (there were then quite a number of Mexicans on Gold Cañon), and gently informed him that he was found out and must disgorge. The Mexican stoutly denied the theft. The boys, however, told him that Mrs. Bowers had seen him in her peep-stone, and the peep-stone never lied. Looking into the peep-stone, she had seen him "gobble the sack" and make off with it. As the miraculous Highland pebble could not lie, the Mexican was told that he would be whipped until he produced the sack of dust.

The boys then went at the fellow and gave him a terrible whipping. The Mexican held out bravely for a time, but concluding that he would be killed if he did not give up the gold, he finally weakened. He guided the party of lynchers to a small cedar tree standing on the banks of Nigger Ravine—just east of where Silver City now stands— and there, at the root of the tree, with his own hands dug up the sack of stolen dust.

The gold recovered, the Mexican was told that he must at once leave the camp. He was not only willing but quite anxious to go. He said he did not want to live in a place where they had "such d——d things" as they "kept there in Johntown." If still alive, that Mexican doubtless has to this day a wholesome dread of all peep-stones.

Snowshoe Thompson had no doubt heard the story of the recovery of the stolen dust through the agency of the peep-stone, and it probably had the effect of inducing him to give greater credit to what was told him about the Washoe Seeress's pointing out the spot where the Comstock lode was first uncovered. He also undoubtedly was somewhat influenced in favor of her predictions from the fact of her being descended from one of those Highland Scotch families who claim to inherit the gift of second sight.

Snowshoe Thompson was one of those unfortunate persons whose lot in life it is to do a great deal of work and endure many hardships for very little pay. For twenty winters he carried the mails across the Sierra Nevada Mountains, at times when they could have been transported in no other way than on snowshoes. After he began the business, he made his home in the mountains, having secured a ranch in Diamond Valley, when for five winters in succession he was constantly engaged in carrying the mails across the snowy range. Two years he carried the United States mails when there was no contract for that service, and he got nothing. On both sides of the mountains he was told that an appropriation would be made and all would come out right with him, but he got nothing except promises.

When Chorpenning had the contract for carrying the mails, Thompson turned out with the oxen from his ranch and kept the roads open for a long time; and when there at last came such a depth of snow that the road could no longer be broken, he mounted his snowshoes and carried the mails on his back. Chorpenning failed, and Thompson never received a dime for his work.

First and last, he did a vast deal of work for nothing. Some seasons our overland mail would not have reached California during the whole winter had not Thompson turned out on his snowshoes and carried the sack across the mountains. He took pride in the work. It challenged the spirit of adventure within him. It was like going forth to battle, and each successive trip was a victory. This being his feeling, he was all the more readily made to believe that in case he turned out and did the work, he would eventually be paid. As Mr. Thompson approached his fiftieth year, he began to think that in his old age he ought to receive something from the government in reward of the services he had performed. He asked but $6,000 for all he had done and endured during twenty years. His petition to Congress was signed by all the state and other officials at Carson City, and by everyone else that was asked to sign it. In the winter of 1874, he himself went to Washington to look after his claim, but all he got was promises. He never got anything but promises while on duty in the Sierras, and when he went to Washington he was still paid in the same coin.

When Thompson went to Washington in 1874, he left Reno, Nevada, January 17. Three days afterwards the train got stuck in a big snowdrift, thirty-five miles this side of Laramie. There it stuck, in spite of the efforts of four locomotives to pull it through, preceded by a full day's shoveling by all the men that could be pressed into service. It was on Sunday that the four engines were tried and found wanting. On Monday morning the wind was still blowing a gale and the snow was still drifting badly. Becoming impatient, Thompson, with one fellow passenger—Rufus Turner, of Idaho—set out on foot and walked to Laramie, where they overtook a train that was also stuck fast in the snow a short distance outside of the village.

At Laramie, Turner came to the conclusion that he wanted no more pedestrian exercise, with the thermometer ranging at from fifteen to thirty degrees below zero. Thompson, however, was undaunted. He pushed on alone. He walked, in two days, fifty-six miles further, which carried him to Cheyenne, he having spent the intervening night at Buford Station, near the summit. At Cheyenne he found a train just starting out, and, boarding it, went through to the Missouri River—the first man directly from the Pacific Coast for about two weeks.

At the time, the newspapers in the East gave Thompson great credit for this achievement, declaring he was the first man who had ever beaten the "iron horse" on so long a stretch. This performance shows that he was still the same Snowshoe Thompson, when his foot was off his native heath. The trip was made without snowshoes—was made in ordinary boots.

If not the swiftest, it was universally conceded that even up to the time of his death, Thompson was the most expert snowshoe runner in the Sierra Nevada Mountains. At Silver Mountain, Alpine County, California, in 1870, when he was forty-three years of age, he ran a distance of sixteen hundred feet in twenty-one seconds. There were many snowshoers at that place, but in daring Thompson surpassed them all. Near the town was a big mountain, where the people of the place were wont to assemble on bright days in winter, to the number of two or three hundred. The ordinary snowshoers would go partway up the mountain to where there was a bench, and then glide down a beaten path. This was too tame for Thompson. He would make a circuit of over a mile, and come out on the top of the mountain. When he appeared on the peak he would give one of his wild High-Sierra whoops, poise his balance pole, and dart down the face of the mountain at lightning speed, leaping all the terraces from top to bottom, and gliding far out on the level before halting.

Snowshoe Thompson seldom performed any feat for the mere name and fame of doing a difficult and daring thing; yet W. P. Merrill, postmaster at Woodford's, Alpine County, writes me as follows, in speaking of some of Thompson's achievements: "He at one time went back of Genoa, on a mountain, on his snowshoes and made a jump of 180 feet without a break." This seems almost incredible, but Mr. Merrill is a reliable man, and for many years Thompson was his near neighbor and a regular customer at his store. Thompson doubtless made this fearful leap at a place where he would land in a great drift of soft snow. I spoke of this feat to Mr. C. P. Gregory, formerly Thompson's neighbor in the mountains, but at present a resident of Virginia City, Nevada, and he answered that although he had never heard of that particular leap, he did not doubt what Mr. Merrill said. "I know," said Mr. Gregory, "that at Silver Mountain he often made clear jumps of fifty and sixty feet."

What Thompson did, however, was generally in the way of business. His neighbors say that only a year or two before his death, while he was superintendent of the Pittsburg mine at the head of I. X. L. Cañon, about twenty miles south of his ranch, he frequently took a quarter of beef on his back and, mounted on his snowshoes, made his way up the cañon to the mine, a distance of one mile and a half. The cañon is described as being "about straight up."

The winter before his death, Thompson left Monitor for Silver Mountain at seven o'clock in the evening on his snowshoes, with a lantern strapped upon his breast, it being pitch dark. Though the road was a most difficult and dangerous one, and a furious snowstorm was beating full in his face, he reached his destination eight miles distant a little before midnight.

Snowshoe Thompson carried across the Sierras much of the material on which the *Territorial Enterprise* was first printed, that paper being first published at Genoa by W. L. Jernegan and Alfred James. It was then a weekly, and the first number was issued on Saturday, December 18, 1858. Thus it is seen that Thompson was called upon in all manner of emergencies. He not only packed newspapers across the mountains, but also the types on which newspapers were printed.

Postmaster Merrill says: "A few years before his death, Thompson one winter made a trip from here [Woodford's] up into Sierra County on his snowshoes, to run a race with the snowshoers up there. But he would not run their way. They had a track beaten down the hill where they ran. They would then squat down on their shoes, and run down along the prepared course. Thompson offered to put up money and go out upon the highest mountains, where there was no track made, and run and jump with them, but no one would take him up." The style of snowshoe racing mentioned by Mr. Merrill is nothing more nor less than coasting on snowshoes, and in Alpine County it is so called—is not dignified with the name of snowshoeing.

At the time of his death, Snowshoe Thompson was a member of the board of commissioners of Alpine County. He was a man who appeared to be well educated, and wrote a bold and beautiful hand. He must have been mainly self-educated. When a lad in Norway, his only chance for the acquirement of book knowledge was in the *omgangs skoler,* or ambulatory schools—schools that shift from place to place at certain periods of the year, following the population in the thinly settled sections. They are so called in contradistinction to the *fast skoler* or stationary schools. As the people of Norway in many places—like those about the Alps in Switzerland work their way up into the mountains in summer with their flocks, and move down again at the approach of winter, the *omgangs skoler* afford the only educational facilities attainable. While moving to and fro in the western states, his opportunities for attending school were probably not much better than they were in his native Norway.

Mr. Thompson was ill but a few days, and was confined to his bed but a day or two before he died. His disease was some derangement of the liver. He was engaged in putting in his spring crop at his ranch when taken sick. Being too ill to carry a sack and sow his barley in the usual way, he mounted a horse and sowed it from a bucket which he carried before him. Sowing grain on horseback was probably never before seen or attempted. He was as anxious and determined about getting in his crops as are the people of his native land, who sow their fields in March with ashes, soil, or sand, to hasten the melting of the snow.

Thompson was forty-nine years and fifteen days old when he died. He was buried at Genoa, and now rests by the side of his son Arthur, his only child and a most promising lad, who died June 22, 1878, at the age of eleven years and four months.

Thompson left his widow a farm of 160 acres in Diamond Valley, just across the Nevada line in California. She married again, and is now Mrs. John Scossa. She recently caused a tombstone to be erected over the grave of her former husband. At the top of the stone are seen a pair of artistically carved snowshoes, crossed and twelve inches in height.

John A. Thompson was the father of all the race of snowshoers in the Sierra Nevada Mountains, and in those mountains he was the pioneer of the pack train, the stage coach, and the locomotive. On the Pacific Coast his equal in his peculiar line will probably never again be seen. The times and conditions are past and gone that called for men possessing the special qualifications that made him famous. It would be hard to find another man combining his courage, physique, and powers of endurance—a man with such thews and sinews, controlled by such a will.

As an explorer in Arctic regions he would have achieved world-wide fame. Less courage than he each winter displayed amid the mountains has secured for hundreds the hero's crown. To ordinary men there is something terrible in the wild winter storms that often sweep through the Sierras; but the louder the howlings of the gale rose, the higher rose the courage of Snowshoe Thompson. He did not fear to beard the Storm King in his own mountain fastnesses and strongholds. Within his breast lived and burned the spirit of the old Vikings. It was this inherited spirit of his daring ancestors that impelled him to embark on difficult and dangerous enterprises—this spirit that incited him to defy even the wildest rage of the elements. In the turmoil of the most fearful tempests that ever beat against the granite walls of the High Sierras, he was undismayed. In the midst of the midnight hurricane, he danced on the rocks as though himself one of the genii of the storm.

Yet for such a man as Thompson, there was no real recklessness in anything he did. He watched every mood of the elements, and guarded against every danger that threatened. It was his knowledge of all the phenomena of the mountains, his calmness and the confidence he felt in his strength that made him victorious in all his undertakings. So modest was he, withal, that what others accounted great feats did not so appear to him. He looked upon the things he did as belonging to the business of everyday life.

He did not boast when he said: "I cannot be lost," for his way was pointed out to him by every star in the heavens; by every tree, rock, and hill—was whispered by the breeze and shouted by the gale. All else might be lost in the wild tumult of a winter storm, but Snowshoe Thompson stood unmoved amid the commotion; there, as everywhere, at home.

And he is still at home, for he rests where the snowy peaks of his loved mountains look down upon his last camping place; where the voices of the pines are borne to him by every breeze, and where the trembling ground often tells of the fall of the avalanche. A most fitting resting place for such a man!

Ho! For Washoe!

Washoe Correspondent

Silver City, Carson Co., Utah T. October 18th, 1860.

*M*y last was from Omega, California; I then promised you some notes from Silverland, and I have now been in Washoe over five months and have not been able to fulfill my promise; but bear with me friend *Gazette*. I promise you on the word of an "honest miner" to amend.

Since coming here I have been almost constantly engaged in prospecting among the neighboring hills and mountains; often I have taken a loaf or two of bread, a few slices of bacon, pick, shovel, blankets, and horn-spoon, and wandered for three or four days in the mountains, seeking at night some spring or rill of fresh water, where

Eight letters from the early days in Silverland, packed with vivid detail about men and mines. The first piece offers first impressions, five months after De Quille's arrival and eighteen after the discovery of the Comstock, from the Cedar Falls *Gazette,* November 30, 1860; the second includes the popular "Arkansaw's Nest," CFG, February 8, 1861; the third makes the case for Winnemucca, *Golden Era,* December 30, 1860; the fourth exhibits the local thirst for cruelty, CFG, April 5, 1861; the fifth introduces Spudder of the Pewterinktum Mine, GE, February 24, 1861; the sixth describes a Washoe sabbath, CFG, September 13, 1861; the seventh sketches an Irish family fight, CFG, December 20, 1861; and the last shows some other ethnic interactions, CFG, January 31, 1862.

after frying a slice of bacon on my shovel and partaking of a frugal repast of such "yarbs" as bread, tea and "inyons," I would roll up in my blankets and in spite of the howling of coyotes and my fears of having a tarantula, rattlesnake, or scorpion for a bed fellow, sleep soundly the sleep that none but a Washoe prospector can know.

This region, but eighteen months since the home of bands of wild Indians and an almost unknown waste, is now peopled by thousands of busy miners; substantial and tastefully constructed adobe cottages, peopled with the cheerful wife and merry and roguish little ones of the miners, merchants, and mechanics, are to be seen in our towns and cities. The steam whistles of our numerous quartz mills resound where but a few months since naught was heard but the war-whoop of the fierce Pah-Ute brave, or the tremendous echoing bleat of the timid mountain sheep. Splendidly graded, wide and smooth thoroughfares have taken the place of the old Indian trail, bridges are built and ferries established; four- and six-horse coaches dash through our streets and express wagons pass conveniently along where but lately jogged in solemn state the skin-dressed Pah-Ute patriarch astride his scrubby steed, while on foot followed a weary train of his women and children, packed like donkeys with the household possessions of the family. In short, we now have (where one year ago a meal could hardly be obtained) splendid hotels, restaurants, saloons, fruit stores, baths, barber shops, drugstores, book and periodical depots, livery stables, laundries, and almost all of the conveniences and luxuries of any country. Hundreds of wagons, heavily laden with machinery, lumber, and merchandise, and drawn by long lines of oxen or mules, come pouring in from California to tumble into our streets and upon our sidewalks impassable piles of bales, bags, boxes, wheels, cranks, stamps, wheel-barrows, and china-mats; long straggling pack trains come winding in and the "ha moola" of the Mexican drivers is constantly ringing in our ears.

Hundreds of stores, shops, and dwellings are now being erected, and all, from the humble 10 × 12 miner's cabin to the large and substantial brick or stone fireproof building of the merchant, spring up with mushroom-like celerity; now is a busy time among our builders, we have already had a foretaste of Washoe winter, and though our hills have rid themselves of their snowy mantle and appear again in sober brown, the warning has not been lost upon our people.

Mining has been carried on with a great deal of energy ever since the conclusion of the Indian war and hundreds—yes, thousands—of veins have been prospected more or less thoroughly. Many new and rich leads of gold- and silver-bearing quartz have been discovered since my arrival here, and claims then selling for four bits per foot are now, in many instances, selling for fifty, one hundred, and as high as three hundred dollars per foot; many lucky "hombres" have left for their homes with their "piles," and others can go whenever they have a mind to say the word.

There is a great variety of metals to be met with in this country; we have iron almost in a malleable state, copper, lead, zinc, cobalt, plumbago, antimony, palladium, platinum, gold, silver, and some other metals. Our miners have found metals which have puzzled our best assayers, and in large quantities at that. There is a place in the Henness pass on the side of a mountain where is found an immense amount of a metal which none of our assayers or those in California are able to name or determine the nature of. It was at first supposed to be platinum, and being lucky enough to secure forty feet in the lode, myself and a few other lucky (?) hombres used to amuse ourselves by getting up at night and making calculations of the amount per ton our rock would be worth.

After a week spent thus happily, and numerous meetings and calculations, we decided that our ore was worth somewhere between forty and one hundred and seventy thousand dollars per ton, and, let the matter go as it would, we were worth millions and tens and hundreds of millions—but alas! there came a telegraph dispatch from San Francisco that our platina was not platina! What was it then? Don't know—insoluble in acids—not affected by heat—don't know what the de—dickens it is. Then we held a sort of indignation meeting and voted the whole tribe of assayers and metallurgists a set of humbugs, who were fit only to steal the honest miner's money and didn't know a good article of platinum when they saw it, or else—yes, that's the idea!—they know its immense value and have only sent this discouraging return to get us to leave so they may get possession of our mine. But we won't be fooled, we'll fight to the last—if we ever catch them near our mine we'll "slaughter the bloody file o' them." And so ended our bright visions of wealth.

We have an almost endless variety of rocks; good limestone, gypsum and a variety of meerschaum almost if not quite equal to the genuine for beauty, lightness, and excellence—the amber mouthpiece of one of which is now between the lips of your humble correspondent.

Dec. 22, 1860.

We, in "Silverado," are having most delightful weather; in fact we have had but an inch or two of snow this winter, to put it altogether, and but one slight shower of rain. Last night the ground was frozen to the depth of an inch, which it has not been before this winter. We sometimes have very high winds, and it is nothing very uncommon for the air to be filled with sand and gravel stones. The other evening we had a pretty severe gale, though only but little damage was done; only one house was blown down. The owner of this house had just stepped out of a saloon and, finding the wind strong, said (addressing the Almighty) "O, blow you old——" (using most blasphemous language), "you can't hurt nothing!" The words were hardly out of his mouth before his house, a large adobe building, lay in a pile of ruins, while not another house, or even tent, in the town was damaged in the least. Verdict of the citizens, "Served him right . . . "

We hear a great deal of the disunion troubles in the States, but people here and in California don't appear to let it trouble them much. They say if it comes to a civil war, they will take no part, but will form out of Oregon, California, and part of Utah, an independent Republic.

In the way of amusements we are pretty hard up here. I once, if I remember rightly, spoke somewhat favorably of the California saloons—remarking that in some of them one might spend an hour or two very pleasantly in reading and chatting with one's friends, and that they were not altogether the "hells" many persons suppose them to be. I am sorry I cannot speak so favorably of the saloons in Washoe; but the fact is that persons who prefer peace and quiet to noise and rowdyism must spend their evenings at home. We did have a theatre here—the performers being amateurs, citizens of the town—but after performing two evenings the thing "went up the flume," i.e. petered. The first evening the effect of the performance "were slightually" injured by an accident which happened to the tights (a pair of woolen drawers) of one of the actors. On the second evening the nerves of the performers were somewhat unsettled by the obduracy of the curtain, which stubbornly refused to rise, notwithstanding divers and sundry frantic efforts made with that very desirable end in view. The bell would ring and the audience lean forward, watching with breathless interest for the striking scene about to be disclosed to their admiring gaze—up would go the curtain about two feet, revealing to the excited and enthusiastic audience a row of legs—here and there a foot planted defiantly forward, and the hems of a pair of petticoats—a frantic tug, a jerk, and down goes the curtain. Then comes a shuffling of feet; the actors fall into attitude, the bell rings, and up goes the curtain about two feet and sticks—another grand and striking display of legs, ditto petticoat hems; down goes the curtain, and the hats and cheers of the delighted and highly edified spectators go up. It is but fair to add that when the curtain did "go loose," the majority of the performers acquitted themselves exceedingly well—all things considered.

Since I wrote last, there has been but three men killed in fights. I had supposed, till after arriving in this fighting country, that the revolver was a weapon sufficiently deadly for any purpose; but here they are considered old-fashioned, slow—and no man who makes the least pretension to being a "blood" will be seen with such a "tool." The derringer is the approved "utensil," and the gamblers, saloon keepers, fancy men, in fact all who are "on the shoot" go about with their derringers at half cock in their pockets. The advantage in this weapon is that you can shoot your enemy before he can make a move towards drawing a revolver—if he should be armed with that weapon. In fact, if necessary, you may shoot through your pocket (as is sometimes done) without bringing your pistol out in sight at all. No fast young man but has his derringers, costing from $50 to $80 per pair.

Having nothing particularly interesting in the way of news to write, I will give you a short sketch of an "Arkansaw's Nest," which I found the other day, while on my way to Fort Churchill with a friend, one Freeman, who knows all sorts of odd people.

In a spot where dark and jagged granite mountains fell back from the river (Carson), leaving a pretty extensive scope of level bottom land, we came upon a newly built log house, or rather a pair of them, with a space of some ten feet between, though both under one roof, similar to the log barns in the western states. A shingle, nailed on the corner of the house, bore the following cheering announcement— "Whiskey and Seegairs fore sale." Freeman, who is acquainted with every man, woman, and child in the country, said he knew the proprietor and must stop and see him and—"especially his daughter." We found the landlord seated on an inverted wash tub in the middle of the floor, which was of the original soil, while a little dried up Dutchman was operating on his straggling locks in the capacity of a barber. On being introduced by Freeman, Arkansaw bounced up with his hair cropped off above his ear on one side of his head and hanging over his shoulder on the other, ducked his head and scraped the dirt floor with one foot, then the other, after the manner of an excited Shanghai—ordered Sal to "set cheers," and then swore he'd "forgot there wasn't sich a thing in the house."

Sal was a green, gawky girl of sixteen, sporting a big old-fashioned sunbonnet, "the whyche" stuck out a foot beyond her face, a dirty, greasy calico dress, with the waist under her arms, and guiltless of the slightest indication of crinoline—nary a hoop! Sal's features were decidedly good, but the smoke of pine wood had got her complexion out of order. Besides Sal and Dad there was Bub, about three years younger than Sal. Bub wore a pair of tow pants with copperas stripe that reached nearly to his chin, effectually precluding all necessity for a vest, and kept in that exalted posture by a pair of knit suspenders of blue woolen yarn.

Arkansaw was a widower; he explained how he'd lost the old woman comin' 'cross the plains and "hadn't been to the white settlements since to get anyone," so he "let Sal boss the consarn and get along how he could."

During our stay Sal stood leaning against the jamb of the fireplace, with her head resting in the crook of her elbow and one heel toasting on the fore-stick of the fire, biting at her nails, and peering at "them fellers" from out the depths profound of her huge bonnet.

Bub was barefoot and put in his time in front of the fire, with his back to the blaze, standing first on one foot then on the other, in order more effectually to toast the soles of a pair of chapped, calloused, and not snow-white "understandings." Says Sal from under her bonnet— "Bub, I'd put them air toad smashers out'r sight; them fellers might think ye's struck with morterfercation."

"Morter, yer granny," says Bub, "yer needn't git so smart cos er's fellers here, elst I tell 'em how yer heels looked fore yer scraped 'em!"

"Do an I'll beat you till ye beller!" says Sal in a fierce whisper.

"Hut, tut! Must you two be jawin' an' jawin' all the time when thar's strangers in?" cries Daddy; then adds—"Come boys, come fellers, let's take suthin'—Sal, clean a cup! Hur's a little the best ole rye in these parts!"

"Well, our regards, sir."

"Hur's my respecks, boys, and hur's hopin' yer may hev luck and may go on bildin' mills at Silver City, an' pound up all the mountains an'—an'—an' git what's in 'em."

Our host was evidently not in the habit of making long speeches and came near breaking down before reaching a climax which, after all, judging from his sheepish looks, did not suit him. He informed us that he owned claims in Silver City, in Esmeraldo, and beyond Mono Lake on Owen's River, and was on the high road to fortune, even if the "hay crop failed."

Bidding our Arkansaw friend good-bye, we traveled on to Miller's Station that evening, and the next day taking a cutoff over mountains so high that for a couple of hours we were enveloped in snow clouds, we reached home just at night, cold and hungry, blessing (?) a miner's lot and thinking of all the warm fires and hot suppers we had ever experienced or read of.

Dec. 23d, 1860.

Having seen several stories going the rounds concerning the Indian who was shot at Chinatown, at first reported to have been Old Winnemucca, then young Winnemucca, I will state the facts in regard to the affair as learned from one who was in the town at the time:

Some fellows, who perhaps were the worse for whisky, went to a cabin in which some Pi-Utes were sleeping, about three o'clock, and demanded admittance, asking at the same time for Winnemucca. Being told by the squaws that Winnemucca was not there, they swore it was a lie, and they were coming in to kill him. With this they burst in the door, and Captain Jim, the only buck in the house, attempted to rush out past them. They fired on and wounded him, believing it to be the old chief, though where he was hit is not known, except that as he passed out he said in the Pi-Ute language, "I am shot in a bad place; you will see me no more." Several shots were fired after him as he retreated, but it is not known that any of them took effect. The Indians say he was killed and thrown into the river. But the probability is that he ran out and caught his pony and escaped to his tribe, though the Indians deny his ever having been seen since.

It is such cowardly acts as the above that stir up Indian wars, and the men who perpetrate them are the ones to run and leave brave men to fight and die when it comes to the fair conflict in the field.

Since I think of it, I will tell you a story of Winnemucca. I tell it as 'twas told to me, not vouching for its truth in every particular. The adventure was related to me by a stout young German lad, some eighteen or twenty years of age, with an honest and good-natured countenance, and I see no reason why it may not be true. The young fellow is certainly of a roving turn, for I met him in a wild and picturesque gorge far east of the Carson, and it was there by the camp fire he told the story. He and his partner were prospecting, at the time the war with the Pi-Utes broke out last Spring, in the vicinity of the Sink of the Humbolt, and were not aware that anything had occurred to disturb the peace which previously existed between the whites and the Indians. This being the case, he and his partner started to come into Chinatown, without the slightest suspicion of anything wrong, until reaching a Station on the Humbolt they found the buildings burned and various articles such as the books and cards strewn about. The thought struck them that a war had broken out, and, being determined that if the Indians did kill them they would not furnish them tools to do it with, they threw away their guns, and pouring their powder on the ground, set fire to it. For some time they saw no Indians, but at length, having camped for the night, an Indian who spoke pretty good English came riding up to their fire and told them to pack up their things and come with him, for if they remained where they were they might be killed, as they were at war with the Californians—"kill heap, great many California men, get heap pony, heap gun; California men heap kill um Injun, heap kill Pi-Ute; white man heap run, like cow."

After a short consultation, the Dutchman and his companion thought it would be best to go with the Indian, and, catching up their ponies, they packed their blankets and camp equipments and announced their readiness to follow. After an hour's travel they reached a large encampment where they found themselves in the midst of at least five hundred warriors. Their guide conducted them to a tent near the middle of the camp, which he informed them was "Winnemucca's house," and soon the old chief made his appearance and catechised them as follows:

"Where do you come from?"

"From beyond the Sink of the Humbolt."

"What were you doing there?"

"Prospecting."

"Did you see many Indians there?"

"We did."

"Did they beg of you much?"

"A great deal."

"Did you give them anything?"

"We gave them all we could spare."

"Did they try to take away your provisions?"

"No."

"Did they steal?"

"Yes, a little."

"Bad, bad Indians! Many white men bad, too; many bad men—some red, some white. What have you in your packs?"

"Blankets and provisions."

"Have you sugar left?"

"A little."

"Will you sell me two pounds?"

"Yes, certainly; or give it to you."

"No, no! I must pay!"

Having measured out the sugar in a tin cup, Winnemucca, on being told the price was one dollar per pound, said it was not enough, and made them take two dollars per pound. He next asked for gunpowder, and on being told they had none, caused their bundles to be opened and searched, but of course was disappointed.

When first brought into the village, they were a good deal alarmed and feared being put to death, but from Winnemucca's manner toward them, they now hoped to escape death, but still felt far from easy. The old man told them they were only at war with the Californians, and would hurt no one that came from the East. Their horses were picketed out with those of the tribe, and they were shown where to spread their blankets. In the morning they went to the tent of Winnemucca and signified their desire to depart. The old man gave orders for their horses to be brought and told them to be sure to travel fast and not stop to prospect. After they had packed their animals and were about to start, Winnemucca gave them a string made of twisted sinews, with a number of knots tied in it, telling them that whenever they were stopped by Indians to show them the string. They were stopped two or three times in the course of the day, but the string operated like magic, for it changed instantly the countenances of the Indians from the savage frown of an enemy to the smiles of friendship. Wherever they were stopped the string was taken from them and one of the knots untied, when it was returned to them. In one place they were fired upon while passing through a cañon, but by calling to the Indians and assuring them they were friends, the Indians approached and, on being shown the pass, shook hands, said they were very sorry for what had happened, and begged them not to mention it to Winnemucca. In another place they passed a hut, but seeing no one but an old woman, did not show her the string. In half an hour they were overtaken by three Indians on horseback and ordered to stop. On showing the string they were asked why they did not show it to the old squaw; however, they took out a knot and went off laughing. A short distance beyond Williams' Station, an Indian stopped them, undid the last knot and kept the string, after that they saw no more Indians and arrived safe at Chinatown. The Dutchman says that when he sees Winnemucca again he is going to ask him to give him a string that he may keep, so that he may prospect where he pleases.

Feb. 2d, 1861.

Some new strikes have been made in Virginia City, in silver. One in a lead called the "Vermillion lead" and "Ironsides Co.," said to be very good; the price per foot went up from 50 cents to $80 in one day. Speculators immediately started out after "outside" owners and in some instances bought their ground for as low as $1.00 per foot. One or two men who owned in it being down in the Esmeralda mines, some half dozen speculators posted off down there to buy them out and will perhaps get their interests for one tenth of their value—this is a fair game here—*homo homini lupus!* or more vulgarly "dog eat dog," is the rule and not the exception. Every fellow for himself and the *gentleman in black* for the majority; best fellow gets the "pile," and don't stop to whine when you're hurt. Old men with blear and watery eyes, snowy locks and shaky, trembling limbs, boys, smooth faced and rosy cheeked, men of middle age and of all colors and conditions crowd, struggle, and snarl for and over various patches of rock supposed to contain their god, the all powerful king Ora; knives gleam, revolvers explode, souls take their flight! but still the tottering old man, the smooth-faced boy, the man in his prime press on, on, ever on! is the cry; they are stricken with the *auri sacra fames!*—the accursed thirst for gold! They are desperate. Gold or death! is written in their faces. Touch one of their leads and you find you were not mistaken in your translation of the lines traced in their countenances—a revolver presses against your brains—a crook of the finger and you're dead!

Well, what of it? Nothing! Folks go on prospecting, play monte and poker, build houses and mills, sink shafts, run tunnels and, among other things, dig a hole and bury you—why didn't you mind your own business? A man may dress himself in the most outlandish style he can invent, he may be naturally ungainly and misshapen, odd, ridiculous, and yet he may travel the country over and no one will call out after him or poke fun at him—why? Because it's *dangerous!* In this country people *must* mind their own business. "Jokes among friends"—*be sure you know them well.* But this rather savage picture is only meant to apply to the population of these mines *en masse* and when mingling promiscuously. There are groups of friends who have by degrees ventured together, who laugh and tell yarns and to a certain point and in certain conditions "poke sly fun" at each other, but *never* to the same degree that I have often seen it done in the States. A certain degree of dignity is accorded to every man and maintained by every man. If a man is used as a butt for the wit of others it must be in such a manner as not to *crowd his dignity,* but rather give him an elevated opinion of himself; and a human being thus inflated often yields quite as much sport to full grown men as his toy balloon does to the boy.

Having traveled quite as far in that direction as I care to at present, and as I don't care particularly where I go or what I do next—which I presume also to be the reader's "awful fix," I will just mention that (speaking of inflating a man, or as is the practice of the feminine portion of humanity—*blowing him up,* reminded me of it) I saw a common bat blown up in a saloon in California, and of all the odd, ludicrous looking specimens of animated nature it was ever my luck to behold, I think this sooty little "connecting link between bird and beast" took the lead—by some distance. It was a Missourian, or Pike as we call them, to their great disgust, that was conducting the operation. At first the little animal's body alone was inflated and this we concluded was the whole *show,* but Pike, taking his mouth off the tube he was using for a moment, said that its wings and all would presently become inflated—*"if he does well!"* In a short time to our great delight "he done well," and of all the laughing and yelling and stamping and pawing the air you have ever heard of, it was there. An *hombre* would go up to the counter, on which rolled and fluttered this literal *rara avis,* bend intently over it a moment, then throw himself back with such a jerk as to send his hat half across the room, emitting at the time a succession of shrieks most horrible to any but uncivilized ears—then another and another would venture up, take *his* dose and *go off* in the same manner. The following recipe for making this *interesting* experiment I procured on the spot from Professor Pike: "Cut a tiny leetle hole atween the varmint's years, then git er leetle, small bit of er holler stick or straw an' perceed to bisness—when his wings are plump, round and tight, take out the tube (the incision will not need to be stopped as no air will escape) and he's fixed." Having an idea that some persons might consider it rather a cruel sport, I mentioned it to Pike and he said in reply—"Hurt 'em? no, fact is, they rather like it!" I am glad now that I thought to make this inquiry of Pike, as small boys hearing of this experiment need have no compunctions nor hesitate about trying this beautiful, entertaining, and instructive experiment on the very first bat they catch.

Feb. 12th, 1861.

My back is elevated—I'm enraged! I gnash my teeth in fury. I kick things about the cabin. I think I should rush out and kick the first man I could find, was it not that I fear *someone* would get hurt. Therefore, I considerately vent my rage within the walls of my own cabin. Most men, when they feel as I do, are so fortunate as to have wives to kick. I am unfortunate; I have only stools and camp kettles to vent my rage upon. Oh, for a wife! I have been in this awful fix for over a week; if something in the line of news don't transpire shortly, you will hear of *some man* getting badly whipped—I *won't* stand it much longer and I *will* kick some feller.

Jones comes rushing into my cabin—you know *how excitable* Jones is? I spring up and run to meet him. I say, "How are you, Jones? Good morning, Jones! Jones, glad to see you! What's up? What's the news?" "News, n-e-w-s concerning what?" queries Jones. "Concerning anything! Concerning everything! What's happened? What's up?"

"Indeed, Mr. De Quille, I'm sure I don't know of anything—what *is* up?"

"Jones, confound you, Jones! Blast you, Jones! Don't you come rushing in here again and not have any news! You're the most excitable man I ever saw, Jones! Why must you always be getting so excited? But don't mind what I say, Jones; I was excited. You disappointed me, Jones, sadly disappointed me!"

"How did I disappoint you? Did I say I had any news?"

"No, but you know, Jones, how you came rushing in here? I thought you had had good news and felt glad, happy, delighted—I thought someone was shot. Oh, Jones, Jones! You can have no idea of my disappointment! You shouldn't come in so; still, I forgive you, Jones, I forgive you, but for heaven's sake, Jones, be careful in the future."

Jones sees he has put his foot in it, and asks in a subdued, trembling voice if I will lend him a cup of sugar, saying that they had not discovered that theirs was out till breakfast was all ready, "and so he run up to borrow a little to do breakfast." I gave Jones the sugar, and as soon as he left, fastened the door, kicked the bottom out of my camp kettle, kicked over the table, kicked a loaf of bread into some seventy-odd pieces, kicked the spout off my teapot, and seizing my hat, rushed up the street. In going uptown I passed a house where lives a little girl I have sometimes been fool enough to think a "sweet, innocent little lamb." She now comes running out to meet me—I feel for my revolver but haven't got it; so I give her a look so savage as to cause her hair to stand straight up on her head, and hurry on. I see Spudder just ahead and again feel for my revolver; but as I don't find it, do the next best thing to get rid of him—cross to the opposite side of the street—for I detest, abhor, abominate, and despise Spudder and his never-ending boasting on his favorite "lead." But Spudder sees me. I felt sure he would—he sees everybody. "Hollo, Dan! Hollo, hold on! *News! News!* Great *news!* Glorious *news!*" I don't wait for Spudder to come to me—I rush across the street again; I could almost hug Spudder to my heart; I feel sure there has just been a fight, and six, at least, shot or cut to pieces. I shake hands with Spudder, ask him where he has been stopping, tell him I have been hunting him all over town, invite him to call round oftener, and when he opens his mouth to speak, say "Not a word, my friend! Not a word *yet,* Mr. Spudder! We'll go in and take something! We *must* take a little something *first,* Spudder! The news afterwards." Spudder is delighted, astonished, joyous, bewildered. We take *something*—Spudder a good deal of it. I draw Spudder's arm within my own and lead him to the extreme far corner of the room. We seat ourselves close together. I lay my hand encouragingly on Spudder's knee. "Now, my dear Spudder, now for the news! But take your time, Spudder, don't hurry!"

"You're too kind, Dan; I never knowed afore ye wur sich a good feller! I hain't been to see ye as often as I orter; but don't think hard, Dan, I'll come every day now, and stay—"

"But the news, Spudder! The *news!*"

"Yes, yes, I wur jist about to tell ye—I know ye'll be delighted— we've struck it richer n-n-ever in er Pewterinktum! Jist as full of sulferts as—"

I kicked the chair from under Spudder, kicked his old "stovepipe" out of the saloon, kicked it halfway down the street and should have been kicking it yet had I not happened upon a Chinaman with a pole and two large baskets of clothes on his back. Him I seized by the tail, and whirling him a few times round my head, let go of him and let him sail down over the embankment and through the canvas roof of a house; then, kicking his baskets after him, went raging down the road. On approaching the house where the "little lamb" lives, I gathered a big rock and watched for her to come out, but, disappointed here again, I rushed home, locked and bolted my door, hung two pairs of blankets before the window, kicked two sacks of "extra self-raising" to pieces, then stood myself up in one corner of my cabin on my head.

After standing on my head three days and two nights I felt a little better. Let myself down and thought I'd go to the post office. Got halfway and saw Spudder coming toward me. Felt worse immediately—got hold of a rock and made at him. Spudder run; I run. I was after Spudder—Spudder knew it. I chased him through town, halfway up Grizzly Hill, and into a tunnel. Built a big fire in the mouth of the tunnel and went back to the post office. Got the *Era* of February 3. Saw the "little lamb" as I went home, patted her head—promised her some candy. Got home feeling pretty good. Felt good a while longer. Put a stool near the wall, put one end of a board on the stool; put the other end of the board on the wall; put a pillow on the board; fixed a box to lay my legs on; got a stool; put my legs on the box; put my head on the pillow. Then I light my candle, open the *Era,* and commence reading "The King of the Mountains." Wish I had got some candy for the "little lamb."

Someone knocks at the door. I say, "Come in." Door opens. "Spudder!" Box slips from under my legs; stool goes after box; board goes after stool; head strikes the hardest rock in the wall. Spudder runs. I get up, lock the door. Go back and bolt the door. Pile a lot of wood against it. Put the table against it. Kick the teapot. Kick the camp kettle. Kick the frying pan. Stand myself on my head in the corner till morning.

In the morning feel better. Commence the story again. Am delighted with Hadgi-Stavros. Feel an affection for the "Corflote." Long to hold "Vasile" in my arms. Hope they'll cut off "Mary Ann's" head—ditto "Mrs. Simons." Wish we had a few such well-disposed gentlemen here. Feel so much better I go uptown. See knots of men here and there on the corners. Heart leaps to my throat. Am in a tremor of delight—think somebody's killed. Inquire and find people are jumping all the cross streets and alleys. Delighted. Recover my usual flow of spirits. Everybody in favor of a *flow of spirits.* Good!— be a fight yet! People rush into saloons—get a drink. Rush out and drive stakes. Stick up notices. "We, the undersigned do claim"—"for building purposes." One man can't find timber for the stakes. Sits down and straddles out his legs—half across the street. Puts notice on his hat: "We, the undersigned." Woman runs out with broom. Hits man with outstretched legs. Man runs. Woman sticks up her broom with notice: "We, the undersigned." Some run to the lumber yards. Buy boards. Make fences across the streets. Tack up cards—"Notice is hereby given." You bet! "Plaza! Plaza! Plaza!" All rush to the plaza. Set stakes. Bring posts—boards, rocks. One man digs a hole— another party pushes him away—puts in his own post. "Fight! Fight! Fight!" Whoops, hurra! Great, good, glorious! No, no, false alarm— no fight! Plaza all gone, all took! "Notice is hereby given" and "we the undersigned." Hurra, hurra! Here we go again for Main Street! Feller gets 200 feet up and 200 feet down through the middle. I take first south extension—"including all dips, spurs, and angles." Also, right of way through Burke & Walsh's mill—with spur up South

Fork, for lager beer saloon. I build a fort—get muskets. Hold out two days. Sell to man from San Francisco—$2,973. Cash—"This indenture," etc., etc. All right! See the little girl—sweet, pretty, *little lamb!* —get her some candy.

Two days have passed; I am fully recovered; and whenever I feel the slightest symptom of a relapse I have only to slap my hand upon my pocket, whereupon arises a chink that most effectually dispels all gloomy thoughts and clothes my visage in radiant smiles.

Aug. 7th, 1861.

A great many families are coming in—women and children are to be seen in every part of town, and we begin to feel like a civilized community. We have preaching nearly every Sunday. To give you an idea of our progress in civilization, I will give you a sketch of

BEAUTIES OF A WASHOE SABBATH AND
CHURCHGOING IN THE MINES

The church is a carpenter's shop on the main street of the city, with the whole front open to the road. The pulpit a workbench, with a number of the Sacramento *Union* doing service as an altar cloth near its center and a lot of paint pots, oil cans, saws, and a lot of jack planes piled on either end. The seats are brandy kegs, nail kegs, and rough boards. Time four o'clock P.M. Congregation begins to arrive. Some secure seats without difficulty; but one or two ladies are so unfortunate as to tear their dresses. One very nice young man, who is seated on the top of a nail keg, arises to accommodate a lady, but the keg is firm for union and won't secede—"Whither thou goest I will go," etc. Nice young man looks very red in the face—some very audible snickering—a r-r-rip! and the agony is over. The house is soon full to overflowing and the holy man arises to "give out" a hymn. A six-mule team, dragging a mountain schooner covered with bells passes the door and the musical clangor rushes into the building and explodes along the rafters in continuous peals. Holy man backs up and takes a fresh start. Singing commences—*Voom!* goes a blast that causes the window panes to rattle and the paint pots to dance. Singing continues. Hack drives slowly past, the driver shouting at the top of his voice— "Oh, yis! gintlemen, here we are now!! All aboard for Go-o-ld Hill and Vergina! Oh, yis, gintlemen, git aboord!"—More teams, another blast, and more bells. Minister reads his text, during which the

"Union Guards" march past with fife and drum. Launches out into his sermon. Bells ring, hackmen yell, a few blasts go off; elevates his voice, shouts, yells till black in the face—a tremendous blast sets the paint pots dancing and jars the spectacles off his nose. Holy man still persists; leans over workbench, gesticulates with hands, sways his body, makes some horrible mouths—but not a word can be heard to fall from his lips; for there is a four-handed dog fight just before the door. Soon there is a man fight—"fight! fight! fight!"—"Shoot the d——d son of a—gun!" "Bang—bang—bang!" A ball crashes through the house over the heads of the worshippers, filling the air with slivers—ladies draw their bonnets forward to protect their faces, and smile. Gents draw their revolvers, cock them, and look out at the door and windows. Holy man takes out his derringer, examines the cap, and lays it beside the bible. Still continues his sermon. More mule teams. More bells and a few light blasts; occasional pistol shot. The theatre folks parade the streets with their brass band; eighteen steam whistles sound the supper hour; Hibernian and Chinaman dispute concerning a "wash bill"; more mule teams; more bells. Holy man pronounces the benediction through a speaking trumpet; a blast in a tunnel immediately under the building jars all the glass from the windows, upsets the paint pots, and hurls the whole in a promiscuous heap into the middle of the room. Holy man leaps over the work-bench and, as fast as members of the congregation get upon their feet, presents his hat for the "regular" two bits. Meetin's out.

Nov. 10th, 1861.

I think I hinted to you in a former letter that I have some rather unpleasant neighbors—in fact, I know I did. Well, the young gentlemen who aspire to become proficients on the "brazen" instruments are at this time in all the agonies of Yankee Doodle. I think they must be striving to "locate" it in all its "dips, spurs, angles and *variations*." God send that they may improve with the utmost possible rapidity!

As for the loving couple of Hibernian antecedents, they, I am happy to announce, are advancing at a "killing" pace. About twice a week the cry of murder is to be heard issuing from their domicile, and I hope the fate of the Kilkenny cats may yet be theirs. In their last engagement the old man rather outgeneraled his worser half and succeeded in fastening her out of the house, himself being strongly intrenched within. The old lady beat the house with clubs, stones, and boards in vain. Her most promising daughter, aged thirteen, a chip off the old block, notwithstanding she is fresh from a San Francisco convent, assisted her in the operation of battering the house; finding they were not making headway at this, old one changed her tactics and urged her daughter to: "Scream, Lizza-beth! scream, ye little divil!" and thus exhorted, "Lizza-beth" set up a series of ear-piercing screeches that would have put to shame the most elaborate vocal efforts of a Black Swamp "painter." Finding this procedure unlikely to produce the desired effect, the little imp struck out in an idea of her own. In a high key, with a heart-broken drawl, she cried: "The God above is good, mother! He'll perteckt us an' He'll punish *him!*" The *old one* thought this might be a good dodge and essayed it; crying out in a loud, sanctimonious tone: "Yis, me darter, G-o-d is gu-u-de! He'll punish 'em to the softenin' of his heart"—then, her wrath getting the better of her, she broke out shrilly and furiously—"an' ef He don't be afther doin' it d——d quick I'll smash in the winde, an' once I come till the cursed, stinkin' ould dthrayman, I'll grip the poker and *soften his haid* for 'im, so I will!" At length, on a promise of good behavior, her "ould mon" admitted her; but no sooner was she within doors than she proceeded to carry out her threat of softenin' Johnny's haid, and "Johnny" gave her a really bad, brutal beating. About a week after this, one McCormick, who knew them both well, met "Johnny" and asked: "And how does the old woman do now'days, Johnny?" "Very well! very well indade, Misther Mac! I broke a broom handle all to smithers over her haid the other night, and kicked her awhile in the ribs—an' she's doin' very well indade now, Misther Mac, I thank ye!"

Dec. 20, 1861.

Did you hear something "drap" out this way a week or ten days ago? Whether you did or not, about that time there was thitherward a fall—of rain here, and, "Oh, what a *fall* my countrymen!" Not in this Washoe region alone, but throughout California. Here it had been raining softly for two or three days, when on Sunday night it set in "on the pour." By ten o'clock the roaring of the swollen cañon, running through the town, was terrific. It is very steep and the bed solid rock, and down this huge boulders chased each other like the balls on a bowling alley. These grinding and crashing together gave out a rumbling that was heard above the howl of the storm. A number of houses were swept away in town and all the mills damaged more or less. The mill of Brook & Co. was undermined and the engine room fell into the flood and broke up. At other mills the water rushed through (they being built in the narrow cañon, which all the "old settlers" stoutly maintained was never known to exceed twenty inches in volume) and tearing out the amalgamating pans, scattered the precious ore promiscuously down the channel—much to the delight of certain *hombres,* of the genus miner, owning surface claims in the bed of the creek. These claims were further enriched by the washing away of great banks of valuable tailings, which had accumulated at all the mills, and which constituted part of the spoils of the mill owners. It is estimated that not less than $100,000 was by these means set adrift. The toll road from Gold Hill to some distance below this city was torn in holes and filled with great blocks of granite, and it will cost the company owning it an immense sum to repair it.

Several houses in town, being built too near the brink of the cañon, were undermined and washed down; others were swept clear from their foundations. The large warehouse of Steiner & Koneman came near being undermined; however, it was saved with the loss of the wall next the cañon. A miner who had made the earthen floor of his cabin a bank of deposit for a purse of $300, found to his cost that even such a *bank* could *cave* under certain circumstances. Taking a walk down the cañon the morning after the flood, I saw a number of stranded houses moored against its banks; the shores strewn with bedding and furniture, wood, lumber, and every imaginable species of wreck. A number of wagon yards on the cañon well cleaned out, and wagons and parts of wagons were strewn from one end of the ravine to the other. The mills on the Carson River were considerably damaged and several dams washed out. At Gold Hill several houses were demolished and one large stone mill, costing some $30,000, washed down. Several mines on the celebrated Gold Hill lead have caved in, one place a space of ground forty feet in width by seventy in length dropped toward the lower regions; the timbers in other claims have been cracking and giving away and it is feared that the cave may become general. All this is owing to insufficient timbering and the amount of water absorbed from the late rains.

At Virginia City but few buildings fell, the town being situated on the summit of a hill. At the town of Flowery, situated in Six-mile Cañon, some damage was sustained by mill owners and two or three houses were washed away. On the cañon below Flowery a large mill was destroyed, and above the town toward Virginia City, just below the Sugar Loaf Mountain, a mill owned by a company of Spaniards went down with a rush from a breaking dam. Many mills and buildings were saved in this place (Silver City), by constructing wing dams above them, and the amount of "rot gut" punished by the Irish and Dutch employed in this work was startling. Toward evening the fighting fluid began to do its work, and in front of the Globe Hotel a free fight ensued between the Pat O'Reileys and the Hans Gunsenhausers. Stones, fists, and clubs were the weapons used—neither party (for a wonder) being armed with anything more deadly. The air was filled with stones, clubs, and curses, and the ground covered with hats, coats, and fallen warriors. The melee commenced indoors, at the bar, and during the preliminary skirmish the greatest execution was done, for there the bottles and glasses of the bar furnished offensive and defensive weapons, and some terrible cuts were given and received with pitchers and porter bottles. I reached the ground just as the two little armies emerged—deployed is, I believe, the proper military term—upon the open field. They formed suddenly into two lines and the "frequency" with which the rocks flew back and forth was delightful—to an outsider, and might be likened to two armies cannonading each other. At last the Teutons were forced to retreat, and this was quite a Leesburgh affair, as there was the raging cañon to cross and the means of "transportation" limited to a single narrow log. Here the Patlanders rushed down to the shore and poured in a deadly fire; most of which, however, took effect upon the back of a burly Dutchlander, who literally covered the retreat. As soon as the front ranks had reached the shore, they wheeled and poured in a fire on the venturesome Irish which made them fall back, and by this most admirable and truly military maneuver, the rear was enabled to effect a safe landing. During the fight a crowd of Americans looked on in disgust and one chiv. gave vent to his mind as follows: "Those fellows ain't as a general thing bad citizens, but d——n them! It takes them a long while to get over their low notions and become used to working with knives and pistols!"

A Day in the Silver Mines

$\mathcal{O}$n a sunny Saturday morning not long since, I concluded to take a stroll to Virginia City. Without incident or accident I reached the famed Comstockian city, and soon after sighted and bore down upon my friend Perry C., who was cruising in the vicinity of Paster's. Having no objection to a more extended voyage, we set sail Ophir-ward, taking an outside peep at the mine and making arrangements for an underground survey at two o'clock. We then for a time wandered and chatted promiscuously, viewing and noting the improvements in the town—which are indeed numerous and substantial. There are new mills, splendid new buildings, and many improvements in and about the various mines.

After perambulating the streets somewhat at random for the space of an hour, and arriving at the conclusion that Virginia was really fast becoming a city, my friend informed me that Mr. B—— of the *Era* was in town, and proposed calling on him at his hotel. It was with many misgivings and much trepidation that I consented, for I pictured a fierce-looking personage with great, shaggy, gray eyebrows

---

An illuminating descent into the Comstock shafts, surtitled "The Wealth of Washoe." From the *Golden Era,* March 31, 1861.

overhanging a pair of piercing, greenish-yellow eyes, with a pair of huge glasses astride a ponderous trumpetlike nose; grizzly hair, standing erect as the bristles of an ireful coyote; a sallow, wrinkled face a yard or more in length; two huge, discolored tushes protruding from his upper jaw, and a perfect *cheveux-de-frise* of pens bristling above his formidable ears. Judge, then, how agreeably I was surprised at finding a brisk, jovial little man, with blue eyes, round face, rosy cheeks, smooth brown locks, and a nose which would be utterly worthless as a pumpkin-splitter. After a half-hour's chat, during which the virtues of a patent beefsteak invented by an ingenious cis-montane *chef de cuisine* came in for a liberal amount of praise from Mr. B———, he having conceived a passionate fondness for this *chef d'oeuvre* in cookery whilst wandering in the region of the West Walker, my friend and I took our departure for the purpose of visiting the Gould and Curry mine.

Gould and Curry Underground

Mr. Strong, the superintendent, was absent, but we found John on hand, ready and willing to show us through. In front of the mine is an embankment, or terrace, some five rods in length by three in width; and enclosing the mouth of the tunnel is a spacious framed building with rooms for storing ore after being sacked, and for breaking and assorting rock; also a neat and substantial dwelling house. John presented me a large and beautiful specimen of sulphuret of silver, or silver glance—called here black ore—also a splendid specimen of a brownish quartz completely covered and resplendent with flakes or scales of metallic silver. From a heap of ore in the assorting room, I selected a very handsome specimen of sulphuret of silver, containing numerous showy veins of green carbonate of copper and glittering spangles of gold.

John now procured candles, and each with his candle in hand, passed through a door in the back part of the building and entered the gloomy portal of the mine. We proceeded along a smooth, straight tunnel in a westerly direction for a distance of 250 feet, when we arrived at a point where a north and south tunnel cut across this main one at right angles; taking the south branch, we soon reached a vast cavern of darkness. Here a large amount of very rich ore has been quarried, and though we were at length enabled, with the combined light of our three candles, to see and make out the dingy walls immediately in front of us, yet above, our feeble light failed to reach the elevated roof, nor could it penetrate the vast profundity of darkness below which, for aught we know, might be the bottomless pit itself. But John, being posted on all of the heights and depths of this bewildering maze of shafts, drifts, and tunnels, came to the rescue and informed us that this vast collection of double-refined darkness extended downward a distance of eighty feet, and that out of this "chimney"—as it is called in miner's phraseology—they had obtained some of their best ore. We now returned to the main tunnel, crossed it and followed a passage running northward through the heart of the lead—which is some thirty feet wide—for a distance of about one hundred feet, passing between walls of ore which will pay from three to eight hundred dollars per ton in silver and gold— though the appearance of the rock in this part of the mine is rather gold-bearing than argentiferous. In the end of the tunnel a shaft has been sunk to the depth of eighty-four feet, and in a number of places drifts have been cut across it at right angles through the lead.

A Deeper Depth

We now descended a perpendicular shaft by means of a ladder, to the depth of eighty feet, and passing through a tunnel to the southward for some sixty feet, struck into a passage running west, which leads again to a dark, yawning abyss of unknown (to me at least) depth, completely studded with cross-ties and braces on which rested planks, at very unequal elevations. Now we were stooping to crawl under a tie, again taking a tremendous upward stride, and anon casting timid glances into the dark profound below, and mentally wondering whether we would ever stop falling were we once precipitated into the dismal chasm, and if we should happen to come to a halt somewhere in the vicinity of the center of gravity, whether John knew of a rope about the establishment long enough to fish us out. But at length we are over, and turning to the east through a large passage, we stand on the verge of that same huge, consolidated chunk of midnight we had been peering into above—i.e., the chimney. Here we see some very rich veins of silver ore, mostly the sulphuret, or black ore, alternating with decomposed vertical strata of auriferous quartz. We passed back again over the gloomy chasm upon the rugged plank pathway, but in what direction or where we went next is altogether impossible for me to say, and I hope John will excuse me if

I do not make the attempt—indeed, I am not as sure as I would like to be that I am right so far. But I am very positive that we did go somewhere else, and "kept a doin' of it" for some time; and am just as positive that John told us where we were going, how far, and all about it; but about all that I can now recollect is that we passed through a multitude of passages, some of great length, and saw a vast amount of gold-bearing rock. From this I conclude we were in some of the more northern galleries, as there the auriferous ores predominate; then we saw in other parts of our bewildering peregrination, veins that were indisputably silver-bearing.

How We Did It

Our gentlemanly and attentive guide now piloted us up to a diabolically dark-looking shaft, and announced that we were to make another descent toward the lower regions of only 104 feet! Another of those confounded ladders! Lord, how I could feel my hair stiffen beneath my hat whenever I thought of the cleats giving way! In passing down the eighty-foot ladder above, I carried a candle in one hand and in the other a walking stick which I had thoughtlessly brought into the mine, and when having made about ten feet of the eighty, it caught between the slats and came within a hair's breadth of sending me to the bottom. Having now another big climb to make, I determined to leave my stick till we returned, and thus have at least one free hand. Our guide started down first, my friend next, and your correspondent, though at the top of the ladder, brought up the rear. I was careful to secure this position, for the reason that besides the thought and prudence necessary to make a safe descent, I imagined it would be a decidedly unpleasant thing to have the additional fear of being knocked into eternity by the fall of a *compagnon du voyage* from above. I thought of what was told the traveler visiting the Kurprinz copper mine at Frieberg, who asked his guide (who had just been telling him that only a few days before a man had fallen to the bottom of the deep shaft they were about to descend), "What became of the man?" "Ah," replied the guide, "he instantly became pan-take-r!" Now, having not the least desire to become "pan-take-r," slap-jack-r, or even to be stove-up shortcake-r, I chose such a position that while apparently *first*, I was in reality *last*, and went down the shaft in the same manner that that most sagacious and rather jocose rattlesnake we read of went into his hole—namely—pshaw, you know. I think my friend and our guide were a little troubled at having me clambering and clawing above them, as they appeared painfully alive to my every move, and were continually calling out: "Long steps here, be careful!" "Stick close to the ladder, here!" "Don't bump against this beam!" But, great Moses! they needn't have been alarmed! Four of the best mules in Utah couldn't have snaked me from that ladder! I'll bet you fifty feet in the "Live Lion" or the "Lame Gipsy"—take your choice—that the impression of my fingers is to be seen on every cleat on that ladder, and at least three fingernails are sticking somewhere between the top and bottom step.

Lower Down—A New Level

On reaching the bottom, we found ourselves in a long passage running north and south, with a great number of drifts and tunnels running across it at right angles and piercing through the lead. We had now descended to the water level, and the floor of this part of the mine was quite wet—varying from mere muddiness to a depth of one or two inches. Shafts have been sunk in the termini of the majority of the tunnels and drifts above; but here the amount of water percolating the strata precluded operations of that kind, and before the mine can be profitably worked to a greater depth a new level will have to be run in. Such a tunnel is now being driven in by the company. The new tunnel will be about two thousand feet in length and will strike the lead 225 feet below the present level. Passing through this part of the mine, a marked improvement was observable over that visited above; though we were shown veins and branches of excellent ore above, yet these deposits had an unstable look—shifting apparently from side to side of the lead and showing, notwithstanding the richness of the deposit, that the metal had as yet assumed no fixed position in the lead and that a greater depth must be attained in order to secure that degree of permanence and concentration necessary to insure successful scientific working. But in the lower part of the mine, not only was the quality of the ore better, but the general appearance of the mine was much more favorable. There was a very flattering increase of metal throughout the lead, filling up between and connecting the hitherto scattered deposits, and showing the most unfailing signs of assuming a position of permanence and perfect consolidation of the contained metals at no great depth below the present waterline.

Brilliant Prospect—Black Ore, Silver Pure

The great tunnel which the enterprising proprietors of this mine will drive in 225 feet below the present greatest depth cannot fail to reward them with a concentrated vein of ore of equal, if not superior, richness to that of any mine in the territory. In this part of the mine we were shown a vast deposit, in a vertical stratum, of the black ore, but owing to the presence of water it is impossible to sink upon it. From a large pile lying near, I obtained a beautiful specimen. We now visited a part of the mine wherein is located the vein of pure, metallic, leaf silver. The vein is cut across at nearly right angles by a drift from the main gallery, and is near four feet in width. Glittering in the light of our candles, it presented a most beautiful appearance. The rock in which it is contained is quite soft, and I scratched out a handful of the glittering "root of evil"—not that I exactly wished for the specimens, for John had given me a specimen of this same ore, which in its perfection was all that heart could desire; but then, standing before a vast bed of silver one likes to be digging at it—you know?

The Ruby Vein—Return

What a shrine, this, for a miner to worship at! Here he might drill in a hole and, crawling into it, literally roll in wealth. Our guide now pointed out a small vein of what he called ruby silver ore, said to assay at the rate of $10,000 per ton in gold—from this fact I am inclined to consider the vein decomposed auriferous sulphuret of iron, rather than the ruby ore, or pyrargyrite, of mineralogists. Having now visited all there was to be seen in the mine, we began to think of getting out to daylight. There were two ways to do this: one was to go up the ladder as we came down, and the other to go out through a long tunnel. It did not take me long to make up my mind as to which route I should prefer, but there was my stick. How was I to get that? John decided this matter by kindly offering to go out that way and bring my cane to me on C Street, where he would find my friend and myself after we had made the trip through the tunnel. Passing out at the tunnel on an east course, we at last emerged into the broad, dazzling light of the sun, some distance below town, and on going up to C Street, found John already there with my stick. After a lunch at

Winn's and a whiff at the Indian weed, we betook ourselves to the works of the Ophir.

Into the Ophir—A 2:40 Plunge

As at the Gould and Curry, there is on the Ophir a roomy terrace in front of the mine, on which and in front of the mouth of the tunnel are spacious buildings for storing and assorting the ore. Being introduced by my friend to Mr. Deidesheimer, a foreman in the mine and a most gentlemanly man and accomplished mining engineer, who politely volunteered to show us through the works, we mounted into the car for a ride into the bowels of the mine. The car is worked by a steam engine, which also operates a pump when there is an influx of water. Perry stowed himself in the bottom of the car, which stood on a track having an inclination of over forty-five degrees, and I piled in on top of him, with one knee stuck into his ribs, an arm clutching the top of the car and the other round his neck, with my chin *hooked* over his head. I now supposed we were about as snugly stowed as possible, when there came an order from above to "Put in that knee!" Finding I was the possessor of the straggling member referred to, I planted it with its mate in the ribs of my fellow passenger with such celerity as to draw from him a grunt of huge disgust, and we were as snugly packed as a pair of sardines. The word being passed to "let'r rip," we went rumbling down this literal "underground railing" at a 2:40 pace.

We went thundering along, and I managed to twist my head half-round and see out of the corners of my eyes as we rushed through the dazzling flash of an occasional lamp fixed on the roof that the passage down which we were coursing, was ceiled with plank kept in place with beams and braces, and that it would not be necessary to raise my head to any great altitude to get my scalp taken. It was at one instant a blinding flash of light, and the next a bunch of dark of a consistency to lift one's hat; another flash and more dark in alternate layers to the bottom. As we went rolling down, said my friend: "Well, this is a little, I imagine, like the descent into the fiery, infernal regions! Can you see anything, Dan?"

"Nary a thing, except a red streak of lamps and a blue streak of night!"

"Well don't you think we must be near the bottom?"

"Can't be over two miles, now, without we have taken the wrong shoot and are going down the bottomless pit!" Bump! and the car has stopped. Hearing a considerable amount of loud laughter, I raise my head and open my eyes during the latter part of my journey. Lights are glancing and glimmering in all directions through the great chamber in which we have landed, and some half-dozen bearded miners are standing about us with candles flashing and flaring in their hands, all laughing fit to split their sides. What at, I didn't know at the time, nor am I better posted yet; but it is barely possible that they may have discovered something ludicrous in the manner in which we were stowed away in our box, and in our lying as still as a pair of pet kittens for some time after the car was down—waiting to be sure the thing had lit!

The Pay Streak

Scrambling out of our carriage, we found Mr. Deidesheimer by our side. How he came down, you can't prove by me. He must have either slid down the cable or took a deck passage on the car—most probably the latter—but at all events, he was on hand, ready to show us the wonders of the mine. Having each received a lighted candle, we started on our subterranean tour. Near the spot where we landed, we entered a series of regular and roomy chambers of a square form, made by the removal of ore. Corresponding with the rooms are huge, square pillars left for the support of the roof. This part of the mine is under the supervision of Mr. Deidesheimer, and evinces a superior knowledge of mining. The timber work is substantial and most scientifically arranged, and in every department there is sufficient room for carrying on work in the various branches without crowding or confusion.

The pay streak is here 30 feet in width, and has been opened a distance of 125 feet along the lead, thus exposing, ready for removal, a body of ore 125 feet in length by 30 in width. The floor, walls, and ceiling of this part of the mine are solid ore, averaging $1,500 per ton. In gazing upon these dingy walls, one can hardly realize the immensity of the wealth by which he is surrounded. Here are black and apparently valueless masses of rock which, touched by a magic wand, are suddenly changed to glittering, metallic silver. The storied splendors of the palaces of the Oriental world would be surpassed by the glitter of these galleries. In the dull, unattractive form of ore, the silver is there, and the metallurgist with his furnace is the magician who is able to bring forth the glittering metal; and allowing that we are not able to see the walls hung with a silver web or silver stalactites pendant from the roof, yet in the solid bars he is able to produce, we have weighty and tangible evidence of the almost incalculable riches hidden beneath the dingy, sootlike covering of these ores, and learn to look upon the sulphurets, arseniurets, chlorides, and seleniurets with almost the same favor as though they were coined dollars. The very floor on which we walk, notwithstanding its dinginess, is one of silver; the very dirt and dust that receives the imprint of our footsteps surpasses in richness the famed Pactolian sands.

The lead might be said to be sixty feet in width at this point, as for that distance there is a preponderance of quartz in veins alternating with streaks of "cassing" or "cab." Some of these veins are from two to three feet in thickness, and are within themselves very respectable leads, and exhibit a very good show of ores. The ore quarried in this part of the mine is wheeled to the incline and hoisted up in the car by which we descended. To show the facility with which the ore is obtained, I will mention that on Thursday, late in the evening, an order was received for a lot of ore, and by nine o'clock on Saturday, it was on the backs of a train of mules, on its way below. This lot weighed 7,510 pounds, and was all picked, or dug, by two men. The lot would average $1,500 per ton.

We now visited a point in the northern part of this section of the mine, where some men were taking out ore. They do not dig it up from the bottom of the vein, but commence what is called a chimney, and work upward by digging the ore down from overhead. In the chimney we visited, the workmen had reached a height of sixty feet. On the sides of the chimney a framework of hewn timbers, put together with mortice and tenon, and as strongly braced as the towers of a first-class bridge, is carried up as the work progresses, and while it serves to support and strengthen the walls of the mine, it also affords a scaffolding for the workmen. The reason for working upward is that every particle of ore, as soon as loosened, falls below out of the way, and the miner, having no loose dirt on his work, can put in every blow to the best advantage, and is not under the necessity of touching the ore after it is dug out.

A Silver-Walled Palace

After wandering through a great number of passages and entering divers rooms and chambers, some of which reminded me of rooms in the great cave at Cave City, in Calaveras County, we came back to the point at which we first landed, and taking passage on a ladder—which mode of underground travel I believe, on the whole, I prefer to the car—(a fellow feels as though he could help himself when he has a tight grip on the slats). Taking our way down the ladder, we at length reached a lower section of the mine. Here the chambers were not so numerous or extensive as above, though still of sufficient magnitude and extent to create surprise. The vein is still of the same size and the quality of the ore equally as good as above. Here, in one place, we ascended several steps cut in the heart of the lead to a chamber cut for some distance in the solid rock. Think of passing up a flight of silver stairs to a silver walled palace! The very walls, floor, and ceiling of this chamber, with the steps leading to it, might be dug down and shipped, for it is all ore, worth at least $1,500 per ton. Viewing the cubic feet—yes, cubic rods—of silver stored in this wonderful vein—the Comstock—one feels that the wealth of an Astor or even a Rothschild is but mere pin money in comparison. Why, the 1,400 feet owned by the Ophir Company would of itself, were its silver made into bricks, build a fair sized city—with enough left to put a brick into the hat of each inhabitant!

Richer Still

We next visited—after numerous turnings and windings through tunnels, passages, and chambers—a part of the mine in which some workmen were engaged in sinking a shaft in the floor of one of the rooms. All of the ore thus excavated was of the best quality, but there was a vein passing through the shaft of almost pure silver. A number of boxes stood near the shaft into which this was thrown as taken out, and the lumps had the weight, glitter, and appearance of pure metallic silver. Indeed, just as thrown up from the shaft it would average two-thirds silver. Mr. D showed me a bar worth $8.25, which was extracted from nine ounces of this ore, and these nine ounces were taken from one pound of ore as it came from the mine, there being a few ounces of rock thrown out in assorting the ore previous to melting. The part of the mine we were now in is two hundred feet in length and lies between the Central on the south and the Spanish on the north; north of the Spanish the Ophir Company owns 1,200 feet more.

The Spanish and Ophir Beyond

Our guide now led us through the Spanish claim to the Ophir ground lying beyond. Our way was along a large tunnel or passage, and over yawning chasms packed full of the very blackest kind of night. Then we were obliged to cross on poles, often a single pole or narrow plank; and in some places where the inclines crossed our way, the path across them was four or five feet higher than that in the tunnel, and we were obliged to seize hold on the timbers and draw ourselves up somewhat after the manner of climbing up the underside of a ladder. In one or two instances I managed to twist myself into such a position that I must inevitably have tumbled into the dark profound but for the ever ready hand of Mr. Deidesheimer, which was always extended just in the nick of time. In passing over these incline chambers in the Spanish mine, which were generally twelve to fifteen feet in width, we noticed in all them the notched poles up which the Mexican miner, with his rawhide sack of ore on his back, makes his way with perfect facility, but down which I would hardly have ventured empty-handed for fifty feet in the Ophir. The vein in the Spanish is hardly as large as in the Ophir, but is well defined and the ore very black, with vertical ribands of pure white quartz passing through it at intervals. No great amount of work has been done on the northern section of the Ophir, and after examining the lead, which presents about the same appearance as the Spanish, we returned to the southern section, visited a number of chambers on the west side of the lead, and met with more ticklish climbing. In a number of places through the mine, we were shown shafts reaching the surface above the mine; some of these were dug in the early days of the mine and are not now used.

A Set of Specimens

We now visited a tunnel which has its outside terminus somewhere down in town, near which was a huge deposit of ore to run out in cars as soon as the track is in order, when most of the ore will pass out through this channel, as it will be more expeditious than hoisting by means of the car and more hands will be worked. The number of men at present employed in the mine is thirty-five. We did not visit the deepest depths of the mine, as there was only a ladder trail and nothing very different from what we had seen above. In going up, we did not make use of the car, but mounted to daylight by means of the ladders, which—as they stand at an inclination of nearly forty-five degrees, and you go on the upper side—is not a "hard road to travel." On reaching the upper regions, we were conducted by Mr. D to a room in one of the company's buildings where we were shown beautiful specimens of the varieties of ore found in the mine, and I was kindly presented with a complete set, for which I can hardly feel sufficiently thankful, as, if there was any one thing I particularly desired, it was these very specimens, which if others could not be procured I would not part with for their weight in gold.

One Foot of Ophir

After having done the Ophir, we felt that we had seen the elephant in the line of silver mines. No one can form an idea of the wealth contained in this mine until after passing through it and having been enclosed within its silver walls. But few of the citizens of Virginia, even, are fully aware of the extent and almost incredible richness of the mine, and some who have lately been persuaded to go through were very greatly astonished at what they beheld. It is said that the company is now free from debt, notwithstanding their vast expenditures in roads, mills, and other improvements; and now, having everything ready for cheap and speedy transportation and working of their ores, with the mine in such shape that an almost unlimited amount of ore can be raised, they cannot fail to realize immense fortunes. In one pile of third-class ore, which will be worked at the company's works on Washoe Lake, is a fortune for a dozen men of moderate desires. This heap contains 12,000 tons of ore, which at the lowest estimate will yield $300 per ton. This mine has never sold for a price even approximating to its real value and there is big money in it at present rates. Recollect that in buying one running foot of Ophir, you get what is equal—in solid ore—to fifteen running feet on a two-foot lead.

In conclusion, I would say to parties visiting Virginia City, "do" the Ophir, and you will say that the half has not been told. It is impossible to convey on paper an adequate idea of its wonders. If you should be so lucky as to secure Mr. Deidesheimer for your guide, you will find him indefatigable in pointing out and explaining whatever is worthy of notice, and withal good-humored, pleasant, and gentlemanly, with no end of patience in answering questions. He intends getting up a model of the mine, showing every cut, tunnel, shaft, and chamber, to be sent to the office in San Francisco, where, by building on the model in such parts as they are informed of the progress of the work in the mine, one may see as well in San Francisco as in Virginia, in what part and to what extent the works are progressing.

Another Strike

*T*his morning the sun rose clear and bright; weather calm, warm, delightful. After breakfast thought I'd go down and have a chat with Jones. You know I told you about how very excitable Jones is and showed up some of his capers? Well, I found him at it again—*at it awful!* Fact is, he didn't much more than let me get into his cabin and get fairly seated before he said—looking and *jerking* his pipe out of his mouth—"Good morning." I saw immediately that something uncommon had occurred or Jones would not be in such a dreadful state of excitement so early in the morning; therefore, I said to him in my calmest manner—so as to rather keep down and cool his excitability—said I, "Jones, good morning!" Jones nodded his head, showing that he was still much inflamed; therefore I continued: "Jones, this is destined to be, when thoroughly prospected and fully developed, one of the richest mineral regions on the globe. Just think for a moment, Jones,—but don't get excited!—of the vast number of leads of unparalleled richness already opened, and think of the new and astonishingly rich strikes made almost every day and hour! There's

---

This and the next piece form two of the three installments of "Washoe Pictures." This one develops further the Silver City characters of Jones and Spudder. From the *Golden Era*, March 24, 1861.

the Grattan; see how immensely valuable it has proved to be within a very few weeks! Why, Jones—*Jones do you hear?*—I could have bought every foot of that lead one month ago for three dollars per foot—five at the very outside—and now it's selling for $60 and $80; and Trench's mill is battering away on the rock which they think will go $500 per ton—some say $1,000! Think of that, Jones; think of that, my friend, and rejoice that you and I are in a country that grows such leads—but still, *don't* get excited! What a great and lasting benefit such leads are to the town, to the country, to the world, to say nothing of the immediate and direct benefit accruing to the lucky individuals who strike them! There is one thing about this strike in the Grattan which gives me great pleasure, Jones—it is that those poor, but industrious and worthy people who live in the little canvas house, where we see the two little boys playing about as we go uptown, you know, happened to have a goodly number of feet in the lead—it will give them quite a boost!

"Oh! I had like to have forgotten about the ball the other evening at Allen's Hotel—the Grand Inauguration Ball! I suppose it's of no use to ask whether you went? I know very well you never go to balls—and you're right, Jones!—fact is, balls ain't the thing; you're too excitable! Come to get among the ladies, you'd be on your head half the time and the other half have your feet on their dresses, tearing off their things and making yourself a sort of general nuisance and terror! But don't become offended at what I say, Jones; you know I esteem you as much as any man in Washoe, and always consider it a perfect treat to be able to run down and listen to your intelligent and entertaining conversation—you know yourself that you're too easily excited; still, as I said before, Jones, I esteem you none the less for it. I bear with you patiently, willingly, and am always ready to say or do anything in my power to keep you calm, cool, and free from agitation!

"But, as I was going to tell you, they say there was a bit of a knock-down at the ball the other evening; all about a man saying 'thing' instead of 'lady'—and the man who should have said 'lady' but said 'thing' got pounded by the lady's husband. So you see, Jones, as I told you a minute ago, it would never do in the world for you to go to balls. Now, supposing you to have been there, you might have become inflamed and said all sorts of 'things' and been pounded to a jelly! It's always good for a man, and a wise thing too, to know his failings. Jones, I consider you—in some respects—a wise man!

137

"By the way, Jones, some of the boys who are sluicing down the cañon, toward and below Johntown, are making a pretty good thing of it—as high as $10 per day, I learn. Jones, I think we must try it! But still, I don't know about *you* either; taking it out that way is *mighty exciting*. Then I saw a fellow last night who is mining somewhere southwest of Washoe Lake, who says they have something good in that locality—tells of getting two to four dollars to the pan, and brags about what big things they will do in the auriferous line as soon as the snow goes off. They have their sluice boxes all made and ready. I am to have word from them as soon as the snow is off sufficiently for prospecting, and will then go over and strike something lousy—something worse infested with the raw material than you have ever dreamed of in your philosophy, or even in your most frenzied moments.

"I shall put you in, Jones, of course, and then we'll get each of us a 2-40 dog and pointer, hoss, and go round cutting big Gould and Curry swells. Jones! *Jones!* Don't shake your head that way and begin to get excited; wait till I get back, and then I will sit down and tell you all about the new placer diggings.

"Oh, yes, Jones! Come near forgetting it—they report big assays from the Churchill lead in Churchill district; all the way from $400 up to $1,000, and down again to $20 in croppings, perhaps; we must look into this Jones.

"You heard anything, Jones? New discoveries; new strikes; sales, deaths, murders, robberies, fights, marriages, divorces, births, larcenies, or extreme cases of borrowing? Take your time to answer, and don't allow yourself to become agitated." Jones says, "I was told yesterday evening that something pretty good had been struck on Nigger ravine."

"My God, Jones, how excited you are! You're in a perfect ferment! You've exhausted yourself completely in spite of all my cautions— you'll be raving in a minute. What do they call it? Where is it? Who struck it? Silver or gold? How big's the lead? Any dispute about it? How many claims are taken? Extensions all gone—no chance to get first, second, third, fourth, tenth, twentieth extensions on the poor end? How big does it prospect anyhow? But Great Heaven, Jones! *Jones, my friend!* Speak to me! How awful you do look! You've gone and got yourself so agitated you can't open your mouth! You'll have the lockjaw before an hour, I'll bet my life. Come up to my cabin and get a dose of salts to cool your blood, or you'll become inflamed to such an extent as to commit larceny, matrimony, suicide, or some such low thing. But I see by the way you shake your head that you will allow me to do nothing for you, and I'll be forced, however much you or I may regret it, to leave you! I leave you. Good-bye Jones, good-bye, my unhappy friend. Ah! you've *got it awful!*"

I saw the moment that Jones, in his hurried way, had managed to gulp out that a strike had been made in Nigger ravine—a locality, by the way, celebrated for its numerous rich veins of gold-bearing quartz, that he was certain to become so thoroughly inflamed and frenzied as to unfit himself for answering coherently even the most deliberately proposed question; therefore, I refrained from distressing him or aggravating his unhappy disorder, withdrawing from his presence as kindly as possible to seek elsewhere what little information I desired. I rush deliberately up Main Street, and as I pass along I see little knots of men on the corners with their hands full of rocks, all talking of the late strike. Two men meet, both put their hands into their pockets, pull out and exchange specimens. Some are busy along the cañon panning, others horning, and every second or third house appears to have a mortar, with some half-dozen pestles, all in full blast. Passing up the street, I hear from the groups on the corners such remarks as the following: "Richest thing in the country." "Looks like the Comstock." "See gold all through the dust." "Looks like the Lucerne." "Them fellers are in luck." "Looks like the Fashion." "A big thing." "Looks like the Grattan." "$50 won't touch it." "Looks like the Del Rey." "Got on 14th extension—just in time." "Looks like St. Louis." "Six feet wide." "Looks like Boston." "It's our lead and they shan't work it." "Looks like the Sucker." "Interferes with nothing." "Looks like the Dana." "Muggings is in." "Looks like the Last Rose of Summer."

As I pass along, I keep a bright lookout for some of my friends, and have great hopes that they may have put me in on some one of the extension claims. At length I find David, my friend David, promenading in front of the Eastern Slope as contentedly as a pig on the sunny side of a straw rick. This David is not the psalmist, but David of the eternal immaculate collar. I say, "Friend David, good morning."

"Ah, Dan'l, that you, hey? Good morning, Dan'l, fine morning, hey?"

After waiting calmly and coolly for some time for my friend to speak of the subject nearest my heart, and after conversing for some time on various subjects in my usual deliberate manner, I am obliged to ask: "Any new thing lately, David?"

"Well, Dan'l, nothing to call recent—heh? Strike in Nigger ravine yesterday evening; very good one—indeed, quite passable—heh? Got on fifth extension north, myself—heh? Call it the 'Hitinahita-wanachiwatabuster'—name'll be apt to take, heh?—good thing, quite fair—heh?"

"David, *friend* David. A—*m* I i—*n?*"

Friend David looks serious—puts up his hands and bends the almost dangerously sharp points of above-mentioned dazzling collar so as to cause it to hug in loving embrace his plump, smooth-shaven cheeks, then puts down his hands, and taking his cane from under his arm where he had deposited it whilst adjusting his collar, bores divers and sundry holes in the ground while he commences: "I'm sorry, Dan'l, very sorry, heh? but there was so many friends—"

I don't wait for him to finish—"Good morning, David, say no more. I'm off, David-good-bye!"

I feel distressed that David should be so thoughtless—got in so nigh the original location too—only fifth extension! It's too bad—I am really vexed with David—such a nice name too—the Hoi-ta-toi-ta-bus-no-matter! I'll find, not my brother, the Colonel, but my *friend* the Colonel; if any man has got me in it's the Colonel."

Find the Colonel just coming in with his buckskin breeches stuck into his boots, his hat awry, and his snowy and venerable beard of patriarchal length waving in the breeze, while his rosy, youthful countenance smiles from out aforesaid beard in a jolly good humor—though loaded with a sack containing some few hundred pounds of rock, pick, and shovel.

"Good morning, Colonel!"

"Ah, that you, Dan? Oh, it's a splendid thing. Good morning, Dan!—it's a beautiful thing—a pretty thing!—the biggest thing in the country!"

"What is it, Colonel? Is it the Hoity-toi—?"

"Hoity-fiddlesticks! It's the Hitinahitawanachiwatabuster! and the biggest thing ever struck! Oh! it's a delightful thing, and I'm in on tenth extension; just as good as the original! Find it in two hours!"

"Colonel, *Colonel, my dear friend!* I suppose then, of course, that *I a—m i—n?*"

"Sorry Dan! You ought to be on hand—so many friends right on the ground that 'twas impossible, sir! Altogether im—"

"Good-bye, Colonel, good-bye, I'm off!"

"Good-bye, Dan, come tomorrow, I know of a thing I'll put you—"

"Good-bye, Colonel, I'm in a hurry!"

I next came across Perry, who has just rushed down from Virginia City. He sees me and calls out—"Say, Dan, am I in? Did you put me in?"

"In! In what?"

"Why, in the Hiwaterbuster, of course! You're in, aint you?"

"No—good-bye, Perry. I'm in a hurry!"

Next I see Isaac, his flaxen locks glistening in the sun and both hands full of rocks, coming into town like a wild locomotive! Isaac has not been long among us, but he's always "in at the death" and "birth" too, for that matter! This time he managed to "come within one" of the *bull's-eye.*

As I pass the Recorder's office, I see a portly, fine-looking, good-natured old gentleman standing in the door who calls out: "Say, Dan! I'm in eighth south—whoa, Laura!"

"Good on your head, Uncle John! I'm out o' luck!"

"Why, aint you in, Dan? Seems to me you ought to have been in!"

"It's been seeming to me that way all the morning—good-bye Uncle John, I'm off!"

As I go down the street, I think—"It does beat thunder! Now, there's the Colonel, and David, and Isaac, and John, all in! And if Garry was not off "slaminading" round San Francisco he'd be in too! Confound it, somebody must have put me in! I've a notion to go and examine the books—no, I'll go and read all the notices—that's what I'll do—and immediately!"

I find the Hiwaterbuster, and see a line of stakes extending out of sight both ways from it, presenting the appearance of a minature line of telegraph. I read the notice on the original—sure enough, Muggins *is* in—blast it all, why didn't I never cultivate that Muggins? Very true, he is not an overly lovable subject; but one never knows what such men may have it in their power to do for one! Now, this very blaze-faced, slab-sided, knock-kneed, squint-eyed, sandy-headed

Muggins might have got me in on the Hiperlowaterbuster. But hold! What do I see? Slocum Piper, as I live! He in too? The very fellow who begged so hard for me to let him into the Live Lion, and by all that's lousy! Here's Plug Scrawney, that I wouldn't let come into the Cream of the Joke—no chance for me in this institution—couldn't make an opening with a maul and wedge! Let's look at the extensions. First South, and very first name on the notice—Tim Squealwell— had a fuss with him about the Lame Gipsy—couldn't get in here by blasting! First North—Jim Stuart, good fellow; put me in the Home- ward Bound—Tom Hill, so-so—Bill Ames, cheated me in a trade— bad sign! Pliny Plausible, lent him \$20—an earthquake would not open a crack here big enough for me to insert a cambric needle. Go through all the notices for four miles both ways, and find that "Dan De Quille" ain't in the papers—nary time! Think I'll go down town and trade some of my Live Lion to someone, and get in somewhere— just that I may say I'm in—I'm in the Hiperpiperwaterbuster. Sounds grand, don't it?

I go to my friend, the Colonel: "Colonel, the Live Lion is a good thing!"

"Yes." says the Colonel, "the Live Lion is a pretty thing!"

"So well defined, Colonel.

"Beautiful, Dan, splendid!"

"Runs well, Colonel."

"Elegant, Dan, elegant!"

"Good color, Colonel."

"Charming, Dan, exquisite, perfect!"

"Colonel it's a good idea to have one's ground pretty well dis- tributed—a little here and a little there; not too much in one thing."

"Excellent, Dan, prudent, very prudent."

"Well, Colonel I've been thinking—that—perhaps—you'd like some Live Lion for a little Hipopernowaterbus—"

"Not a foot of it!—trash; Live Lion is trash. I've got too much now—if that's what you're up to, Dan, I ain't on it!"

"No harm done, Colonel. I'll try David—but, by the way, Colonel, what did you get out of that sack of rock I saw you bring in— pounded it up, I suppose?"

"Pounded it up! No such thing; just a specimen or two for my cabinet!"

"Oh! Good day, Colonel."

"Good day, Dan, good day, sir."

I find my friend David. "David, friend David, the Lame Gipsy is looking well."

"Very well indeed, Dan'l, very well indeed—heh?"

"She has good points, David."

"Very excellent, Dan'l, very excellent—heh?"

"She may not run as well as some, but she has the right dip, David."

"Perfection, Dan'l, perfection—heh?"

"Widens out every day, David."

"Good sign, Dan'l, good sign—heh?"

"It's a good plan to scatter one's ground a little, David."

"Very excellent, Dan'l, very excellent indeed—heh?"

"I've been thinking, David, that I ought to let you have an interest in the Lame Gipsy, and, just to accommodate you, you know! I wouldn't mind taking a little Hiperhipoticust."

"Can't stand it, Dan'l, heh? Can't stand the press—heh? Miserable, split-up thing—can't stand it—heh?"

"Good-bye David! I'm off!"

"Good day, Dan'l, can't quite endure the pressure—ha, ha, ha! Dan'l—heh?"

I rush down the street as calmly as any man possibly could under the pressure of such a vast accommodation of disappointments; I see Spudder on a corner hanging on to a hitching post, and looking wistfully at the saloon across the way, only waiting for his head to stop whirling a minute to and down upon it. I think Spudder may know of someone who would like a little Lame Gipsy for Hi-ten-ti-ch-wa-buster, so I ask him the question.

"No-sur-ee-sur, ain't tin-n-t'self, an' don't want er be! Little ticky upstart, new-fangled gimcrack. Wi, don'ter folks make a fuss 'bout ter lead-das is er lead; wi don'ter roar'n howl, 'bout er Pewterink-um! er glitter' star of er Easern zlope, er peerless queen, er Utah, er very cream of er cream! Fer Stilton among smeer-kase, er big dog of er tom-yard! Wi done-ter, I zay *wi,* wi don't er 'owl 'bout it? Stick'n out'er groun' all'v vorty feet bove zurfus an' extendin' down'rd *ad liberatum, ne plus bonum,* without money an' wir'out price—you bes you? Yar, you zee zis peice o' rock? Ritc vrom under er cap-rock, long zide of er casin'. Pure horn zilver-action boplipe its *got it big* nomer stake! With er acid 'tis yields gobules."

Spudder's head is too many for him; after getting him halfway to the ground several times, it at last proves victorious; he loses his hold on the post and tumbles forward on his nose, while his old stovepipe rolls into the gutter and lands in a puddle of dirty water. But Spudder is unconquerable, irrepressible; he raises himself up on his hands and knees and mutters something about "percipertatin' chloride," but a sudden spasm seizes him and he is forced to give a practical illustration—when I suddenly depart.

Spudder is awful tight today; must have been firing up on tarantula juice. *En passant* I may be allowed in this connection to relate a little tarantula-juice joke.

A dashing buck came clashing into one of our saloons the other day with immense jingle of spurs and high-price airs, and halting in front of the bar and spreading himself out like a bale of hay which had suddenly busted its fastenings, called out, "Say, you thar, give us some tarantula juice!"

Now, it so happened that bar-keep was something of a naturalist and among other curious things had a pint bottle in which were some half-dozen fine, large, hairy specimens of the tarantula, preserved in alcohol; this bottle happened to be under the bar immediately in front of the customer, and bar-keep, with a face which would have been no disgrace to a down-east deacon, reached down, drew out the bottle, set it before the customer, and placed a glass before him, filling another with water from the pitcher. Dashing buck looked at the bottle till his eyes had assumed the dimensions of Mexican dollars, then turning his expanded visual organs upon bar-keep, whose face was gravity itself, he drew out a quarter dollar, placed it on the counter, and as he clashed out at the door some of the loungers thought they distinguished amid the jingle of spurs something very like the naughty word "h——l!"

I have now but little more to say; after leaving Spudder I went home, where I found the excitable Jones, but looking much better. He managed to tell me that he had a full claim in the First South on the Hiperbuster, and as he didn't want to "keep up" so much, I might have half. I immediately open my arms and take Jones, and the 100 feet, to my bosom; Jones further said that he had intended telling me this in the morning if I had not rushed off in such a hurry.

Strange what singular notions Jones gets into his head—now, he really believes I rushed off, when I never was more calm, cool, and deliberate in my life, and he was perfectly speechless with excitement; if he had only been in possession of his senses he might have saved me a great deal of vexation. Jones is a good fellow—fine, splendid fellow, but he gives me a great deal of trouble.

P.S.—I trust such of my Silver City friends as may find some of their little peculiarities touched at above will take it all as good-naturedly as it is meant—that I would, on no account, knowingly wound their feelings they can rest assured.

No Wife nor Mother's Care

*H*ere we are, some thousands in number—poor, miserable "wusser" halves; dilapidated lords of creation; fallen monarchs reduced to the humiliating necessity of frying our own slapjacks, washing our own shirts, and performing perplexing surgical operations on our don't-mention-'ems. Poor forlorn wretches! What a confounded dull thing a house is without a woman, anyhow. It's merely a house, a den; nothing more. It can never be a *home*. The carver may display his skill, the painter spread his most brilliant pigments, the gilder exhaust his art and the upholsterer his stock; but until you put a *woman* in your house you have no home. It is but a splendid wilderness, a gilded desert. Your house has no *soul. Homes* have souls! *Par example,* here am I dwelling in a splendid *brownstone* mansion, built, I might almost be allowed to say, in the Tudor style—it has *one door*—yet I have no home. I have a den. The mice thrust their heads out at me from the crevices in the walls, and screech out their shrill raillery; great bushy-tailed rats mount upon my table before my very eyes and, sitting erect upon their haunches, munch the loaf still smoking from the bake

---

A revealing, sentimental fantasy about his little daughter Lura and his alter ego, Markham, the hopeful drunk. From the *Golden Era,* April 14, 1861. Third installment of "Washoe Pictures."

kettle. Spiders solve geometrical problems upon the rafters of my dwelling and demonstrate the laws of gravitation by letting themselves down into my last cup of coffee. Lizards make frequent calls, and scorpions are frightfully familiar. Cockroaches glide among my domestic utensils, and ants travel in caravans across the floor of my *casa*. My salt and sugar become unaccountably mingled; my beefsteaks take fire and my mutton chops become what a chemist would term carbonaceous. My shirts are buttonless; my pants are seatless; my coats are tailless; my stockings are heelless and toeless, and with a house I am homeless. Ah, me, I'm a disconsolate set—I am—*estoy inconsolable!*

Now, a few yards of calico fluttering in and out of my domicile would put all these ills to flight, and every dull crystal in the rocks composing the walls of my castle would blaze like a diamond of the first water. The fire would burn brighter, the teakettle resume its almost forgotten tune, and the cricket again sing on the hearth. But, good Lord! There's an infernal, great rat going up the wall with six inches of sausage in his mouth. Broke my pickle jar and upset the coffee pot into the sugar bowl—confound it, I can never kill one of those rats! I've got myself into such a flutter that I hardly remember what I was saying. Blast a rat anyhow!

The other day I was thinking of home, wife, little ones, mothers, sisters, brothers, friends, and home comforts and enjoyments in general; and to prevent having a fit of the blues, determined to go down and have a chat with Jones about things in the States, and our dear ones away back yonder. I found my friend engaged in re-seating a pair of clay-colored pants—or rather re-re-seating them.

"Ah, Jones," cried I, "I find you engaged in the devil's own occupation! I have always had a better opinion of you, Jones; sorry to see you assuming his part and performing his task—sorry indeed, Jones!"

Jones immediately becomes nearly suffocated with excitement, and says, with an effort to appear calm, "How so?"

"Why, Jones, you are *sowing tares!*" Jones looks at me for the space of two minutes, with eyes wide open and such a wooden expression of countenance that I fear I have done for him and thrown him into a perpetual spasm; then the rigidity of his facial muscles relaxes, a faint glimmer of light breaks over his visage, and I hear a low chuckling sound which appears to emanate from underneath the stool on which he is seated. I say, "Jones, for heaven's sake, be calm; I am glad to see you get over that awful look, but I pray you keep cool. Jones, I have stayed at my cabin thinking of home until I hate the very sight of the walls. I hate every stone in it, and every pot, kettle, and pan. I want to talk with you about our homes, our wives, and our babies! I always feel better after talking with you, Jones; you always interest me, and I am pleased to be with you, except when you get into one of your infernal fits of excitement."

Jones hitched back and forth on his stool in an uneasy manner when I spoke of talking of wives and homes, and I almost feared the subject would be too much for his excitable temperament. Some of the boys have told me that Jones's wife used to wear the breeches, and was seen on one occasion to pursue him with a carving knife. I have no faith in these idle stories. It's true, Mrs. Jones may sometimes have found it necessary to soothe and check her excitable spouse, and use her influence to quiet his mind; but to pursue him with a murderous weapon—impossible!

"Now, Jones," said I, "we will suppose that you and I are at home—no, not at *home*—going home, almost home. We have landed from the steamboat or cars, and hired a hack to take us to *our home*. But we don't let the hack go quite there—not quite. We stop at the post office and leave our trunks. We don't wish to have the appearance of a traveler; we will take them by surprise—pop in when they least expect us. Now, we will suppose that we have a schoolhouse to pass before we get home, and that the school is just dismissed for the day. It is evening, and a perfect avalanche of little boys and girls rush, shouting and laughing, into the street. You have a little girl about seven years old, with a wavy mass of curls floating about her dimpled shoulders, and the merriest dancing blue—dark blue—eyes, pearly teeth, and the sweetest little rosebud of a mouth that is capable of assuming more primps and rogueish shapes than any other you ever saw. And haven't you often thought so, as plucking at the buttons of your coat, with her head thrown back and set archly on one side, and her glossy tresses tossing about her snowy throat, she teased you to get her that doll with the 'prettiest blue eyes, and curls almost as long as mine, and red cheeks and hands, and feet with the pretty red slippers—now won't you, pa?' You have such a little girl as that, Jones?" Jones shakes his head and yawns—sure sign, with him, of incipient excitement. "Jones, what have you got?"

"Seven boys!"

"Great heaven! But I mean nothing wrong, Jones; all right, only, you see, you spoke so sudden, and—and—excuse me, Jones—I thought excitedly, that—but all right, all right, Jones, only you don't know what you've missed by not having a girl or two. Poor fellow, you'll never be able to comprehend little-girl-ism. You'll never understand their arch, tantalizing, sweet, love-provoking primps and quirks. But we will suppose you to have such a little girl—a boy would not do so well. Jones—you see we had better *suppose* you have a girl. Well, we pass along with the schoolchildren swarming about us and casting curious glances at the stranger; and we see tripping along before us such a queenly little lady, with the tiniest, daintiest little boots twinkling along over the sward; the jauntiest little cloak, showing the least mite of scarlet lining where the little arm is thrust out; and the sauciest bit of a hood, from under which sunny curls are rambling. We overtake the little flirt, and at the first look into those great blue wells of eyes, feel our heart give a great thump and something rise up in our throat. Then we take the hand of the little one in our own and she looks up and smiles—a trusting smile, Jones—and does not pull away nor look scared. We ask her to tell us her name. She looks up again, and again we look down into those great liquid blue eyes—and she says, (I'm sorry, Jones, that you have no little girl) she says: 'I am little Lura De Quille.' (Our heart gives another tremendous thump.) The most delightful, flutelike little voice, Jones! Then we say: 'Does your pa live near here, my little lady?' And again the music-bubbles of the little voice rise up—but the music has a slight shade of sadness, Jones, just the least bit—as she says: 'I did have a pa that lived here once, long, long ago; but now he's away, away, ever so far off in California!' Then we ask: 'How' (and our voice trembles a little, Jones, and that something is in our throat again) 'would you like me for your pa, Lura?' The little witch claps her hands and laughs a ringing silvery laugh, as though it was a great joke, and asks in return—'And would you like to be my pa?'

"Jones, hold my hat—Jones—whoop, whoop-ee! I'll have to catch the little one up in my arms and tell her who I am—I can't stand it much longer! Whoop, whoop-ee! come to your father's—but, Jones, great heaven, man! you're excited—don't deny it, I know you *have it* again by your filling that pipe. That's what makes you nervous, getting yourself into a perfect frenzy, then smoking to settle your nerves. It's killing you! But then on the present occasion it is, perhaps, not out of place to give way to your feelings to a moderate extent—a *moderate* extent, Jones. Now, just to see with what archness and enchanting witchery the little minx, with her head held a very little to one side, her rosebud mouth primped into the most roguish shapes and her eyes twinkling fun, asked—'And *would you* like to be *my* pa?' Oh, Jones, Jones, what a pity you have no little girl! 'But Lura'— and we stoop down and put our hands on her little shoulders—'but Lura, I am your pa—your own pa—come home all the way from California to see his little girl.' Then we take the little one to our bosom and almost smother her with kisses, and as soon as she can get her breath she says: 'Oh, I'm so glad you are my pa! I like you so much! You are a good-looking pa, too'—she's talking to me now, Jones—'and you'll let me sit on your lap and you'll tell me ever so many pretty stories of giants and castles all covered with silver that steals a little girl and her brother with a bright sword and a horse as black as a coal that kills the nasty mean giant and gets the little girl and the castle all covered with silver—now won't you?'

"Jones, you know that 'Old Block,' in the introduction to one of his books, says: 'Oh, I feel at this moment as if I wished for power to take California in my arms as I would a darling child.' Now, Jones, at 'this moment' I have an idea that I 'feel as if *I* wished for power' to take— not California, but all of her little girls (those of sixteen not too old) in *my* arms, and while showering kisses on their lips, ask heaven to shower blessings on their heads through the whole course of their mundane pilgrimage! I once had a partner who was always singing:

> If all the gals on this 'ere crick
>   War melted inter one,
> I'd marry 'em all ef I see fit,
> Or elst I'd let 'em run!

Now, Jones, if I had 'em all in the melted state, I'll tell you what I'd do—come to think, Jones, it's too exciting for you, and besides you will do better to imagine something for yourself. Bacon has said: 'The honorablest part of talk is to give the occasion; and again to moderate and pass to somewhat else.' So, Jones, I'll 'moderate,' and pass on.

"Well, Jones, we take our little girl by the hand—no, we will have it the little boy now—and we will go to *your* house, *your* home, and it will be *your* wife we will meet—we take—what is your boy's name?—we take little Moses by the hand, and soon we reach the gate.

We catch a glimpse of a face at the window, and the next instant an angelic being with auburn ringlets tossing wildly on her swanlike neck, and her form of exquisite slenderness exhibiting the grace of a gazelle and the litheness of a willow, comes bounding forth and springs into our—your—arms, clings about *your* neck, and her cherry red lips are eagerly seeking—Oh! Jones, I never heard you say, but I hope your wife is not a great, fat woman weighing 240 pounds. Jones, did you groan? Those pigs outside, I suppose. As I was saying, I hope your wife is not a great bunch of blubber—Ah! did you burn your mouth, Jones? Well, I'd not smoke. I hope she is not, for you—now, I wouldn't wound your feelings for the world, Jones, but a bosom friend may be allowed some liberties. You are—to be plain and use an old-fashioned phrase—not bigger than a pint of cider, and a good deal dried up, withal. Now, if your wife was a big, fat woman, the same thing might happen to you that happened to Smith's friend. I will tell you about Smith's friend:

"Smith and his friend, whom I will call Hobbs, and another man, whom I will call Boggs, all went home together in '56; they all lived in the same New England village. Hobbs's wife was an immense woman, weighing near three hundred, and Hobbs himself, a diminutive remnant of a man, just about your size, Jones. Well, as Hobbs was about to rush into the house, his wife saw him and came rushing—rolling—out; so they met upon the doorsteps—the fifth step from the bottom and second from the top—and Mrs. Hobbs precipitated herself upon her trying-to-reach-up husband, threw her arms about his neck and gave way to the whole weight of her body and feelings. Poor Hobbs couldn't stand the press of both affection and bulk, and in turn 'gave way'—though principally in the knees—and over and over, down the steps they rolled till they landed in the gutter, Mrs. Hobbs, as cruel fate would have it, on top, and as soon as Hobbs wriggled his head out she commenced kissing at him—a remarkable example of woman's love under difficulties, Jones. But Hobbs escaped, and leaving his wife rolling on the ground, rushed hatless into the house. Mrs. Hobbs presently rolled in the right direction, and got her feet on the ground, when she picked up that 'fancy plug,' lately so smooth and glossy, now smashed flatter than a pancake, as the neighbors said (and they know, for they were all watching) and started puffing and blowing, to renew the attack within, and as that was all the neighbors could see, I cannot say how they made it in the second encounter, but we have seen enough to show that it is necessary for a man that marries a big woman to be not only stouthearted, but stout in the legs!

"But to resume; let me see, where did I leave off? Oh, I have it. Your wife was about to kiss you. Jones, do you care particularly about me letting her do it, or shall I pass on? Well, then, I'll let it go; you are doubtless right—it would, perhaps, be too much for your nerves. You ain't like Davis, Jones. Now, Davis would want me to go on.

"I'll tell you what Davis told me the other day about how he used to 'fool his wife.' Said he: 'I would come in at night from the store, and throwing myself into a chair, heave a most horrible sigh, then roll my eyes up toward the ceiling, commence to groan, but suddenly check myself and finish off with a second edition of the horrid sigh; by this time my wife was aroused, and with a look of alarm rushing toward me—another awful sigh and roll of my eyes and she was seated on my knee, with her soft, white hands on my brow and smoothing my hair—"Davis, love, are you sick?" "No, dearest, not sick." "Oh, Davis! You have met some loss and are fretting on my account; but, dearest, as I have the love of my husband I am happy!" Then she would throw her arms about my neck and—.' Davis wouldn't tell me any more, but he says it's surprising how often he has fooled her that way.

"Did you ever fool your wife that way, Jones? But good heavens, Jones! What's the matter? Got the toothache? What faces you make! Now go to filling that pipe again! Ah, Jones, your excitable brain is devouring your body. Be calm, be cool, be like me! Jones, now do try to acquire something near the same degree of calmness you observe me invariably display. You have quite a snug house, here, Jones. Now if you only had Mrs. Jones and those boys—especially Moses—here, how happy you might all be. What a pleasure it would be to Mrs. Jones to take that little job of re-seating off your hands; and then when you met with losses and came home despondent, how she would—Jones, you groaned; don't deny it!—you groaned; it's that tooth—I'm sorry it troubles you so. I've done wrong to stay so long; but your conversation is so very interesting that I can hardly tear myself away at all. What a pleasure it is to have sympathizing friends with whom to talk of those we love! But good-bye, Jones; better go to bed with that tooth and try to forget it!"

It's a pity about that tooth of Jones's. Fine fellow as ever was—little excitable or so—it's too bad he should have such an infernal tooth! I'd get it pulled if I was Jones.

Leaving Jones's cabin, I wandered on down the ravine and in a bend saw Spudder—Spudder P. V. lying dead drunk, his old plug hat lying above him near the path, proving that he had tumbled down the hill to his present position. A couple of small loaves of bread were lying beside him, showing that he was homeward-bound when his enemy overwhelmed him. I shook him, pulled his hair, and called out that we had struck it in the Pewterincktum, but could not arouse him; he was thoroughly stupid and steaming with gin, and as insensible as a log.

Continuing down the cañon, I at length found myself in front of Markham's den—a sort of hole, neither square, oblong, or round, scooped out in the bank and covered with boards, canvas and gun-nysacks. Markham is, if possible, a greater sot than Spudder, and I was surprised to find him at home and quite sober—the first time I ever saw him when not in some degree of intoxication. He was sitting just within his door with his head resting in his hands. Hearing my footsteps, he raised his head, and I was shocked to observe the hol-lowness of his cheeks and the dimness of his blear and sunken eyes. He looked much older and more haggard than when intoxicated, for then his cheek has an artificial bloom and his eye a borrowed fire. Markham is not an old man—not over thirty-five at the furthest—yet his hair is grizzled and his cheeks and brow ploughed in furrows. When he saw me standing at his door, he rose up, tossed his hair back from his eyes, smiled a dim, sickly smile, and, drawing aside the blanket which formed his door, asked me to enter. Having a curiosity to see what manner of man he was when sober, I accepted his invita-tion and seated myself opposite to him on a three-legged bench.

"Markham, you look unwell; have you been sick?"

"I don't feel well; yet I cannot say that I am sick—I feel low-spirited and nervous."

"Yes, I notice your hands shake—what do you suppose to be the cause?"

Markham colored slightly, cast an uneasy inquiring glance at me, then, letting his eyes fall to the floor, remained silent for some mo-ments. Then he raised his head and said in a voice at first thick and tremulous, but growing gradually more firm and clear: "I know it as well as you do; it would eventually have killed me; but, God being my

helper, I hope to be a man once more. I have too long been a beast—
yes, a *beast!* I can say it and I care not if *you* say it. You *think* it!
Everybody but beasts like myself think it, or have thought it—why
not say it! Why did you not, the first time you saw me reeling along
the streets, say, 'Markham, you are a beast?' I believe that when I first
drank to excess, if someone whom I felt to be my friend had said to
me—instead of laughing and making a joke of it as they did—
'Markham, you are making a beast of yourself, you are a disgrace to
the human species and only fit to be classed with wallowing swine'—
it would have saved me; for as a celebrated author has said, 'There is
in every man that innate dread of scorn which is a perpetual spur to
him to rescue and deliver himself from it.'"

"Well, how does it happen that you have resolved to abstain from
drink?"

"You will better comprehend that if I give you a short sketch of my
life. You will also have more faith in my reformation, and perhaps
give me your countenance and friendship, which I feel would greatly
assist me. I was born, and lived till I started for California, in Knox
County, Ohio, near Mount Vernon. My parents were wealthy and
respectable, and very kind and indulgent to me, their only son. At the
age of twenty-two I married the daughter of a neighbor, a beautiful
and most lovable young lady. My father was able to give me a farm,
and Mary's father being also wealthy, gave us money to stock it and
make the necessary improvements.

"The ensuing five years were the happiest I have ever seen. We had
two children, a boy and a little girl the very image of her mother; I
thought them the handsomest in the world. In '53 I determined to
join a company then fitting out to cross the plains to California—alas,
that I ever made that move! I was not in debt and everything on my
farm was prospering; but I had an ardent desire to see something of
the world—to cross the plains and visit the golden land beyond the
Sierras. Then I promised Mary that at the furthest I would be gone
but two years. Alas, I am still here! When I first began to talk of
coming, Mary thought me jesting, and laughingly said I could not
leave her and the children long enough to make half the journey. But
when she found that I really would leave her, she wept bitterly
enough; and when I started, clung to me and begged and prayed me
to take her along. Oh, that I had done it! I would not now be as you
see me! Here, sir, is her likeness; I have always kept that, though until

today have not for many months dared to look upon those features. You would not think, to look at me now, that that woman was my wife; that she had pressed those lips to mine; that those hands had soothed my brow, those taper fingers toyed with these locks, or those lovely eyes gazed fondly into these inflamed and sunken orbs! But I must hasten; I left Mary and the children at her father's, and after many hardships reached California and made money as fast as I could desire. At the end of eighteen months I wrote to Mary that in two months more I would be at home. I even mentioned near the day. I had $6,000 in coin and dust—enough with my farm to make me independent for life.

"But now I have to relate what to this day gives me great pain and remorse. My partners were all in the habit of using liquors daily, and often to excess; and in a very short time I was ready to drink upon every occasion, and had several times been led or carried to our cabin helplessly drunk. The night before I was to start home, it was determined among my friends that we must have a sort of parting spree. This I did not like, as I had determined to reform; but thinking it best not to refuse, I went to the saloon intending to drink but once or twice and then make my escape to the cabin. Alas, for my resolution! By ten o'clock I was raving drunk, and I can remember little that happened that night. I had but a few dollars in my pockets and did not feel alarmed the next morning on coming to my senses to find them missing, but on being told that I had lost $500 at *monte,* I began to feel uneasy and asked who lent me the money. I was told that it was my own; that at first I had lost a few dollars and then went out and soon after returned and lost about $500. To this I said nothing at the time, but I felt a dreadful, chilly, sinking sensation at my heart, for I had a dim recollection of having visited the spot where I had my money secreted. I hastened thither. It was gone—all, every dollar! Some prowling villain had followed me and stolen it.

"I wrote home that I had lost my money and would remain another year—sad news for Mary. That is the last letter I have written her. Since then I have been a beast! I have wandered from place to place and have heard from Mary but once since—that was about five months after losing my money. All was well then, and Mary said it would break her heart if I disappointed her a second time. But I did, poor woman; there has been nothing for her but disappointment. I have sometimes thought of the hundreds of times she has gone to the

155

post office, hoping and fearing. Then how she would imagine me on
the road home as the only reason for my silence; and when that hope
had died away, return again to the post office. Oh, I'm a beast. Yes,
worse; a beast would not so desert its mate! There have been long
seasons—yes, years—when I have hardly thought of home. I tried to
banish it from my thoughts or to imagine everything as when I last
heard from there. It seemed a far-off happy place where I could never
go, and where I was not fit to be welcomed. But last night I saw
Mary—saw her as plain as I see you now, sir! She looked nearly as in
the picture you hold in your hand, but thinner and very pale. She was
dressed in a flowing robe of white that rustled as she moved. She
came across from near your seat and stood at the side of my bed and
gazed sorrowfully upon me. Her lips moved as in prayer, and tears
were on her pale cheeks. She stooped down and pressed her lips to
mine. I tried to speak, but shame kept me silent. She moved slowly
toward the door, and, fearing to lose her, I rose up in my bed and
cried out—'Oh, Mary!' She turned again toward me, slowly drew the
blanket aside from the door and pointed out with her hand. I looked
in the direction she pointed, and saw just before the door my old
home—the white paling about the dooryard, the old locusts waving
in the wind, the vines clinging to the porch and windows, and there in
the shade of the vines on the porch sat another Mary with precisely
the same look of sadness as the one that stood pointing at the scene;
but near this one—my own, long-forgotten, cruelly neglected Mary—
stood a slender, brave-looking boy with brown curls clustering about
his fair young brow, and at her feet, resting her hands on her mother's
knees, was a young girl with the face and expression of an angel,
gazing sadly upon her mother, who points with her hand toward me.
The Mary in my door, with uplifted hand still pointing, says in a low
and mournful, yet thrilling voice, 'They ask for their father!'

"My God! It may all have been a dream, but I will never forget the
feeling that thrilled through my being at those words. I leaped from
my bed and found that the day was just dawning; the blanket was
pulled aside from my door, but I found no other trace of Mary—for I
shall ever believe or try to believe it was her I saw! Then, upon my
knees I vowed never again to allow a drop of strong drink to pass my
lips, and that as soon as I can earn enough to pay my passage home, to
go to Mary and the children—for I now feel that they are alive and
still expecting me. I have been gazing on Mary's picture all the morn-

ing, and will now carry it next to my heart; and not a day shall pass but I will look on those features and renew my vow."

"Markham, may God enable you to carry out your noble resolves! Come with me!"

Without a word of explanation I led him up the ravine to where Spudder was wallowing in his vomit, with a white froth oozing from between his lips and covering his beard; and pointing to him, I said, "Markham, behold how *I have seen you!*"

"May God help me!" cried he and dropped upon his knees. I made a move to raise him, thinking in his weak state he had fainted, but with his hand he motioned me back, and in a low but perfectly audible voice prayed most earnestly for strength to uphold him in the new course he had marked out, while I turning my face aside, bowed my head upon my breast and listened in awe and silence. My proud knees would not come to the ground, and I felt that I was in the presence of one much my superior in goodness. May he find the strength for which he so fervently prayed!

Petrified!
Or the
Stewed Chicken Monster

Home Again from the Gold Fields of California—Home from the Silver Mountains of Washoe!

Stewed Chicken and Crab Apple Sauce

There I take my text—that's what's the matter!

Fool that I was to dream of stewed chicken while wandering among the auriferous hills of California! Fool, to encourage visions of stewed chicken while roving amid the argentiferous wilds of Silverado! Idiot, to sit dozing over thoughts of stewed chicken while rolling day and night over the broad plains separating the valley of the Mississippi from the golden shores of the Pacific! But most consummate fool, most uncalculating and driveling of idiots was I to confess, upon landing in Iowa, that I felt a hankering after stewed chicken and crab apple sauce.

It has now come to be the firm conviction of every human being in this county that stewed chicken and crab apple sauce are necessary to my existence. My system is supposed to crave stewed chicken—without stewed chicken I would pine, dwindle, and go into the sear and yellow, etc.

It's not use for me to say that I care nothing about stewed chicken; every good, motherly woman in the country knows better—she has

---

Bizarre fantasy that established Dan as the "Washoe Giant" of letters on his return from Iowa and serious rival of the young Mark Twain. From the *Golden Era,* August 30, 1863.

always, ever since her earliest infancy, known better. Can't cheat her in that way out of the pleasure of providing me with my favorite dish.

All the little boys and girls in the country—the very school-children—know that my principal article of diet is stewed chicken; and as I pass they whisper to each other slyly, with their hands held to their mouths, "There goes the new man from Washoe—the man who eats nothing but stewed chicken." Doubtless, in their minds, I occupy a place side by side with the horrible creatures they have read of in their storybooks—creatures whose existence could only be maintained by sucking daily the blood of an infant. I am become a stewed chicken ghoul—a crab apple sauce monster.

Oh, that I could hit upon some way of convincing the good people hereabouts that I have had enough stewed chicken, that for me crab apple sauce has lost its ancient charms! When I approach a homestead, the farmyard is instantly in an uproar. Tall and valorous Shanghai cocks feel their hearts sink, and scud away with necks outstretched and wings outspread, to hide under convenient pigpens and haystacks, shouting with might and main, "He's come, he's come! Oh, Lord!"

Again, I say, I am tired of stewed chicken and sick unto death of crab apple sauce—oh, that folks would become convinced of this fact! But they won't—no, I feel in my bones that they won't.

I am to visit the Joneses. Because I am to visit the Joneses I can't sleep well o' nights. It has now been some days since I promised to visit this family. They are a very clever and respectable family. When they have visitors, they do all in their power to make them feel at home, to please and amuse them.

Every night since I promised to visit the Joneses I have had the nightmare. Stewed chicken and crab apple sauce have been in all my dreams. As soon as Sleep has bound me fast, his son, Morpheus, god of dreams, seizes me, and in an instant his swift wings have transported me to Washoe; there I discover rich silver veins cropping out from mountains of stewed chickens; I build mills in ravines to be run by chicken gravy, and run tunnels through miles of stewed chicken bedrock; but at last, however well I may be getting on, my mine caves and I find myself buried thousands of feet under mountains of chicken stew, and die in agony with eyes and ears full of chicken gravy.

The Joneses' children have heard their parents talking about me, I am confident. They look at me from head to foot and nod—as much as to say, "Yes, this is he—this is the man!"—then they whisper together. They are dying to see me eat. If Jones allows one of his brats to stay in the room, I won't eat a bite. I've made up my mind to that.

Every time I meet Jones he asks when I am coming. I am getting afraid to see him. My hair rises and a cold perspiration breaks out on my brow at the sound of his voice. Not more terrible was the voice of Pan in the ears of the Titans. I feel as though the props supporting my mountain of stewed chicken were beginning to give way; my breath comes hard and I can hardly resist the desire to toss aloft my arms and cry out for help. Nothing but the great respect I feel for Jones as a man and a neighbor prevents me from doing this. I shall do it yet; I know I shall. Then what will Jones think? What will Mrs. Jones and all the little Joneses think?

I hope I may not do it; I shall strive hard against the temptation, but I shall do it yet—do it just when striving hardest not to. I know if I should act in such a manner, Jones would think me crazy—he would tell his wife so; the little Joneses would hear it, then they would all run from me as the chickens do now.

I am not certain but I am becoming insane—on the subject of stewed chicken and crab apple sauce. I am sometimes afraid that others think the same. I have been thinking for several nights past of asking my wife if she saw any change—whether she could see anything to remind her of stewed chicken and apple sauce. Yes, that, I decided, was the best way to put the question; I would say nothing about my mind—that would show an uneasiness I did not care to have her perceive. But simply to ask if there was anything about me to remind her of stewed chicken or crab apple sauce was a very quiet way of putting the question. I whispered this over to myself for several nights, and two or three times came very near asking the question aloud. I think I should have done so, but I fell asleep and was soon tunneling my mountain, only to be tortured at last by the insecure timbering of chicken bones giving away and letting down the whole to crush and smother me.

I saw Jones again yesterday. Somehow I now see him wherever I go. He wants me to come—will expect me in a day or two. Said I could depend on having a "grand feast of stewed"—I did not hear the rest; my head swam; I think I came near fainting.

What could I do? What say? Jones mistakes me—everybody mistakes me. Just as sure as the sun rises or the earth revolves, I shall be obliged to eat six plates of stewed chicken and half as many of crab apple sauce when I visit the Joneses! Tonight I shall dream of it all again, commencing with the dinner at Joneses', and ending with the falling of the mountain—though last night it did not end so:

I was smothered and died—I knew I was dead, for I pinched my nose and felt no pain. (I remembered that during my lifetime my nose was much hurt by pinching—that tears sprang into my eyes when it was pinched.) Then I was really dead—dead; of course I was, and I laughed to think I had doubted the fact. After lying in a kind of trance for a few hours, days, years, hundreds or thousands of years— for I could not judge of time—I heard the sound of picks and shovels. Every day—as I supposed, at least for what seemed some space of time—the sound drew nearer, nearer; at last they reached me. A pick struck my leg. I felt the jar, but the blow did not pain me. I would then have bet high that I was dead. I was so much pleased that my first conclusion founded on the experiment of pinching my nose was substantiated by this accident that I made an attempt to laugh, and tried to sing out to the adventurous miners that I would bet them four ounces that I was dead. But somehow my tongue was so benumbed that it refused to wag. Finally I heard an exclamation of surprise. Then there was a hum, as of persons consulting in a low tone. Soon they commenced digging about me—digging very carefully. Shortly afterwards I felt myself slide down upon a pile of loose gravel. I had been expecting this and had made up my mind as to how I would act. I felt very thankful to the men for digging me out, and I would tell them so. I would then explain to them the manner of my death; tell them who I was, when I was killed, and get them to bury me in some nice retired spot. But to my great terror and discomfiture, I found myself incapable of uttering a single word, moving a limb, or even of winking an eye. I was very dead indeed. If I could only have said ten words I would now have doubled my bet, and bet them eight ounces that I was the *deadest* man they had ever seen. But as I couldn't make the bet, I concluded, after chuckling a little at the idea of what a dead sure thing I would have if they should take my bet, to listen and see if I could gather from their talk what their notion of me was. They were quite busy cleaning me off—scratching the dirt from my eyes and boring out my ears.

"A petrified man, by all that's howly!" cried one.

"Be jabbers, an' ye may well say it!" cried another. "I've niver seen a more peterfieder feller in all my life."

"Our fortunes are made, sure!" cried a third.

"It's a bigger strike by a goldarned sight than the Comstock was in the days of old."

"We can sell it for fifty thousand dollars!" cried out a sanguine fellow with a nasal twang which proclaimed him a Yankee.

Heavens, then I was not only dead but an *it*—and Petrified!

Petrified!

I had never thought of being petrified and did not much like the notion. I had long since become accustomed to being dead; in fact, prided myself upon being the deadest among the dead, but this thing of being petrified rather frightened me.

Then, blast it, I should have lost my bet; I wasn't dead after all. *Only* petrified. That must have been what ailed me all the time. And I had been fool enough to think myself dead.

When I was pinching my nose I must have just begun to harden. What a fool I was not to think I might be petrifying! By keeping my blood in circulation I might have arrested the petrifaction before it spread to other parts of my body. That would have been so gay! And I laughed at the idea of my going about with a stone nose—a nose that would never need blowing, would never get frostbitten and couldn't be pinched. But my laugh died away and softened down into a moan of despair when I thought of my situation.

"Petrified! Of all things! Why must *I* petrify?" and I vainly strove to toss my arms aloft.

The men who had dug me out went away and were gone for some time, how long I could not tell. They might have been gone an hour, a day, a month or a year, but they returned. A crowd came with them. They talked a great deal, and very fast, all in a shrill, piping tone so that I could scarce understand them. I soon found out, however, that I was considered to be a man of monstrous size—in short, a giant— and *petrified!*

No doubt, now, about my being in that fix. A learned professor made one of the crowd, and he pronounced me the most perfect case of petrifaction that had ever been dug up in any age.

"Heavens, me—me who never harmed a soul—*me* a petrified giant!"

I wouldn't stand it! I'd get up and kick the old fool. No use. Not a limb would move. I was petrified after all; to quote the language of the professor, I was one of the most perfect specimens ever dug up in any age. Well, that was not so bad after all. What if my nose had been lacking? What if one of my ears were missing, or an arm or leg? I should make a pretty appearance in that case!

I was immediately filled with delight when I came to consider that I was all on hand, and tried to bet the professor fifty dollars that there *never would* be another such perfect case of petrifaction dug up as I presented. But I couldn't speak, and concluded that on the whole, I would prefer not being petrified.

The professor was now busy examining the dirt in which I had been confined, and presently declared that the hill for several yards about the spot where I had been found was composed of the remains of some fowl, he believed chicken, with a slight trace of some acid fruit. He could not be positive, but he would be able to tell all about it as soon as he had analyzed it.

I should have liked very much to have bet him a hundred or two that the stuff was stewed chicken and crab apple sauce, but the thing was out of the question, so I only moaned in spirit, and waited to see what would next be done.

Niobe, after being turned to stone by Jupiter, continued, as she rested in her metamorphosed condition on Mount Sipylus, to feel and mourn the misfortunes with which the gods had visited her; so I, though powerless to move, and with a tongue of stone that forbade all utterance, seemed still in possession of a brain capable of exercising all its proper functions, and of ears whose tympanums still had enough of elasticity and sensitiveness to catch all the sounds about me.

I found shortly that I had been hoisted upon some kind of vehicle and was being conveyed away. As I lay helpless upon my back, listening to the screeching of numerous slow-moving wheels and a Babel of shrill voices, I was very forcibly reminded of Swift's description of the manner in which the Emperor of Lilliput caused Gulliver to be conveyed to his capital.

From the labor it cost my discoverers to hoist me upon the vehicle, I arrived at the conclusion that I must have become very heavy by having undergone the petrifying process, and was about ready to offer to bet that I was the heaviest man on the Pacific Coast, when it occurred to me that while I was lying in the ground hardening, some hundreds of thousands of years might have passed, during which the human race might have degenerated in stature, till they were now no larger than the celebrated race of Pygmæi, who were wont, as Homer, Ovid, Juvenal, Pliny, and many other writers tell us, to fight many bloody battles with cranes for possession of that part of India in which they dwell. The sound of their voices in the immense cheering which followed the successful hoisting of my body upon the vehicle confirmed me in this opinion, once I came to dwell upon the matter and give the circumstance its proper weight and value.

To these people, then, I was really a giant.

According to the Rabbins, Adam, the first man, was so tall that his head, upon his first creation, reached the heavens; though they say that afterward, upon the angels complaining that the great height of our common father was a source of much annoyance to them, God put his hand upon Adam's head and squeezed him down some thousand cubits; and Eve, his wife, was herself no doll, if we may credit certain learned Mahommedan doctors, who assert that when her head lay on a hill near Mecca, her knees rested on two others in the plain, two bow-shots asunder.

Now, if the men of my age of the world—the Comstock age—were so much inferior in stature to our first parents, was there anything strange in my appearing a giant in the eyes of people living on the earth a thousand years later than the Comstock period? I thought not.

After being hauled a considerable distance, as I supposed, I was unloaded, carried somewhere—into a large room, apparently—and finally placed upon my feet, much to the satisfaction of those at work about me, among whom I recognized the professor and some of those who dug me out of the mountain. These, I now found, called themselves my owners. I thought of making them a small bet on that; but as I couldn't, I let it pass.

All was quiet for a time after these busy fellows departed, then I heard music and the patter of many feet—as of a multitude crowding into a room. I could hear these people utter a great many exclamations of astonishment, such as: "What a monster!" "Look at its great claws!" and "Ain't he a buster!" from the juveniles.

Some kind of label had been pasted upon my breast, and at length it was read aloud by one of the pigmies, so that I understood the whole of it. Blast them, they were making a show of me! The label read:

"A PETRIFIED WASHOE GIANT, belonging to the COMSTOCK PERIOD;

found 2513 feet below the surface of Shanghæ Hill, and 5610 feet from its base, following a water level; being almost immediately in the center of the mountain. It has been ascertained that the food of this MAN MONSTER consists wholly of STEWED CHICKEN and CRAB APPLE SAUCE."

The learned professor now arose and commenced a lecture on the Great Man Monster, as he was pleased to call me. He first entered into a minute description of the strata under which I was found. In this he had much to say of various shells he had picked out of the strata above and below me; of carbonaceous matter, ferns, mosses, and other cryptogamic productions, and also of deposits or substances forming the basis of, or being at least favorable to, petrifaction. A few of these I remember were marl, calcsinter, calctuff and stalactitic tufa.

Then he spoke long and eloquently of the mastodon and other monster animals of the Comstock period and drew the conclusion that the men of that age doubtless corresponded in size with the animals, birds, etc. He then made mention of one Og, king of Basan, spoken of by the Rabbins, who was so tall that the flood which drowned the world in Noah's time only came up to his knees, and he further stated, on the authority of the Rabbins, that this Og was still alive when Moses led the Israelites out of Egypt and that he undertook to oppose the march of the Israelites, whose army covered a space of nine miles, by taking a stone on his head sufficiently large to cover up the entire host; but as he was preparing to launch this vast rock, the Almighty sent a lapwing that picked a hole through the stone and caused it to slip over his neck and throw him upon the ground, when Moses attacked and slew him, though he could only reach his heels, notwithstanding that he threw his spear ten cubits high. The body of this Og, he proceeded to say, lay stretched on the ground for a whole year, reaching as far as the river Nile, in Egypt.

Next he proceeded to show that the flood was much more recent than was supposed, that the location of Egypt and the Nile was doubtful, and finally declared it to be his firm conviction that the Great Man Monster before them was none other but the celebrated Og. He said he was aware that there were some few links wanting in his chain of evidence, and that some other flaws might be picked, as, for instance, that the mountain under which the giant was found buried was a little too large to pass for the remains of the rock which

Og bore on his head when he threatened to exterminate the Israelites—there was some disagreement of proportion—but then a part might be the original rock, and a part more recent accumulation.

As the professor thus discoursed, I was burning with indignation: "Og indeed!"

But, like a second Prometheus, I was chained to a rock and the professor, as a vulture, tore my liver. Yet I could but chafe and rage under the torture of his foul break, and all at once, when my anger was highest, I felt a hot gush of blood through all my limbs and every fiber of my frame. I was no longer petrified! My dead eyeballs were no longer lustreless. I could see, and I felt my eyes flaming as living coals.

I was in a glass case—the devils!

"Revenge! Death to the professor!"

A crash—and I was out of the case.

A strike—and I clutched the professor by his long flowing locks.

He screamed—heavens, how wildly!

What cared I?

I laughed, "Ha, ha, ha! Ho, ho, ho!"

Dragging the professor after me by his long hair, I danced about the room.

I kicked the swarms of pigmies that were struggling in the wildest consternation to escape from the room, hither and thither, like so many footballs.

I seized a little old bald-headed fellow, who had been torturing a bass viol, by one of his legs, held him aloft, and swung him about my head, causing him to scream quite as lustily as the professor was doing: "Glorious!" and I took another turn across the room, doing the scalp-dance square through the center of the thickest bunch of pigmies I could find—tossing aloft the bass viol player, and jerking the professor so ferociously that his hair was ready to part from his scalp.

"Ha, ha!—glorious!"—and I kicked a female pigmy such a lifter that she passed through a chandelier that hung from the ceiling. But no sooner was this light out than another appeared—not borne by pigmies, but in the hands of giants—giants equal in every respect to myself.

"Heavens! Now I am a gone specimen! Back to my case I must go. That infernal label will again be pasted on my breast!"

I was so terribly frightened at the ferocious look of an aged giantess that led the Titan host that I relinquished my hold on the professor and dropped the bald-headed bass viol player.

The ferocious giantess spoke: "Dan De Quille, are you insane? Do you want to murder your wife and child? Say!"

"No," cried I, "only the professor, and his blood I will have!"

I stared about me to seize him, but only saw my wife sobbing at my side, with hair disheveled and eyes staring wildly—only her and my boy, darling Ebenezer, standing on his head at the foot of the bed, with his legs bent over the footboard, in imminent danger of breaking his neck.

Bedclothes were strewn in every direction; a lock of brown hair hung in a tangled skein from the fingers of my right hand. My last pigmy—a pillow—had smashed a lamp burning on a table near the bed; a washbowl and pitcher lay in fragments!

When my good-natured old mother-in-law asked me if I "didn't feel ashamed of myself," I answered without a moment's hesitation: "I am!" When other sympathizing members of the household asked me whether or not they were to "consider me a brute," I answered promptly: "You are!"

My wife looks at me in such a suspicious, penetrating, and sometimes fearful manner that I have almost abandoned the idea of asking her whether she sees anything about me to remind her of stewed chicken and crab apple sauce. I feel that I shall have to find some more delicate way of putting the question, or leave it unasked.

There is still that visit to the Joneses.

Great heaven! Can stewed chicken and crab apple sauce drive a man to the lunatic asylum?

Quien sabe?

A Silver Man

The Goblin Frog

*The Demon Frog Bears a Charmed Life—He
Chases Peter O'Reilly Out of Gold Canyon—
Drives Him from Golden Sands to Caverns
of Silver—Through the Frog the
Comstock Lode is Discovered.*

*P*eter O'Reilly was one of the pioneer miners of Washoe and
one of the discoverers of the Comstock silver mines—one of the men
who turned up to the light of day that glittering ore which was the
first of over $200 million since taken from the great vein then hit
upon.

Before going to work on Six-Mile Canon, at the head of which the
great silver discovery was made, Peter O'Reilly mined on Gold Cañon, a long and large ravine heading on the opposite side of Mount
Davidson, a mile south of the canyon first named. There he wrought
with pan and rocker at washing placer gold from the sand and gravel
of the bed and bars of the cañon.

"Pete" was fond of rambling away alone along the meanderings of
the stream in search of rich spots, where he could be by himself and
mine in his own way. Provided he could find a few "colors" (small
specks of gold) he would dig and pan away for days, quite confident
that his luck would at last lead him to the right spot and that in the
end his labors would be richly rewarded.

Pete was not only a spiritualist, but was also a firm believer in luck
and in all manner of signs and omens. The last mining he ever did on

Mythologizing the founding of the Comstock and one-upping Twain's Calaveras amphibian. From the *Territorial Enterprise*, January 30, 1876.

Gold Cañon was when he started in to prospect a bar on which he found already located a squatter in the person of a frog, which frog began in a short time to give him a great deal of trouble.

He constructed a small dam or reservoir to turn the small rill running in the ravine into a little ditch leading to his panning hole near the bar. The reservoir held but about a dozen hogsheads of water, and it was soon after this was completed and filled that Pete first had notice of the presence on his claim of the frog. He had sunk a pit almost down to the bedrock and had washed out two or three pans of dirt that yielded well. He was down in his prospect hole digging up and filling his pan with some particularly fine-looking gravel when he heard a small, squeaky voice sing out, "Struck it?"

Pete was at the moment deeply absorbed in the work in which he was engaged, and the shrill, squeaking voice ringing out so near at hand and asking a question that so exactly chimed in with the train of the thought running through his head so startled him that his pick almost fell from his hands. He pricked up his ears and looked about in all directions to see whence proceeded the cheery little voice. He half expected to see a little red-mantled fairy standing in some neighboring clump of willows or peering out at him through a tuft of the rank grass growing along the margin of the rill. As he thus stood gazing about in open-mouthed amazement, the little voice again piped out: "Struck it? Struck it? Struck it?"

Turning his eyes in the direction whence proceeded the inquiring voice, Pete presently descried a small green frog mounted upon a stick that projected an inch or two above the surface of the water in his reservoir. The frog was but a rod or two away and seemed, as Pete thought, to be looking inquiringly into his eyes.

"Struck it?" again said the frog.

"It is a good omen," said Pete. "The little fellow says I have struck it. Though he is no countryman of mine, I belave in me sowl I have struck it in this very hole."

So saying, Pete carried the pan of dirt he had dug to his panning place, panned it out, and did not get a color. He was not a little astonished at this result and had a notion to call the frog a liar, but on turning to look for him the little fellow was gone. Pete went back to his pit and dug another pan of dirt—listening all the time to hear what the frog would say about it. Not a word did the frog say, however.

Pete washed out the pan of dirt and got nearly a dollar. "Aha! ye little divil!" cried he, "where air ye now? Ye hadn't a word to say this time!"

Well pleased with his luck, Pete began digging another pan of dirt from the place where he had got the last, expecting a rich haul. He had been at work but half a minute when the voice rang out sharp and clear: "Struck it? Struck it? Struck it?"

"Oh, yes, ye little fool; it's aisy for ye to say 'Sthruck it! Sthruck it!' afther seein' what I got in me last pan!"

"Struck it! Struck it! Struck it!" cried the frog in what to Pete seemed a triumphant tone.

"All right, me bye!" cheerily assented Pete, nodding his head toward the little fellow that sat winking and blinking on the end of the stick. "All right, me bye—av course I've sthruck it!"

He carried the pan to his water hole, washed it out, and didn't get a color. "Ye'r the warst liar I iver saw!" cried Pete, rising up from his work and shaking his fist in the direction of the frog. Not a sign of the frog did he see, however; the little fellow having very prudently retired to the bottom of the pond.

Pete grumbled for a time and then went and dug another pan of gravel; the frog again stuck his head above the water and said "Struck it?" and again the dirt yielded no gold when washed out. Thus it went; when the frog said nothing he got a good yield of gold, but when he made his usual inquiry—sneering inquiry, Pete now considered it to be—no gold was found.

At last Pete had washed so many pans of dirt out of which the frog had charmed all the gold that he began to grow very angry. He was also not a little discouraged. Finally, just as he began to scrape the dirt out of the bottom of a very promising crevice, and just as he was beginning to think the frog would this time hold his tongue, out came the little fellow with his "Struck it? Struck it?"

Pete quietly laid down his crevicing spoon, slyly gathered two or three big rocks, then softly, on tiptoe, began stealing toward his little persecutor, and just as the frog cried, "Struck it?" Pete let drive at him with a rock so huge that it could have been hurled by no lesser than Ajax, missing his mark but raising a great commotion in the pond.

Thinking he had given his bad angel a fright that would last him a fortnight, Pete returned to his work. He had almost filled his pan with very rich-looking dirt when up came the frog's head and out came his tantalizing, "Struck it? Struck it?"

Pete threw the pan of dirt as far as he could send it and made for the frog, determined on its destruction. He would stand no more of its infernal nonsense. Shovel in hand, he waded into the middle of the little reservoir and scooped and tore about in it with the vigor and venom of a mad bull. Once or twice he saw, or imagined he saw, the frog dart through the discolored water and brought down the back of his shovel upon the spot with such a "spat" that the blow might have been heard half a mile away. At length, not seeing anything more of the frog, Pete concluded that he had killed him. He gave him a parting curse and, being now wrought up to such a pitch of excitement and nervousness that he could work no more that afternoon, strode away, put on his coat, and went home.

The next morning he returned to his claim and his work. He had washed out several pans of dirt and was getting good pay out of them when suddenly there fell upon his ear the shrill cry of "Struck it?"

The first note sent a thrill through Pete's frame like the sharp shock of an electrical battery, then a chill fell upon his heart, and his hair almost rose on end. His evil genius, as he now firmly believed the little green frog to be, was still there, alive and at his old tricks.

He kicked over the pan of dirt he had dug and made a rush for the reservoir, the frog plumping under the water at his approach. Pete again went into the reservoir with his long-handled shovel and charged about at a furious rate, but he could see nothing of the frog or anything that looked like it. Being determined to do for his tormentor this time, Pete went for his pan and began trying to bail out the reservoir. Finding this too great a task, he got a pick, dug down the embankment of dirt and rocks forming the little dam, and eagerly watched, with uplifted shovel, for the frog as the water ran off. The water all ran out but the frog was nowhere to be seen.

Pete then waded out in the oozy bed of the pond, digging and plowing about with his shovel, but he failed to start the goblin frog. He then arrived at the very reasonable conclusion that the little imp had gone down the stream with the body of water that rushed out of the reservoir when it was opened. He cruised about the spot for an hour or two, going down the channel of the ravine, turning over rocks and beating tufts of grass with his shovel, but saw nothing of the frog. Thinking his evil genius had been washed down through the cañon into the Carson River, Pete concluded to rebuild his dam in order that he might have water ready for use in the morning. This job done he went home, feeling quite sure that he had either killed or permanently ousted his little enemy.

The next day he returned to his work. Before starting in, however, he walked around the reservoir several times, peering keenly into the water and kicking every bunch of grass about its margin. The frog was nowhere to be seen or started. Pete then went to his prospect hole and began to dig, stopping occasionally to cock an eye toward the pond and to listen for the frog. All promised well for Pete. He had dug a pan of dirt without the hated interruption and was on his way to wash it out when "Struck it? Struck it?" was squeaked from the pond by the goblin frog.

This was too much for Pete. The pan dropped from his hands, his under jaw fell, and he sank down upon the nearest rock, where he sat and considered the matter. As he was wondering if it was possible for him ever in any way to rid him himself of the evil thing that destroyed his luck, the frog again sang out, cheerily as ever, "Struck it? Struck it?"

"May the divil burn ye!" cried Pete. "I haven't *sthruck it,* and what's more I never will wid ye there, ye dirty little blackguard! Must I come afther ye again, ye unclane baste of the divil?"

"Struck it?" said the frog.

"Ye think so!" said Pete, and catching up his pick, he rushed to the reservoir and began digging down the embankment.

Presently he paused in this work and said: "It's of no use. Haven't I tried to get him in all ways? No; when I get the wather off he'll be gone. He's no human frog! I'll jist let him howld possession and I'll hunt me another place. Divil the lick will I ever sthrike here again; it's the divil's own child he is!"

Pete began to gather up his clothes and tools with the intention of vacating the place, when he stopped and gazed wistfully at his prospecting hole. "A promising place it was, too, in the main," said he. "Now, shall I be tormented away by a dirty little baste like yon? No; I'll give him a warmin' yet and all the likes of him. I'll pepper him tomorrow!" So saying, Pete put on his coat and struck out for home, turning to shake his fist toward the pond as he departed.

The next morning Pete went up to Johntown and borrowed a shotgun; he then bought a quantity of powder and shot and returned to his claim, saying as he strode along: "I'll kill that frog if it's among the possibilities!"

On reaching his claim, he crawled to a rock near the edge of the pond and, seating himself upon it, watched for some hours, but the goblin frog was neither to be seen nor heard.

"He has run away," said Pete, "but I'll kill him if he is anywhere on the face of the green earth!"

He then moved along down the cañon and presently saw what seemed to be his tormentor. He blazed away and stretched the creature dead on the margin of the rill. He was just beginning to rejoice over the victory he had gained when up from the spot sprung another frog, the very picture of that he had killed. Pete looked at this new apparition and then turned and gazed upon the slaughtered animal to be sure it was dead. Finding it stretched lifeless on the ground, he went after the second frog. This was finally slaughtered, and he continued his hunt down the cañon. All that day he hunted frogs, blazing away at everything that moved in the water or that looked at all like a frog.

The next day he bought more ammunition and again went on the warpath along the cañon, firing so frequently that some of the miners above thought that the Piutes had attacked the settlers at the mouth of the cañon. The next day and the next, and right along for a week, Pete hunted the cañon, always beginning with the pond on his claim, and keeping up a murderous fire as often as he saw a frog or the suspicion of one. Not satisfied with this, he hunted the banks of the Carson River for a mile or two up and down the mouth of the cañon. He talked of nothing but frogs for a fortnight, bought and fired away whole sacks of shot and pound after pound of powder, and seemed to be almost insane on frogs. But he at last concluded that he had cleaned them all out and the goblin frog among the rest.

One morning, to the surprise of his neighbors in the camp who had been watching him curiously for some days, instead of starting out with his gun he took his pan and crevicing spoon and departed down the cañon in the direction of his claim.

An hour later Pete came tearing back to camp. "I'll niver sthrike pick intil the cañon again!" cried he. "That imp o' hell is still there on me claim! I was but liftin' me dirt for me second pan whin he raised his head from the wattur and says, 'Pete, have he sthruck it?' sez he. 'May the divil bless me,' said I, 'if ye can't have the whole bloody cañon; I'll niver sthrike pick intil it again.' No more I will. That frog is no human frog—it's a child o' hell!"

Pete kept his word; he never mined in the cañon again. He left for Six-Mile Cañon to hunt a place not haunted by a demon frog, and he had not mined many weeks before he and his partner, Pat McLaughlin, struck it! struck it! struck it!—struck the great Comstock silver lode, the hidden treasure house of the gnomes and the wonder of the whole mining world. He was, as he always believed, driven into this great good fortune by a goblin frog.

The Wonder of the Age, a Silver Man

*E*verybody, no doubt, has heard of the discovery of the wonderful "Silver Man," found in a mine between Esmeralda and Owen's River. Everybody, however, has not heard the full particulars of the discovery, and many will hoot the idea of any such discovery ever having been made. They will at once say that it is impossible for a human body to be changed to silver ore. Let them have their say!

Although the story is almost too much for belief, yet I hope to be able to show before finishing this account that, startling as the assertion may appear, such a change in the substance of the human body is not only possible, but that there is on record one well-authenticated instance of a similar changing of a human body into a mass of ore.

We have had all kinds of astonishing discoveries. Many things formerly classed among the impossibilities are now familiar, everyday possibilities. We are now to acknowledge that it is not impossible for a human body to be changed—through contact in a mineral vein with solutions of certain salts, carbonic and hydrosulphuric gases, and the electrical currents induced by the reaction of said solutions upon each other—into a mass of sulphuret of silver.

As no particular account of the discovery of the Silver Man has ever

Sparkling pseudo-paleontology. From the *Golden Era*, February 5, 1865.

been published, and as all who have heard of the wonder will be pleased to know something in regard to the finding of the body thus curiously mineralized, I will venture to give a full history.

Mr. Peter Kuhlman, a gentleman who has for some months past been engaged prospecting in a range of mountains lying to the southeast of Mono Lake, between Esmeralda and Owen's River, has kindly furnished me with the particulars given below:

The body is that of a full-grown man, and was found in what is known as the Hot Springs Lead. The body, when first found, was almost perfect, even to the fingers and toes. The features are distinctly traceable, but not wholly perfect. They present a blurred appearance.

In removing the body from its resting place, an arm was broken off. It was from observing the peculiar appearance of the fractured arm that Mr. Kuhlman—who is not only a good practical miner, but an excellent chemist and mineralogist—was induced to make a careful assay of pieces taken from the severed limb.

When it was announced to the miners that what they had looked upon as merely a most remarkable petrifaction was a mass of sulphuret of silver slightly mixed with copper and iron (in the shape of pyrites), they were at first incredulous. But repeated and careful tests, made before their own eyes, at length convinced them that such was the indisputable fact. The iron and copper pyrites are found lining the cavities of the bones and filling the spaces occurring between the body and the robe in which it was found partially enveloped, as these minerals often occur in holes and crevices in petrified wood. Pieces taken from the arm were tested with acids, with the blowpipe, and in other ways—always with the same result. A small button of pure silver, extracted by means of the blowpipe, was shown me by Mr. Kuhlman. He started for this city with part of the hand from the severed arm, with the thumb and two fingers attached and entire, but was induced to leave it with a scientific friend at Aurora, Esmeralda.

The body is supposed to be, and doubtless is, that of an Indian; but in its present changed state it is impossible to be certain on that point. The robe found about the body, part of which crumbled away on being exposed to the air, appears to have been of some kind of coarse cloth. Nothing but a few sticks of charred wood, also mineralized, was found with the body.

The lead in which the Silver Man, as he is popularly termed, was found was discovered last year, about the first of May, by three prospectors—Wm. R. Prescott, Oscar E. Hartman, and Patrick O'Haloran. On account of there being several hot springs on the cañon, some twenty rods above the vein, they called it the Hot Springs Lead. The lead was discovered at a point where it was laid bare by the action of the water of the cañon in passing over it. Here the cañon is very deep, the mountains rising in rugged walls on either side. Getting the course of the vein, the miners opened a cut on the side of the mountain about sixty feet above the bed of the cañon. On striking the lead, a tunnel was driven in upon it to the distance of seventy-five feet. The lead being found of rather a loose structure, it was thought best to start a shaft at the end of the tunnel and follow the lead down to where it became more solid, in the hope that the metal it contained would there be found more concentrated. While sinking this shaft, and after it had reached the depth of forty-five feet, a blow with a pick by the man working below was followed by a tremendous rush of air, and the terrified miner shouted lustily to his partners above to haul him up. The upward rush of air continued for some minutes after he had reached the surface, coming out with a noise like that made in blowing off a steam boiler, much to the astonishment and consternation of the three honest miners, who stood quaking in the tunnel above.

Upon consultation, after the startling noise had ceased, the true cause of the singular phenomenon was conjectured. Having made up their minds that the noise was caused by the escape of a large body of air compressed in a cavern in the lead, they at once determined to cut through into it and see what it might contain. Tying the windlass rope securely about his waist, one of the men descended and with a heavy drill succeeded, after a few minutes' labor, in staving out a hole nearly the full size of the bottom of the shaft; the shell left being little more than a mass of metallic concretions of a pyritous nature. On sounding the cavern with a rope, it was found to be no more than twelve to fifteen feet deep. As a candle burned clearly at the bottom, which looked safe and solid, two of the men were let down to explore the opening. It was found to be nothing more than a huge crevice in the rock, four or five feet in width at the point where cut into by the shaft, but back in the direction of the mountain closing in till not more than ten inches in width.

The body I have been talking about was found stretched upon the ground, lying face upwards, a few feet from where the men landed.

Had the finders been any other than California or Washoe miners, there would have been a jolly stampede and some frantic climbing of the windlass rope. Although startled and greatly astonished, they stood their ground and soon sufficiently regained their composure to make a critical examination of the singular object before them.

The news of the wonderful strike soon spread through the neighborhood, and the "Petrified Man," as he was then called, was visited by all living near—that is to say, within twenty or thirty miles.

When Mr. Kuhlman first visited the Silver Man, which was three days after the discovery—he living twenty-three miles southwest of Hot Springs—that argentiferous *homo* was still reposing, as found, in the cavern. At his suggestion the body was loosened from the floor, where it was held by an accumulation of pyritous concretions, and hoisted out to the light of day. During this operation, one of the arms—the right one—was broken off, as has been stated. The left arm, being pressed across the body as though in the act of clutching the robe, was saved.

Mr. Kuhlman describes the walls of the cavern as presenting the most magnificent appearance imaginable, being a complete mass of pyrites of the most perfect and brilliant description—all as fresh as the crystals in the heart of an unbroken geode. The cavern, or crevice, widens in the direction of the cañon and is blocked up by a mass of rocks; all, however, covered, as well as the walls, with a thick and bristling incrustation of pyrites.

The opinion of Mr. Kuhlman—which is very reasonable—is that the body so singularly discovered is that of an Indian who ages ago sought shelter in this cleft in the rocks during a rainstorm, and that the face of the mountain, worn perpendicularly by the water of the cañon and softened by the rain, slid down, confining the lone red man in the cavity, and leaving him to die of starvation and become mineralized—to become, in short, a Silver Man, for us in this age to wonder about.

The miners who have this great curiosity intend taking it to San Francisco, thence to New York, and expect to make fortunes by its exhibition; but Mr. Kuhlman says it is certain soon to fall to pieces and be destroyed by the action of the atmosphere—in fact, that it is already crumbling.

As I said at the outset, this story of a human body turning to silver ore will doubtless strike the majority of my readers as a thing wholly impossible and absurd in the extreme, but I will try to show that it is neither one nor the other.

In Sweden is an old mining town called Falun, situated on Lake Runn, and about fifty-four miles southwest of Gefle. This town is the capital of the Swedish laen, or province, of the same name, though sometimes called Kopparburg's Laen on account of its extensive copper mines. The mines, which are west of the town, are worked for copper, though the ore contains a small percent of gold, silver, and lead. These mines have been worked hundreds of years, and are still quite productive. By the falling in of ancient galleries, a vast chasm has been formed on the surface, the opening being no less than 300 feet deep, 1,200 long, and 600 wide. Stairs now lead down the sides of this chasm to its bottom, whence, by means of ladders, the workmen descend to the pits and galleries below. The works extend for miles underground, and far below are many vast galleries. In one of these immense chambers, magnificently illuminated for the occasion, Bernadotte and his queen once banqueted.

But with all this we have nothing to do, further than to understand that the mines are of very ancient date and that they contain many great galleries, a portion of which were once broken in and filled up, and doubtless great loss of life was occasioned by the accident. In reopening these old galleries, bodies of miners are often found, more or less preserved by the action of the copper and gases of the mine. The particular case which I wish to quote is one mentioned by Breithaupt, who says: "In one instance, the body of a miner was recovered from a very deep part of the mine, where it had remained no longer than sixty years, yet it was found converted into iron pyrites which had slowly and completely replaced the organic materials, retaining their forms."

Here is positive proof, on indisputable authority, that this supposed great absurdity of a Silver Man is not so absurd after all.

All who have the least knowledge of paleontology know that all those wonderful remains of fishes, animals, etc., found in limestone and other rocks, and about which so much is said and written, are not the creatures themselves, but merely their shapes replaced by mineral substances.

There are many instances of veins once worked out being filled afresh with mineral deposited by gases ascending from the depths of the mine, in connection, perhaps, with water holding in solution various mineral salts. Often the ore and vein stone have been found in a position so natural that but for the finding of the tools of the ancient miners embedded in the solid quartz, the fact of its being other than the primitive deposit would never have been suspected. So certain is it that many ores are thus deposited that the operations of nature may in this respect be imitated by artificial means. M. de Senarmont has made numerous experiments with such solutions as are found in hot springs, and by ingenious combinations in vessels hermetically sealed and properly heated, has succeeded in producing not only perfect quartz crystals, but the ores of iron, copper, silver, etc.

From what I have said, it will readily be seen that what appears so very wonderful in the fact of a human body being changed into a mass of mineral, is not so very strange after all. The place where the body was found, be it remembered, was most admirably calculated to produce such a change. Sealed up by a not uncommon accident in a cavity in the very heart of a metallic vein, and this again hermetically closed in every part by an accumulation on all its walls of pyritous concretions, while from below steamed upward gasses loaded with volatilized minerals, it would have been strange if no remarkable change had been produced in the organic remains subjected to these combined influences. There is every sign that the hot springs near the mine were at one time situated as far below the lead in which the body was found as they are now above it. Hot springs are generally caused by the decomposition of pyrites in contact with water. Once this operation commences, it proceeds in pretty much the same manner as the burning of a stratum of coal, following the unburnt portions of the deposit. The course of this burning at Steamboat Springs, Washoe, is northward. Even within the memory of the present generation, certain hot springs in California have moved several rods up the ravine on which they are situated, following the bed of pyritous matter to which they owe their existence. The strong subterranean heat of the Springs I have mentioned, during the time they were passing under the lead in which the mineralized body was found, doubtless caused immense volumes of various gases to be evolved, and this, besides the production of a favorable temperature, must most assuredly have had much to do in the production of the Silver Man.

I might say much more in proof not only of the fact of a human body so changed having been found, but of the simple and natural causes which have operated to produce a change which at the first glance appears so wonderful; however, as many would not believe, even though I should produce the body and melt it up into buttons before their very eyes, I refrain.

In conclusion, I have only to say that in my opinion the greatest wonder that Washoe has yet produced—the greatest wonder of the age—is this marvelous Silver Man!

Sad Fate of an Inventor
(Solar Armor)

A gentleman who has just arrived from the borax fields of the desert regions surrounding the town of Columbus, in the eastern part of this state, gives us the following account of the sad fate of Mr. Jonathan Newhouse, a man of considerable inventive genius. Mr. Newhouse had constructed what he called a "solar armor," an apparatus intended to protect the wearer from the fierce heat of the sun in crossing deserts and burning alkali plains. The armor consisted of a long, close-fitting jacket made of common sponge and a cap or hood of the same material, both jacket and hood being about an inch in thickness. Before starting across a desert, this armor was to be saturated with water. Under the right arm was suspended an India rubber sack filled with water and having a small gutta percha tube leading to the top of the hood. In order to keep the armor moist, all that was necessary to be done by the traveler as he progressed over the burning sands was to press the sack occasionally, when a small quantity of

---

What started as a filler hoax grew into the tale better known as "Solar Armor." From the *Territorial Enterprise*, July 2, 1874. Also the *San Francisco Examiner*, July 7, 1874; *Scientific American*, 31 (July 25, 1874), p. 51. The hoax was never taken seriously according to De Lancey Ferguson in his discussion "The Petrified Truth," *Colophon*, 2 (Winter 1937), pp. 189–96.

water would be forced up and thoroughly saturate the hood and the jacket below it. Thus, by the evaporation of the moisture in the armor it was calculated might be produced almost any degree of cold.

Mr. Newhouse went down to Death Valley, determined to try the experiment of crossing that terrible place in his armor. He started out into the valley one morning from the camp nearest its borders, telling the men at the camp as they laced his armor on his back that he would return in two days. The next day an Indian who could speak but a few words of English came to the camp in a great state of excitement. He made the men understand that he wanted them to follow him. At the distance of about twenty miles out into the desert the Indian pointed to a human figure seated against a rock. Approaching, they found it to be Newhouse still in his armor. He was dead and frozen stiff. His beard was covered with frost and—though the noonday sun poured down its fiercest rays—an icicle over a foot in length hung from his nose. There he had perished miserably, because his armor had worked but too well, and because it was laced up behind where he could not reach the fastenings.

A Mystery Explained

The Sequel to the Strange Death of Jonathan Newhouse, the Inventor of the Solar Armor.

$\mathcal{T}$he *Daily Telegraph*, London, England, appears to doubt the truth of the account we some time since published of the strange death of Jonathan Newhouse, in Death Valley, where he fell a victim to an apparatus of his own invention, styled a "solar armor." Under the date of August 3 the *Telegraph* says:

> A curious story reaches us from Virginia City, which, to quote transatlantic phraseology, is the "last new thing in the town line" that the young State of Nevada has produced. Virginia City is the child of the celebrated Comstock lode, which is in its immediate neighborhood. "The city," says Mr. Ross Browne, "lies on a rugged slope, and is singularly diversified in its up-risings and down-fallings. It is difficult to see upon what principle it was laid out. My impression is, it was never laid out at all, but followed the dips, spurs, and angles of the immortal Comstock." Be this as it may, the alkaline plains lying between the young capital of Nevada and the eastern border of the state have a terrible reputation for burning heat and waterless sterility. It is not uncommon for men—and

Sequel to "Solar Armor," giving Dan the opportunity to send up the London *Daily Telegraph*. From the *Territorial Enterprise*, August 30, 1874.

even wagons, with their teams of from eight to sixteen mules or oxen—to sink overwhelmed with heat and thirst when an effort is made to cross this desert during the height of summer. The Virginia City *Enterprise* tells us that a Mr. Jonathan Newhouse, being a man endowed with considerable inventive faculties, devised what he called a "solar armor," which he proposed to don before taking to the alkaline plains. This armor "consisted of a long, close-fitting jacket, made of common sponge, with a hood of the same material, both being saturated with water." Under the right arm its wearer had an india rubber pouch filled with water, and connecting with the top of the hood by means of a gutta-percha tube. As the traveler proceeds and feels the sun scorching his head, he compresses his right arm and squirts water into the hood, whence it percolates through the entire jacket. Clothed in this strange outfit, Mr. Newhouse set out from Virginia City for a place called "Death Valley," which, if this story be true, has more than ever earned the name that it bears. He expected to be absent for a couple of days. The heat of the sun was torrid, and, on the second day after his departure, an Indian, in a terrible state of "scare," rushed into a camp of white men on the edge of the desert, announcing that a man was lying frozen to death under a rock towards which he pointed his finger. Followed by his startled companions, the Indian led them to the body of poor Mr. Newhouse. It was then found that the traveler had been unable to unlace the jacket which his friends had fastened with thongs before he started, and the evaporation of moisture from the saturated sponge vestment had produced such intensity of cold that its wearer and inventor paid the penalty of his too successful ingenuity with his life. His beard is represented as having been covered with frost, and a large icicle hung from his nose and lips. The marvelous stories which come from "the plains" are apt to be received with incredulity by our transatlantic kinsmen who dwell upon the Eastern seaboard of the United States. We confess that, although the fate of Mr. Newhouse is related by the Western journal *au grande serieux,* we should require some additional confirmation before we unhesitatingly accept it. But everyone who has iced a bottle of wine by wrapping a wet cloth round it and putting it in a draught must have noticed how great is the cold that evaporation of moisture produces. For these reasons we are disposed to accept the tale from Virginia City in the same frame of mind which Herodotus, the Father of History, usually assumed when he repeated some marvel that had reached him—that is to say, we are

188

neither prepared to disbelieve it wholly nor to credit it without question.

Had not our attention been called to the above by Mr. Duncan McKay, superintendent of the Santiago mill, Carson River, who is in the weekly receipt of several English newspapers, we should probably never again have referred to the strange matter and manner of the death of Mr. Newhouse. However, as the truth of our narration appears to be called in question—if not directly, at least impliedly— by a paper which enjoys the reputation of having the largest circulation of any daily newspaper in the world, we feel that it is but right that we should make public some further particulars in regard to the strange affair—particulars which throw a flood of light upon what, we must admit, did appear almost incredible in our account of the sad occurrence as published. It seemed strange that so great a degree of cold could be produced simply by the evaporation of water, but it now appears that it was not water—at least not water alone—that was used by the unfortunate gentlemen.

We are glad that the *Telegraph* has given us the opportunity, long awaited, of publishing in detail the sequel to the curious affair. (The *Telegraph* is mistaken in supposing Death Valley to be near Virginia City. It is 250 or 300 miles distant.)

A fortnight after our account of the sad affair was published, we received a letter in regard to the matter from one David Baxter, who states that he is Justice of the Peace and ex officio Coroner at Salt Wells, a station in Inyo County, California, situated at the head of the Sink of Amargosa River, at the north end of Death Valley. Mr. Baxter states that he held an inquest on the body of the deceased, Newhouse, in due form, and that the verdict rendered was as follows: "We find that the name of the deceased was Jonathan Newhouse, a native of Knox County, Ohio, aged forty-seven years; and we further find that deceased came to his death in Death Valley, Inyo County, California, on the 27th day of June, A.D. 1874, by being frozen in a sort of coat of sponge called a 'solar armor,' of which he was the inventor and in which he was tightly laced at his own request, said 'solar armor' being moistened with some frigorific mixture, with the precise nature of which we are unacquainted."

Mr. Baxter further states in his letter that he had before him as witnesses the men stopping at the camp on the borders of Death Valley where Mr. Newhouse was last seen alive. These men produced what Mr. Baxter had not before heard mentioned, namely the carpet-sack of deceased, which he had left at their camp. In this was found, besides a few light articles of wearing apparel, several bottles and small glass jars containing liquids and powders or salts of various kinds, with the nature of the most of which no person in the settlement was acquainted. One of the largest bottles was labeled "Ether," known to them to be a very volatile liquid and capable of producing an intense degree of cold by evaporation.

From this they were able to give a shrewd guess at the nature of the contents of the other vessels. Although it was at first stated—and generally believed until after the contents of the carpetsack had been overhauled and the inquest held—that deceased had used water only in filling the little india rubber sack used in supplying moisture to the armor, one of the witnesses, Mr. Robert Purcell, testified that he had observed Mr. Newhouse at a spring about fifty yards from camp half an hour previous to his donning the armor, and recollects distinctly to have seen him handling one or two of the bottles and jars found in the carpetsack; though at the time he thought nothing of it, and did not approach very near to deceased, as he did not wish to be thought inquisitive.

Besides the bottle containing the ether, there was another in which was a liquid labeled "Bisulphide of Carbon." There were small glass jars containing what appeared to be salts. They were labeled "Ammonic Nitrate"; "Sodic Nitrate"; "Ammonic Chloride"; "Sodic Sulphate"; and "Sodic Phosphate."

Mr. Baxter is firmly convinced that with these chemicals, either alone or diluted with water, the degree of cold was produced which caused the death of the unfortunate man. He thinks that in his attempts to reach the fastenings of his armor, on his back, when he began to experience a painful degree of cold, he unavoidably compressed the india rubber pouch and thus constantly ejected more and more of the freezing fluid into the headpiece of his armor. As he stiffened in death, his arm, under which the sack was suspended, naturally pressed more strongly upon his side and thus caused a steady flow of the fluid. Mr. Baxter is of the opinion that the frost and icicle found on the beard and depending from the nose of deceased were formed from the water mingled with the more volatile fluids comprising the frigorific mixture.

He states as a remarkable fact—and it is strange that this was not mentioned by the gentleman from Columbus, Mr. Abner Wade, who gave us our first brief and imperfect account of the affair—that the men who went out with the Indian to find the remains of Mr. Newhouse came near having their hands frozen in handling the body when trying to place it upon the back of a horse. The freezing mixture oozed out of the spongy armor upon their hands and gave them intense pain. Finally—after they found they could handle the body in no other way—they were obliged to cut the lacings to the armor; when, after an infinite deal of pain to their hands and fingers, the armor was peeled off the body and left lying in the desert, where it probably still remains.

One of the men, Alexander Martin, suffered for about three weeks from the freezing his left hand received and he came near losing the middle finger, gangrene supervening at the root of the nail.

Viewed in the flood of light which Mr. Baxter throws upon the strange death of Mr. Newhouse, we think there can be but one opinion in regard to it; which is, that he fell a victim to a rash experiment with chemicals with the nature of which he was but imperfectly acquainted.

In conclusion, it only remains for us to state that Mr. Baxter informed us that it was his intention to send the bottles and jars of chemicals to the Academy of Sciences at San Francisco; also, the solar armor, in case he could recover it. Whether or not he has done so we cannot say. For several weeks we have closely watched the reports of the proceedings of the learned body named, but as yet have seen no mention made of either the chemicals or the armor.

The Boss Rainmaker

*Uncle Jess Slade's Strange Discovery. Tapping the
Clouds With a Shotgun. Rain and Snow Produced
to Order—The Veracious Tale of an Old-Timer.*

*Y*as, yas, let 'em go on with their racket!" cried old Uncle Jess
Slade, looking up from his newspaper. "Let 'em go right along
with their poppin', bangin', explodin' of dynermite an' making' of
kimickle smokes, but I'm the boss rainmaker as far as heerd from,
and I'll bet on it all the time."

"You a rainmaker, Uncle Jess? Why, you're about the last man I'd
have suspected," said I.

"Well, jist by lookin' at her you can't tell how fur a cat kin jump. I
don't go about blowin' and advertisin' myself as sich, like them fellers
over in Tulary; nevertheless, I'm the boss of all the rainmakers and
cloud-busters. I onct performed a feat in cloud-bustin' never ekaled
before or sinct by mortal man."

"What! Did you actually produce a storm, Uncle Jess?"

"Perjuce a storm? Well, if I didn't perjuce a reglar out-and-out
storm I astonished natur most damnably!"

"Got hold of one of the old dame's secrets, eh? How came you to
hit on it, Uncle Jess?"

A late spoof set in the high Sierra. From the San Francisco *Chronicle,* April
10, 1892.

192

"Well, jist by accidin'—jist by a sort of fool caper, as you may say. It were 'bout ten year ago in the High Sierra—away up at the very head of the headwaters of the Middle Tuollermy. It were on the old Walker River trail. There wur 'bout ten of us up there on the very backbone of the old range. We all had mules, burros, or some kind of pack animals an' were strung out injun file on a part of the trail high above the timberline. It were away up on the very top ridge where there were a little trough of a pass betwixt two bare granite peaks. Castle Peak were to the north and to the south wur Mount Dana and Mount Lyell. In the main the sky were clear, but there were floatin' about tolerable numerous a lot of them sort of woolly cotton-ball clouds of the piled-up kind that some people calls 'thunderheads.' They wus all sizes, from a haystack up to a good chunk of a mountain. They wur goin' through the pass in a kind of percission, follerin' the current of air that drawed through the notch in the mountains jist as icebergs float along in a current in the ocean. Some were draggin' right along on the ground, some wur five foot high, some twenty, and some fifty foot high.

"We wur travlin' west, meetin' these masses of cloud, and so thick wur they that when a man or a hoss ahead went into one of 'em he disappeared same as if he'd gone inter the side of a solid mountain. You stepped right out of sunshine into midnight darkness.

"These big piles of cloud stuff had a smell and taste of swamps and tules, and an awful damp, cold feelin'. I were bringin' up the rear of the train, leadin' my donkey and carryin' my shotgun on my shoulder. Well, sir, finally along comes one of them big fat clouds, one about as big as a meetin'-house. It were 'bout ten feet 'bove my head, and jist when it got square over me I up with my big No. 9 shotgun and let drive right inter the middle of it with both barrels. Well, sir, blast my buttons, didn't I git astonished! At the crack of my gun every particle of that cloud vanished. Down upon me fell a shower of snow and out flashed the bright sunlight. On my hat and on the pack of my burro's back were 'bout four inches of snow, and the whole ground were whitened for a space of forty feet in every direction.

"You brought the whole thing down at your first shot, Uncle Jess?"

"Yas, and blast my buttons if I wasn't skeered. For 'bout three seconds I thought I'd busted a hole in the roof of the heavens."

"Your old No. 9 was a powerful strong shooting gun."

"Pow'ful, sir! You may grin, but I'm only tellin' facts. I spose I'm the only livin' man that ever tried the like. I reckon most anybody might do the same thing, but so far as heerd from I'm the boss rainmaker."

"But, Uncle Jess, you made snow."

"Yas, I did, an' lots of it, considerin' the small patch of cloud I had to work on. I made snow because it were nigh onto the fust of November, and that were the nat'ral thing to make at that season and at that altertude."

"Well, Uncle Jess, I'm willing to admit that it wasn't bad as a beginning."

"No, sir, it weren't, and it were only a beginnin'. You hain't heerd all; the wust is to come."

"What! More cloud bursting?"

"My God, yes; a thing to ha'nt me to my dyin' day. But it was owin' to my inexperience. After I'd got over my fust skeer I busted a number more of clouds of various sizes as I traveled along. It wur big fun to see the snow tumble down, so I let go old No. 9 inter every cloud that come in reach. But the last time I turned loose on one I awfully overdid the business.

"We'd left the Tuollermy and turned south, the trail leadin' down a tremenjus gorge to Lake Tenizer, three thousand feet below. All my party wur a long ways ahead down the big cañon when I got to the top of it, I'd been foolin' along so much at cloud bustin'.

"Well, sir, jist as I got to the head of the gorge along comes a cloud so big that it seemed to fill all the space between the mountains. It was so heavy that it dragged along on the ground, and inside of it wur black as night. I let her move on, my hair and whiskers drippin', till I thought I were 'bout the middle of her, then I lets go both barrels to once and busted her wide open. She hit back at me with a flash of lightnin' and a clap of thunder, then she tumbled. Talk about your cloudbusts and waterspouts, this were the boss of 'em all. It were jist like I'd knocked the bottom outer Lake Tahoe. I tuck a hitch of my lead rope round a big fir tree when I see what I'd done and then me and the burro held on, but I couldn't have held my ground half a minit if I'd been down in the gorge.

"All were over in a second or two and I then tuck my way down the gorge. The further I went the more skeert I got. Bowlders, sile, trees, and all elst in the cañon to a height of fifty feet on both sides had been swept as clean as a shotgun. 'My God!' cries I, 'why didn't I hev sense enough not to fool with the clouds when I knowed I were gittin' down below the snowline!'

"I felt purty sure I'd killed my whole party, and for a time I were jist about crazy. But after a bit one after another come climbin' down the rocky sides of the cañon, though every hoss, mule, and burro was gone, with all the pervisions and traps they carried. This were bad enough, but when we come to count noses we found poor Bob Gilchrist gone—swept away inter Lake Tenizer along with the animals, the trees, and the other debray.

"I were blamed for the whole trouble. All drawed their revolvers, turned upon me and accused me of bustin' the cloud. In less'n two minits it were decided to shoot me. I had to lie to save my life—a thing I've been ashamed of ever since. I put the blame of the whole business upon the Lord, askin' the fellers if they hadn't heerd the thunderclap. They couldn't deny havin' heerd it. That clap of thunder was all that saved me.

"That certainly was big work, Uncle Jess."

"Yaas, tolerable fair for a shotgun. You jist give me a big bell-muzzled howitzer and put me up on the main ridge of the Sierra anytime in the spring or summer months and I'll drap every cloud that comes along jist as easy as a sportin' man draps pigeons when let outen a trap. I'll fetch 'em down in reglar cloudbursts, now on the Nevada side of the ridge and now on the California side—jist sendin' a rush of water down the East Walker, then a rush down the Tuollermy. It's no trouble to bust open the clouds when you git up in fair range of 'em, but these fellers in the valley bangin' away 5,000 feet below 'em are only a wastin' their amernition."

"Uncle Jess, I am afraid you are not a true sportsman. Judging from your methods you are a rascally pot-hunter."

"Well, sir, there's allers plenty of ——— fools in the world to make light of a big discovery. But, turn up your nose at me and sneer at me till you tire of it; still the fact remains that I'm the boss rainmaker, so far as heerd from."

195

A Strange Monomania

A Man with a Beef's Liver in His Nose— His Sufferings and How He was Cured.

*A*late resident of Owen's Valley, who arrived in this city a day or two since, tells a remarkable story of a curious monomania which took possession, some weeks since, of a man who was his partner in a ranch in the valley named. The case is so curious that we think our readers will not find fault with us if we relate it as fully as it was detailed to us by the gentleman mentioned above, who observed it from first to last.

The man first began picking at his nose one evening while seated on the porch of his dwelling after finishing a hard day's work in the fields. He was then in excellent health and spirits. He remarked to our informant, who was seated near him, that it was curious, but there was some little thing in his nose that annoyed him greatly, yet he could not get it out nor move it in any direction. During the evening he spent a good deal of time picking at and blowing his nose, and finally went to bed grumbling about being unable to get rid of the

---

More in the horrible style, about a man with beef's liver in his nose— reminiscent of the fate De Quille wished on Twain. See pp. 19–20 above. From the *Territorial Enterprise,* September 13, 1874.

substance, whatever it was. The next morning he was still picking at his nose, and worrying because he could not remove the obstruction.

However, after breakfast he went out into the fields as usual. Before noon he left off work, and going home, got his wife to look into his nose to see if she could discover the nature of the thing which was annoying him. She could see nothing, and told him so. He did not seem altogether satisfied, but said nothing, and presently went off to the barn to work, taking his little boy with him.

Half an hour after the boy came back and said: "Mamma, when I was at the barn, Papa made me look in his nose ever so many times, but I couldn't see anything." This somewhat alarmed the wife, and she went in search of her husband. She found him seated beside a horse bucket partially filled with water. He was gazing down at his face as reflected there, at the same time distending his right nostril—where his trouble was—with his thumb and finger. He appeared a good deal ashamed when he saw his wife, and pretended that he was trying to adjust the bail of the bucket, which had, as he said, got "out of fix."

For two or three days he moped about. He would go out into the fields to work, but in an hour or two was back looking terribly melancholy and distressed. At last he one morning made a clean breast of it. Calling his partner—our informant—and his wife to draw near to where he was seated on his porch, he said: "I know I have not long to live. My dear wife—" Here he burst into tears and broke down for a time, but he soon rallied and continued: "My dear wife, I fully appreciate your goodness and the kindness of your intentions when you told me you could see nothing in my nose. You did not wish to distress me, but I know now that you saw it. I knew you was deceiving me, so I looked in a bucket of water when I went to the barn to water the horses, and there for the first time I saw it—saw it distinctly. I didn't know what it was then, it was so small, but since then I have looked in the looking glass and seen it. It is growing all the time and filling up my nose so that I cannot get my breath. It is a—oh! It's horrible to think of it!—It is a beef's liver! How it got there I don't know, but that is what it is. I must soon die. I shall suffocate. It's a mere matter of time!"

All arguments were vain. No reasoning could convince him that there was not a beef's liver growing in his nose. His wife at length became so much alarmed that a doctor was sent for. He proved to be a rough and gruff old fellow and, besides, was a good deal intoxicated when he arrived. He looked into the sufferer's nose and told him it was "all d——d nonsense!" There was nothing in it—not even a pimple, let alone a beef's liver. In short, the doctor went away leaving the patient worse than he found him. He knew the liver was there—that the doctor had seen it and that it was incurable.

What to do next they did not know. The case stood thus for several days—the husband expecting every day would be his last and frequently calling wife, children, and partner to his side to give them his dying instructions.

The partner was a single man and was living in the house. The husband took it into his head that on some occasions he had seen things—looks and actions—which showed that his wife and partner were a little inclined to be fond of each other. His hobby in giving his deathbed directions was to get the pair to agree to marry as soon as he had shuffled off his mortal coil. He would tell his boy that he knew "John"—his partner's name—would be a good father to him. "And Maria," he would say, "I know John will make you a good husband. He loves you! I have seen it!—I have seen it!" These scenes were most annoying both to the wife and the partner—particularly to the wife, who was so shocked and shamed on the first occasion of the kind that she could hardly hold up her head.

The house was near a road a good deal traveled, and persons passing were calling several times every day. The husband was very cunning when any strangers were about. He suddenly pretended to be feeling in excellent spirits. He would smile and walk about whistling cheerfully—as gaily as any lark. As soon as he could find the opportunity he would get one of the strangers off about the grounds under pretense of showing some tree, plant, or other curiosity, and the next thing would be to get him to look into his nose. When the stranger could see nothing he would leave him abruptly, rush into the house, and hastening to his bedroom would throw himself upon the bed. Then he would bury his face in the pillows and sob for hours. He would say he knew the stranger had seen the liver in his nose but would not tell him, because he was incurable and it was "too horrible." When told that his nose was too small to contain a thing as large as the liver of a beef, a new notion took possession of him. He declared that his nose was swollen to a prodigious size, and asserted that he knew they could all see it and that they all knew it to be the case. After this he tied a handkerchief across his nose, saying that its weight hurt him without this support.

He was all this time preparing to die and thought every day would be his last on earth. When he found that he was still alive the next day, he explained that it was because the liver had shifted in position at the last moment. He was in this condition when the partner encountered one day, while in the town of Independence, a young physician who had heard something about the case and who seemed much interested in it. After hearing full particulars, the young doctor said he believed he could cure the man. That same day he went out to the ranch to see the strangely afflicted man. He asked his patient very particularly all the symptoms of his disease, listening gravely to all that was said. He then informed him that the disease was by no means new to him; that in Texas, where he had resided for some years, it was quite prevalent among those who had much to do with cattle. He gave the particulars of several bad cases which he had successfully treated while in Texas.

While the physician was talking, the sick man was constantly glancing triumphantly at his wife and partner. When the doctor at last looked into his nose and declared that there was plainly to be seen in it a liver of the largest size, the patient could no longer restrain himself: "I told you so!" he cried, glancing first at his wife and then at his partner; "I could not be mistaken! I knew all the time it was there, and so did both of you, but you feared to tell me so."

Seeing the doctor's drift, the wife and partner owned that they were well aware of the existence of the liver in the patient's nose and had watched its growth from the very beginning in great alarm, but had thought best to assert to the contrary.

The doctor finally arranged to come the next day armed with proper instruments for the removal of the hideous parasite. When the wife pretended to fear that the operation would be dangerous, the doctor cried: "Perfectly safe, madam! Perfectly safe! It amounts to no more than the prick of a needle." At this the afflicted man laughed aloud, for he felt confident he had found a man who would cure him. Before leaving, the doctor took the partner aside and told him to secretly convey into the house the fresh liver of a beef, so that it might be there in readiness at ten o'clock the next morning, when he would arrive with his instruments.

At the appointed hour the next day the doctor made his appearance with a most formidable assortment of surgical instruments—almost every instrument he had in his office, in fact. The man with the liver in his nose was observed to grow somewhat pale as this grand array of ugly-looking tools was spread out before him upon a table.

In accordance with the doctor's instructions, the patient was placed in a large rocking chair. The chair was then tilted back to the proper angle, when it was blocked up in the desired position. The patient was then securely tied to its back—the doctor saying that he wanted his man in such shape that he could not move a single muscle.

After the patient's arms had been pinioned and his head drawn back into the proper position, the doctor looked into his nose and declared that he could perceive that the liver had slightly increased in size since the previous day. He then ordered a large washbowl to be brought and held under the patient's chin, in which to catch the liver when he should detach it with his instruments.

This being done, the doctor selected a long, slender, glittering knife, which appeared to be as keen as a razor. He took hold of the patient's nose and, opening his nostrils, made a movement as though about to insert the instrument. He then declared that his patient had winced, and said he would not undertake to operate until his eyes had been bandaged. A strip of cloth was then procured and tied over the man's eyes. When this had been done, the doctor said he was ready to begin the operation.

Two or three men from neighboring ranches had been called in to assist in performing the operation, and while one of these held the huge bowl under the sick man's chin, the partner brought in a large fresh beef's liver. He had received his instructions from the doctor. Holding the liver over the bowl he stood ready to act his part.

Taking a small instrument shaped like an awl, being slightly crooked at the point, the doctor inserted it in the man's nostril, and after scratching about for a time gave the inside of the nose a smart prick, at the same time crying out in a tone of exultation: "There, I've got it!" At this the liver was dropped into the bowl, and all present uttered loud cries of astonishment. They talked about its great size and declared that after all it was a real liver. They said they had not expected this, but had thought it would prove to be a mass of flesh somewhat resembling a liver.

The monomaniac all this time was clamoring to have the bandage removed from his eyes that he might feast them upon that which had so long tormented him.

After some delay his wish was gratified, and he was shown the liver lying in the bloody bowl. He uttered a fervent, "Thank God!" and then began to pour out his thanks to the doctor. The doctor cut him short by thrusting into his nose a bit of sponge fastened at the end of a slip of whalebone, and containing some kind of wash composed largely of ammonia.

After a sufficient delay to prevent his observing that the liver was cold—for he was supernaturally cunning—the patient was released from the chair, and examined the contents of the bowl with great satisfaction. At last, at the suggestion of the wife, a hole was dug in the garden and the ugly liver buried out of sight.

From the moment the man was released from the chair, he was as well as ever he was in his life and has so remained ever since. He is perfectly sane in every other respect, but still thinks a beef's liver was cut out of his nose, though it was observed after a week or two that he did not like to hear it mentioned and at length would blush deeply when it was spoken of.

After the light he had obtained during the leave-taking scenes, the partner thought it not well to remain longer with the family and so sold to the cured monomaniac his half of the ranch and left to push his fortune in this part of the state.

Covering the Comstock

Reporting with Mark Twain

$\mathcal{I}$t was in the early days of the Comstock, just when the great boom in silver mining had fairly commenced, that I first met Samuel L. Clemens, now better known as Mark Twain. It was in the days when Washoe was still the popular name of all the silver mining regions of Nevada. Mr. Clemens had been engaged in prospecting at Aurora, Esmeralda County (then a lively camp), whence he sent to the *Territorial Enterprise,* of Virginia City, some humorous letters signed "Josh." The *Enterprise* was then not only the leading paper of "Silverland," but also was one of the liveliest and most prosperous newspapers on the Pacific Coast.

I had been at work on the *Enterprise* about two years, when, in December, 1862, I concluded to take a trip to the States, whereupon the proprietors of the paper—J. T. Goodman and D. E. McCarthy— engaged Josh (Mr. Clemens) to come in from Aurora and take a position on their paper as reporter. I was absent from the Comstock about nine months—on the Plains and in the States—and when I

Fairly genial fun poking and embroidery of Twain's Comstock- and Mother-Lode days. Less unreliable in its facts than Twain's recollection of Dan in the *Autobiography.* From the *Californian Illustrated Magazine,* 4 (July 1893), pp. 170–78.

returned, Mr. Clemens had shed his nom de plume of Josh and taken that which he still retains and has made famous. Mark did not much relish the work of writing reports of mines and mining affairs, and for that reason, and because of the boom in business and rush of events demanding reportorial notice, I was asked to return posthaste and resume work on the paper—everything being, as my letter of recall said, "red-hot."

I found things red-hot indeed. Reaching San Francisco in the evening after dark, the first news I heard, even before our steamer had reached the wharf, was that Virginia City was on fire and was being "wiped out." At once there was great excitement, for a score or more of Washoe people were on board the vessel. Upon landing, we rushed to the newspaper offices and there heard that the town was still burning. I also learned that there had been a big fight among the firemen and that some of my friends and acquaintances had been killed and wounded. It was midnight before we heard that the fire was under control, and I then ascertained, to my great relief, that the *Enterprise* office had escaped, while all about it had been destroyed.

Thus I resumed business at the old stand in the thick of red-hot times—in the midst of flames and war. It was also in the midst of the cutting and shooting days—the days of stage robberies, of mining fights, wonderful finds of ore, and all manner of excitements. As may be imagined, Mark and I had our hands full, and no grass grew under our feet. There was a constant rush of startling events; they came tumbling over one another as though playing at leapfrog. While a stage robbery was being written up, a shooting affray started; and perhaps before the pistol shots had ceased to echo among the surrounding hills, the firebells were banging out an alarm.

The crowding of the whole population into that part of the town which had escaped the fire led to many bloody battles. Fighters, sports, and adventurers, burned out of their old haunts, thronged the saloons and gaming houses remaining, where many of them were by no means welcome visitors; and, as in the case of cats in strange garrets, battles were of nightly occurrence. Everybody was armed, and no man threw away his life by making an attack with his fists.

Mark and I agreed well in our work, which we divided when there was a rush of events, but we often cruised in company—he taking the items of news he could best handle, and I such as I felt myself competent to work up. However, we wrote at the same table and frequently helped each other with such suggestions as occurred to us during the brief consultations we held in regard to the handling of any matters of importance. Never was there an angry word between us in all the time we worked together.

Mark Twain, as a reporter, was earnest and enthusiastic in such work as suited him—really industrious—but when it came to "cast-iron" items, he gave them a lick and a promise. He hated to have to do with figures, measurements, and solid facts, such as were called for in matters pertaining to mines and machinery.

Mark displayed a peculiarity when at work that was very detrimental to the integrity of office property. In case he wished to clip an item or a paragraph out of a paper, and could not at once lay his hand upon his scissors, he would cut out the required matter with his knife, at the same time slashing into the baize covering of the table. His end of the cover was so mutilated that little was left of the original cloth. In its place appeared what might have passed for a representation of the polar star, spiritedly darting forth a thousand rays. Some years ago, when at Mark's house in Hartford, I found myself almost unconsciously examining the top of the fine writing desk in his library for evidences of his old knife-slashing habit, but did not find so much as a scratch.

Mark Twain was pretty apt in sketching in a rude way, and when reporting meetings where there were long waits or uninteresting debates, he would cover the margins of his copy paper with drawings. When reporting the meetings of the Board of Aldermen, where there was often much tedious talk, he would frequently make sketches illustrative of the subjects under discussion. Some of his offhand sketches were very good—good in the same way that a pun is sometimes good, though farfetched and ridiculous. I have forgotten the subjects of most of these pencil sketches. I recall one, however, that might have been labeled "The Captured Menagerie." There had been some trouble about collecting city license from a menagerie (it had paid county license) and the matter came up before the Board of Aldermen. Mark was amused at the talk of what could be done and what would be done with the show and showmen if the license was not paid at once, and so he pictured it all out. He depicted the city marshal leading away the elephant by its trunk, and the mayor mounted upon a giraffe which he had captured, while one policeman had a lion by the tail, and another had captured a rhinoceros. Still others had shouldered kangaroos, strings of monkeys, and the like.

This was about his best effort, and after writing out his report of the meeting, he kept his sheets of notes for some time, working up and improving the several pictures. At his home in Hartford, Mark sometimes dabbles in oil colors, he having taken lessons in art since the Comstock days. He points with pride to the curly head of a dove-colored bull on an easel in his library, and hints that the best effects were all achieved without the assistance of his teacher.

Mark Twain was fond of manufacturing items of the horrible style, but on one occasion he overdid this business, and the disease worked its own cure. He wrote an account of a terrible murder, supposed to have occurred at Dutch Nick's, a station on the Carson River where Empire City now stands. He made a man cut his wife's throat and those of his nine children, after which diabolical deed the murderer mounted his horse, cut his own throat from ear to ear, rode to Carson City (a distance of three and a half miles), and fell dead in front of Pete Hopkins's saloon.

All the California papers copied the item, and several made editorial comment upon it as being the most shocking occurrence of the kind ever known on the Pacific Coast. Of course rival Virginia City papers at once denounced the item as a "cruel and idiotic hoax." They showed how the publication of such "shocking and reckless falsehoods" disgraced and injured the state, and they made it as sultry as possible for the *Enterprise* and its "fool reporter."

When the California papers saw all this and found they had been sold, there was a howl from Siskiyou to San Diego. Some papers demanded the immediate discharge of the author of the item by the *Enterprise* proprietors. They said they would never quote another line from that paper while the reporter who wrote the shocking item remained on its force. All this worried Mark as I had never seen him worried. Said he: "I am being burned alive on both sides of the mountains." We roomed together, and one night when the persecution was hottest, he was so distressed that he could not sleep. He tossed, tumbled, and groaned aloud. So I set to work to comfort him. "Mark," said I, "never mind this bit of a gale; it will soon blow itself out. This item of yours will be remembered and talked about when all your other work is forgotten. The murder at Dutch Nick's will be quoted years from now as the big sell of these times."

Said Mark: "I believe you are right; I remember I once did a thing at home in Missouri, was caught at it, and worried almost to death. I was a mere lad and was going to school in a little town where I had an uncle living. I at once left the town and did not return to it for three years. When I finally came back I found I was only remembered as 'the boy that played the trick on the schoolmaster.'"

Mark then told me the story, began to laugh over it, and from that moment ceased to groan. He was not discharged, and in less than a month people everywhere were laughing and joking about the "murder at Dutch Nick's."

When Mark wrote the item he read it over to me, and I asked him how he was going to wind it up so as to make it plain that it was a mere invention.

"Oh, it is wound up now," was the reply. "It is all plain enough. I have said that the family lived in a little cabin at the edge of the great pine forest near Dutch Nick's, when everybody knows there's not a pine tree within ten miles of Nick's. Then I make the man ride nearly four miles after he has cut his throat from ear to ear, when any fool must see that he would fall dead in a moment."

But the people were all so shocked at first with the wholesale throat-cutting that they did not stop to think of these points. Mark's whole object in writing the story was to make the murderer go to Pete Hopkins's saloon and fall dead in front of it—Pete having in some way offended him. I could never quite see how this was to hurt Pete Hopkins. Mark probably meant to insinuate that the murderer had been rendered insane by the kind of liquor sold over Hopkins's bar, or that he was one of Pete's bosom friends.

Today not one man in a hundred in Nevada can remember anything written by Mark Twain while he was connected with the *Enterprise,* except this one item in regard to the shocking murder at Dutch Nick's; all else is forgotten, even by his oldest and most intimate friends.

First and last, many newspapers, daily and weekly, have been published in Virginia City. The life of one of these was so short, however, that only a few persons are now aware that it ever had an existence. It opened its eyes to the light only to close them again forever. This was the *Occidental,* an eight-page weekly literary paper started by Honorable Tom Fitch, the "Silver-tongued Orator of Nevada." But one number of the paper was issued. The good die young—the *Occidental* was good. Why the paper died as soon as born I never exactly knew, but think it would be safe to say that all the "powder" in the magazine was used up in the first shot.

Twain and I were rooming together at the time in what was known as the Daggett building, a large brick structure where there were many lodgers. Tom Fitch and family were our across-the-hall neighbors. Of course we were informed in regard to Tom's newspaper venture and took a lively interest in all his literary plans. The paper was intended to constitute a sort of safety valve for the red-hot and hissing Comstock literary boiler. Writers on the other papers, and writers at large were to contribute to its columns.

In the number of this paper that was published, a romance was commenced that was to have been continued almost indefinitely. At least, in discussing the plan of it nothing was ever said about how it was to be ended, and had the story been carried forward in accordance with the original plan, it would have been one of the curiosities of literature, and probably running yet.

Honorable R. M. Daggett, late minister to the Hawaiian Islands, wrote the opening chapters of the story. A striking character in the story, as begun by Mr. Daggett, was an old hermit, "reported a Rosycrucian," who dwelt in a partially subterranean castle situated in a dark and secret mountain gorge where, "in the dead waist and middle of the night," smoke and flames were to be seen issuing from his chimneys while lights—red, blue, and green—flashed up in his heavily barred windows. The building had no visible door—all was solid masonry—and the person viewing it from the outside could only imagine a subterranean entrance, which no man could discover "for the dews that dripped all over."

The old white-haired alchemist had a pupil, of course, and this pupil was the hero of the romance, as it was begun by Mr. Daggett. In the great outside world dwelt the heroine, who started out—began business—as a very lovable young lady. The opening was full of mystery, and was very interesting. Mr. Daggett left the hero in a position of such peril that it seemed impossible he could be rescued, except through means and wisdom more than human.

Mrs. Tom Fitch was to have written the chapters for the next number of the paper; she would have been followed by Mark Twain, and he, in due course, by J. T. Goodman, Tom Fitch, and myself, when Mr. Daggett would again come in and take up the thread of the exciting tale.

Each person would have been obliged to extricate the hero, heroine (or any other useful character) from whatever sad predicament the writer preceding him might have devised, and would have aimed to puzzle the one who was to follow him. It would have been a sort of literary game of chess.

It was thought that Mrs. Fitch would respect Daggett's lovely heroine, and carry her along in unsullied beauty of both person and soul; but Mark Twain was sharpening his scalping knife for her. The old Rosycrucian was Daggett's pet. He wanted to carry the old fellow all through the story, but was afraid Mrs. Fitch would find him unmanageable and would roast him in one of his own furnaces. In case she did anything of the kind, Mr. Daggett was resolved to take a terrible revenge when he got hold of her pet character—he would do "a deed that the ibis and the crocodile would tremble at."

Although Mark and I had promised to let Mr. Daggett's old hermit live, we had secretly conjured up a demon fiddler who was to make his appearance in the mysterious barred castle at critical moments, and with rosined bow torment both the quivering string and the old alchemist. In case Daggett provided the old fellow with some spell sufficiently potent to "lay" the fiddler, we intended to introduce into the secret laboratory a spectral owl that should worry the occupant by watching his every movement; and following the owl we would send the whole progeny of devils—ærial, aquatic, and terrestial—said to have been born of Adam's first wife, Lilis.

Mrs. Fitch and her lady friends and advisers doubtless had their plans for "warming" Mark and all the rest of us. However, with the death of the *Occidental,* all passed away into the realms of nothingness, "wie ein schatten vergehen"—as a shadow goes.

The story of the presentation to Mark Twain of a bogus meerschaum pipe has often been told, but in most instances without touching upon that which was the fine point of the whole affair. Major Steve Gillis, C. A. V. Putnam, D. E. McCarthy, and several other newspaper men put up a job to present Mark an imitation meerschaum pipe. They selected one they knew he would not like because of its shape, had its German silver mounting polished up, and on this the inscription, "To Mark Twain, from his Friends" was neatly engraved. A cherry stem about a yard long, with a genuine amber mouthpiece, was procured, and the present was ready. The presentation was to take place on a Saturday night, after the paper was up, at Harris's saloon, in Maguire's Opera House. Charley Pope, now proprietor of a theater in St. Louis, Missouri, was then playing at the Opera House, and he was engaged to make the presentation speech. All this being arranged, I said to Mark one night after we had gone to bed: "Mark, I don't know that I ought to tell you, but the boys are going to make you a present of a fine meerschaum pipe next Saturday night. Charley Pope is to make the presentation speech, and as it will doubtless be rather fine, I have thought it best to post you, in order that you may think up a suitable reply."

Mark thanked me most cordially for giving the business away—not once suspecting that the boys had made it my part to thus thoroughly post him, in order that we might all have the fun of watching him in his effort to convey the impression that the presentation was a genuine surprise.

This was really the point, and the big sell of the whole affair. Even Charley Pope was aware that Mark had been fully posted, therefore to us all it was deliciously ridiculous to observe Mark's pretended unawareness.

From the moment of our assembling until the ceremonies ended, every eye was fixed upon him, watching every shade of expression on his countenance.

Even with the enticing of Mark down to the Opera House saloon, the fun began, as he assumed a certain degree of coyness, pretending to hold back, and couldn't "see why we wanted him to go there." When our victim and all the conspirators had been assembled for some time round the center table in a private parlor of the saloon, Charley Pope made his appearance. Mark seemed surprised at seeing him enter the room.

Mr. Pope carried under his arm, wrapped in a newspaper, a bundle about a yard in length. Advancing to the table he proceeded to unroll the bundle, producing a ridiculous-looking pipe, with a straight bowl about five inches high, and about a yard of blue ribbon floating from the stem.

"That is a mighty fine pipe you have there, Charley," said Mark in an offhand, unconcerned tone of voice.

Mr. Pope made no reply, but throwing the newspapers upon the floor held the pipe aloft by the middle of the stem, as in the great paintings of the presentation of the Pipe of Peace, and began his speech with: "Mr. Clemens, on behalf of your friends and admirers, those you see here assembled and many others, I present you this magnificent meerschaum pipe as a slight," etc., etc.

Mr. Pope spoke about twenty minutes, making a really admirable speech. In parts it was very feeling, and again it was witty and jolly. Of course we applauded it from Alpha to Omega.

Then Mark Twain arose. In his hand he held the mighty calumet. He was sorry that he would be unable fittingly to reply to a speech so able and excellent as that of Mr. Pope—a speech that had touched his heart and stirred in his bosom feelings he could not find words to express. But the truth was that he had been taken by surprise. The presentation was a thing wholly unexpected.

He then launched forth into what we all knew was his prepared speech. He began with the introduction of tobacco into England by Sir Walter Raleigh, and wound up with George Washington. Just how he managed to bring in the father of his country I have forgotten; but he had him there in the wind-up, and showed him off to good advantage.

Often the thunders of applause brought him to a halt. He was made to feel that he was a success. Then he called for sparkling Moselle— no other wine would do him—and before the session was over six bottles, at five dollars a bottle, had vanished.

A day or two afterwards a printer let the cat out of the bag—told Mark his pipe was a "mere sham." Mark had suspected as much. Even on the night of the presentation, before we had consumed more than two of the six bottles of Moselle, I had detected him inspecting the bowl of the pipe with a sort of reproachful look in his eye.

I was alone in the "local room," one day, when Mark suddenly made his appearance with the pipe in his hand. He locked the door on the inside and put the key in his pocket. "I want to know from you, now," said he, "whether this pipe is bogus."

"It is just as bogus as they make 'em," said I.

"Did you know that when you capped me into preparing a speech?"

"Certainly. That was where the fun came in."

"'Et tu Brute!'" said Mark in a hollow voice; then he began to pace the room with his face on his breast.

I told Mark to take it easy and say nothing, as a really fine pipe—one that cost $45—was back of the bogus one and would be given him without ceremony or cost. Mark then subsided, but was by no means satisfied with the business. However, years after he told me that he thought more of the bogus pipe than he did of the genuine one. Like his Dutch Nick item, time ripened it.

At the time Mark Twain was on the *Enterprise* he wrote no long stories or sketches for that paper. Occasionally, however, he sent a sketch to the *Golden Era,* of San Francisco. After going to San Francisco he was for a time regularly employed on one or two papers, then wrote sketches and did piecework of various kinds. He did not much like reporting in the city by the sea. For a long time after going down to San Francisco, he wrote a weekly letter to the *Enterprise* in which he gave such chat as would not be sent by telegraph—chat made up in good part of personals in regard to the doings of Comstockers at the Bay, the humors of the stock market and the like.

In 1865, Mark Twain grew tired of a life of literary drudgery in San Francisco and went up into the mining regions of Calaveras County to rusticate and rejuvenate with some old friends—Steve, Billy, and Jim Gillis. The cabin of Jim Gillis is, and always has been, a friendly place of retreat in the mountain wilds for writers desirous of respite from the vanities and vexations of spirit incident to a life of literary labor in San Francisco. At his cabin the latchstring is always on the outside. Many are the well-known California writers who have at various times been sojourners in the hospitable mountain home of Jim Gillis. His cabin is a sort of Bohemian infirmary. There the sick are made well, and the well are made better—physically, mentally, and morally.

Mark Twain found life pleasant in this literary mountain retreat. He found the Bohemian style of mining practiced by the Gillis boys much more attractive than those more regular kinds which call for a large outlay of muscle. The business of the pocket miner is much like that of the bee hunter. The trail of the latter leads him to the tree stored with golden sweets, and that of the former ends in a pocket of sweetest gold.

Soon after Mark's arrival at the "Gillis Bohemian Infirmary," he and Jim Gillis took to the hills in search of golden pockets. They soon found and spent some days in working up the undisturbed trail of an undiscovered deposit. They were on the golden beeline, and stuck to it faithfully, though it was necessary to carry each sample of dirt a considerable distance to a small stream in the bed of a cañon in order to wash it. However, Mark hungered and thirsted to find a big, rich pocket, and he pitched in after the manner of Joe Bowers of old—just like a thousand of brick.

Each step made sure by the finding of golden grains, they at last came upon the pocket whence these grains had trailed out down the slope of the mountain. It was a cold, dreary, drizzling day when the home deposit was found. The first sample of dirt carried to the stream and washed out yielded only a few cents. Although the right vein had been discovered, they had as yet found only the tail end of the pocket.

Returning to the vein, they dug a sample of the decomposed ore from a new place and were about to carry it down to the ravine and test it, when the rain increased to a lively downpour. With chattering teeth, Mark declared he would remain no longer. He said there was no sense in freezing to death, as in a day or two when it was bright and warm they could return and pursue their investigations in comfort.

Yielding to Mark's entreaties, backed as they were by his blue nose, humped back, and generally miserable and dejected appearance, Jim Gillis emptied the sacks of dirt just dug upon the ground—first having hastily written and posted a notice claiming a certain number of feet on the vein, which notice would hold good for thirty days. This done they left the claim.

Angel's Camp being at no great distance from the spot, whereas their cabin was some miles away, Mark and Jim struck out for that place.

The only hotel in Angel's Camp was kept by Coon Drayton, an old Mississippi river pilot, and at his house the half-drowned pocket miners found shelter. Mark Twain having in his youthful days been a cub pilot on the Mississippi, he and Coon were soon great friends and swapped yarns by the dozen. It continued to rain for three days, and until the weather cleared up, Mark and Jim remained at Coon's hotel.

Among the stories told Mark by Coon during the three days' session was that of the "Jumping Frog," and it struck him as being so comical that he concluded to write it up. When he returned to the

Gillis cabin, Mark set to work on the frog story. He also wrote some sketches of life in the mountains and the mines for some of the San Francisco papers.

Even after he had given it the finishing touches, Mark did not think much of the frog story. He gave the preference to some other sketches, and sent them to the papers for which he was writing. The frog story lay about the cabin for some time, when Steve Gillis told him it was the best thing he had written, and advised him to save it for a book of sketches he was talking of publishing.

A literary turn having thus been given to the thoughts of the inmates of the Gillis cabin, a month passed without a return to the business of pocket mining. While the days were passed by Mark and his friends in discussing the merits of the "Jumping Frog" and other literary matters, other prospectors were not idle. A trio of Austrian miners who were out in search of gold-bearing quartz happened upon the spot where Mark and Jim had dug into their ledge. It was but a few days after Twain and Gillis had retreated in a pouring rain. The Austrians were astonished at seeing the ground glittering with gold. Where the dirt emptied from the sacks had been dissolved away by the rain, lay over three ounces of bright quartz gold. The foreigners were not long in gathering this harvest, but soon discovering the notice posted on the claim, they dared not venture to delve in the deposit whence it came. They could only wait and watch and pray. Their hope was that the parties who had posted up the notice would not return while it held good.

The sun that rose on the day after the Twain-Gillis notice expired saw the Austrians in possession of the ground, with a notice of their own conspicuously and defiantly posted. The new owners soon cleaned out the pocket, obtaining from it in a few days a little over $7,500.

Had Mark Twain's backbone held out a few minutes longer, the sacks of dirt would have been panned out and the richness of the pocket discovered. He would not then have gone to Angel's Camp, and would probably never have heard or written the story of the "Jumping Frog," the story that gave him his first boost in the literary world, as the "Heathen Chinee" gave Bret Harte his first lift up the ladder of fame. Had Mark found the gold that was captured by the Austrians, he would have settled down as a pocket miner, and probably to this day would have been pounding quartz in a little cabin in the Sierras somewhere along about the snowline.

Returning to San Francisco from the mountains, Mark for a time resumed his literary hackwork. He then arranged to make a trip to the Hawaiian Islands, and wrote up the beauties and wonders thereof for the old Sacramento *Union.* While engaged in this work he conceived the idea of writing a lecture on the Sandwich Islands, wisely judging that he could in that way get more money out of a certain amount of writing than by toiling for the newspapers.

He delivered his lecture very successfully, both on the Pacific Coast and in the Atlantic States. On the Pacific Coast D. E. McCarthy, who had then sold his interest in the *Enterprise,* was with Mark as his agent. When they reached Nevada the lecture was first delivered in Virginia City. Next they went to Gold Hill, a mile south of Virginia City and just over a low ridge known as the Divide, a place noted in the annals of the Comstock for a thousand robberies by footpads.

A sham robbery was planned of which Mark was to be the victim. He was to be halted on the Divide as he was returning on foot from Gold Hill, and robbed of the proceeds of his lecture. Mark's agent, McCarthy, was in the plot, as also was his old friend Major Steve Gillis and other friends, with Captain Jack Perry, George Birdsall, and one or two other members of the police force. Twain and one or two friends (who were in the secret) were held up on a trail called the cut-off. The job was done in the regular road-agent style. The pretended robbers not only took the gripsack of coin—some $300—but also Mark's fine gold watch.

When he reached Virginia City, Mark was raging mad, as the watch taken from him was a present from a friend. He did not in the least doubt the genuineness of the robbery, and it so soured him against the Comstock that he determined to leave the next morning.

The robbery had been planned by Mark's old friends as a sort of advertising dodge. It was intended to create sympathy for him, and by having him deliver a second lecture in Virginia City afford the people an opportunity of redeeming the good name of the Comstock. He would have had a rousing benefit, and after all was over his agent would have returned him his watch and money. Of course, it would not have done to ask Mark to consent to be robbed for this purpose. His friends meant well, but like other schemes of mice and men this particular one failed to work. Mark was too hot to be handled, and when at last it was explained to him that the robbery was a sham affair he became still hotter—he boiled over with wrath.

His money and watch were returned to him after he had taken his seat in the stage, and his friends begged him to remain, but he refused to disembark. Upon observing some of his friends of the police force engaged in violent demonstrations of mirth, he turned his attention to them and fired at them a tremendous broadside of anathemas as the stage rolled away. Had he kept cool, he would have had a benefit that would have put at least a thousand dollars in his pocket, for the papers had made a great sensation of the robbery.

A good deal has been said of Mark Twain's drawling speech. This peculiarity is not natural, but acquired. When he was a small boy he spoke so rapidly that his family constantly remonstrated with him with the result that he went to the opposite extreme. When angry or excited, he can snap his words off as short as anyone.

The cabin in which Mark and Bob Howland lived in Aurora, in 1862, endured until a few years ago. It was a sort of dugout, to the roof of which the wandering billy goat of inquiring mind had access from the hillside above. A picture of this cabin—the old Nevada home—would form a striking contrast to Mark's present fine residence in Hartford. The Hartford dwelling is a structure of many gables and angles, and at the rear or east end projects a veranda, intended to represent the hurricane deck of a Mississippi steamboat. In summer, with the shade of the surrounding chestnut trees cooling the air, this open deck is a pleasant lounging-place. Seated in it, dressed in white linen, Mark imagines himself on board one of the floating palaces of the Father of Waters, while his thoughts often revert to the still earlier days of reportorial work in the mining regions of the wild Washoe.

Artemus Ward in Nevada

$\mathscr{I}$n 1863, the Comstock mines of Nevada were in the full swing of
their youthful prosperity. Already Virginia City contained about
12,000 inhabitants when, staging it over the mountains by the old
Placerville route, Artemus Ward arrived under an engagement to
deliver his famous lecture entitled the "Babes in the Wood"—a lecture in which not the slightest reference was made to the "poor
innocents" that wandered in the wood "till death did end their grief."

Artemus had been lecturing in San Francisco, and other places in
California, and expectation was on the tiptoe when he arrived in
Virginia City. He was hail, fellow, well met with everyone the moment he reached town. All had so often read and laughed over the
letters and sketches of the proprietor of the Great Moral Show that
when he appeared on the Comstock he was greeted as an old
acquaintance.

Ward was then in fine health and spirits. Everything he saw called
forth a joke or a quaint saying. His drollery was without effort. His
fun, like the quality of mercy, was not strained. It was natural to him

More potboiling reminiscence, about Twain as well. From *Californian Illustrated Magazine,* 4 (August 1893), 403–406. Overlaps material presented in
"Salad Days of Mark Twain," San Francisco *Examiner,* March 19, 1893.

to see the comical side of everything. He teemed with waggery which on the slightest provocation expanded into a surprising flow of face-tiousness—into a merry, sportive string of pleasantries. There was nothing malicious in his fun, and he harbored no feeling of resentment when he himself was the victim. Even when that poor old chestnut of "an oat" being in waiting for him at a certain place was played off on him, he did not lose his temper. He said it merely made him feel sad, as it detracted from the "high opinion he had formed of the wit and originality of the Comstockers." Said he, "I could weep for the poor man."

Artemus remained in Virginia City about a week, spending much of his leisure time in the editorial rooms of the *Enterprise*. It devolved upon Mark Twain and myself to show him the silver mines and the wonders of the town—a very agreeable task, as the novelty of many sights and situations aroused in his soul the spirit of the "wax figger" man, and drew from him whole trains of witty remarks. He was as much at home among the miners a thousand feet below the light of day as on the surface among the people on the street. The talk of the miners amused him and he treasured up all the mining terms and phrases he heard, asking the meaning of them as he jotted them down. "These are the things," he would say, "that give the life touch-es to a sketch." He made no elaborate notes. I never saw him write to exceed half a dozen words at any one time. "A line," said he, "if you can hit the right thing, will give as good an idea of a place as whole pages."

The serious manner and solemn face assumed by Artemus Ward added not a little to the fun of his impromptu "quaints." A stranger would gaze at the man for a moment in blank amazement. Then the oddity of the thing would prove too much for him and he would be obliged to let go all holds and indulge in a regular explosion of laughter—Artemus the while, more solemn than ever, gazing from face to face, as though astonished and somewhat hurt at being inter-rupted by the sudden outburst of merriment. He worked this trick with telling effect in his lectures. He had wonderful control of his facial muscles, and could make his face absolutely wooden. Nothing could surprise him into a laugh at such times, or even into the slightest approach to a smile.

Artemus had a favorite trick that he loved to indulge in, and out of which he appeared to get a good deal of congenial fun. This was the disbursing of a rigmarole of nonsense in a solemn and impressive manner, as though he was saying something of unusual weight and importance. It was a game of mystification in which he greatly delighted. At a dinner given him by leading Comstockers at the International Hotel, Ward played this trick on Mark Twain, all present being let into the secret beforehand. Artemus was seated beside Mark near the head of the table. Presently something was said about genius. Artemus at once cleared his throat and turning to Mark began in a voice loud enough to attract the attention of all present and put a stop to general conversation, about as follows: "Ah—speaking of genius, Mr. Clemens, now, genius appears to me to be a sort of luminous quality of the mind, allied to a warm and inflammable constitution, which is inherent in the man, and supersedes in him whatever constitutional tendency he may possess, to permit himself to be influenced by such things as do not coincide with his preconceived notions and established convictions to the contrary. Does not my definition hit the nail squarely on the head, Mr. Clemens?"

"I don't know that I exactly understand you," returned Mark. "Somehow I—I didn't fully grasp your meaning."

"No?" queried Artemus. And then he elevated his eyebrows and gazed at Mark with a countenance expressive of profound astonishment and some shifting shades of pity.

All at the table gave utterance to half-smothered "humphs," snorts, and grunts of disgust at Mark's stupidity. "Didn't grasp my meaning?" said Artemus. "Why, that is very singular. However," he added, pulling himself together more hopefully, "I will try and express my idea more clearly. Genius, Mr. Clemens, does not appear to me to consist, or rest, merely in sensibility to that degree of beauty which is perceived by all, as there is an inherent illuminating power, the possession of which causes luminous ideas to dart like meteors across the intellectual firmament, and which, I say, checks in the person possessing it a tendency to permit himself to be influenced by preconceived opinions in regard to those beauties in nature, which all objects display to the eye of one of a warm and inflammable temperament, and which is not at all understood by those detractors who are constitutionally incapable of seeing those beauties. The—but I must have already made it plain to you, Mr. Clemens?"

"I am almost ashamed to say it," drawled Mark, "but, to tell you the truth, I was not able to catch your exact meaning. I will admit, however, that what you say appears reasonable enough, and you speak it in a very logical and convincing tone of voice; still I somehow fail to grasp your idea of genius."

"Indeed!" exclaimed Artemus, and for half a minute he gazed at Mark with a face in which a shade of impatience began to mingle with astonishment and compassion. Then heaving a sigh, he said, "Well, perhaps I was not sufficiently explicit. What I wished to say was simply that genius is a sort of illuminating quality of the mind inherent in those of constitutionally inflammable natures and whose conceptions are not of that ambiguous and disputable kind which may be said—"

"Hold on, Artemus," interrupted Mark, "it is useless for you to repeat your definition. The wine, or the brandy, or the whisky or some other thing has gone to my head. Tell it to me some other time; or, better still, write it down for me and I'll study it at my leisure."

"Good!" cried Artemus, his face beaming with pleasure. "I'll give it to you tomorrow in black and white. I have been much misunderstood in this matter and it is important that I should set myself right. You see that to the eye of a person of a warm and inflammable nature and in whose self-luminous mind ideas arise that are by no means confined to the material which conception furnishes, but may be—"

"For God's sake!" cried Mark; "if you go at that again you'll drive me mad!"

The general burst of laughter which followed this feeling and half-angry protest made it plain to Mark that Artemus had been set to work on him with malice aforethought, and that all present were in the plot and had been amusing themselves at his expense.

Mark was in no amiable mood the remainder of the evening. He said such a thing "might be thought by some to be smart," but he failed to see "where the fun came in."

Artemus Ward gave no thought to money—not enough to take care of it when he had earned it. In the midst of a whirl of speculation on the Comstock, and with mines of gold and silver all about him, he envied no one the millions that were being hoisted up to the light of day. He never thought of such a thing as joining in the stock speculations about which all with whom he came in contact were running mad. Had the mines been of copper, iron, or coal he would have shown quite as much interest in them. He was wholly interested in the people he found in the mines, and the ordinary miner received as large a share of his attention as did the millionaire owner. Indeed, of the two, he preferred the miner as being the more picturesque.

At the time Artemus was in Virginia City, he said his peculiar style would soon surfeit the public if he wrote too much. For this reason he said he was going to give the people a rest. "But," he said, "I am taking notes of the queer words and expressions I hear in different regions. These I shall sometimes use in sketches located in those places where heard." He told me that he had one book filled with notes of queer things he picked up among the boatmen about the wharves of the towns on the great lakes. He also contemplated altering his style as regarded spelling, except in letters in which he appeared as the "wax figger" showman. Had he not died at the early age of thirty-two, he would doubtless have worked into stories and sketches much material that he had accumulated.

Although Artemus made no pretension to a knowledge of fine points of art, he frequently made hasty pencil sketches of places and persons that struck his fancy. In a letter he wrote me from Austin, Nevada, he sent me on the back of a program a sketch of a brush-roofed saloon in which he lectured at Big Creek. That sketch has disappeared, but I still have two small ones made, I think, in New York at the waterfront. I am of the opinion that he made most of his rude pencil drawings as hints for artists in making illustrations for his sketches.

As I said above, he did not take extended notes. He wanted only a few words. "Let me get that," he would say, and down went the expression that had struck him, with the name of the place. For the rest he trusted to his memory. In a few words he was able to give the local color of a place. In leaving Aspinwall it is "Adios, Americanos!"

On the Panama Railroad—"There are huts all along the route, and half-naked savages gaze patronizingly upon us from their doorways."

Central America—"The Central American is lazy. The only exercise he ever takes is to occasionally produce a revolution."

Acapulco—"The pretty peasant girls peddle necklaces made of shells."

Arriving at San Francisco it was—"Ki hi-hi ki! Shoolah!"

Stockton—"A vivacious maniac invites me to ride in a chariot drawn by eight lions and a rhinoceros."

Carson City—"I hain't killed a man for over two weeks! What'll yer poison yourself with?"

Virginia City—"Its splendid streets paved with silver."

Artemus Ward was fond of theatricals and theatrical people. His head was full of scraps of plays, which he constantly quoted in a comical way. While in Virginia City he blackened his face one night and appeared as end man in a minstrel show that was performing at Niagara Hall on B street. He happened to be acquainted with some of the leading members of the company and good-naturedly volunteered in order to help them along. Also he probably wished to see what he could do in that line. He made a good deal of fun, and of a kind that was fresh and droll. Though he appeared among them but once, Artemus gave the company many telling jokes and funny little stories.

Artemus at times contemplated taking to the stage as a comedian, but feared he was too old. He was of the opinion that he ought to have made a beginning when he was about nineteen or twenty years of age. Yet at the time of his visit to the Comstock he thought quite seriously of writing a play for himself; one that could be performed by a small company and in which he would have appeared in his great character of showman. His play would have introduced "Betsy Jane" and other "Baldinville" folk, also some of the "wax figgers." His show, with the characters he intended using, would undoubtedly have been a success on the stage, as it had been thoroughly advertised throughout the country by his letters and sketches, and would have added new luster to the career of the gifted humorist.

No Head nor Tail

*B*last my buttons! Blast everybody's buttons! Curse the Chinese nation, the African race! Mrs. Gummidge and the laundresses far out in the hills! Curse everybody or anybody that washed, ironed, and pretended to sew the buttons on that shirt! Oh, that I knew the delinquent! But that is something which (as I "gobbled" the shirt out of Mark Twain's trunk) I may not consistently attempt to trace to any man's (washhouse) door.

[Thus far had my pen recorded my wrath when it occurred to me that, as I had promised to send something to the *Era,* I might as well put a head into my wrath—seeing that it had almost come to a head of itself. Now, the words standing at the head of this article do not particularly refer to the shirt I have abstracted from the trunk of my absent roommate; for—though it is true enough that said article of apparel has no head—it has, when unfolded a tremendous—but whither are we drifting? I simply mean to say that the reason of my writing the words that stand at the head of this paper was because there will be neither head nor tail to what I am going to write—

Maniacal housekeeping with Mark. From *Golden Era,* December 6, 1863. Discussed by C. Grant Loomis, *Pacific Historical Quarterly;* and Ivan Benson, *Mark Twain's Western Years* (Stanford, 1938), p. 73.

which is as good luck as any. What matters it whether it turn out a song or a sermon?]

Now, having fenced up all these explanations in brackets, to keep them from meddling with matters that concern them not, I will get back to where I was when I commenced building the fence.

The person who sewed on those buttons should be boiled in oil!

Mark Twain and I

If I had known that Mark Twain's shirts were all without collars, I would never have gone into partnership with him in rooms. I should have sternly refused having such a partner—all his many excellent qualities and his useful little accomplishments, as those of foraging for little luxuries, and staving off the demands of our landlord for rent, I should have counted as nought—yea, as vanities. Now, when after much trouble I had succeeded in prying open his trunk (why need he have left it locked, as though he had something in it?), all I found fit for any white man to wear was one shirt, and it without a collar. I rejoiced then to think that I had broken the lock of his old Saratoga bandbox. I spread out the shirt, pulled it this way and that, thinking the collar was turned down or that it was fastened on in some out-landish place—halfway down the back, perhaps—for who could tell where such an oddity as Mark Twain might choose to wear his collars? I held it out at arms length by the sleeves and gazed on it—not a sign of a collar! In the first outburst of my rage and disappoint-ment, I threw the shirt as far as I could send it, flew at his old horsehide-covered abortion of a trunk and kicked the lid and half of one side to pieces—though I have since repented somewhat of my hastiness, and tried to fix it up—exclaiming: "The vagrant hound! the deceitful wretch! to have a shirt to his trunk with no collar!"

Being somewhat exhausted with my efforts at kicking the old trunk, I seated myself on our washstand (Mark's and mine) and counted one hundred twice over, when I grew calmer and began to see in its proper light the absurdity of my late proceedings. All, I saw, was not yet lost. I took another look at the shirt. It was as square off at the shoulders as though the last man who had worn it had had his head chopped off close to his body by old Hopkins's bloody axe. While looking at the shirt, I discovered some buttons which, I judged, were put in the peculiar position they occupied for the purpose of fastening a collar to the garment. Elated by this discovery, I rushed forth into the streets and of an accommodating Israelite procured the needed collar. Coming home, I managed, by a strategic movement or series of movements, to get into the collarless garment.

Next I set to work to attach the collar. There was a button on the shirt somewhere back of my neck. On this I essayed to fasten the stiff, parchmentlike collar. I tried for about six consecutive times—standing in front of our splendid (Mark's and mine) oval mirror, twisting my neck till every joint in it cracked with trying to see just where that infernal button was—before I discovered that the buttonhole in the collar was pasted tight shut with some kind of devilish glue. I took the end of a penholder and pretty effectually opened it—I think so. Then I tried again to coax the button to enter the breach. I got one edge of it through, got my finger firmly on the other edge—that was not through—then twisted my neck, raised upon the tips of my toes, made such horrible faces and rolled my eyes so frightfully that if I had not known for certain it was a reflection of my own face I saw in the glass, I should have sworn I beheld some poor fellow dying in an apoplectic fit. After trying as long as I could stand on my toes, I let myself down, and puffing and blowing for a few minutes, went at it again. I started the same way, only that after getting the edge of the button through I got my thumb nail firmly hooked under it—with my right thumb thus gripping the part that was through and the forefinger of my left hand pressing against the part that it was desirable to get through—I raised again upon the tips of my toes, holding my breath and quivering in every nerve—"spat," something struck against the wall behind me, on the opposite side of the room. About the same time, my clutching fingers failed to find the button. I tried to twist my neck around sufficiently to see if it was really gone, or only hiding somewhere. I failed to either see or feel it, so I stopped and ruminated upon the matter. Remembering the sound I had heard of something striking the wall, a light broke in upon me and going across the room I succeeded after a short search in finding the missing button, but of what use was it to me when I had neither needle nor thread to refasten it? Never mind, there is another button—a button in front. At it I go to fasten the two ends of the linen hoop to the front button. This, at the very first pass I make, flies whizzing against the glass before me. I am mad then—I throw the crumpled bit of linen as far as I can send it and go—like a stray dog—without a collar. I feel like saying bad words, but as there are ladies in the rooms all about me, I dare not; so I seize my pen and write the sentences which commence this article, with "No Head nor Tail" for a head. Don't think from what I have said that I am hard up for shirts—we (Mark and I) have thousands of shirts, and we are going to get them all home one of these days—as soon as we get money enough. But I may as well, now that I think of it, tell you about our housekeeping.

We (Mark and I) have the sweetest little parlor and the snuggest little bedroom (and it's only three floors from the ground) all to ourselves. Here we come every night and live—breathe, move, and have our being, also our toddies. As Mark has already hinted to the world in his modest way, through the columns of the *Territorial Enterprise,* that "our furniture alone cost $28,000, in Europe," I need only add that our upholstery, etc., cost $15,000 more, in—a horn. We have a very good dodge for getting wood; we leave our door open when we go out (we have nothing in our rooms but is so fearfully and wonderfully made, and of such valuable materials, that we have no fear of thieves—why, a thief would run from them at first sight! He would feel, just to gaze on them, as though a rope were already about his neck), so we leave our door open when we go out, and the fellows that are hired to carry up wood to the rooms make a mistake nearly every day and pile a lot in our parlor. I never have seen the fellow making these mistakes, but Mark assures me that the wood all gets into our parlor that way. I suppose he was right—it looks very plausible—but lately I've been thinking that it was rather strange that the fellow quit making these mistakes the very day that Mark went down to Carson to report the proceedings of the Constitutional Convention, and hasn't made a single mistake since. Now, it would be a most singular coincidence if the fellow should commence piling wood into our parlor again the very night Mark returns. I think I shall remember to observe if anything of the kind occurs; it would really be *remarkable* if his presence should so confuse the poor man.

I used to feel quite uneasy in mind at times while these awkward mistakes about rooms were occurring, as the neighbors used to nearly always branch out about the enormity of the sin of wood-stealing when Mark or I came about. Mark said there was no use in listening to what they were saying, as he could prove by history that in all ages there were found wicked persons who took a sort of fiendish delight in persecuting the modest, the virtuous, and the innocent; then he cited the case of our Savior who was crucified by wicked men, "and," said he, "I think there are those who, being envious of our great reputation for virtue and honesty, are laying plans to injure us in the eyes of the world. But, Dan'l," said he, "we can live them down—yes, live them down!" "Do you know," said he, whispering in my ear, "that I sometimes think our enemies *bring this wood into our room!*" And he looked with a look so unfathomably deep, so sagacious and wise, just as he turned to walk off, that I could not help admiring him.

That night, when we reached home near midnight, a bigger lot than ever of wood was found in our room. Poor Mark saw it, and clapping his hands to his forehead, heaved a great sigh and pointing to the goodly heap of billets, said, "Behold the work of the persecutors!" then staggered to a seat. I supposed he had fainted and was about to seize the water pitcher and pour its contents over his head, when, seeing the movement, with a wave of his hand, he said, "Never mind, 'twas but a passing throe of agony wrung from my iron soul by the persistency of our secret foes! Slap in a few sticks of that nice nut-pine and make up a jolly fire; methinks a toddy, piping hot, would rid this breast of the woes planted there by our skulking enemies!" This second view of the case may possibly have been the correct one— instead of the wood having been placed in our room through the mistake of a low-born hireling, it may have been cunningly insinuated into our apartment by an enemy to work out upon us some hellish plot against our purity of character. As the persecution ceased the very day my friend and partner left, I cannot feel that these persecutions— if such they really were—were aimed particularly against my poor guileless Mark. If there should be a recurrence of these singular proceedings on his return, I shall feel very uneasy for him. The above is about all that has occurred to mar our peace since we began house-keeping. To be sure, soap, candles, towels, etc., have been mysteriously left in our rooms, but these are minor troubles and give us little uneasiness.

The Baby Crop

$\mathscr{N}$early every day we find a little slip of paper in our drawer headed in big letters: "BORN. To the wife of Mr. John Henry So-and-so, a son," generally follows. One day we went to our drawer and to our unspeakable astonishment found three sons in it, all brand new. As we pulled out one slip after the other and read thereon—"son, son, son!"—our eyes began to expand. We could hardly believe our eyes. We shuffled the pack over again. Same result—"son! son! son!" "Lord!" thought we, "here is at last one sunny spot in our experience!" We then were seized with a wild notion that sons must be raining down, like the angleworms in Grass Valley, from the clouds. We felt pretty certain that there must be more about. We pulled out our drawer and looked through it very carefully. No son met our gaze. We pulled the drawer clear out of the desk and there, behind it, found what looked very much like a son—or a wash-bill—but what was our indignation to find it nothing more than a poor, puny, little daughter that had been stowed away there for six months.

Formerly these mysterious little slips came so seldom that we were not—we blush to own it—so careful of the precious documents as we

---

One of Dan's occasional spoofs on the local reporter's line of work. See the follow-up piece in the next item. From the *Golden Era,* January 1, 1865.

ought to have been. By our carelessness we had been the means of suppressing this tender bud. Nor—as we now remember in sorrow—was this the sum of our guiltiness. We recollect quite distinctly that once, and not more than two or three months ago, we rolled three newborn babes, two boys and a girl, into a wad and stuffed them into our vest pocket and there carried them till they were worn out. We might never have thought of the little dears again during our mortal career, but for a gentleman who had entrusted us with his firstborn, a son, and a fine healthy child, weighing, we believe he said, twelve pounds. We were dumbfounded. Instinctively we placed our thumb and forefinger in our vest pocket. The state of the infants entrusted to our care was not, as well as we could judge by our sense of feeling, exactly such as would prove satisfactory to their fond parents. For some time we fumbled and cogitated. At last we determined upon a bold front. Bringing out the whole of the infants in one pulpy mass we placed them in the gentleman's hand and told him if he could pick out his boy he was quite welcome to him. Would you believe it? That man has never spoken to us since.

One night, in a fit of abstraction, we lighted our pipe with an infant but one day old. We have almost forgotten, but we think it was a boy, weighing somewhere between seven and forty pounds. But all this was before we began to feel an interest and take pride in our babies. Now we are becoming very fond of them. We love to contemplate them, to set them up in rows and count them over, figure up their average weight and make other instructive calculations. During the past week we have had some very fine ones—one that weighed fifteen pounds, one fourteen, one thirteen, and plenty of them ranging between nine and twelve pounds. A fifteen-pound baby is very good, but we expect still greater ponderosity will yet be obtained. Send along your babies. We are now fully satisfied of their importance, and will see that they are properly cared for. They are fast becoming the great staple productions of Washoe.

A Shocking Mistake

*W*e sometime since wrote an item about the "Baby Crop of Wash-oe." We wrote it because it was necessary to write something, and because we, at the moment, could think of nothing else to write about. We certainly wrote the item in a good humor and with the very best intentions. If we do not love all the women in the land, we must plead guilty to loving *nearly* all the babes. We would do nothing to interfere with the largest possible production of what we in our item assumed to consider the great Washoe staple—babies.

Since the publication of our first article relating to the "Baby Crop" we have been troubled daily by calls from men—careworn family-looking men—who have remonstrated with us about the publication of the said article or rather item. They have assured us that the said item was considered by the ladies as being somewhat—that is, slightly, very slightly—disrespectful to the mothers of the little house-hold angels mentioned by us; and that a great many—a very great many—ladies of their acquaintance had determined to send us no more babies to abuse. When thus assailed, we of course felt very badly and did our best to assure the indignant Benedicts that the item about

---

More journalistic overkill. From the *Golden Era,* February 19, 1865. See also "The Local Editor—His Duties and Delights," TE, June 28, 1868.

the "Baby Crop" was merely a bit of fun. But all this would not do. We were assured that it was really a very serious matter, and one that was likely to very seriously effect what we had been pleased to style the "great Washoe staple." In proof of this, our assailants triumphantly referred us to our paper and to a certain department thereof. "You see that since your item, that department has been as good as vacant. Another such item and there would be no babies at all!"

Of course we felt very sorry for all this, and began to think we had done a very injudicious thing. Having still a faint hope that things were not so bad as represented, we every day looked in our drawer in expectation of finding—well, even a little three-pound daughter would have been some comfort. We found nothing of the kind, however, and when assailed by indignant Benedicts, could only throw ourself upon their generosity and beg them to be merciful.

A day or two since we went to our drawer as usual, to see what it might contain. About the first thing we found was a newly wedded pair and—great Heaven!—tucked in beside them a very young son. Shocked at this catastrophe, we turned away and paced our room in agitation, fanning our flushed cheek with the lid of a cigar box. Several times we made up our mind to having nothing to do with the lot, but finally—being anxious to prove the predictions of the indignant Benedicts fallacious, we ventured a more critical examination—came down to dates. We are not ashamed to confess that we blushed to the roots of our hair—now becoming very gray—as we seated ourself for this delicate investigation. A moment sufficed to convince us that all was right, and, bounding from our seat, we cried, "Thank God!" (We afterwards took our hat and gave several—we were not particular about the number—cheers.) The baby did not belong to the newly married couple. The happy father of the little newcomer was also the happy(?) father of eleven other "comers" of more mature age. Our trials are many, but we hope, through patience and the kind indulgence of a good-natured public, to long remain in a position to watch over the various and vital interests of our loved Washoe.

Comstock Characters

Butter-mouth Bill

Some of His Professional Adventures.

---

*T*he original patronymic of the subject of this little sketch is unknown to us. "Butter-mouth Bill," his sobriquet, is, however, infinite-
ly more suggestive of the nature and manner of the man than could
possibly be the name borne by his father, whatever that may have
been.

The names which men are born unto are usually most meaningless,
while these they have thrust upon them are ever pregnant of meaning.
They speak volumes and should always be noted.

"Butter-mouth" stands before our reader the moment we mention
his name, and almost are his mellifluent accents heard. In oily
smoothness of discourse and plausibility of manner, he is a man
without compare. Virulent polemics are not his forte. His occupation,
that of a dealer of the noble game of faro, is one which furnishes him
endless opportunity for the exercise of his peculiar talent of tongue.

The subject of our sketch is so smooth and oily in all of his walks in
life that it is hard to find anywhere in his life any protruding point
upon which to lay hold. He seems at the first glance a promising

---

One of the local "sports." From the *Territorial Enterprise,* November 8, 1874.
See Dan's letter to Lou on p. 34 in this book.

237

subject, but, like the Irishman's flea, when we put our finger on him, he is not there. However, as we have said this much in regard to him, we shall do our best in order that at least one leaf of "Daphne's deathless plant" may rest upon the broad, unwrinkled brow of Butter-mouth Bill.

Butter-mouth Soothes a Den of Lions—His Narrow Escape

As we have said, Butter-mouth is a dealer of the game of faro; we may add that he generally deals his own game, moving from town to town as the grass grows short.

To exemplify the truth of the divine aphorism: "A soft answer turneth away wrath," we may give a brief account of Butter-mouth's professional visit to Sulphuropolis, a well-known town in this state, which would smell as sweet by any other name. Butter-mouth had heard much of this town as being one in which shekels abounded, but he had also heard from such of his fellow-craftsmen as had visited it, that its inhabitants were not such as yielded kindly to the hand of the spoiler.

Half of the knife-scarred cheekbones, broken noses, and deficient ears that were boasted by his friends and followers of the fortunes of the Egyptian king were mementos of the genial and gushing race who made Sulphuropolis their home. Coin being, as it were, a reminiscence of the past in all the towns through which he was wont to range, Butter-mouth finally made up his mind to venture into the town with the name savoring of the here-after home of men of his ungodly craft.

As the gentle dove goes cooing into the strange dove-cot, so Butter-mouth entered the town of Sulphuropolis; unostentatiously he secured a large room in the rear of the barroom of the principal hotel, and smilingly he spread forth his net.

The people came—for it had been long since the beast of the jungle had ventured to show himself in the town, and they thirsted for the fray—the people came, they saw, and were conquered. Smilingly, Butter-mouth raked their shekels into his drawer. With oily tongue he deprecated their losses and almost tore his hair when one whom he was cheering on, and in whom he seemed to feel an almost fatherly interest, was a continual loser.

Many of those gathered about the lair of Butter-mouth's pet Bengal were fiery sons of the chivalrous South, men of the half-horse, half-alligator strain. To guide his bark and ride serene in the midst of this turbulent element taxed the peculiar talent of Butter-mouth to the uttermost, yet he was equal to the situation.

As they saw their golden pieces depart and their piles of silver melt away, not unfrequently was there heard among those surrounding Butter-mouth's board the sound of grinding teeth; sighs that shook strong frames forced their way from brazen breasts, and often hands that twitched nervously went back and toyed with the buckhorn of a bowie or rested upon the ivory hilt of Colt's incomparable invention. At such times—times that try men's souls!—Butter-mouth shone forth in almost godlike greatness. He saw nothing. A serene smile of peace and goodwill to all mankind played upon his lips; and his eyes, soft in their gaze as a maiden's, sought the ceiling as in oily tones he recounted other scenes in other lands. Not a thought gave he to the board or the piles of gold before him; his soul was not in these, but absent in the sunny land of his childhood.

Amazed, the wretched and ruined men would then stand and impotently gaze into each other's faces. Horny hands would slowly relax their grasp upon the hilts of gleaming weapons and a perfect calm would ensue—the troubled waters acknowledging the soothing oil.

Thus, time—a whole month—passed on, and there in the day and in the dead vast middle of the night sat Butter-mouth, raking in the spoils of the people of Sulphuropolis. At length he had gathered in the last slick quarter; the town was cleaned, the grass mown to the very roots. Butter-mouth had packed his apparatus and was prepared to go in search of fresh fields and pastures new.

The stage which was to bear him away, and with him his heavy sacks of coin, was soon to drive around to the front of the hotel. Many of his old customers thronged the barroom and to these Butter-mouth made a little speech. He told them of all the stories he had heard against them previous to his coming among them, and wound up by declaring he was happy to be able to say that he was now convinced that these were all malicious lies; that more pleasant or agreeable gentlemen it had never been his good fortune to meet with than those whose acquaintance he had had the pleasure of making in the charming village of Sulphuropolis. Butter-mouth smiled in various directions about the room, but no answering smile met his gaze. A dogged and somewhat ominous silence prevailed.

Butter-mouth was glad when he was safely stowed away inside of the coach, for he liked not the fierce and sullen looks of those who began to throng about him on the eve of his departure. Just as the whip of the driver cracked and the unwilling team began to feel the way into their collars, Butter-mouth heard a gruff voice say, in anger-thickened tones, these words: "Just thar, whar he said 'more pleasant or agreeable gentleman,' is whar you ought'r struck him!"

Butter-mouth felt in his inmost soul that he had made a narrow escape. But, true to his nature, as the coach rolled away from the gloomy group of coinless men, he bent forward from its window and with his lily hand waved them from his radiant countenance a smiling adieu—for he was yet within reach of a pistol ball, and the words "Just thar is whar you ought'r struck him!" still rang in his ears.

Butter-mouth Shears a Sheep of His Own Color

Once upon a time—after all there is no better way in which to begin a truthful narrative—once upon a time, then, Butter-mouth Bill made his appearance in the brisk little town of Smelterville, famous for its furnaces and argentiferous ores. He walked about the town in a gloomy and dejected manner. Yet was he unctuous to the core; and, even as he seemed to sorrow, the oil of gladness exuded from his every pore.

In the town was but one suitable room in which to display to the full the attractions of the royal beast of Bengal. This room was occupied by a brother sport who was driving quite a thriving trade. To obtain possession of this room was the secret desire of Butter-mouth's soul; but there was Wasatch Sam in full and flourishing possession. Haman looked not on Mordecai sitting in the king's gate with more envious eye than did Butter-mouth Bill observe Wasatch Sam seated behind his green baize offering forth his lay-out.

At the first opportunity, Butter-mouth, in tones all greasy with grief, informed Wasatch that he was dead broke. He was even then, as he said, on his way to Virginia City to raise a sum with which to start afresh in the world. It was hard, he went on to say, for a man like him, who had always rejoiced in the possession of almost unnumbered shekels, to be reduced to this dire extremity; but to this complexion must sometimes come the man who tempts dame Fortune too far.

He then descended to particulars and informed the sympathetic Sam—for so Sam strove to appear—that he had been in the town of Chloridetta, where he had spread forth his lure. The town was full of pigeons ripe for the plucking; coin abounded in every man's pocket and was rattling in every man's hand. There seemed spread abroad and ready for the sickle of the reaper a harvest of at least $30,000 or $40,000.

But, alas! the run of the cards was villainously against him. No expedient served to give him a turn of luck. Fortune favored alone those who fought against him and at last his bank was broken, his last dime gone, and his fangless tiger grinned ghastfully through naked gums.

As Butter-mouth concluded the story of his woes, tears stood in his angel eyes; he heaved a heartbroken sigh, affectionately wrung his dear friend Sam's soft hand, and rushed away to his room to hide—a smile of exultation.

When Butter-mouth thus rushed away from the sympathetic gaze of his friend Sam, it was late—somewhat beyond that witching time of night when churchyards yawn—and Sam's game had closed. Gazing in the direction taken by the departed Butter-mouth for some seconds, Wasatch began assiduously to pace the floor of his place of traffic, meanwhile most vigorously puffing his fragrant Havana. The mind of the man was busy!

"The saffron morn," as Homer hath it, had long passed and the sun rode high in the heavens when Butter-mouth made his appearance the next day. A sort of premonitory symptom of a smile for a moment curled along his full, ripe upper lip—as a flaw of wind is sometimes seen to ripple the placid surface of a lake—when it was told him that through some sudden and unaccountable freak, Wasatch Sam had given up the room in which he was wont to exhibit his small but energetic menagerie and had departed, bag and baggage, by the early coach for someplace to his friends and foes alike unknown.

This bit of news was imparted to Butter-mouth as he imbibed his morning cocktail at the bar of the saloon in the rear of which was situated the coveted faro-room. The man who furnished the intelligence was proprietor of the place, and after about three flourishes of Butter-mouth's oily tongue, the landlord had deposited in his till a month's rent in advance, and our hero, with hands in breeches pockets, was leisurely viewing his newly acquired quarters and estimating the capabilities thereof.

Now turn we to Wasatch Sam. Arrived in the town of Chloridetta, his first care was to secure a spacious room suited to his purpose, making sure of it by planking down the rent for a month in advance.

Until he had done this he said not a word of his business or his intentions to living soul. All being made sure, however, he at length walked forth to view the bleating herds of the place and begin in anticipation the pleasing task of shearing them.

Sam had none of the faults of the weak, the vain, the vacillating good; he meant business, and he was in a hurry to set about it. He had not sauntered far along the principal street of the town before he met a brother sport.

"Hello!" cried the cheerful member of mighty confraternity. "Hello, Sam! What brings you here. Thought you had a good, easy-going game down at Smelterville? I had about made up my mind to go down there myself."

"Nonsense!" cried Sam, "from what I hear it is ten times better picking up here. I just landed here this morning, and I've got me a room already and am going to open a game tonight."

"The bloody blazes you are!" cried the cheerful sport. "What *to* I should like to know? There is not a splitter left in the town. Butter-mouth Bill left here but four days ago, and he carried away with him the last slick quarter in the town!"

"Butter-mouth Bill!" yelled Sam, "the infernal, tear-shedding croc-odile!—the oily-tongued, thieving liar! Why, he told me that he got broke here, that the town was lousy with money and that he could have won $50,000 if luck had not turned against him. The infernal, lying, solemn-faced scoundrel! Just see what he has made me do! Town teetotally cleaned out, hey?"

"Cleaned and scraped—the last slick quarter and old battered bit gone! Look at all the 'huskies' going 'round here with their backs humped," said the cheerful, man, "not one of 'em has had a square meal since Butter-mouth Bill left town! By the great bull of Bashan, and everything else that roars and rumbles, even my belly is beginning to believe my throat is cut, so long has it been since communication between the two has taken place! There is not money enough left in the town to buy a louse a pair of boxing gloves!"

"D——n Butter-mouth!" cried Sam. "Good day, old pard; I've business on my hands. D——n that Butter-mouth Bill!" and thus, grumbling and wearing a musing look, Sam went in search of the man of whom he had so gleefully rented his room in the morning. After a hard battle of words, he finally succeeded in getting $25 of the $50 he had a few hours before paid into the landlord's hands. As he busied himself with packing his traps, blood was in his eye. He was bound to be off that night by the return coach in order to settle down in his old place, for it was much too good to lose.

We once more breathe the stuffy atmosphere of Smelterville. How serene and smiling sits Butter-mouth behind the baize. He reminds us of the priest of whom Chaucer said:

> Full sweetly heard he confession.
> And pleasant was his absolution.

To lose to such a man was a greater pleasure than to win from the average of mankind.

Butter-mouth has an immense game going—better than has been seen in the town for months, for all desire to try their luck at the new bank—and he is raking in coin right royally. Just when all is going on most swimmingly, Wasatch Sam arrives in town. Without waiting to look after his baggage—at least nothing more than his bags of coin— he rushes from the coach and in a moment is at the bar confronting his old landlord.

"The room!" he cries, "the room! I'll take the room again at the old rent! Here is your money for the first month!"

"I don't understand you," said the landlord. "What about a room?"

"The room I had—the faro-room! I'll take it again! I've just got back and I want to take the room again—to keep it right along, same as before!"

"Ah! ahem! Well, yes; but you see you went away, and as Butter-mouth Bill said that rather than see it lyin' idle—and as he always felt like helpin' a man when it came in his way—he'd try if he could manage to keep it going on as a sort of help to the bar, why, I—"

"Rented it to him?" yelled Sam.

"Well, yes; he put up for it for the first month in advance, with the refusal for as long as he wants it."

"D——n Butter-mouth! He beats me at every turn! Butter-mouth here, Butter-mouth there—Butter-mouth everywhere! D——n Butter-mouth!"

Sam then went and took a look into the back room where the tiger was rending his prey right and left. The evidences of prosperity that he there saw made him sick at heart.

He came back to the bar and took half a tumbler of raw tarantula, sat down and mused for a time, then went and called Butter-mouth, requesting that gentleman to come out for discourse.

Butter-mouth called upon the man in the lookout chair to take his seat and deal; winked a friend into the lookout chair, and then, serene as a summer's morn, came forth to meet and affectionately greet his dear and ever-sympathetic friend, Wasatch Sam. Most cordially did he advance and grasp Sam's half-extended hand. It was like David going for Jonathan after a six weeks' absence.

The torrent of abuse which Sam poured forth upon the devoted head of the apparently thoroughly crushed Butter-mouth shall find no place here. Already have we been pained by several profane expressions from Wasatch—we will have no more of them!

The most ingenious and, we may add, gentle and lamblike (such was the tone that accompanied the argument) explanation of Butter-mouth, it gives us pleasure to record.

"Why, my dear friend!" said he, "just to see how curiously things sometimes turn out. You see, I had a dream in which I saw myself overtaken by the very misfortune I related to you. I saw all who played at my game winning my gold till at last all was gone and I was left penniless—I will not say a beggar—and I was almost kicked out of the town. This dream made a deep and lasting impression on my mind. I said to myself, 'What if it were so; really and truly so!—what should I do?' Then I thought I would try my friends by telling to them my dream as a fact.

"To you, Sam—you being my dearest and most valued friend on earth—I first related as being a fact what was indeed an idle dream. Forgive me my cruelty, for as I poured into your private sympathetic ear the story of my losses and my despair, I saw that your very soul was wrung—that your heart of hearts was bleeding for me! Yet had I the cruelty to rush away from you and leave you thus sorrowing for your friend. No sooner was I composed in my bed and had taken the second thought than my heart wept for the anguish I had so foolishly and lightly caused you. More than once I was on the point of rising and rushing away to find you, to tell you that it was I, Samson, who had spoiled the Philistines, and not the Philistines Samson!

"Long I lingered in my room the next morning—startled, confused, and blushing at every step that sounded on the stairs, for, said I: 'There, now, comes Sam to offer—nay, to thrust upon me—half of his wealth. What a sorry figure I shall cut in trying to give a sane reason for having kept him a whole night stretched upon the rack! How pitiful and small will look my joke when I tell him it was all a dream!'

"Thus I tortured myself till I could no longer endure my own society. I then sallied forth and great was my astonishment at learning of your sudden departure. At one time I meditated putting a pistol to my head, for I thought that grief at the woes of a friend might have turned your brain; or, again, that you had gone to some distant place, there to dispose of some possessions in order to assist me—me who needed no assistance.

"To make a long story short, I then, to assist this poor man and make him some amends for having deprived him of a paying tenant, rented of him his empty room. Thus, my dear friend, you see, from a mere idle dream came about all of these wonderful and perplexing complications. But let them not impair that friendship which has so long reached out from heart to heart and grappled us together as it were with hooks of steel. On your manly and loving breast I thus throw myself and sob my prayer for forgiveness—"

"Butter-mouth!" cried Sam, aghast as he beheld that weeping and subjugated individual advancing upon him—"Butter-mouth, keep away from me, or so help me God, I'll give you a mash in the jaw. You played your game well! You caught my jack—and much good may it do you, but if you ever deal me such a hand again and get away with the trick, I hope that I may never more hold deuce high till Gabriel toots his old dinner horn!" Thus saying, Wasatch, Ajaxlike, in silence turns, and sullen stalks away.

All night Wasatch tossed restless in his bed, and, soon as the morn restored the day, he mounted the outgoing coach and left the town.

The ever-serene Butter-mouth remained master of the situation, and still sits in Sam's warm nest behind the baize, smiling whole handfuls of gold into his spacious drawer. For this is he—Butter-mouth Bill!

Sleepy Pete

He Communes With Big Horn Smith.

---

*A*few evenings since, a wild-eyed individual, of the Buffalo Bill style in hair, entered a North C Street saloon and introduced himself in a general way as Big Horn Smith, of the Goose Creek mountains, and a real Kentucky gentleman. He said he was becoming moldy for want of congenial exercise. The Comstock range pleased him sufficiently well, except that the people were too good to afford him any amusement. They agreed too readily to any and every proposition. What was the utility of his announcing himself as being dangerous and ugly to handle when nobody disputed the assertion? On the frontiers men were true men. There the souls of men were not cowed by civilization. There each man declared himself and passed for what he was worth. There, on the frontiers, a man would not agree with you if you told him white was black and black was white. On the frontiers could at all times be found spirited and instructive argument supplemented with invigorating exercise.

"Now," said the apostle from the Goose Creek mountains, "when I tell you that I think you are the biggest set of white-livered curs that I have ever encountered in my travels, I don't expect any of you to

---

A blowhard mountain man, Big Horn Smith, gets his comeuppance. From the *Territorial Enterprise,* June 6, 1878.

dispute the assertion; when I tell you that I believe there is not one among you but would shed tears were I to spit in his face, I do not expect a man among you to show that he is aware of my presence; when I tell you that the man who is saying these things is right here and easy to be found, I have not the least fear that one among you will come to hunt him!"

Having concluded this speech, the long-haired being sneeringly surveyed those in the room. No one said a word, as no one felt it to be his duty to engage in a rough-and-tumble fight with a man for whose opinions, good or bad, he did not care a straw. A man is not obliged to turn scavenger and undertake to abate every nuisance that comes in his way, though he may encounter some that are very offensive.

"I see that I have estimated you at your true value," said the Goose Creek mountaineer. "Now, if it would be any credit to me, I'd just haul you all up here by your noses and knock your heads together."

"Somebody ought to teach this windy fool a lesson," said one of those in the saloon, to his neighbor. "I do not feel personally aggrieved, but it's a work that should be done for the good of society at large. He is evidently all wind, a bubble that would be easily pricked, but even in pricking a bubble you must come in contact with foul air."

Said the neighbor: "Sleepy Pete went into the card room, back, a while ago. He would think it no hardship to come out and abate the nuisance—he would do it for a dollar."

The two men left their seats and went toward the card room.

"I have always observed coyotes leave the plain when the grizzly bear comes down from the mountains," sneered the Goose Creek man, following the pair with his eyes.

The two citizens made no reply. They found Pete with his head on a card table, sound asleep. They awoke him and told him that a man outside was spoiling for a sound thrashing, and a dollar was ready for him as soon as he had finished the job.

Yawning till the top of his head seemed coming off, Pete said: "Yo-o-aw hoo-oo-yaw-yum! A dollar's small to be waked up for—ya-aw oo-yum—but I reckon I'll take it. Ya-oo-yum! I've got nothing else to do just now."

As Pete walked into the barroom, his eyes fell upon the long-haired stranger.

"This him?" was all he said.

An affirmative nod from one of the men was his answer.

Pete slouched forward, lazily stretching his brawny limbs and yawning in the stranger's face, said: "Well, let's (hoo-yaw-um) begin."

Pete's arms shot out two or three times, like the pistons of a double-cylinder engine, the apostle from the Goose Creek mountains went to the floor and was kicked under a table and against the wall, like a wet dishrag.

Pete held out his hand for the dollar, and muttering: "Small money (yaw-oo-yum), small money," retired to the rear room to finish his nap.

Big Horn Smith, the apostle of chivalry from the Goose Creek mountains, presently recovered his consciousness, crawled out from under the table, blew and wiped his nose, got his hat and placed it on his head, hauled up the waistband of his pantaloons, shook himself into shape, then turned to those present and said: "Gentlemen, I humbly beg pardon for any disparaging remarks that I may have let fall in regard to the people of this town. I find there are places in it where a man who is pining for those comforts to which he may have become habituated on the frontiers may meet gentlemen who are both able and willing to minister to his wants. Gentlemen, you have among you good Samaritans. How call you the gentleman with whom I just now held a very satisfying and instructive colloquy?"

"He is known as Sleepy Pete," said someone.

"Think you 'Somnolent Peter' likely to be inclined to partake of something in the way of refreshment after his exercise?"

"He is doubtless asleep ere now," was the reply, "but should you at anytime during your sojourn in our town find yourself wasting away for the comforts of the frontier, call round, and for your benefit we will awake Sleepy Pete."

"Thank you, gentlemen, thank you; but I feel that I shall not again desire to commune with our sleepy friend, except at very long range," and the apostle wandered forth.

The Boss Snorer

*A*fter the fire old man Bullard found lodgings on South C Street. He got a bed in a large room containing two other beds that were occupied. Mr. Bullard is a huge, fat, good-natured, and very entertaining man. The proprietor of the lodging house was much pleased with Bullard, and laughed at his jokes the first evening of his arrival at his place till tears ran down his cheeks. The men who were to be Bullard's roommates also thought well of him—that evening. The next morning, however, they looked sad and red-eyed. Then they went to the landlord and told him that he must find some other place for Mr. Bullard, as he was such a terrific snorer they couldn't stand him. The landlord's rooms were all occupied, and he had no place for Bullard but just where he was. The complaining lodgers left and in two or three days two other men were put into the vacant bed. Bullard made short work of them; one night let them out. The landlord sought an interview with Bullard and remonstrated with him. Bullard stoutly asserted that he did not snore—had never been known to snore.

On one of the drawbacks of boardinghouse life. From the *Territorial Enterprise,* January 1, 1876.

The landlord had to give Bullard up as a bad bargain and turned his attention to looking up lodgers with which to fill his vacant beds. He found men to take the beds, but again Bullard cleaned them out in a single night. Growing desperate, the landlord again went to Bullard. He told them he must either leave the house or pay rent for all the beds in the room—$45 per month. Bullard said a bargain was a bargain; he had paid $15 for his bed and he intended keeping it till his month was up, and he didn't propose to pay for beds he had no use for; he didn't snore, and the man who asserted to the contrary was a "liar and a horse thief!" The landlord felt very much depressed after this last interview with Bullard, as he saw he was determined not to be removed from his quarters. A morning or two after, as Bullard's landlord was going downtown, he saw standing in his door a brother lodging house man.

"Thank heaven he's gone!" said the man as Bullard's landlord came up. "Thank heaven I'm rid of him at last!"

"Rid of whom?"

"Why, of the big fat man you see yonder, waddling down the street."

"What of him?"

"Enough of him! He cleaned nearly every man out of my house before he left. They wouldn't stop in the same block with that snorting, Falstaffian porpoise, sir!"

"He's a good one, is he?"

"A good one? He's a perfect terror! He's more different kinds of a snorer than any man I ever heard, and every time he changes his key it is for the worse. While I had him here, crowds were gathering in front of the house nightly wondering what was the matter within, and the police came in one night thinking someone was being murdered. My dog ran away, and all the cats left the house, sir!"

"And the man you pointed out to me is this snorer?"

"Yes, sir, he is, and may he burst!"

"Good day, sir!" And Bullard's landlord hastened down the street. The next morning, with the first peep of day, Bullard, puffing and blowing, rushed into the presence of his landlord.

"What are you trying to play on me?" cried he. "I never slept a wink all night. Of all the infernal noises I ever heard, that man in my room got off the worst. He is going to stay here?"

"Stay? Of course he is. Hain't he got the bed for a month?"

"Then I leave," and Bullard was as good as his word.

An hour afterward the man who had ousted Bullard arose and waddled serenely into the presence of the landlord.

"You've cleaned him out," said the landlord. "You raised him; he's gone for good," and the landlord gleefully rubbed his hands. "Now," continued the landlord, "I'll give you a good, square breakfast and then you can go."

"Go?" said the fat man; "not much I don't. Didn't you say last evening in the presence of Bullard and half a dozen others that I was to stay here a month?"

"But that you know was only to—"

"I know nothing of the kind, and I shall stay here! I am human; I must have someplace in which to repose!"

The landlord is now trying to get some man to set up some kind of machine in his house that will oust the boss snorer, who now has the whole place to himself except a small room in a corner of the third story where he and his wife spend their nights in a miserable way.

Old Tunneling Pete

What He Has Done and What He Threatens.

*O*ld Tunneling Pete was what he was always called, and if he had any other name it was never heard on the Pacific Coast. It is said that he was from the lead mines of Galena, Illinois, where they to this day tell how he burrowed his way through the limestone from cave to cave in his search for mineral, making the cave last found his abiding place.

Even in those days he was nearly always underground. How he managed to endure the light of day long enough to cross the plains has always been a mystery to all who knew him. Some assert that he traveled only during the night, and others that he wore a huge pair of goggles of black glass.

Old Pete landed in California in 1849, and as soon as he struck the golden soil, took pick and shovel and went out of sight beneath it. During the ten years he mined in California he was under the ground most of the time, only coming out to the light of day at night, as a son of Erin would say.

Old Pete was a regular ground mole, and like that little animal appeared to hate the light of the sun, which kept him winking and

The lifestyle of a human mole. From the *Territorial Enterprise,* September 29, 1878.

blinking, even when his eyes were half closed, as they always were when he was on the surface.

In California old Pete mined the gravel banks Mexican fashion, running coyote holes in them till they were a greater puzzle than was the famed labyrinth of Crete. What he did with the gold he found no one ever knew, as he was never seen to have any in his possession, nor was he ever seen to purchase either food or drink. It was the same in the lead mines, and a story came from Galena that he was not a human being, but a gnome, in disgrace in some shape with the beings of his race.

He was seen here on the Comstock soon after silver was found, but straightway disappeared underground. No one saw him on his way hither or knew he was coming; the first information had of his migration was when he was seen here. There were those among the prospectors of that day who swore that old Pete had merely extended one of his California holes and so "come square through the Sierra Nevada mountains." It is reported that after the day of his arrival he was not seen for over two years, when he finally came out near where the town of Sutro now stands. Some now say that Mr. Sutro followed in on old Pete's hole when he dug his tunnel, otherwise he would never have found his way to the Comstock.

The story goes that when old Pete's head popped out through the ground down by the verge of the valley, it was daylight, and when he saw the cottonwood trees along the Carson River he is said to have been in a terrible rage, as he had supposed he was deep enough to pass under the channel of the Carson and get beneath the big peaks of Como. All day he sat winking and blinking and cursing and swearing in the mouth of his hole—for old Pete was fearfully wicked—and at night he gathered up his drifting bar, pick, and shovel, and crossed over the hills to Flowery District, where he set to work and was out of sight under the base of a big hill long before morning.

He was seen on the surface, in the twilight and of moonlight nights, two or three times each year by the miners of Flowery until about three years ago, when he seemed to have disappeared for good. No one cared much whither he had gone, for he was an unsightly old man and exceedingly snappish and disagreeable.

One morning about six months ago some Indians rushed into the little village of Flowery in a terrible fright, saying the devil had appeared in their camp. A few miners went with the Indians and found old Pete sitting in the middle of their rancheria beside a hole, through which it was evident he had just risen. The old man's eyes were glassy and his grey hairs were matted with clay, like those of a badger just dragged from his hole, and it was easy to see that he was on his last legs. He said he had come to the surface to get a mouthful of fresh air in order that he might have strength to die. He had just life enough left to say that he had been away up under the roots of the Comstock during the past three years and had there seen more wealth than Fair, Mackay, or any mining millionaire of them all had ever dreamed of.

"They will never find it, though," chuckled he; "they will never find it! They will never go down to where it is. They will become discouraged far above, up among the twisting clays and cross-courses, and faults and great horses of porphyry. I must die now and go to hell, as I well know, but none of them will ever find what I have seen—no, never!"

So saying, the old fellow suddenly pressed his hands to his breast, a rattling came from his throat, he fell back upon the ground, gasped and clutched the gravel with his bony fingers, a tremor passed through his frame; he straightened out and was dead.

The miners buried him and his pick, shovel, and bar with him, thinking that was the last of him. Last week, however, about twelve o'clock one gusty night, he came up fair and square in the center of the dirt floor of a miner's cabin down by the Lady Bryan, and there sat winking and blinking in his old way at the owner, who was lying in his bunk regaling himself with the yellow fever news in the *Enterprise*. The miner was one of those who had assisted in burying the old fellow, therefore he was naturally a good deal surprised to see him come back.

"Why, Pete," cried he, "Where in h——l do you come from?"

"You have named the place," said old Pete. "I am fresh from the brimstone diggings of his Satanic Majesty. I always knew I should go there, and I told you so just before I died."

"Why didn't you stay there? What brought you back?" said the miner.

"Well, I should have stayed there, and would have been comfortable enough, if I had not been able to see all that was going on outside. I tell you when I saw Johnny Skae going straight down into that private treasure house of mine, the devil couldn't keep me. You fellows buried my tools with me, and when the imps of the lower regions came for me, I was such a bag of bones that, in trying to get the whole of me, they gathered out tools and all by mistake and dumped all down together in the devil's dominions. I heard the clatter of pick, shovel, and bar when they tumbled me down over the red-hot cliffs of hell, and when I wanted to get out I just hunted up my tools, tunneled under the walls—and here I am."

"Yes, you are here—what next?" said the miner.

"Don't you fear. I am not come to stop with you—I am going up to the Sierra Nevada to keep an eye on things. There has got to be a square deal up there, now that they are into the edge of it."

"Otherwise, what? What can you do?" queried the miner.

"What can I do?" and here the ghost of old Pete chuckled horribly—"What did I do when in the life?—such life as it was. Let Skae displease me and see what I will do! Who let the water into the lower levels of the Savage and Hale and Norcross? Who did it? Answer me that."

"How do I know—I wasn't there when it came?" said the miner, becoming a little alarmed at the shrill and rather fierce tones of old Pete's ghost.

"Ha, ha, ha! No, *you* wasn't, but *I* was, and aren't they pumping yet?—aren't they pumping yet? Oh, ho! Aren't they a-pumping yet? Let them pump; let them pump! I have brought in seas—I'll bring in the ocean! Thus far all goes well at the Sierra Nevada, but there must be a square deal or I'll—"

There was a clatter of tools, the door of the cabin flew open, a blast of wind came in, the miner's candle went out, a faint "ha! ha!" seemed to come from a distance along the mountainside, and all was hushed again.

When the miner had closed his door and relighted his candle, not a trace of old Pete could be seen and, strangest of all, the hole through which he came up was closed, and it could not be discovered that the earth of the floor had ever been broken.

The Scholarly Tramp

*The Soliloquy of a Highly Educated Wanderer as
Taken by a Nevada Miner.*

*O*ld Ben is a well-known tramp. He is about sixty-five years old,
and is said to be a graduate of Harvard College, and once the editor of
a prominent newspaper in Philadelphia. No one here knows his full
name, but in Carson City and other Nevada towns his face is as well
known as was the face of the lime-kiln man in New York years ago.
James Peters is a young Cornish miner who improves his evenings by
studying phonography. He caught Old Ben in a gruesome mood not
long ago, soliloquizing. With ready pencil he took down the words of
the Parson of the Tramps, as Ben is sometimes called. It was in the
dead waste and middle of the night, that noon of thought when
wisdom mounts her zenith with the stars. Ben stood as prop most
unstable to an awning post.

"Did I hear a voice?" he said. "Did some mortal whisper 'Old
Ben'? No one! Ah, 'twas but some distant sound; but yet, this is the
hour when the sheeted dead do squeak and gibber. Ah me! I am Old
Ben now. It seems ages ago that I was Young Ben, and, with diploma
in pouch pranced forth into the blazing, flaring world from my
college, an erudite incapable—an inflated nihility.

A literary fantasy of the sort De Quille belabored in his "Dives and Lazarus."
From the New York *Sun,* June 21, 1885.

"'Old Ben! Old Ben!' like the rhythmic tick of a clock pulsates upon my strained tympanum; yet no one calls. Strange, now—passing strange—the hallucinations that are born to my eager and fecund brain. At times it seems that the very dogs bark my name—that the cocks crow it, cattle low it, horses neigh it, asses bray it, winds sigh it, infants cry it, senility mumbles it, each passing car rumbles it—it rolls and surges to and fro, mingling with the roar of the city. Even the prayer-blest bells in the church towers boom forth—'Old Ben! Old Ben! Old Ben!'

"But, ah, 'tis cold, bitter cold. This ancient coat is thin, thin, and awning posts a full furlong apart are not umbrageous groves of shelter, yet even one of the smallest outgirths my body. Lean, lean and shriveled is poor old Ben! Hungry, too, and thirsty—beloved Bacchus, how thirsty! My belly has now so long been empty that it must suspect my throat is cut. Even my throat is dusty as a garret. I feel that I must be a lineal descendant of Gargantua, who at birth cried out 'Drink! drink!' so lustily that the words were heard in distant cities. My voice, uttering the same cry, has also been heard in many cities, for I have out-walked the Ewige Jude—the Wandering Jew.

"Had I but a watch now—a paltry silver watch—an old gold ring, any pawnable thing, I soon would feast. Even the ring of Hans Carvel, presented him by the devil, as told by Rabelais, would I spout in this mine emergency. But all my treasures have long since been laid up beyond the reach of all impecunious mortal moths—have gone to that bourne whence no unredeemed pledge returns—

> Oh, my prophetic soul,
> Mine uncle!

"Mine uncle, thou receiver of all good and precious gifts! Into thy hands are gone all 'mine ancient, most domestic ornaments.' I would that I were now possessed of the ring of Odin, which dropped eight other rings every ninth night, or all the rings the Doges of Venice have flung from the Bucentaur in wedding the Adriatic. But all wishes are vain. In the language of Jeremiah, the inspired Hebrew, let me cry, 'Vanitas vanitatum et omnia vanitas!'

"Down, Belly; good fellow, down! Thinkest thou, clamorous fool, that I am unmindful of thee? This instant would I give thee, had I the power, a suffocating fill of pork and beans. A fig, say I—and a fig wouldst thou, too, say, were the savory dish now before us—for either

257

Moses or Pythagoras. What care we for the Hebrew lawgiver's bad opinion of pork, or the long-haired Samian's interdiction of beans? Pork and beans! Ye gods! The thought of their rising steam and spreading aroma warms and perfumes the night. What ho, good waiter, bestir thyself! Pork and beans for nine! Alas, I do but dream. Brave words—noble commands, but coin is required to back them up. Though I stretch my fingers to reach to heaven. I have one heel nailed in hell.

"And now, behold, stalking through the night hitherward comes a policeman, a—to speak the detestable slang of the swinish multitude—a peeler. Sad is my fate; I am beneath the dignity of arrest; he will pass me by in scorn as not worthy of a glance of the policial eye. Would I were a hoodlum, now—a villainous, low-browed, dangerous hoodlum! Then might I hope to be taken in. Many very excellent meals have I eaten in their station houses, and in their jails have I spent many happy, musing days. But now, in my time of sorest need, they will not put hand to my collar. I am but a vapor, scud, rack; a nimbus on the face of nature; am too unsubstantial to even be bodied forth in the form of a vagrant—technically, 'vag.' I am now an example of what the hoodlum ripens into—am a hoodlum in the sere and yellow leaf, dropping overripe and rotten fruit. Was it thus with my aged good sire in the days of his decline?

"A vision rises before mine eyes. In the far east I see a green and noble mountain. By the door of a far-up cottage, where the river is but a rill, sits a man, gray-haired and old. On a rude bench, with bared head, he sits beneath the contemporaneous trees. On his knee rests the book of books. His is a happy household, though exceeding poor. From within the humble dwelling comes a slender girl; her face is an angel's, and golden is the hair that floats about her neck and rests upon her bosom. Bright is the light in her eyes, and their color is not dimmed under the blue of heaven. Gently her hand, so small and white, falls upon the old man's shoulder. Aroused, he lifts his head and smiles, and she, smiling, kisses his withered cheek. Oh, God! My sister—my father!

"Great Niobe, a tear! Ha, ha, ha—a tear! Welcome, stranger! but thrice welcome wouldst thou be wert thou a tear such as 'tis written once fell from heaven—fell upon the camps of Israel's murmuring children. Manna, manna! Would I make moan were bread to fall to me from heaven? Would I complain of sameness of diet and howl for the flesh pots of bondage? Never! Besides, if we may credit the Talmudical writers, the manna—this bread from heaven—for the truly good had the taste of fish, flesh, and fowl—the taste of all things under heaven.

"Though not wholly given up to ungodliness—*Gottvergessenheit*—could I now be seated at old Belshazzar's feast, the ghostly handwriting on the wall should not make me miss a dish nor pass untasted a single goblet.

"We should never, good Sancho tells us, 'speak of ropes in the houses of the hanged,' nor to my mind should we speak of wine in the presence of those who are dying of thirst. Oh, could I but achieve a drink—a fierce, soul-searching drink—a drink that would thrill my nerves till each became vibrant and vocal as the strings of a windswept harp! Since to eat is out of the question, beyond my hopes, let me drink. Deep calleth unto deep, and whether I am most tortured by hunger or by thirst is difficult to decide—both gnaw like the worm that dieth not.

"*Digna canis pablo*—a dog is worth his food. Would I were a dog. I would be a Cerberus—three-mouthed and three-throated! I may once have been a dog—perhaps a dog of high degree—before appearing in this ignoble biped form. Pythagoras remembered having occupied other forms before birth, and the Ettrick shepherd, in *Noctes Ambrosianæ*, tells of his prehuman life and loves as a lion in the wilds of Africa. What form I next may take remains with the fates. I feel that I am not yet fit, though sufficiently ethereal, to become an angel. Yet a while I must remain and fight the world, the flesh, and the devil.

"The corpse of the man slain in battle looks better than the living soldier who has saved himself by flight; therefore will I still do battle. Flight in my case means suicide, or euthanasia, as the modern advocates of the right of man to shuffle off this mortal coil are pleased by a Greek euphemism to term it.

"'Where's Gerunto now? And what's become of him? Gerunto's dead because he could not swim.' For Gerunto, let One-eyed Pete be understood; and for 'could not swim,' be more definite and say could not swim the great deep of gin he carried within, and which in its undertow carried him off, probably landing him—

In the Domdaniel caverns
Under the roots of the ocean.

"A good man was the One-eyed. With his many faults he still had his virtues, and often had a 'half.'

"'Old Ben'—my name! Now, by the two-headed Janus, mine ears hear aright, and are not deceived by wizards that mow and mutter. And oh, doubly blest in hearing, they hear an invitation to 'stand in'—to sacrifice to the rosy god. 'Tis Fiddler Phil invites, a very Philip of Macedon for drink, but for any judgment he may ever give there will be no appeal; he is never 'Philip sober.' Drink! I would now drink with a pig-eyed Mongolian—a painted Piute, shock-headed autochthon of the deserts! Drink! Yes, I would drink with the base-born Judean himself—would drink from a skull in the halls of Valhalla—drink anything, if it were but drink! My humble bowels make no aristocratic suggestions. The paltry heats and animosities of the day are forgotten. I embrace my Trinkbruder. Philip, my brother, I smell the sweet winds of the wild groves of Blarney, suggestive of illicit stills and mountain dew! My voice is for whiskey:

> Whate'er the standard tipple, whiskey's best
> To greet the coming, speed the parting guest!
> And he that will this truth deny,
> Down among the dead men let him lie.

"In, in, my noble Philip! Let's 'vex with mirth the drowsy ear of night.' What is wealthy, bloated ease to jocund content? We'll sing a reckless roundelay:

> Gin by pailfuls, wine in rivers,
> Dash the window glass to shivers.

"Produce, Philip—bring forth! Behold, dispenser of stimulants, behold the filthy lucre, the root of evil! Set forth thy flagons—put the enemy in battle array!

"Ha! the timepiece smites one, but we heed it not. We're not of the weak, the vain, the vacillating good. We are of the living dead.

"Custodian of intoxicants, the enemy!—set forth—no frowns. On my soul, I'd rather be cursed in Hungarian by a female gypsy than see thee frown!

"Here's to thee, Philip! Man, thou'rt a credit to thy great namesake and to this dædal earth. With such men as thee let me live; with such let me be buried!

"Fiddler Philip, wielder of a sceptre of ebony and horse hair! we'll make a night of it; we'll emulate the fate of Milo of old, who tore the oak and by the oak was torn! And again, here's to thee, my noble Philip! I look toward you."

Washoe Zephyrs

Marier's Room

A Washoe Lodging-house Experience.

$\mathcal{A}$mong the keepers of lodging houses in this argentiferous land one occasionally finds a landlady who far excels the heathen Chinee in ways that are dark and tricks that are vain. She is, to all outward appearance, serene as a summer's day, and, seemingly, her ways are ways of pleasantness, and all her paths are peace; but in reality she is at war with all mankind, and in artifices she is simply Luciferian.

When you sally forth in search of lodgings, the smiling landlady no sooner learns your business than her voice mellows and she stands before you one of the most kindhearted and motherly middle-aged female personages it has ever been your good fortune to meet.

Mrs. Tabitha Smiley

Thus, when I called at Mrs. Smiley's, Mrs. Smiley, a most robust inveigler of the weary and heavy laden, put on her receiving face and said: "My child, I have just what will suit you. You don't look strong. Have you been sick, my poor boy? Just step this way, please. Here we are. Ah! The door is locked. I must always keep my doors locked—

One of the best of Dan's many boardinghouse dramas. See his novelette, "Tom Bently; or Love, Art and Gold." From the *Territorial Enterprise*, December 6, 1874.

there is so many sneak thieves about nowadays, you know, sir. Now, you must always keep your door locked, sir—the sneak thieves are so bad. Ah! yes; the door is locked; the Chinaman has the key, but I'll call him. Wing Lee! Ho! Wing Lee! You, Wing Lee! You good-for-nothing, where are you?"

The Chinaman, a shrewd-looking, pig-eyed rascal, who was chambermaid and also man-of-all-work, finally made his appearance with the key, and the door of the room in front of which we stood was unlocked. When the door swung open Mrs. Smiley struck an attitude at the entrance, crying: "There, sir! Ain't it lovely? There is a bed, sir, fit for a prince! Double-spring mattress, with genuine curled hair—no pulu there, sir—and all the kivers of the best! Chairs, washstand, readin' stand—to put at the head of your bed if you are fond of readin' o'nights, sir, as some is—towel rack, beautiful lamp, and everything heart could desire!

"You see, sir," continued she, "all of them alabastered vases, them bronge statutes, the purcelain fixtures, the chromoed picturs and them air imidges in terra-incognita—lovely, ain't they?"

Beginning to warm to her work, she cried, with great enthusiasm: "This, sir, is 'Little Mary and her Lamb,' and this is a pictur of the 'Crucifixtion'—shows how our Savior suffered on Cavalry. This here, in bronge, is Don Quickset, a powerful knight who went and fit with the Crewsajers, in werry ancient times."

Sainted Marier!

"Ah, poor fellow!" said I; "poor fellow"—for I was thinking of the Don.

"You may well say so," remarked Mrs. Smiley; "you may well say so, for I believe he was killed by the bustin' of a windmill. Also, sir, you may be supprised at seein' of everything so tasty; but sir, it was my dear darter's room," and Mrs. Smiley lifted a corner of her apron to her left eye.

"Ah!" sighed I, looking solemnly heavenward.

"She's not dead! Oh, no, sir!" cried Mrs. Smiley.

"Ha!" cried I; "she lives?"

"She does, sir," said Mrs. Smiley, "and I believe she's quite hearty—thank you, sir. She is over to school in California—over to the high school at Bernecia, where I hear she is makin' great progress in the French tung. I hate offully to rent her room, but these 'ere times, sir—what with the licenses, taxes, and all that—why, we must do a many things as we don't like."

Turning suddenly toward a window, she said: "Beautiful view you'll obsarve, sir, from this 'ere south winder? From this winder, you'll obsarve, you can see the top of Mount Davinson—you can even see the flagstafft up at the top! Marier—the name of my dear child, now over to Bernecia, sir—Marier she us't to admire to look up there at that air landscape. You'll have the use of the bal-*cony*, too, sir. From the bal-*cony* the view off east is perfectly charming, as the sweet child very frekently would remark. You can see clean out to the Twenty-two-mile Desert!"

Making the Bargain

"But the rent, madam! What rent do you ask?" cried I.

"The price of the room, my dear child? I hardly know what to say. The fact is, I've not bin rentin' this 'ere room. Bein' as it were formerly my darters boodwo-*ra*, I've in a manner kept it sakerd."

"Well," said I, "the price?"

"Oh, yes, the price!" cried Mrs. Smiley. Well, sir, I'm sure you won't think $45 a month out o' the way for sich a room—with any little thing I can do for you in case of sickness, and a bed fit for a prince, and busts and picturs, and bronges and terra incog—."

"Thirty dollars is all I can give," was my answer, firmly spoken.

"What! *Thirty dollars* for this room? Oh, no, sir! Why, my dear child, wherever could you a bin stoppin' at previously? See the home comforts!" cried Mrs. Smiley, growing red in the face with enthusiasm; "see the works of art! But, hows'ever, as I like your looks, we'll say $40. Dear me! what would Marier say to this? Her own room, too!—the dear child's boodwo-*ra!* There, now, it is over!—the room is yours at $40! Will you send your trunks and things this afternoon? You, Wing Lee! That Chinaman has gone again, and you will want the key to the room. Oh, but you will be snug here, sir!—What! You can't pay $40?"

Thus we fight it down—$5, and, finally, $2.50 a round—till at last Mrs. Smiley, very red in the face and apparently completely exhausted, says: "It would break the heart of that poor child if she knowed it, but somehow I've taken sich a likin' to you—jist as I may say while we have bin a talkin' together—that to help you—as I see that you're not in any big payin' business—to help you, my child, I'm willin' to sakerfize my own intrusts. Well, then, if I must I must, and you can have it for the $30—$30 in advance, understand!"

Mysterious Disappearances

To make a long story short, I took the room—the room, "Mary and Her Lamb," Don "Quickset," and all the rest of the "bronges" and "terra incognitas."

For about four days all went well. The fifth night, when I came home, I observed that I had a broken-nosed pitcher; also, my easy chair had disappeared. "Doubtless the Chinaman's mistake," I said.

In a day or two I missed "Mary and Her Lamb" and the "Crucifixtion" on "Cavalry"; next went a few of the vases and some of the more startling terra incognita imidges; after these departed the warlike old Don and all of his fellows in bronge.

"Rather strange!" say I, but I arrive at the conclusion that Mrs. Smiley thinks that I do not appreciate these works of art as I should; or that she has concluded that they—they being the goods and gods of her sweet Marier—should not be profaned by the daily gaze of sacrilegious eyes.

Soon my reading stand, towel rack, my lamp, and even the lace curtains from the windows disappeared—also my last chair goes. The sneak thieves so dreaded by Mrs. Smiley now came into my head—they were gradually stripping the room!

I now, for the first time, remembered that I had not seen Mrs. Smiley since taking the room. I also recollected that in the last interview, when she said "Thirty dollars in advance, understand!" she forgot her dulcet, motherly tone, and her voice had a harsh, metallic ring—the chink of hard gold!

I resolved to see her and tell her how things were going, but every day the Chinaman, Wing Lee, met me with: "Madam gone out; she gone downtown. Yes; *sure* she go downtown!"

The end of my first month was now approaching, and one fine night I went home and found my fine bed—fit for a prince—gone, while in its place stood a little rickety three-quarter concern.

Tabitha Was Equal to the Emergency

This was the feather too much, and I besieged the house in season and out of season, rushing in whenever I could snatch a moment from my business. Finally, I pounced down upon the old lady and turned

loose upon her all the batteries of my wrath. Bless me! She was as
serene as a Mayday morning. She had known all along how things
had been going. She didn't blame me for the loss of the bronges and
other fine things—"no, poor child, he wasn't to blame!" She had had
the "perlice to work constantly for three weeks. It's the nasty sneak
thieves!" said she.

"But," said I, "how about that fine bed? The sneak thieves didn't
take that and bring in a little, old, rickety three-quarter—"

"Oh, my, no! But the bed—you must have noticed it, sir?—the
bed was sadly out of repair. The little spirous springs was all smashed
down and I've sent it to the upholster man to have it fixed. It will be
home tomorrer; then you can have it again."

About the broken-nosed pitcher she gave Wing Lee all the blame;
also, about the chairs and many other things—but all should be
"'tended to." The curtains were "taken down to be washed," and
finally all seemed right enough, except that there was not a decent
article of furniture of any kind left in my room, and for over a
fortnight I had been reduced to a tallow candle.

The next day, and the next, and the next, I saw no Mrs. Tabitha,
but I finally saw her, and she abused the upholster man at a great rate.

Petard Takes Marier's Room

A day or two after, as I was leaving my denuded room, I met in the
hall my friend Petard, secretary of the Hoist Gold and Silver Mining
Company.

"Hello!" said he, and "Hello!" said I. Petard informed me that he
was rooming in the house, and invited me into his room to take a
cigar.

"Been lodging here nearly a week," says Petard, as we enter his
room.

No sooner have I entered than my eyes begin to expand, as they
roam about the room. There before me on the mantel stands that
masterpiece of modern art, "Little Mary and Her Lamb"; nearby is
Don "Quickset," the warlike, and all the other bronges, while on the
wall fames the "Crucifixtion," and other familiar "picturs." Looking
further, I see my lamp, lace curtains, reading stand, and, last but not
least, my bed! That bed, "fit for a prince!" and nearly all lost from my
room I here see snug and safe in the room of my friend Petard.

I vigorously puff the cigar, which by this time I have lighted, and neither by word nor look give Petard any hint of the discovery I have made. Finally, I venture the remark: "Petard, this is a very snug room in which I find you quartered."

"Yes," complacently assents Petard.

"Good many works of art?" said I.

"Well," said Petard, "the room is good enough, but as for the works of art, as you are pleased to call them—bah! Horrible things, most of them! It is a room," continued Petard, "that the landlady has never before let. It was formerly occupied by her daughter Maria, a young lady who is now at school at Benicia, California. She must be an exceedingly romantic young lady! Why, Mrs. Smiley tells me that she would sit for hours at that north window, gazing out there at that old pile of rotten granite called Cedar Hill—that she thought that dirty old wart on the face of creation perfectly magnificent! Queer taste, I must say!" sneers Petard.

Marier's Room Again Becoming Restive

All this time Petard is seated on the side of that bed, while I occupy the only chair in the room. Presently he says: "I did have a nice easy chair in the room when I first came, but it disappeared a day or two since. Some of the Chinaman's blundering, I presume; and—blast his almond eyes!—I see that he has given me an old cracked washbowl! also, is throwing off on some other little things."

I see that the game has been commenced with my friend Petard; but I only ask what rent he is paying. He tells me $40 per month, and thinks it rather high; but says he could do no better at the time he took it—"didn't have time to look about much." I take my departure, leaving Petard smoking his cigar and musingly studying the "Crucifixtion."

In going downtown I made inquiries of two or three friends in regard to furnished rooms. One of them carelessly asked my present camping place. When I mentioned Mrs. Smiley's, a gleam of light, showing suddenly awakened interest, flashed across his broad, good-humored countenance. "What!" cried he, "are you housed in Marier's room?—her boodwo-ra?—and is the sweet child still at Bernicia studying the Frentch tung?"

I fear that I blushed slightly as I made answer that, for a time, the boodwo-ra was mine; but I lost no time in explaining that our mutual friend, Petard, was now the happy possessor of that mythical apartment—the "Crucifixtion," the knightly Don, and all the movables.

Sainted Marier, but a Beautiful Dream

My friend laughed long and heartily before proceeding to explain that he, too, at one time reveled in the possession of Marier's room. He then went on to tell me that Maria was a myth; at least as painted by Mrs. Smiley. "The only daughter she ever had," said my friend, "was a grass widow when she first struck the Comstock range, and she was not here a month before she ran away to Montana with a faro dealer. Mrs. Smiley," proceeded he, "has but about three sets of decent furniture in her whole house and these, or the component parts thereof, she is constantly moving from room to room, in order to catch anywhere from $25 to $45 in the shape of rent in advance. Her other rooms—those not Marier's—only bring her in from $12 to $15 per month. I have known her to get $40 three times in one month for Marier's room, just by parties raising a row and leaving when the work of stripping began. Few persons have ever stuck to the old lady as faithfully as you have done. She must have been fearfully disgusted with your powers of endurance, your forbearance, and your infernal good nature!"

I saw it all. That very day I found new quarters. A fortnight after, I met Petard and asked him how he liked Marier's room.

"D——n Marier's room!" cried he. "Do you know that—?"

But I knew it all. My friend Abijah Clayton now has Marier's room; he moved in only two days ago and is very happy among all those bronges and terra incognitas.

Angry Wives of Virginia

Red Hair Almost as Dangerous as Fire as a Plaything.

---

*B*rown and Jones are partners in the dry goods business. One morning early when Brown was wending his way from his residence on Howard Street to his place of business on South C Street, he found lying at the edge of the sidewalk, where it had evidently blown from the planks, a small wisp of fiery red hair—what the ladies call a "switch." Picking it up, he said to himself: "Now I'll have some fun with that steady-going old partner of mine. Before the week is out it'll be hot for him at his house. I'll get Mrs. Jones into his wool!"

Three or four days after this, when Jones came back from his dinner, he said to his partner, Brown: "Brown, do you know rather a curious thing happened to me yesterday and the day before and has happened to me again today—a devilish strange kind of thing! Day before yesterday my wife found a long, red, undoubted female hair on my coat collar. I thought nothing of it and she didn't seem to think much about it—easy enough for it to get there by accident, you know—but yesterday when I went home she found two such hairs on my coat and naturally was a little riled. Today, however, I'll be blowed if she didn't find three or four long red hairs on my coat and picked them off and showed them to me. Where I could have got

---

A backfired practical joke. From *Territorial Enterprise,* April 11, 1878.

them beats my time. Told my wife so—told her I had no idea how they got there. She said 'of course I hadn't,' that I 'must have caught them floating in the breeze.' Then I said: 'In passing some lady on the street her switch might have blown across my shoulder and left the hairs there.' She said: 'Nothing more likely, and nothing more likely than that you should meet a woman three evenings in succession whose switch blew across your shoulders, and nothing more likely than that in each instance the switch should belong to a woman with red hair.' She said all this coolly and calmly, but with a little twitching about the corners of her mouth and a sort of quivering of the nostrils that I never like to see, then dropped the subject.

Now, how those hairs came on my coat I can't imagine, without I did accidentally brush against some lady with auburn ringlets. But I am confident my wife don't believe that possible. During dinner, and while I was at home, I several times caught her looking at me in such a way as I never observed before—like she was trying to study out in me some unknown and hitherto unsuspected capacity. Now tell, Brown, have there been many redheaded women in the store during the past three days?"

"Not one, as you well know. Oh, you old innocent, just as though you didn't know how those hairs came there and from whose head! Oh, Jones, you sly old rat! A redhead has brought you at last—has fired your venerable heart!"

"Nonsense, sir—d——d nonsense! Do you suppose I've lived to the age of fifty in a quiet and correct way to at last lose my head all on a sudden and begin running after suspicious characters?"

"That's the way you steady, exemplary old cocks generally go when you make a flop of it."

"Why, blast me, Brown, you talk and look just as though you thought it all over with me. I haven't been near any woman—I don't know a thing about those hairs!"

"Oh, no, it's not all over with you; not at all, but you must own that the finding of the hairs was rather a suspicious circumstance—you yourself thought it was curious, or you would not have spoken of it, and your wife evidently thought it not only curious but also rather suspicious."

"My wife," said Jones, and a troubled expression for a moment shaded his face, "well, yes, but then you know when there is a thing of the kind that you are unable to fully explain, a woman is liable to see more in it than there really is. It is of no use that you tell her the plain, unvarnished truth, that it is a thing you know nothing about, and which you can in no way account for; her active brain will imagine beyond all you can say."

"Yes, that is very true. Now, seeing two or three long, red hairs that have by some accident become attached to your clothing, she at once takes the very extravagant notion that those hairs must have belonged to some redheaded woman, and is so unreasonable as to suppose that the head from which the hairs came must have been near the place where they were found; and even the fact of finding these hairs on your coat three days in succession don't seem to convince her of the utter groundlessness of her suspicions."

"I know—there is no use of denying it—things do look rather against me, but I swear to you that no redheaded woman has, to my knowledge, been within a rod of me, and that no woman's head has been on my shoulder!"

"Very well; I am sure you tell the truth, but the great point is to convince your wife."

"My wife—aye, there's the rub!"

The very next evening after this conversation Jones rushed into the store and cried:

"Brown, the devil is in it! More hairs—half a dozen of 'em and all the same old color! My wife has lost patience, and what can I say? How can I explain a thing I know nothing about? The more I tell her this the more vexed she becomes, and says I ought at least to have the decency to brush the hairs off my coat before making my appearance in the streets. This thing is beginning to worry me. I shall brush my coat every day hereafter before going home."

The next day Jones brushed his coat before leaving the store. Brown accompanied him to the door to see that he was all right, but when he came back from dinner he was like a wild man. More hairs than ever before had been found on his coat, and there had been a regular scene between him and his wife.

The next day Jones got Brown to brush his coat, to make sure that it was all right. He happened to stand between two mirrors that hung on opposite walls of the store, and just as Brown was pronouncing him all right he made a discovery. All was plain to him in a moment, and he said to himself: "So, so, Mr. Brown; I'll show you that two can play at that game!"

274

Without appearing to notice anything, Jones saw where Brown tucked away the snarl of hair and then took his departure, stopping at a barber shop on his way home, however, to get his coat brushed.

When he returned to the store he growled more than ever about the hairs on his coat, all of which Brown enjoyed hugely.

Meantime, Mrs. Jones had visited Mrs. Brown and told her of her suspicions in regard to some of the visitors of the store over which their husbands presided—told her all about the red hairs, in fact. Mrs. Brown had never seen any red hairs on her husband's clothing, and was therefore of the opinion that the woman did not visit the store.

Three or four days after this talk between two wives, Mrs. Brown called upon Mrs. Jones in a state of great heat and excitement. Said she: "Do you know, Mrs. Jones, that for two or three days past my husband has come home with a lot of just such hairs as you described to me on his coat. At first there were but one or two, then more and more of them. I never said a word to him about them, the deceitful wretch, but I'll find out who that redheaded hussey is before I am many days older. Let them think I am not on the watch; it will then be all the easier to catch them."

"How long has it been since you began to see the hairs on your husband's coat?" said Mrs. Jones.

"Just three days," was the answer.

"It is strange," said Mrs. Jones, musingly, "but do you know that for the past three days I have seen nothing of the kind on my husband's clothes."

The ladies looked at each other wild eyed for the space of a minute, then Mrs. Brown spoke the mind of both in saying: "Can it be possible that they are partners in everything?"

"That woman visits the store every afternoon as sure as we are alive!" cried Mrs. Jones "If we have a grain of sense we shall be able to surprise the hussey, whoever she may be, when we can give her what she desires."

"You are right. Let us give her a nice little surprise tomorrow," said Mrs. Brown. "I'll send the Chinaman for two good rawhides, and we'll give the hussey a taste of them, no matter how high she may be holding her head at present."

The next day, along in the afternoon, Brown says to Jones: "I wonder what our wives are up to? I've seen them pass along by the opposite side of the street three or four times in the last hour."

"Oh they are just out sauntering about to see how their acquaintances are dressing this spring. Things of that kind are all women think of."

Presently a very stylishly dressed young lady came into the store and asked to see some goods. She was young and handsome, but had a perfect cataract of fiery red hair. As she was the daughter of one of the wealthiest citizens of a neighboring town, the two merchants never gave her red hair a thought but both obsequiously busied themselves in taking down and showing her the costly goods she had asked to see.

The two men were so busy with their goods and the praise of them that neither of them observed the two shawled women who swiftly glided into the store until they were upon their customer, were shouting: "You hussey, you're caught at last!" and were plying their cowhides with fearful effect.

A pile of red hair lay on the floor in an instant, and the three women were locked together, spitting, sputtering, and clawing like a trio of cats.

Brown and Jones recognized their wives, at once understood the whole business, and in a second were over the counter. Each man grasped his wife and, in spite of her struggles, drew her away, when the customer, thus left at liberty, darted hatless and almost hairless into the street, shrieking: "Police! Police!"

Here was a go. Brown undertook to hold the two wives, while Jones ran out after the young lady.

Mrs. Jones clawed Brown with the ferocity of a tigress, seeing which Mrs. Brown got her hands into the hair of Mrs. Jones, and poor Brown had a good deal of business on his hands when Jones and a policeman appeared on the scene with the young lady, who was crying and frightened nearly out of her wits.

"Gentlemen, I hope you will have the goodness to explain this racket?" said the policeman.

Both men began talking when the policeman said: "One at a time, if you please, and we'll get at the business all the sooner."

Brown then told of finding the switch, and the joke he had played on Jones with the hairs extracted from it, and to prove that he was telling the truth produced what remained of the hair. "But," said he, "I can't understand why my wife should feel so venomous about the matter."

"I can," said Jones, and then explained in what way he had detected Brown's little trick, and how he had paid him back in his own coin.

"And so there was no woman coming here after all?" cried both wives in a breath.

"Not the shadow of one!" said the two husbands.

It was then from the wives, "dear George" and "dear Charles," how we have wronged you!

"And how you have both wronged me!" cried the young lady, now thoroughly recovered from her fright, but blazing like a meteor with anger.

"Oh, you dear, good girl; you poor creature; we have indeed done you a great wrong, and we beg your pardon a thousand times!" cried the two wives. "You shall go home with us at once and hereafter you'll have no better friends than we shall show ourselves to be to you," and the two wives patched up the now pacified young lady, and, drawing their veils over their faces, the feminine trio departed.

After they were gone, Jones and Brown gazed at each other for some time in silence, when the latter said: "A nice pair of jokers we are!"

"It's dangerous playing with fire," said Jones, "and I believe red hair is the next thing to it!"

An Untold Tale

*The Great Story About Honey-stealing—
A Disappointed Audience.*

---

*T*he foreman of a certain mine counted among the Comstocks, having reason to think that the men working in a particular drift were doing a good deal of soldiering, took occasion the other day to satisfy himself in regard to their underground operations. Quietly advancing along the drift, without a warning light of any kind, he found the men all comfortably seated with their backs braced against the side walls.

One of them was just saying: "I presume I can tell you the greatest story about stealing honey that any of you ever heard."

"Will you be kind enough to hold on with that story?" said the foreman, coming to the front.

Instantly all the men were on their feet. As they were fairly caught, however, it was useless to make a sudden show of industry. They therefore awaited somewhat anxiously what further their foreman might have to say.

He then proceeded: "You see, if you tell your wonderful honey

---

Storytelling is for newspapers, not for men supposed to be at work. From *Territorial Enterprise*, March 17, 1877.

story here, but few of the men in the mine will be able to hear it. Now, as it is undoubtedly a very amusing thing, I wish all the men to have the pleasure of listening to it. Go on with your work, and this evening you shall tell the story at the boardinghouse, when all may hear it."

With this the foreman turned and marched away, while the men fell to work heartily, feeling much ashamed of having been caught soldiering.

That evening after supper, much to the surprise of the workmen of the mine, all were requested to remain, as a matter of great importance was about to be brought to their notice. All remained, wondering what was coming. Not a few feared there was to be a heavy draft or a general discharge. All were next asked to range themselves around the room on chairs, properly placed for a comfortable lean against the walls. The cooks, waiters, and dishwashers were next called in and seated. A large armchair was then placed at the upper end of the room, to a seat in which the hero of the great honey story was invited.

The foreman then stated to the meeting that he had in store for them a great treat—nothing less, indeed, than the most remarkable story about stealing honey ever heard since the invention of that industrious insect, the honeybee. The story would be told them by the gentleman occupying the armchair at the head of the hall. Said gentleman had intended relating the story to a few men that day in one of the drifts of the mine, but he had been prevailed upon to await the present opportunity, when all would be able to hear the best thing of the age.

All eyes were turned toward the blushing occupant of the armchair, who was so bewildered and stunned that for a time he was unable to utter a word.

"Well, the story," cried the foreman. "Begin the story!"

Something must now be done by the man in the armchair. He arose and said: "I can't tell the story here. I shall not try. You may give me my time—discharge me!"

"We are very sorry to lose the great honey-stealing story," said the foreman, "as we are all ready to hear it from first to last, but if you can't tell it we must do without it, I suppose." Turning to the men, he then said: "Here is the only place where I will have any telling of stories. When a man has a good story to tell, I shall so arrange it that he may have the use of this room and I shall discharge the next man who has a good thing to tell and refuses to relate it when called upon."

The man who is in possession of the great honey story has not yet told it, and not a man in the mine can now be induced to admit that he knows or ever knew a story of any kind. Storytelling is at a discount there.

Torture Unutterable

What a Woman Suffered to Win $50, and Why She Lost.

$\mathcal{M}$r. Morey had seated himself in his easy chair, newspaper in hand, to read up the Turco-Russian business.

"Just the way when I've anything particular to say to you, Mr. Morey; the moment you come into the house you take up your paper," and Mrs. Morey paused for a reply.

"Tell me of a time when you didn't have something to say—and something particular?"

"You speak as though I were a perfect magpie, or a poll parrot. I hope I may be allowed to speak once in a while. There is not a woman in Virginia City that talks less—"

"You are not talking now, my dear?"

"Not when you are taking the conversation to yourself."

"I presume it is the old subject—what your neighbors have got and what you have not got in the way of dress or furniture?"

"No, it is not."

"What then?"

O. Henry-style elaboration of an old wheeze about conning a woman into silence. One of Dan's "Sunday Whims and Frivolities" features. From the *Territorial Enterprise*, October 14, 1877.

"Oh, go on with your reading. I have nothing to say now. I should be sorry to disturb you."

"Nothing to say—for once you have nothing to say!"

"Nothing."

"That is good. Ha, ha, ha!—nothing to say! Now, look here, Mrs. Morey, I'll tell you what I'll do with you. I'll—"

"What?"

"I'll give you a chance for getting some of the fine things you are always talking about."

"You will?"

"I will. Now, provided you do not speak a word during the next two hours, I'll give you $50."

"Honor bright?"

"Honor bright!"

"It's a bargain! I am not to speak a word for two hours and you are to give me $50?"

"That's it."

"It's a bargain! It's a bargain—bargain!" cried Mrs. Morey, and she began dancing about the room.

"Let us have a fair understanding; you are not to speak a word or write a word during two hours, and if you do not I am to give you $50."

"Yes, $50."

"You may laugh, cry, and dance about to your heart's content, but not one intelligible word must you utter."

"I understand—then I get the $50?"

"Of course, if you win."

"If I win! You may just as well give me the $50 now—I am sure of it. Why, I'd be sure of it were the time three hours—four hours—eight hours!"

"All right. It is now three minutes to two o'clock P.M.—at two o'clock you start in, at four o'clock you win—that is, provided you do not speak in the meantime."

At two o'clock, precisely, Mrs. Morey closed her lips hard together. Her eyes twinkled roguishly, and she shook her finger at her husband, as much as to say: "Now I begin—not a word shall you induce me to speak!"

Mr. Morey read quietly for some twenty minutes, then suddenly said: "Hattie, the children were not at school today. What can have become of them?"

Not a word from Mrs. Morey—only a smile and a look that said: "No you don't."

Again Mr. Morey read for some time, when he cried: "Ha! What is that I see! Your sister Ellen married to that old hunks, Hiram Todd!"

Mrs. Morey smiled, shook her head, and, with her eyes, said: "Too thin—try again!" Then she laughed and waltzed about the room, as much as to say: "Oh haven't I a good thing for that $50!"

Mr. Morey tried several similar dodges without avail. Nearly an hour had passed and not a word had his wife yet spoken. Her chance for winning the $50 seemed good. Mrs. Morey was jubilant, and laughed, danced, and snapped her fingers.

Finally Mr. Morey happened to look out at the window, and saw at his front gate Mrs. Brownson, the wife of his partner. Assuming a serious and frightened look, he ran to meet the lady. In a few words he told her that he had just started in search of her—that his wife had suddenly lost her speech, and, he feared, her reason as well.

Mrs. Brownson, a timid little creature, turned pale at once and looked much frightened. She even showed signs of beating a retreat, but Mr. Morey caught her by the arm and hurried her into the house, begging her to see his wife and do all she could to restore her speech and reason.

"Oh, my dear Mrs. Morey," cried Mrs. Brownson, "your husband has been telling me that you are very, very ill—that you have lost your speech."

Mrs. Morey burst into a merry peal of laughter, as though she thought it an excellent joke. Mrs. Brownson stared wildly at her and was evidently not a little alarmed, but finally managed to say: "Speak to me, Hattie, dear—tell me that your tongue is not paralyzed!"

Mrs. Morey laughed loudly and merrily, then put out her tongue to show that she had full use of that member. To further explain she went to the clock. She pointed to the figure 2, then to 4, when she took some silver coins from her pocket and made believe she was counting a considerable sum of money, looking at her husband and laughing as she did so.

"Just the way she has been going on for nearly an hour; she

evidently thinks there is something wrong with the clock," said Mr. Morey, speaking in a low tone, yet so loud that his wife might overhear.

Mrs. Morey darted upon him and boxed his ears in a playful way that was meant to express some such thing as "Why, you great story-teller, how can you talk so?" Then she hugged and kissed Mrs. Brownson, to show that lady that she was perfectly sane.

Mrs. Brownson did not so construe her actions, however. On the contrary, she thought Mrs. Morey was rapidly growing violent, and instead of returning her caresses, released herself as soon as possible, and, throwing herself into a chair, burst into tears, trembling in every limb.

To reassure her, Mrs. Morey ran to her side, and, laughing immod-erately, again tried to embrace her.

"Take her away! Take her away!" cried Mrs. Brownson, springing to her feet and running to Mr. Morey for protection.

Mrs. Morey began to look serious and puzzled. Soon, however, she ran to the clock and pointing again to the figures 2 and 4, opened her mouth, put out her tongue and laughed merrily, as she thought, but insanely as a bedlamite, as it appeared to Mrs. Brownson.

At this juncture the little boy and girl of the Moreys, aged respec-tively nine and six, came darting in from school. Their faces were radiant with happiness, and both at once began to tell their mother some wonderful bit of news.

"Why don't you say something, mama?" cried they, looking astonished.

"Your poor mama has lost her speech—she can't talk," said Mr. Morey.

"Can't you talk, mama?" cried they.

Mrs. Morey nodded her head, laughed and kissed them, but the little ones looked frightened and clamored for her to speak to them.

"My poor dears, your mother has lost her speech," said Mr. Morey, solemnly.

"Poor little dears!" cried Mrs. Brownson, and burst into tears. Both children followed her example, crying bitterly.

It was after three o'clock. In less than an hour Mrs. Morey would win the $50 if she remained silent, and she determined that as she had gone so far, no power on earth should make her speak. She pointed to the clock, laughed, and tried all manner of pantomime in order to show that she was all right and could speak if she chose to do so, but this only served to frighten Mrs. Brownson and the children all the more. Hastily whispering a few words to Mr. Morey, Mrs. Brownson left the house. She ran to the houses of two or three of the neighbors and told them the terrible news that Mrs. Morey had suddenly lost her power of speech and was, beside, a raving maniac; that she had tried to kill Mr. Morey, and she feared that ere now she might have killed her children. Three or four boys were sent for physicians, and soon half a dozen women were found who had the courage to move upon the house of the Moreys in a solid body.

They found Mrs. Morey weeping and laughing by turns, while Mr. Morey, apparently utterly broken down and hopeless, sat with his face buried in his handkerchief, sobbing convulsively, as it seemed. He merely looked up when the female delegation arrived, pointed to his wife, then buried his face in his handkerchief and again visibly shook in every limb.

Mrs. Morey's face was flushed, her eyes were red and had a wild look, yet she tried to laugh, and by various gestures and embraces strove to reassure her friends.

It was 3:30 o'clock. In half an hour she would be at liberty to relate the joke—in half an hour she would have the $50. It would then be a big joke on her husband and it would be a triumph for her sex—all would applaud her self-control and courage. Nothing should make her utter a word—no, nothing!

Finding that she could not be made to utter a word; that she only laughed or wept hysterically, and kept her eyes fixed upon or with her fingers pointed to the clock, the ladies, her neighbors, decided that she must be put to bed and, if need be, tied there.

The ladies advanced upon Mrs. Morey in full force, Mr. Morey, poor soul, seeming to be utterly broken down and unable to do anything to assist them. They were in the midst of a fearful struggle with Mrs. Morey—who was a large and strong woman—when the doctors began to arrive. The children were screaming at the top of their voices; the women were all coaxing and scolding at once; Mrs. Morey's long golden tresses were streaming below her waist, and Mr. Morey was moaning and groaning with his face in his handkerchief, when two physicians came rushing in together.

They at once seized upon Mrs. Morey and tried to force her down into a chair. This she at first stoutly resisted, pointing to the clock and gesticulating wildly, but she was finally obliged to seat herself.

"It's in the clock—it's something about the clock that is troubling her! She's constantly watching and pointing toward the clock!" cried the ladies.

A gleam of hope passed over the face of Mrs. Morey. She thought she might in some way make the doctors understand the situation, therefore she again pointed toward the clock, though she was not permitted to rise and approach it; went through the pantomime of counting money and pointing to her husband, who was staring at her with his eyes just peeping over his handkerchief.

"Yes, it is evidently in the clock or about money matters or in regard to her husband—they take all manner of queer cranks," said one of the physicians.

"It's strange she is unable to speak," said the other, "as I see she puts out and moves her tongue quite freely—evidently it is not paralyzed."

"The lolling of the tongue," said the first physician, "is a mere animal movement and may be quite involuntary; I've often seen 'em do it—it proves nothing."

Two more physicians arrived about this time, and soon all four quite understood each other. The poor lady was insane, but it might be only temporarily so. They would do all they could for her relief.

"Poor thing! poor thing!" moaned the neighbor women. "Oh, oh!" groaned Mr. Morey within his handkerchief.

Mrs. Morey saw that in five minutes more she would win, and she pointed to the clock and laughed loud and long. Soon she would be at liberty to speak, and oh, the fun she would have.

One of the doctors whispered to a lady, who nodded and went into another room; two doctors then tightly grasped Mrs. Morey's arms and held her firmly in her chair. The lady who had left the room returned with a pair of scissors in her hand.

"It is a great pity that we are obliged to do it," said one of the physicians, taking the scissors, "but her hair must come off, her head must be shaved, a blister must be applied and she must then be put to bed and kept there."

"Oh, oh!" groaned Mr. Morey.

The doctor had grasped a large tress near the top of Mrs. Morey's head and she felt the cold scissors pushed across her scalp. In two minutes the clock would strike four and she would win the $50. She struggled to free herself, but the two strong men held her in the chair.

"Oh, you wretches—you fools!" cried she—"you call yourselves doctors! I am as well as any of you and have a thousand times more sense this minute. You have made me lose $50! Release me, you idiots!"

The doctors looked surprised at hearing Mrs. Morey speak, but it was only for a moment. One of them said: "Hold her fast. Her silence was only a freak. They do all manner of curious things."

The man with the scissors again had his hands in Mrs. Morey's hair, but her tongue was now free and she made good use of it. "My husband was to give me $50 not to speak a word in two hours and you four fools have made me lose by two minutes!" cried she, and then rapidly proceeded to tell the whole story.

The doctors looked confused, but still incredulous, and turned toward Mr. Morey for an explanation, provided he had any to offer.

Throwing aside his handkerchief and his lugubrious air, Mr. Morey burst out in a roar of laughter that almost shook the room, and crying: "It's all true that she says!" advanced to release and embrace his wife, declaring that she was a greater heroine than Joan of Arc or any of them; but Mrs. Morey boxed his ears and broke into a torrent of tears.

"We have heard that in heaven there was once silence for the 'space of half an hour,'" said one of the doctors, "but, then, we don't know that there were any women there."

"A woman not speak a word for two hours, lacking two minutes!" said another of the wise men. "She has vindicated her sex—her praise should be sounded to the farthest corners of the earth. Such a thing has never before been known."

"Here are your $50, Hattie," said Mr. Morey, "I brought the money home today on purpose to give it to you, and without any conditions, but things happened to take that curious turn, you know."

All the women were crying in concert by this time, and retired to another room to hold a regular indignation meeting; but, sobbing bitterly as she was, Mrs. Morey first went to her husband and held out her hand for the $50.

One of the Lost

$\mathcal{B}$usiness was dull with Jacob Seibner last Sunday evening. He stood behind the bar of his saloon and yawned. Two or three pairs of old-stagers seated at tables in the further part of the saloon were playing bean poker, but there was nothing in it for Jacob. Not one of them had called for a pot of beer in the last hour. Jacob yawned again, looked at the clock, and wished it was time to turn the old stiffs out and close up, but it was not yet ten o'clock.

In order to do something that had a little the look of business, Jacob drew a glass of beer and cocking an eye at the old stove sharps over the top of the mug, drank it off at a breath.

After resting his elbows on the bar for a time, sleepily watching the door for customers that did not come, Jacob drew and drank another mug of beer, again cocking an impatient eye over its top at his unprofitable customers. He then passed out from behind his bar and took a seat by his stove, thinking it useless to tire his legs by standing when there was just as much money in resting comfortably in his chair by a good fire.

There he sat, dreamily sucking the stem of his ancient meer-

Beer drinking and logic. From the *Territorial Enterprise*, February 6, 1876.

schaum, when the door opened and there entered a tall, well-dressed, and genial-looking stranger. Jacob was behind his bar in an instant, both eyes living interrogation points.

The smooth-looking stranger advanced to the bar and called for lager beer, asking Jacob to join him in a glass, which Jacob did. The stranger praised Jacob's bar and admired the neat manner in which the saloon was arranged, saying that he had not seen a snugger place in town, or one in which there was a greater display of good taste. Jacob felt that his taste was rather good, so he asked the stranger to take a glass of beer with him.

The stranger was so well pleased with Jacob that he took some pains to amuse him. He told him a great number of wonderful stories of adventures in strange lands; about elephant hunting in India, lion hunting in Africa, kangaroo hunting in Australia, and white bear hunting among the Esquimaux at the North Pole, Jacob passing the beer every five minutes, so utterly regardless of money matters had he become while listening to the marvelous yarns of the stranger.

They had tired of standing and, with a gallon measure of beer between them, which came there Jacob did not know how, were snugly seated at a table near the stove. The stranger was still talking on, helping himself to the beer occasionally—smilingly talking and smilingly drinking on—while Jacob, with half-closed eyes, sucked at his pipe and dreamily listened.

As time passed, the fumes of the beer, those of the pipe, and the heat of the room began visibly to tell on Jacob, who had been his own best customer all day. It was only when he aroused himself and by a great effort brought all his faculties to a focus, as it were, that he understood the half of what the stranger was saying.

After a time, having exhausted his store of wonderful adventures among the wild animals and savage tribes of all parts of the world, the stranger said: "You have heard all about that fearful disaster, the loss of the steamer *Pacific*, Mr. Seibner?"

The stranger had for some time been in possession of Jacob's name, though Jacob did not remember telling it.

"Yaw; boud der *Bacific*, yaw," said Jacob.

"That was a fearful, a terrible disaster—the sinking of that magnificent steamer with her valuable cargo and her living freight of precious souls!"

"Yaw."

"Millions in precious commodities and many, many noble and beautiful women, fair and innocent children, and accomplished and brave men there went down!"

"Y-yaw," said Jacob, yawningly.

"Nothing could save them—their doom was sealed!"

"Ya-aw."

"Yet they died through no fault, no carelessness, no lack of foresight, no mismanagement of their own!"

"Ya-a-w."

"Down into the blue bosom of the broad Pacific Ocean sank the shrieking multitude."

"Y-ya-aw," and Jacob seemed almost asleep.

"Of all those who that fearful night trod the deck of that doomed steamer there are but two survivors; I am one of them—one of the two men that was saved!"

"Dat bees von tam lies!" roared Jacob, suddenly arousing himself and bringing his huge fist down upon the table with such force as to cause the beer measure to dance. "Dat bees all von tam lies!" reiterated he.

"Softly, softly, my good friend Jacob!" cried the stranger. "Why become belligerent and disagreeable? Now, understand me, if I am not one of the only two men saved on the occasion of that fearful marine disaster, you surely will not attempt to contradict me when I most solemnly assure you on my word and honor as a gentleman that I am one of the 170 that were lost?"

"Yaw, vell dot I von't disbute. Vare dare vas so many lost dat may be. Yaw, dot ish all right. Took anoder glass peer!"

A Tough Pair

The Miner and the Pill Peddler.

$\mathscr{A}$ peddler of patent medicines, whose torch had illuminated a street stand earlier in the evening, was a few nights ago seated at a table in a Comstock saloon regaling himself with a glass or two of beer, and at the same time regaling those about him with stories of his wonderful adventures in all parts of the world. He mingled a good deal of the shop with his stories and in the course of half an hour had managed to ring in two or three puffs of his wonderful mandrake pills. He had been to India, China, Japan, Mexico, South America, and many other countries and could show medals and badges of honor from a great number of princes and potentates. He had a good deal of curiosity about the mines and asked many questions in regard to the dangers and the peculiar diseases to which men working in the lower levels were exposed.

Finally a miner said that he did not know of any peculiar diseases caused by the work in the lower levels. He had heard of miners subject to attacks of soldiering, but had never been troubled that way himself. He believed the diseases of the miners were about the same as those to which persons working on the surface were exposed in this

Putting on a pill peddler, in vain. From the Carson *Free Lance,* November 9, 1885.

climate. "But," said he, "we are of course exposed to many and great dangers in the mines. I have had some pretty close calls myself."

"Indeed," said the pill peddler, "from caves or from blasts?"

"Well, a little of all kinds. About as close a call as I ever had was in a big old tunnel down at American Flat a few years ago."

"In a tunnel, eh? A deep one?"

"Well, one end of it was tolerably deep—a couple of hundred feet or so. I was working in the face of the tunnel, not dreaming of danger, when, without the slightest warning, down came about a hundred tons of dirt and rock."

"Fell near you, did it?"

"Within about fifty feet of where I was working; but that wasn't the worst of it. The cave completely blocked up the tunnel."

"You were regularly imprisoned?"

"Yes, but that wasn't the worst of it."

"What could be worse?"

"The water! The water began to rise. A stream of about twenty inches of water was coming in at the face. The cave formed a dam and the tunnel was rapidly filling up. As the water rose I went to the pile of dirt that had caved down and got upon that as the highest point. For hours the water steadily rose and before night it was two feet over the pile of dirt."

"And no one came to your assistance?"

"No, and that was not the worst of it. No one knew I was in there. I was prospecting the old tunnel on the sly."

"Why, you were in a fearful position!"

"Pretty bad, for when only the arched cavity above the tunnel remained to be filled, the water came up very rapidly. A timber had floated up into the hole and I secured it. Placing it on end, I managed to climb up and gain a footing on top of it, but in doing so I dropped my last candle and was left in the dark—nasty, moist dark that got inside of me and clogged up my lungs."

"That was the compressed air," said the pill peddler.

"Perhaps," said the miner, "but if you want darkness that you can taste, just get into such a hole. Well, finally as I sat crouched on top of my post I began to feel the water creeping up over my breast."

"My God, what a situation to be placed in!"

"Very dark and wet, I assure you. Presently the water came up to my mouth, and then to my nostrils."

"And still no help came?"

"No, I could expect none from the outside. I held my head as high as possible, but the water was in my nostrils and I could not breathe."

"I wonder you did not lose your senses!"

"I did not. I held both my breath and my senses. Yes, held my breath till my eyes almost started from their sockets, and till there seemed to dance before and around me a thousand flashes of brilliant light of all colors."

"And still you escaped?"

"I must have escaped—for I am here to tell of it."

"Of course—of course! But your case was so utterly hopeless!"

"I know—I know. Yes, it seemed hopeless, but at my last gasp—just when I was about falling from my post—a happy thought struck me, and I felt that I was saved."

"What could possibly save you from death in such a situation?"

"But one thing. In that last moment with my brain reeling and all the colors of the rainbow flashing before my eyes, I suddenly remembered that I had in the pocket of my shirt a box of your justly celebrated mandrake pills. Quick as thought I opened the box and poured its contents down into the tunnel. Instantly there was a great rumbling and gurgling below me. I found that I could breathe, and in less than three minutes that tunnel was cleaned out as clean as a shotgun!"

For a single instant the jaw of the pill peddler fell. It was but for an instant, however. In another moment his face was wreathed in smiles and leaning across the table he grasped the hand of the miner, crying: "I do not doubt it! I do not doubt it! My dear sir, do me the favor to put your statement in the form of an affidavit. It will be invaluable to me in the mining regions!"

"Well, I'll be blowed!" cried the miner, "if you ain't about the toughest I ever did see, and the beer is on me!"

Then that miner leaned back in his seat and heaved a great sigh, as he gazed in awed silence upon the calm, cast-iron countenance of the pill peddler.

Courting an Emigrant Female

$\mathcal{O}$ur Washoe bachelors are always on the *qui vive* during the last months of summer and the first and second fall months, when the emigrant trains are rolling in off the plains with whole troops of sun-browned damsels. The girls have all heard that the chances for getting husbands are awful good in Washoe. They know there are sights of chances, so they begin primping shortly after passing Independence Rock, and by the time they strike the waters of the Carson they are in a perfect state of wiggle.

My friend Condrick wanted a wife. He wanted a piece of un-sophisticated bit calico from the States. He talked much of when the trains would arrive and of pretty emigrant girls. He swore he would gobble one up this fall, sure.

At last it was reported that a big train was camped on the Carson, two miles below Dayton.

Condrick mounted his mustang and departed with alacrity.

The report proved true, and what was better—"Women absolutely abounded!" as Condrick afterwards informed me in his enthusiastic way. He rode among the tents and wagons, ostensibly much con-

---

Dan toys with his San Francisco readers in the erotic genre. From the *Golden Era,* October 2, 1864.

cerned to know exactly the state, county, and town from which each family hailed, but in reality taking notes of the fine points of all the marriageable looking females in the camp. At last he struck one that suited him to a dot.

Long afterwards, he said to me with a great sigh, which he tried to smother in a laugh, "Oh! she was a clipper! Trim as a gazelle; lithe as a willow; cheeks which (though sun-browned) showed a peachy ruddiness, with eyes—ah! such great brown swimming eyes!—that drove your soul down into your boots, dragged your heart up into your throat, and left you speechless and slaughtered.

To this sumptuous female, Condrick laid siege. His progress was good. As the shades of evening settled down upon valley and hill, he and his charmer took a stroll. As they walked along the meandering banks of the Carson, the full face of the moon rose up from behind the eastern hills. All nature seemed filled and quivering with love.

Love danced in the rays of moonlight that glanced on the stream; the willows rustled their leaves to the passing breezes and so sweetly told the story of their love that even the restless winds were for a while enticed to linger, forgetful of their journey; enamored nighthawks were skimming the love-laden air in voluptuous circles, rays of languishing light gleaming in answering flashes from their lazy wings; crickets, peeping from their holes in neighboring hillocks, chirped to each other in mellow, tremulous notes the ripe and gushing love of their surcharged hearts; beetles, crazy with love, thundered hoarsely their plaints of the tender pain that racked their mailed bodies, and the sweet honeydew of heaven fell softly into the heart-cup that each meek plant held trustingly up.

The sympathetic hearts of the lovers acknowledged the tender influences surrounding them, and shared the sweet thrills with which all nature quivered. Slowly the pair, in fond discourse, wandered on. What throbs of affection stirred Condrick's heart! What fires of love burned in Condrick's eyes. As his charmer leaned trustingly upon his arm, heaven seemed to descend and rest on the lower and nearest hills. As the murmur of a bee in a rose was her voice to his soul.

Seating themselves on a grassy bank, they gazed together on the darkling eddies of the gliding stream. In glowing colors Condrick painted for the fair being by his side a picture of the wonderful wealth hidden within the rocky vaults of the Whippoorwill mine.

Charmed by his eloquence and absorbed in the contemplation of the picture he placed before her, she forgot all else and gradually her beautiful head drooped—drooped lower and lower—and finally rested upon his bosom—his manly chest. Great heaven! A thrill darted through his frame and so affected him that it was only by a tremendous effort that he could smother the volcano of emotions swelling within his bosom. He felt a desire to bound to his feet and utter a wild whoop! But he didn't. No; he constrained his emotions; he resisted the impulse. Her head was now fairly and snugly nestled upon his breast.

As she lay gazing into his handsome face, her parted tresses of richest brown fell backward in affluent waves from her broad forehead, unkissed by the sun and of marble texture and whiteness. Her great liquid eyes looked into his and he gazed down in their unfathomable depths till all the past, all the future seemed to center there.

Heaven came down still lower and rested on the valley. But this could not always last. He felt that it could not. She seemed expecting something.

Her great eyes closed wearily and the silken fringes of their curtains rested on her cheek. He was happy as he was, but he could not be as he was forever. She seemed to have the same thoughts. She slightly raised her head. Its pressure on his chest was not so great as formerly.

He was distressed. Would she rise? Was he about to lose her? The thought was agony.

His head grew dizzy. He felt himself standing on a precipice. He was losing his balance. He was toppling over. Courage!

He gasped—gasped out his tale of love. It was not a long one. But it was to the point.

She sighed—sighed a long, long, tremendous, convulsive sigh. But she said nothing.

In a murmuring tone, he asked her if she hadn't some feelings of the same kind for him. She put her arms about his neck, and hiding her sweet face in his shirt front sobbed out in a broken voice that that was what ailed her.

Heaven let go all holds, and fell at his feet! Here followed several deep, searching, delicious kisses.

(For the gratification of my lady readers, and that they may know the exact number and duration of these kisses, I have put them all down. They were as follows, the stars representing their number, and the dashes, the duration of each: ******__*____*****_____**__ __*_*_*_____*____**_____***__**__*_____ _____-* It will be observed that the last one was of immense length. It has a tail to it like a comet. I am not sure that it was not even longer than I have represented. Condrick is not sure about it. He thinks about here he was insensible for a time.)

After all these kisses came an awkward pause. The situation, to be sure, was not an unhappy one. But again my friend felt that it was time for something more.

He had made the leap from one precipice—another was before him. He was tottering to its brink. He must speak of marriage. How would she take that?

She had acknowledged that she loved him. Good! This gave him courage. He gasped, and chokingly gulped out the question—in fear, and with his eyes tightly closed.

She clasped him more tightly about the neck, and sighed deeply. Poor Condrick! all sorts of fears attacked him. The very blood in his heart seemed congealing. He felt a drop of something moist fall on his hand. At first he thought her nose was bleeding. He held his hand aloft in the moonlight, and on it beheld a glittering tear. He felt better then. His heart gave a great leap, and he said: "Thank Heaven!"

He was now much encouraged. He again made inquiry as to her love for him. She said then, in words, that she loved him—"Oh! so, *so* much!" which for a time comforted him greatly.

Condrick now began to urge immediate marriage. She objected, but clung more closely to him, and said, "Wait awhile." Condrick wanted to know if there was any obstacle to their immediate union.

She kissed him (****____*_____*_____-*) and said there was a slight one. He then tenderly kissed her (**_____-*) and asked if they could not be married in a week. She raised her great swimming eyes to his face and gazed fondly upon him, but said nothing.

Her pouting lips were in tempting proximity to his own, (***____ *____*_____*)

He now repeated his question, when in an agonized voice she cried out: "Oh! dear, I can't tell! I've got a phthisicy old cuss of a husband out in one o' them wagons, and he's jist spiteful enough to live a month yet!"

Condrick is still a bachelor.

He had a bad spell of something like mountain fever the next day after he visited the emigrant train—at least, he went off into the mountains and shunned mankind and womankind for about two months.

But he is all right now.

Ghosts

The Frenchman's Ghost

*The Story of a Lost Mine. A Nevada Prospector's
Strange Adventure.*

---

*S*ome very rich mines are now being washed in Red Cañon district, some thirty or forty miles south of this place and off to the eastward of Genoa, Douglas County. The veins found in the district are
principally gold-bearing, and in some of them are found very rich
pockets. From these pockets, or small bonanzas, lumps of quartz are
often taken that are literally glittering with spangles of gold. Very
snug little fortunes are sometimes taken out of a single pocket.

Speaking of these mines a few days ago to Robert Morrison, our
present chief of police, he said: "Yes, there are some very rich little
mines in Red Cañon district, and there are still richer ones that
remain to be found. Among others, there is the lost mine of the old
Frenchman. The man who finds that will find a fortune. I believe that
I once saw it, but I have never since been able to find it."

"If you once found and saw the mine, why were you not able to
return to it?" I asked.

"Well, it was in the night, and in the midst of a heavy snowstorm
that I was in it; then I left it rather hurriedly. But I will tell you how I
once saw the mine, and you may then form your own opinion. It is a

---

A lost mine tale, with all the formulae of its kind, including much incidental
verisimilitude. From the San Francisco *Post,* November 28, 1885.

strange story, and one that I don't often tell since coming into my present position, as some might put me down as being a little too superstitious for the place of chief of police. However, I will relate my adventure. After all, what I saw may not have been anything super-natural—I try to think it was not."

The Chief's Story

"In 1876, early in October, I mounted a mustang, and, taking the trail by way of El Dorado Cañon and Hines' Hot Springs, I struck into the hills about Pinenut Valley, and east of the head of Red Cañon. I had heard of rich float quartz being found in that region, though at that time not much mining was being done out there. Several parties of men were engaged in cutting wood and burning charcoal at and about Pinenut, and some cattle were being tended there; also, two or three large flocks of sheep from Mariposa County, California.

"Soon after I arrived in the Red Cañon region, a sheepherder told me of a place where some of his men had frequently found pieces of quartz that showed free gold. I prospected for a day or two, and discovered several narrow veins of gold-bearing quartz that were very promising. The prospects I obtained were so good that I at once came back to the Comstock to make arrangements for opening one of the veins by means of a tunnel.

"The specimens that I was able to show were so rich that Officer Daniels, then on the police force of Virginia City, but now somewhere in New Mexico, begged me to take him in as a partner, saying that he would resign his place, go with me to the mine, and assist in its development.

"I took Daniels as a partner, and, purchasing a supply of provisions, we packed it over to the mine. At no great distance from the mine was a deserted milk ranch and on it was a cabin, of which we took possession. The cabin was just what we wanted, as it had under it a cellar in which we could keep our vegetables.

"As soon as we had put the cabin in order for the winter, we set to work in earnest at running a tunnel for the development of our mine. We hardly missed a day in the tunnel till along about the middle of November, when we one morning found that an inch or two of snow had fallen. On seeing the snow, Daniels said: 'I don't feel much in the humor for work today. Suppose we take the guns and see if we can't find a deer or two.'"

"'Agreed,' said I. 'You take the rifle and go in one direction, while I'll take the shotgun, load her with buckshot, and try my luck in the opposite quarter.'

"This being arranged, Daniels started off to the eastward, while I struck out southwest towards a black-looking mountain many miles away. I knew that the black appearance of the mountain was owing to the heavy growth of nut pine with which it was covered, and thought that there, if anywhere, I should find a herd or two of deer.

"Almost as soon as I reached the timber, I saw signs of deer, and in about half an hour saw three, one of which I killed. About this time it began blowing and snowing heavily. I therefore concluded not to attempt to pack my deer home. The storm was so bad that I thought I would be doing well to make the cabin by nightfall without any greater encumbrance than my gun. Hanging the carcass of the deer so high in a nut pine tree as to place it out of the reach of foxes and coyotes, I struck out for home. After leaving the shelter of the timber, I found the storm almost blinding. It was a regular blizzard. Though it was not very cold, yet it was a rough storm. The snow fell thick and fast, and was so whirled about by the wind that at times I could not see five rods ahead. After I had traveled for two or three hours, a lull in the storm allowed me to get a pretty good view of my surroundings, when I found that I had lost my reckoning. The hills were all new to me. I pushed ahead, however, for another hour, hoping to be able to find some known landmark; but the country grew more wild and unfamiliar as I advanced. Recognizing the fact that I was thoroughly lost, I determined not to wander too far away, but to set about hunting up a camping place before night came on.

"I first went to a big cliff that loomed up before me, hoping to find among its rocks a cavern of some kind, or at least a shelf that would protect me from the storm. I spent half an hour searching the cliff, but found no place that was tenable. Traveling on, I presently found on the side of a mountain a large, spreading nut pine tree, the branches of which were bent nearly to the ground by the snow that loaded them. The tree looked like a big tent. I crawled through an opening between the branches and found bare ground inside. I soon discovered, however, that the place was disagreeably wet. Owing to the warmth ascending from the ground—for it was the first cold spell of the season—the snow was melting and there was a constant dripping from the overarching branches. I soon found it was no good place in which to attempt to pass the night, and so I crawled out to look for better shelter. My mind still ran upon caverns and my eyes searched the hills as far as they could reach for a bluff or a big pile of rocks. Among heaped fragments of rock I might find a dry and substantial shelter in a place where I could build a fire. However, very few rocks were to be seen and the few visible were small—mere boulders.

The Haunted Tunnel

"While thus surveying my surroundings, I faced about and looked up toward the top of the hill opposite that on the slope of which I was standing. Halfway up I saw a pile of dirt that looked as if it had been dumped from a tunnel. I at once crossed over the dividing canyon and climbed the hill to inspect the place. To my great joy I found that there was indeed an old tunnel running into the face of the hill. It had so caved about the entrance, and so much debris had tumbled down from the slope of the hill that the mouth was almost closed. However, by pushing some rocks inside and dragging others out, I soon made an opening through which I could crowd.

"I found the tunnel to be about forty feet in length, with an incline at the end some thirty feet in depth. The tunnel was perfectly dry and quite warm. It was just such a place as I had been longing to find. I went outside, and with my hunting knife cut a lot of pine and cedar boughs for a bed. These I beat against the sides of the tunnel until all moisture was knocked off them, and till they were pretty thoroughly bruised and softened, when I made of them a rude couch.

"I constructed this couch at a point back some ten feet from the top of the incline, as I did not wish to lie so near that hole as to tumble into it during the night, should my sleep prove restless. I had found in one of my coat pockets a bit of candle—a stump about an inch in length, such as miners use in lighting their fuse in blasting—and this I had lighted and used while making my bed, sticking it upon a point of rock that projected from the wall of the tunnel.

"The bit of candle seemed to warm the air of the place considerably, and soon after the wick tumbled over in a last dying flicker, I fell asleep, for I was pretty well tired out. I would have liked something to eat, but there being nothing eatable at hand, I took the next best thing, which was sleep.

The Ghost at Work

"Just how long I had slept I do not know, when I was awakened by hearing the sound of a pick. At first, in my sleepy condition, I paid but little attention to this, it being a sound so familiar to my ears. But as soon as I became thoroughly awakened, I was not a little astonished at hearing the steady click, click, click of a pick in that place.

"I rose to a sitting position to listen. As I did so I observed a light reflected against the roof of the incline. I then, for the first time, perceived that the sounds of picking and hammering came from the incline. How a man could have passed through the tunnel and gone to work without awakening me I could not conceive. Then I became curious to know what the man looked like and what he was doing.

"On my hands and knees I crept to the top of the incline and peeped down into it. At the bottom I saw busily at work a man somewhat beyond middle age. He was short of stature, and an iron-gray beard covered his face. He had two candles burning, and at the moment was engaged in breaking and assorting some fragments of quartz. He was breaking the quartz on a large stone with the back of poll-pick. Near to where he was squatted stood a sack in which he placed some pieces of ore, while he threw others upon the ground.

"The man had on a pair of black pantaloons and a gray woolen shirt, and wore a small cloth cap with a large and long front piece. On a pile of rock behind him lay a brown cloth coat. I judged from the appearance of things that the man, whoever he was, had but just come into the tunnel and set to work. At first I thought he was some rambling prospector, then it occurred to me that it must be a man who was well acquainted with the spot. No stranger would be likely to find his way to such a place in the night and in the midst of a storm.

"By the light of the two candles burning down there, I could see that quite a large opening had been chambered out at the foot of the incline. Every moment I expected to see the old man look up, but his whole mind seemed to be concentrated upon the work in which he was engaged. He acted as if he had no knowledge of any person being within fifty miles of him.

The Death Scene

"Finding that the old man was so much absorbed in his occupation of breaking and assorting rock that he did not raise his head, I was about to call out to him when he arose. While he was seated I was able to obtain an imperfect view of the side of his face, but he now turned his back toward me and began picking and hammering at a large boulder that projected from the wall or breast of rock before him. This boulder was a little above the level of his head, and he appeared to be trying to break off a portion of the lower part of it with the back of his pick.

"Suddenly the boulder fell from its place. As it left its bed in the wall it appeared to pitch forward. I saw it strike the old man on the breast and bear him toward the ground. At the same instant the two candles were extinguished and there came up from the bottom of the incline the most blood-freezing shriek I ever heard.

"Until I saw the fall of the boulder and heard that fearful scream I had felt no alarm. It is true that I was a good deal astonished at seeing a man in the bottom of the incline in the dead of night and I could not imagine how he came there, yet there might have been another entrance to the chamber in which he was at work. When, however, that awful cry of agony smote upon my ears I became thoroughly frightened—I was utterly unnerved and panic-stricken.

"My wits were gone. Instinct alone remained, and that told me to make a dash for the mouth of the tunnel and the open air. Forgetting where I was, I bounded to my feet and struck my head against the rocky roof of the tunnel. This dazed me to such a degree that I do not remember how I got to the mouth of the tunnel. I may have fallen to the floor and lain unconscious for some minutes. However, I have a distinct recollection of bumping and cutting my head in my frantic efforts to get out through the small opening at the mouth of the tunnel, where I could see a gleam of sky and catch a smell of the open air.

"Once out, I ran down the side of the mountain so recklessly that I was much cut and bruised by falling over rocks, and my clothes were torn half off me by the thorny bushes through which I passed. It was not until I was completely exhausted that I ceased rushing forward at this dangerous pace. The moment I saw the fall of the rock, heard the old man's dying scream, and saw the lights go out, it flashed into my mind that the whole scene was unreal—was supernatural—and as I ran I was in constant fear of feeling the ghost clutch me from behind or leap upon my back.

"With exhaustion came some degree of calmness and reflection. In a short time I so far recovered from my fears that I no longer entertained the idea of having seen a ghost. I began to accuse myself of cowardice and lack of feeling in running away from a man whose life I might have saved; for it now occurred to me that the old man might not have been instantly killed.

"I now observed that the storm was over and that the stars were shining brightly in all parts of the heavens. I thought of trying to find my way back to the old tunnel, as I might still be in time to do some good; but I did not know in what direction to travel, for it was too dark to follow my tracks back in the snow; indeed, they could hardly have been followed in the daytime, among rocks and through patches of brush. Just at this time, too, I felt warm blood trickling down over my face. Putting up my hands, I found that I was hatless, and discovered that I had several bad cuts on various parts of my head.

The Cabin Found at Last

"After discovering my wounded condition I determined to get home as soon as possible. I did not know in what direction to move, but not wishing to stand still till daylight, I pushed forward at a tolerably brisk pace, hoping that I might be traveling toward the cabin.

"When daylight came I found that I was still in a section of country that was unfamiliar to my eyes. All the hills and mountains being covered to a depth of three or four inches with snow served to disguise them. The white coating gave to the whole face of the country a sort of uniform look. This being the case, I made my way to the highest mountain in the neighborhood, in the hope of being able to get sight of some known landmark. When I reached the summit of the mountain, I could see no familiar hill or valley; therefore, I struck out for another big mountain, two or three miles away. Before I reached this the sun was well up in the heavens, and the snow had become a slippery slush, through which it was very fatiguing to travel in my weak condition, for through want of food and loss of blood I was a good deal reduced in strength. To my great joy, when I reached the top of the second mountain, I saw my cabin and the well-known little valley in which it stood.

"The cabin was nearly three miles away, but I hobbled forward at a pretty lively gait, considering the many cuts and bruises that began to make themselves felt on all parts of my body. At last I reached the cabin, opened the door, and marched in.

"Within I found my partner, Daniels, and a man from a wood ranch about two miles away.

"'My God! What is the matter? What has happened?' cried both men as I appeared before them hatless and covered with blood.

"'Give me something to drink,' said I; 'then get me something to eat, when I'll tell you all you want to know. I am nearly famished, and must have something to eat before I tell any long stories.'

"Daniels at once set about getting me some breakfast, but could not refrain from asking me many questions. Had I encountered a bear, a California lion, a wildcat or a pack of wolves? None of these had I seen. Then what had happened? How did I become covered with blood? To all these questions I made reply that I would give them my story after breakfast, and not before. I never knew Daniels to cook a meal in less time than he did on that occasion.

"Meantime, the man from the wood ranch informed me that he and Daniels were just on the point of setting out in search of me. My absence during the whole night in the storm had alarmed Daniels, and early in the morning he had gone to the wood ranch and obtained the assistance of its owner, one of the oldest residents in that part of the country, to try to hunt me up.

The Old Frenchman and His Mine

"After breakfast I gave the two men a minute account of all that had happened [to] me from the time I left the grove where I killed the deer till I arrived in sight of the cabin. While I was describing my adventures in the old tunnel, the wood rancher interrupted me with several questions in regard to the dress and appearance of the old man I had seen at work in the bottom of the incline. When I had finished my story, he cried out:

"'Morrison, do you know that what you saw last night was the lost mine of the old Frenchman? And the man you saw at work there was no living man. You saw the ghost of the old Frenchman, who has been dead these ten years. You saw enacted the scene of his death; I am confident that he lost his life in his mine in just that way. Your fortune is made if you can again find that mine.'

"'Find it? Of course, I can,' said I. 'I may not be able to go directly to it, but I can easily find it. All I have to do is to go to the grove where I killed the deer, then strike out northeasterly till I sight the cliff of rocks where I first tried to find a camping place, when I shall soon find the spreading pine and the damp of the old tunnel. But what about the old Frenchman and his mine?'

"'Has no one told you the story of the old Frenchman and his mine?'

"'No; I've never heard a word about them,' said I.

"'That is strange. However, you are but newcomers, and not so much is now said about the old man and his mine as was heard some years ago.

"'Well, about ten years ago,' began the ranchman, 'an old Frenchman made his appearance in this neighborhood. He spent every hour of his time in prospecting for gold quartz. However, we who were engaged in cutting wood and burning charcoal paid very little attention to what he was doing—never went out of our way to observe his movements.

"'After a time the old man built a small cabin, and had a whole winter's supply of grub packed in. The old fellow either knew very little English or pretended to understand only a few words. We used to call at his cabin in passing to see how he was getting along, for he was alone and in a lonely place— you see, we thought he might be taken sick or meet with an accident of some kind. Often did I hear the ringing of a pestle in a mortar on approaching his place, but never did I see mortar, pestle, or quartz in his cabin.

"'Before opening his door to a knock he always spread a blanket over those tools and over any quartz he may have had in his cabin at the time. I often noticed his blanket in a corner of the cabin, and knew as well what was under it as if he had lifted the covering and shown me. But I was in another branch of business, and cared very little about what the old man was doing; I only wanted to see that he was alive and well.

"'Things went on about in this way till one day in November, when one of my men told me he thought the old French must have gone away, as he had knocked at his door and had received no answer. The next day two of us went to the cabin. After knocking a long time without hearing either voice or movement within, we broke open the door.

"'On entering, we found everything in place, but there was no sign of a fire having been kindled on the hearth for several days, and the bread left on the table was as dry as bone. On lifting the blanket in the corner we found beneath it a mortar, pestle, a sack of quartz, a gold pan, and a horn spoon.

"'Thinking the old man might have taken a trip to Virginia City or some other town, we left everything about as found, fastened the door on the outside, and left. Several times during the next three months we went to the cabin, or halted there in passing, but saw nothing of the old Frenchman, nor was he ever again seen by any man among us.

"'The next spring a man who was prospecting in the neighborhood pounded out the sack of quartz that was left in the cabin and obtained about $160 from it. He spent weeks and weeks in searching for the vein from which the quartz was procured, but without success. He said that the man who had the good fortune to find that vein would be fixed for life.

"'I do not doubt it, as the quartz I saw in the cabin was filled with flakes and seams of gold. My boys have spent much time, first and last, in looking for the lost lead; the sheepherders have searched the hills, and all the prospectors that came this way for five years after hunted for it; but to this day it has not been found—if you did not find it last night.

"'Now, you may laugh at me,' said the wood rancher, 'but as sure as you are a living man, you were last night in the old Frenchman's mine, and you saw exactly the manner in which he lost his life ten years ago! I am just as sure of this as I am that I now see you before me. You have exactly described the appearance of the old man, and every article of his usual dress—little old blue cloth cap and all. I have seen him fifty times, just as you saw him last night. Were you to give one of my men the same description, without saying where you met such a man, he would at once say: "Why, that is our little old lost Frenchman!"

"'You have seen him, Morrison—you've seen him, and have been in his mine! Now, if you can find your way back to that old tunnel, you will not only find a fortune, but will also find the skeleton of the old Frenchman lying under that boulder you saw fall upon him—or upon his ghost—last night. I have not the least doubt that his death occurred just as the scene was enacted before you last night.'

Searching for the Haunted Tunnel

"I was too stiff and sore to move that day, but Daniels borrowed the wood rancher's horse and went out and got the deer I had killed, finding it without the least trouble from the description I gave him of the place where I hung it in the tree, but he said he saw no such cliff as I spoke of, though he had looked for it, both going out and returning. I told him I would be all right in a day or two, when I would go out with him, and not only find the cliff, but also the old tunnel. I must find it, for I had left in it my hat, gun, and hunting knife.

"The third day I was well enough to travel, and, accompanied by Daniels, struck out for the old tunnel. I was so sure that I could find the big cliff that I did not think it worthwhile to go all the way to where I had killed the deer; but no cliff could we find. We spent the whole day in a vain search for the cliff, the spreading pine, and the dump pile I had seen at the mouth of the tunnel.

"We found a few small bluffs of rock, plenty of spreading pines, and not a few piles of dirt and patches of colored ground, which at a distance looked like dump piles, but no real dump pile or old tunnel could we discover.

"A day or two later we renewed the search, making the place where I killed the deer our point of departure. We, however, saw only the places we had visited on the occasion of our first trip. Afterwards we traveled in various directions—branching off to all points of the compass—and, though we spent over two months in the search, first and last, we never did find the old tunnel, nor has it been found to this day. My shotgun, hat, and hunting knife lie in it to this hour—wherever it is.

"Think what you may of this story," said the chief. "I have told you nothing more than what I saw or thought I saw. Had we found my hat, gun, and knife in an old tunnel, with an incline at the back in which was no skeleton crushed under a rock, I might have been made to believe that the death scene was all a dream; but as the matter now stands, I am much inclined to believe with the old wood rancher.

"When the lost mine is found—if ever—there will be found in it the rock-pressed skeleton of the old Frenchman, the remains of my hat, gun, and knife—with, perhaps, some bunches of sandy hair on the jagged rocks forming the roof of the tunnel."

Spooks of the High Trails

I can assure the reader that there is more truth than poetry in
the incidents related in the following sketch. Some of the old-
timers had queer notions regarding spooks. Many among the
miners of the early days will remember old Jake Fisher; also
the dilapidated cabin at the mouth of Scotchman's Creek,
with the big pine tree lying across it.   D. D. Q.

---

*G*hosts! Ghosts in the mountains?" cried Omega Joe, as he tossed
a flapjack in the air and flopped it over in his frying pan. "No,
pard, I hain't never seen nothin' of the kind. I never think of sich
things when I'm up in the mountains."

"Spooks hev allers 'peard to me," said Tehama, as he turned the
slice of beef he was broiling at the end of a stick, "to be a sorter
product of civilization. My ideas is that they belong to the settlements
whar thar's lots of graveyards for 'em to live in and old houses whar
they kin meet of nights and hold fo'th in ther specialties."

"So you two men think there's no such thing as—as a ghost up in
these mountains?" said the man from Sonora, who seemed to have
something on his mind that rather worried him and had set him to
questioning Joe.

"Oh, no, not in the mountains," said Omega. "Up in the mountains
of nights I never think of anything wuss nor a grizzly bar, a Calerfor-
ny lion or some sich varments, but down in the settlements, in pokin'

For these late dialect yarns, De Quille returns to Omega, the scene of his
earliest adventures in the Sierra. From the San Francisco *Call,* December 23,
1894.

about an old, empty, musty house after dark, I'm a little skeerish, pard. Yes, pard, I'll own up to that."

"Them kind of feelin's is nat'ral to man." said Tehama. "They's born in him. Old houses is the reg'lar stampin' ground of spooks, and man's got a nat'ral instink in him that tells him when ther's invisible things pokin' about that would be ugly to look at."

"Well," said the Sonora man, "ghost or no ghost, I got a pretty good scare about a week ago. I'm either getting wrong in my head or I last Saturday afternoon saw a thing of air in the shape of some old miner."

"What's that about a ghost?" sung out some of the men cooking and lounging at the other end of the big camp fire. "What sort of er thing was it yer seed?"

"Why," said the Omega man, "it seems our Sonora chum has had an experience of some kind with the ghost of one of the 'old boys.'"

"Yes, had a devil of a time with it," said Tehama, "and all in broad daylight! If the spooks is leavin' the settlements and comin' up inter the wilds of the mountains, it behooves me to know it."

The attention of all in the camp was by this time drawn to the man who hailed from Sonora. Every man pricked up his ears at the mention of ghosts in the mountains. It was looked upon as a sort of unholy invasion of territory rightfully belonging to the prospecting brotherhood by some. Others said if it was really the ghost of one of the old boys—an old '49er—it had some right to be up in the mountains, but it would be cheeky in a cow-country spook to take to haunting the high trails. But before forming an opinion, all wanted to hear the Sonora man's experience.

We were camped in a grove at the edge of a patch of meadow on Bear River, Nevada County, California. All were prospectors, and in parties of two and three had turned from the main road toward sunset to halt for the night in a place that was a favorite camping ground. The party that first arrived lighted a camp fire, and for this fire each new party coming in at once headed, as for a well-known home.

We were all leisurely retreating from the High Sierras, where it was no longer safe to remain, as winter was near at hand and big snowstorms might soon be expected. By nightfall ten or twelve men, with nearly as many burros and pack mules, were collected in the camp. All were soon chatting as though they had known one another for years, whereas the fact was that the members of no one party were acquainted with any of the men composing the others. However, it was found that most of us had mutual friends in various mining camps, and, all being engaged in the same business, we were soon like so many brothers.

Finding all faces turned toward him expectantly, the Sonora man proceeded to satisfy the general curiosity. Said he: "Last Saturday I was camped on the South Yuba, a little above Washington, near the mouth of Scotchman's Creek. In the afternoon, having nothing better to do, I went up to a large pool on the creek where I had seen a fine lot of trout, and began fishing.

"After I had been engaged in this sport for about half an hour I began to have a feeling that someone was near at hand behind me. I turned about and saw standing within three or four paces an old man dressed as a miner. He was a man at least six feet in height, broad chested and stalwart. A long gray beard reached far down his breast, and he had but one eye.

"The man gazed at me very intently—in a fixed sort of way, I thought. His lips parted and he seemed about to speak, but instead he began to stroke his beard, first with one hand then the other, all the time gazing at me in a queer, wistful way.

"I thought he was some miner working on the creek and was about to speak to him when I felt a trout take my hook. I turned and gave such a jerk to my rod that I flung the fish quite behind me.

"Following the trout with my eyes as I thus threw it out, I saw it strike full in the breast of the old man, pass through him, and fall to the ground. At the same moment the miner disappeared. He seemed to fade out just when the trout reached and passed through his image.

"Now, what I saw was either the ghost of some old miner or I am getting to be wrong in the head. Why the shape of such a man should have appeared to me I cannot understand. I have never known such a man in California, yet there seemed to be something familiar to me in his general appearance."

"I guess, pard," said Omega, "it's safe to say that you saw a ghost. Yes, pard, thar ain't no doubt about that. What you saw was the ghost of old Jake Fisher. I knowed old Jake for years, and you have described him to a dot. I mined for years in the hills on both sides of Scotchman's Creek—at Alpha and Omega—and I often saw old man Fisher. Pard, you've got him down to a dot; his build, his one eye, and even his fashion of strokin' his beard. Old Jake mined on Scotchman's

Creek—his diggin's was just below the rich Brookshire claim—and first and last he must have got out a pile of money. Did you notice near the mouth of the creek, on the west bank, an old rotten cabin with a big pine tree layin' across the middle of it and smashin' it almost flat to the ground? You did? Well, that was old Jake's cabin, and in it he met his death under that tree. It was many years ago, and about this time o' year that he was killed.

"In an awful storm one night the big tree crashed down and killed the old man as he was sleepin' in his bunk.

"We got his body out from under the tree by choppin' away part of the sleepin' bunk and buried him jist above the cabin on the hillside. Old Jake had a mighty rich claim and was close as the bark on a tree, but we could find neither gold dust nor coin about his cabin, though we sarched high and low, bein' sure he had a pile hid somewhar. So we wur obliged to write to his family back in Illinois, at Galena—he was an old lead miner—that he left nothing. However, we auctioned off his claim and sent back to his widder the $1,500 it fetched."

"So the old man was from Galena, Illinois?" said Sonora. "I also lived in Galena at one time, and knew a one-eyed man there whose name was Fisher. The man killed here was probably the same. I can now see why there seemed to be something familiar about the apparition, though I was a mere lad when I lived in Galena. I used to go to Fisher's house to play with his boy Jim, who was about my own age."

"Yes, pard, true enough," said Omega, "thar was a son Jim. He come out here in the hope that his father had left money with someone, or that he could find gold buried about the cabin, for the old man told in his letters home of the big finds he was makin'. But Jim found nothin'. He stopped on the creek a month or so, then wandered off north to some camp in Plumas where the old man used to mine. So you used to live in Galena, and knowed the old man? Now we begin to see the sense of his ghost appearin' to you."

"Yes, that was nat'ral instink," said Tehama, "and if Sonora hadn't flung that air trout in the ghost's face, and kinder flumixed it, it would have up an' told him whar its pile of gold was buried."

"That was what it was after, sure," said Omega, "for Jim was one of the kind that would have blowed it all in at faro, and the folks at home would never got a cent."

"You two fellers are trying mighty hard to set up your ghost on solid ground," said the man from Red Dog, "but I don't go a cent on him. Pooh! The idea of a ghost in broad daylight! Who ever heard of sich a thing before?"

One man said he had heard of a ghost putting in an appearance on a very dark cloudy day in the midst of a thunderstorm. Then there was started a war of words as to whether it was not against the laws of spookdom for a ghost to appear in daylight. Tehama, who found himself worsted in his attempt to show that because of the absence of graveyards there could be no spooks in the wilds of the mountains, at last said: "Well, of course, it would be nat'ral enough for the ghost of an old prospector that wur killed by a bar or got lost and perished in the snow to hant the place whar the body was planted or scattered, 'cause it hain't got no reg'lar home. Ghosts seem to hev a sorter nat'ral instink for doin' that; or maybe it's one of the rules they've got. Whar the man passed in his chips is whar his ghost holds forth if it's got anything pressin' on its mind. It nat'rally wants to be on the spot to clear up somethin'. No, boys, I ain't agin the ghost of an old miner showin' up in the wilds, but I'm blowed if I wants to see any of the reg'larly buried of the valley graveyards comin' up inter the mountains."

"Now pards," said Omega, "what's agin a decent miner ghost, like that of old Jake Fisher—a man I knowed for years—showin' up in the daylight? Sonora, here, has told you it dressed natural an' didn't try to look nasty. If they strolls about in the quiet places in and about the high trails in daylight it ain't often there's anyone to see 'em. Besides, if they've got something on their minds they want to make known they've got ter show up in daylight, for people ain't often travelin' in wild places of nights."

"Since so much has been said in regard to the ghosts of miners bein' out and about in daylight," put in Dan Davis, an old mountain man who had been a silent listener, "I've got a case in pint that's evidence to me that Sonora seed jist what he said he did, an' it's a thing like I seed myself."

"Let's hear your 'sperience, pard," said Omega. "I don't reckon we need ter be ashamed of the ghosts of any of the old boys that's walkin' beats on the high trails. They ain't of the fool valley kind that thinks it smart to git out in their shrouds and skeer folks."

There being a general call for old Dan's experience with mountain spooks, he knocked the ashes from his pipe and, clearing his throat with a pint cup of black coffee, told the following story:

"Last fall a year, 'bout this time, I was diggin' down out in the mountains on an old trail that leads down from the headwaters of the Feather. It was in the afternoon and hot as blazes, for I was on the north side of the river and close up by a wall of rock that poured more heat onto my head than come out of the sun. At last I got down to a big flat and was glad to halt at a spring in the shade of some willers.

"Thar was some nice patches of grass on the spring branch for my old burro, Turk. So I unpacked him, turned him loose, and sat down in the shade to a lunch of cold slapjacks and bacon.

"I'd finished my lunch and was taking a pull at my pipe when I sees a man coming up the trail. It was an old man, with a long, gray beard. He had on a reg'lar miner's rig, with a six-shooter slung to his belt. I was kinder astonished, for I hadn't s'posed thar was airy man within twenty mile of the spot. Howsumever, I concluded the old feller was walkin' in ahead of some party of prospectors that were climbin' up to the flat. So I sot and waited for him to come up to the shade and water.

"But when he was within fifty yards of me he halted. Then he faced about, and looking to the north, started across the flat. Turk then got sight of him, stopped feedin', and stood gazin' at him, with his ears stuck forrard.

"Out, 'bout the middle of the flat, a hundred yards away, the old feller stopped and stood looking down at the ground. I thought he was waitin' for his pards to come up. I turned and looked down the trail, but no one hove in sight. Turnin' again to the old man, I found him gazin' straight at me. As I looked up, he lifted his right hand and beckoned me to come to him. 'What do you want?' says I.

"Not a word does the old feller say, but again he beckons to me. I rose to my feet and then could see some dirt piled up, as if at a prospect hole. Thinks I, the old chap may have struck it rich. 'What is it?' I sung out.

"The old feller made no answer, but still beckoned me to come out to him.

"I concluded to go and see what the old coon wanted. As I moved toward the old feller, he began to disappear. He seemed to be sinkin' into the ground. When he had sunk to the waist I halted, for I didn't like the looks of the business. While I stood still, the old man didn't move, but as soon as I started on down, he sank till I could only see his head and shoulders.

"I had got up so near the old chap that I could plainly see the stare of his cold and fishy eyes. Cold chills run up and down my back, and my hair began to raise. Thar was su'thin' so unwholesome in the steady stare of the glassy eyes that I began to crawfish.

"Then was developed a new featur. As I moved back foot by foot up rose the old man. Inch by inch he come up till I could almost see the tops of his boots. Then, holdin' onto me with his cold, glassy eyes, he again beckoned me to come to him.

"I was about to take to my heels when a thought struck me. 'What a fool I am!' says I. 'There's a ladder in the shaft that the old creetur is movin' up and down upon.'

"It still struck me that the old chap's eyes were no good, but I concluded that he might be built that way. So I again moved forrard. Down, down went the old man as I went toward him, but as I thought he was on a ladder I marched on.

"At the spot whar the old feller disappeared I found an old shaft, but no ladder was in it—not even a notched pole. It looked about twenty-five feet deep, and not a thing was in it on which any human bein' could have stood. At the bottom was not a thing but some loose dirt, a dead rabbit or two, and on one side a little puddle of water.

"Soon as I seed that the old man had been dancin' up and down in the air, my legs began to weaken, my teeth chattered, and the squeak of a mouse would have stampeded me. I wanted to run away, but was afeerd to turn my back lest the old creetur would spring out uv the hole and mount me.

"So I began to walk backwards, keepin' my eyes on the shaft. When I had moved back a rod or two up came the old man's head, the eyes starin' wuss 'n ever. I shuffled backwards till the thing stood waist high above the ground, then turned tail and made the gravel fly till I was back at the spring.

"Turnin' toward the shaft, I seed the old man of the hole standin' as if on top of the ground. As I stood gazin', with cold sweat pourin' out of me, the old chap lifted his right hand and beckoned to me as at first.

"'No you don't, old cock,' say I; 'I've got my dose.'

"Lookin' about for old Turk, I found he'd got sight of the thing and was workin' his ears and starin' at it. In less'n a minit I had Turk's pack on his back and was raisin' a dust down the trail.

"The old creetur at the shaft followed me with his eyes, turnin' his head like an owl, till I got to where the trail pitched down from the flat into a tremenjous cañon, and as I turned for a last look he raised his hand and beckoned me back. At that moment, so help me Moses, if my old burro didn't twist his head round, stick his ears forrard at the old man at the shaft and give a rousin' yee-haw!

"'Git up, Turk, you tormented old fool!' yells I, givin' the old jack a kick in the rear, and down we dove into the shadder of the big cañon. And more'n once, as we went down, at the sound of a little racket behind me, I came near jumpin' clean over my old burro's back.

"Now, what do you make of that? If I wasn't sunstruck and crazy, I seed jist what I've told you. Besides, old Turk saw the same thing, and 'tain't likely he, too, was sunstruck."

"My verdic," said Tehama, "is that thar's rich gravel in the bottom of that old shaft. The ghost bein' that of an old miner and you bein' a prospector, it wanted you to take up the ground. As for your old jack seein' the ghost, I don't doubt it. Burros has got a nat'ral instink for seein' sich things. The Bible tells us that Balaam's donkey seed the angel that stood in the way when Balaam couldn't see a sign of it, though he was a big prophet as worked mirkles. You often see burros standin' workin' of ther ears and lookin' dreamy. Who knows but it's then they're communin' with spirits?"

"Ketch me diggin' in that old shaft?" said Dan Davis. "I'd expect to hear a groan come up at the first stroke of the pick. I've had all I want of the old man of the hole."

Said Mike Maroney: "I'm acquainted wid a little ould praste down at Oroville that bates the divil on spooks. He'd put a quiatus on that ghost at wanst. Joost a few words in Latin, then a couple o' squirts of holy wather and the ghost would be could as a wedge."

"Get yer priest and take the diggin's," said Dan. "I don't want 'em.

"My opinion is," said Omega, "that the old man had suthin' on his mind. He 'pears to have been dressed decent—had his six-shooter on, and was proverbally a good old man. He wasn't off his beat, and as for his eyes bein' sot in his head I don't reckon that was his fault. Now, I think his bones is at the bottom of that shaft. All he's after is to have 'em took out and buried in a dry place."

"If that's your opinion," said Dan Davis, "s'pose you go up the Feather and dig him out? You're welcome to him."

Spirit of the Rock

*The Haunted Sluicer of the Comstock. Tragedy of
Six-Mile Canyon Recalled. The Old Miner Who
Heard His Dead Partner's Voice in the Wind.*

$\mathcal{G}$od of nature, what a picture the great rock will make!" cried I.
"Now, if I can sketch it as I see and feel it, I shall have a fine and
a striking picture. Yes," said I, seating myself up on a grassy bank,
"the rock will make a fine sketch. I shall have the little cabin well in
the foreground and may bring it out strong and with full details."

All this I muttered in a mild frenzy of delight such as is felt not
alone by the skilled artist but often by lovers of nature who are able to
see and feel more than they are capable of expressing with their
unpracticed pencils. I might weakly transfer the rock and its surroundings to my portfolio, but the sight of it aroused my artistic
instincts, and I hungered to set to work upon it.

With my sketching pad on my knees and my pencil held at arm's
length I began my work, happy as the miner whose pick is turning up
a socket of golden nuggets. The rock in front of which I had sat
myself down, as in ancient times a warrior chief pitched his camp
before a castle he desired to capture, is a singular freak of nature. It
stands on a great rock-walled cleft, which, starting from the Comstock lode, cuts its way eastward from Virginia City through several

---

For this tale of the haunted sluicer of Six-Mile Canyon, Dan provides an
artistic frame. From the San Francisco *Chronicle,* July 30, 1893.

ranges of hills down to the desert bordering the Carson River. This rock-bound gorge is known as Six-Mile Cañon.

In this cañon is a round-topped rock, which is the most striking object seen in looking eastward from Virginia City. This huge conical mass of rock is known as the Sugar-loaf, and is only about two miles east of the town. The rock is not visible from the Comstock, being hidden by a high range of rugged hills. It stands alone on the south side of the cañon at the point of a low hill. It rises sheer from the bottom of the gorge to a height of over five hundred feet, and looks like some huge old fortress. The mass is composed of rock of a kind different from any in the neighborhood, and appears to have been thrust up from a great depth in the subterranean regions at a single supreme effort of nature in some one of her tremendous convulsions. The face of this castlelike rock fronting on the cañon is perpendicular and quite smooth. It is gray in color, though it shows many broad patches of orange, red, and brown lichens. In the face of the rock are clefts and holes that resemble narrow doors and windows. Several of the openings, however, are of depth sufficient to give shelter to bats and owls; are probably caverns of considerable extent.

At the base of this towering cliff and built against one of its lower buttresses stands a little cabin constructed of rough stones and a mortar of yellow clay. It has a low and narrow door, beside which is a small window. The little cabin thus stuck against the base of the big rock resembles the nest of some Brobdingnagian species of swallow.

In front of the cabin is a rod-square patch of garden, and adjoining this, running along the foot of the cliff, is a thin row of tall willow trees. The willows stand so close to the foot of the rock that their boughs sweep across its face as they sway in the wind, for there is only a narrow pathway of soil between the base of the cliff and the cañon.

In the ravine was a little string of blanket sluices, showing the occupant of the cabin to be one of those who earn a scanty subsistence by sluicing the tailings flowing down the cañon from the mills above. This was at one time a lucrative business, but the occupation of blanket sluicer is now gone.

I had been at work for some time on my sketch when I noticed that the door of the little cabin had been opened an inch or two. By looking sharply I was able to discern what appeared to be a face peering out at me—the face of an old man. Presently, as I worked on, the door was more widely opened. Then an ancient sluicer made his appearance in the doorway. He was hatless and coatless, and after watching me for some moments with a hand shading his eyes, came out through the little garden. Crossing the stream on an old sluicebox, he timidly advanced a few steps, then halted and stood alternately gazing at me and up at the rock I was sketching.

He was a man apparently about seventy years of age. His grizzled locks hung upon his shoulders and his beard almost reached his shiny old leathern waist belt. He wore a faded blue woolen shirt and a pair of clay-colored canvas pantaloons, the legs of which were thrust into rubber boots that came up to his knees. He was tall and gaunt, and his back was bent like the rainbow.

Soon the old man's curiosity mastered any scruples he may have entertained about the propriety of approaching and addressing me. On tiptoes he glided to my side, and peering keenly down into my face, said in a low but very earnest tone of voice: "Ah, you hear it. You must hear it, for you are taking down what it says. I hear it often, particularly of nights, and I can understand a good deal of what it says."

"Hear what?" I asked. "What do you mean?"

"Why, the spirit—the voice of the spirit in the rock, of course. What else? Yes, I often hear it—often and often. And by lying awake of nights and listening, I can make out a great deal of what it says."

"And what does the spirit say?"

"It says many things—talks to me about almost everything. On nights when I am in bed it is often restless. Then it rouses itself and calls out to me: 'Joe, Joe, Joe! Oh, oh, wake up, Joe! Oh, oh, old man! Woe, woe, old man! No, they don't treat the old man well!' and so the voice from the rock goes on moaning and lamenting."

I looked up from my work, thinking I was being given a game by one of the queer old jokers of the days of '49, but when I saw the man's sad, wrinkled old face and the wild glitter of his eyes, I felt that he was in solemn earnest. The poor old fellow had so long lived a solitary life in his little cabin and had so long struggled with poverty and disappointments that, like the sheepherders who lose their minds out in the wilds, he was fast becoming a mental wreck.

"Uncle," said I, "the voice you hear is the voice of the winds over your head in the rock—the winds playing across the crevices and holes and caverns in the face of the cliff."

"Ah, yes! The wind is necessary, of course. The wind gives a voice that the spirit may use, having no vocal organs of its own. But for the air we would be unable to give utterance to audible speech though we have all the necessary organs. Having neither mouth nor tongue, the spirit must so modulate the voice of the winds as to make itself understood."

"You speak of a spirit, Uncle Joe. What spirit is it that dwells in the rock? Is it the spirit of the rock itself or some spirit that has taken up its residence in the rock?"

"Why, then you do not know, you have not heard, that it is the spirit of Tom Hawkins, my old pardner, that lives in the rock? Of course the men here in the cañon will not believe this, but I know his voice too well to be deceived. How should I be deceived when almost every night I hear him call out to me, 'Oh, Joe! Joe! Poor old Joe! They don't treat the old grandfather right. No, no—oh, dear, no.' Tom is always fretting that way about me, the same as when he was alive."

"When did your pardner die, Uncle Joe?"

"Ten years ago. He was killed at the foot of the rock, almost in front of where the cabin stands. He was at work in the bottom of a deep ground sluice, and a big slab of rock from one side of it fell on him. He had not a bone broken, but the rock held him down till the water rose over his head and drowned him. I heard him call, 'Oh, Joe, Joe!' and I ran out of the cabin—I had gone in to cook supper—but by the time I got to him all was still—all was over. He had been caught by the legs, with his head upstream. He lay flat on his back, and at once the water, dammed up by the cave, rose over his head. Poor Tom! He was more to me than any brother I ever had.

"I fear something bad is going to happen to me. I didn't hear Tom's voice lamenting of nights until times began to grow bad here in the mines, but now he moans and groans more and more. This winter and spring he has been calling to me and waking me at all hours of the night."

"Don't you think, Uncle Joe, that the raking of the willows on the face of the cliff and the howling of the gale in the clefts and crevices may produce sounds that you imagine to be words? Then there are the owls up there in the caverns of the rock."

"Ah! but I am not deceived by the voices of the owls, nor by the voices of the fiends that visit and wrangle with them up there in the caves."

323

"Why don't you move away from here, old man—why not go to some new place?"

"What! Go away and leave poor Tom! No, no, he is lonely now up there in the rock and he'd be worse—would have no peace at all—if I were to go away. It is a comfort to him to talk to me. Besides," said the old man, with a cunning twinkle in his eye, "besides, he is trying to make me understand where the old gang of Flowery stage robbers buried a lot of gold. I am searching for it now and I think I am near it. Only last night Tom called out to me: 'Joe, Joe, go slow! Have patience, Joe!' Then pretty soon he said: 'Gold, Joe—gold!'

"Tom tries to tell me exactly where the treasure is, and speaks of two letters on a rock, but as he is obliged to make his voice heard through the winds, what he says is often broken off by sudden gusts or calms and I lose his meaning just when I seem almost to have got hold of it. Then, too, at times when Tom is beginning to tell me just where the gold is buried, the owls and imps begin screeching, 'He lies, old man, he lies! There is no gold for you. No, you are on your last legs. The grave is for you.' But this talk of the owls and devils does not long worry me. Tom soon comes back and says: 'Don't mind them, Joe. I see the gold. Go slow, old man.'"

Again the weird sounds were heard, and the old miner, lifting his skinny right arm and shaking it at the imaginary spirits, cried out: "Who lies? Ah, you sons and daughters of Satan!" Then, after a moment of quiet listening, he turned to me and said earnestly: "There! Did you hear that? That was Tom's call. 'Joe! Joe!' he cried. I must away! Every day I understand him better. Before long I shall be able to talk with him the same as when he was alive. Then, if not before, I shall find the buried gold."

The old man then left me and started back toward his cabin. When he had reached the stream and was about stepping up on the old sluice box to cross it, he suddenly halted, and gazing fixedly up at the rock cried out: "Who lies? Ah, you sons and daughters of Satan, you well know that I have told you nothing but the truth!" And shaking his fist at the rock, he hastened across the stream and shut himself up in his hut.

As I was still looking at the little den into which the old man had rushed, I saw poked out from a hole at one end, near the low roof, a sheet-iron contrivance resembling a big speaking trumpet. The old man was listening for the voices.

324

Having finished my sketch of the rock after a poor fashion, I took my way up the cañon toward Virginia City in rather a gloomy state of mind. It was not a walk that was calculated to dispel the feeling of melancholy that had taken possession of me. Where once all was life and bustle was now little but ruin and desolation. The once flourishing town of Flowery was no more, and no more was heard the thunder of stamps and the scream of the steam whistle. Piles of rubbish marked the sites of the big mills and great works. Bordering the stream were still visible in places the remains of massive walls of cut stone, with occasional dilapidated reservoirs and wrecked waterwheels. Pitching down from tall trestlework were broken flumes, and here and there were sections of dry ditches.

Clambering up the cañon over boulders, piles of loose rock, and strings of old, rotten sluices, I seemed to hear in the wind that roared above in the rocky walls a cry of: "Oh, oh, the ruin! Woe, woe, the desolation!"

I passed, perched upon the banks against the rocks, a number of little cabins that were of the same pattern as that of Uncle Joe. Some of these were inhabited, and from out their doors were now and again thrust a bushy gray head and a blinking old blanket-sluicer, owllike, peered down at me.

"Here," said I, "are more men who will soon be hearing voices in the rocks, unless times change—perhaps some besides Uncle Joe are already at it!"

The Musical Coffin

How Barney Dolan's Partner Came Back.

---

*I*t was at a wake, and when it came to Barney Dolan's turn to tell
a story he gave the following:

"Tim McShae's schtory 'minds me of the warst fright I iver got in
all me born days. It was in the spring of '57 that I was minin' on Rush
Creek, near Nevada City, in California. Four of us had a cabin there
and diggin's that was payin' us well; but jist then Frazer River was all
the talk, and we all got that faver. I held out against it for a while, but
whin I found that Bill Johnson was dead set on goin' I tould him I
would go and take me chance along wid him, for Bill was the best of
all my partners, and we were like twin brothers—God rest his sowl!

"Well, off we all wint to the Frazer River, lavin' our claim and
cabin on Rush Creek to be looked out for by our neighbors in the next
cabin below, till they would hear from us what luck we were matin'
wid in the new mines.

"It was a bad speculation, that trip to the Frazer River—for me at
laste, as I niver wint intil the mines at all.

"Well, as we were all goin' up the river in canoes the murtherin'
wild Injuns got afther us, firin' from behind rocks and trees along the

---

How Barney Dolan's partner came back, in stage-Irish dialect. From the
Territorial Enterprise, November 4, 1877.

shore. The bullets struck the wather all about us, whistled about our heads and, before we could get paddled out into the stream far enough to be out of their reach, Bill Johnson was shot through the head and fell over the side of the canoe and disappeared under the wather, and Mike Casey, another of me pardners, got a bullet in his left shouldther.

"Whin we got over to the other shore we found a camp of white men and a docther, who fixed up Mike's shouldther. The men in the camp was goin' down the river—most o' them—and I tould the byes, my pardners, to take all my share of the pervisions and traps, for I was goin' down the river and back to California, to the ould cabin and diggin's.

"They thried to laugh me out of it, sayin' the brush wid the Injuns had sickened me, but I had made up me mind an' down the river I wint. The truth was that as soon as poor Johnson was kilt, I felt myself all alone, and was sick to get out of the counthry and back to me ould home in California.

"In the steamer, all the way down the coast, I thought of Johnson and wondthered if his body had dhrifted out intil the great ocean on which I was sailin', for we niver was able to find his corpse, though we stopped at the camp and sarched along down the river for two whole days. In the storms I sometimes consaited I heard his voice, and lookin' over the side of the vessel on moonlight nights I often seemed to see his face sinkin' down and down in the water, like when he fell dead over the side of the canoe.

"Whin at last I got back to Rush Creek and the ould cabin, I was more lonesome than iver. Johnson was always in my thoughts, whether I was at work in the claim or sittin' alone by the fire in me cabin. I thought if I could have found the body and buried it high and dhry on the shore, I would have been more aisy in me mind. Where the corpse wint to and what became of it throubled me not a little.

"It was soon winter, and I still stuck to me claim and cabin all alone, for the ground was payin' well and I did not know how soon Mike Casey and the ither byes would be back down, for they wrote me they had no luck in the Frazer mines.

"About 300 or 400 yards below me on the creek, four men had a cabin and a claim. They were makin' big wages and were a jolly crowd. They would fraquently come up to my cabin o' nights and sing songs an' tell yarns to thry to cheer me up a bit, but as soon as they were away I'd be thinkin' of Johnson again and that onlucky thrip to Frazer River.

"Often of nights the byes from the ither cabin would dhrop in as they passed and thry to get me to go into town wid 'em, to have a bit o' fun, as they called it, whin they came home wid black eyes and broken heads. But I had no heart for it, as I had whin I used to have Johnson—my fightin' Yankee, as I used to call him—wid me.

"One night—it was a Christmas night—the byes of the ither cabin come by, all full of the divil, on their way to town to have a good time. They swore I should go wid them and not sit moping at home, but that night I somehow felt less like seein' anybody than usual and they all went away, almost mad wid me.

"After they had been gone a short time I wint to bed, for there was four or five inches of snow on the ground and it was cold sitting up. I was soon asleep. I slept sound as a log for a long time, then I began drhamin' of Johnson. I thought he had come back and was in the cabin wid me, whistlin' about, just as merry as in the days before we wint to the Frazer River. I was so glad that he was not shot afther all, to be washed away intil the ocean and ate up by the crabs, sharks, aligathors, and other blagard fishes, that at wanst I was wide awake.

"I could hardly belave me ears, for there in the cabin was bein' played 'Yankee Doodle' in the most beautiful way, and all on some insthrument the likes of which I had niver heard before in all me life.

"It was dark as pitch in the cabin as I sot up and gazed about. Where all the music came from I could not tell. 'Sure,' said I, 'it's the music of the ither warld.' The could chills wint up and down me back as I thought of this. I strained me eyes almost out of me head, but could see nothing white—nothing like a ghost would be.

"All at once, as I was sittin' up in me bed shiverin' wid the cold and the fright, the music stopped a bit; then, clear and beautiful, it sthruck up 'St. Patrick's Day in the Mornin'.' Howly mother of Moses, at this I was sure it was Johnson, an' the hair stood straight up on me head!

"I could stand it no longer in the dark. I must see what was in the house. Me hand shook so I could hardly light the candle that stood by me bed. Somehow—I don't know how—I lit it. Holdin' it high over my head, I began to look about for Johnson.

"At first I looked up, expectin' to see the whole roof of me cabin gone and Johnson sittin' above on a bit of a cloud, thumpin' away on a goolden harp. A glance showed me the roof of the cabin still on; thin I noticed that the music seemed to be below in the room.

"Takin' a step or two forward and holdin' out my light toward where the sounds seemed to come from, I saw on the floor in a corner of the cabin a coffin, out of which was comin' the tune.

"One look was all I wanted. All barefoot and in my shirt as I was, I darted out of the door and ran like a deer to the cabin below. I did not wait to open the door. Plungin' against it, I sint it flying off its hinges against the next wall.

"'Hello, byes!' sez I; 'hello! air ye here?'

"'Faith, we air all here, Barney,' said Dennis McGunnigal, spakin' from his bunk. 'What the divil is the matther wid you? Air ye clane gone crazy that ye brak down the door of the house and howl at that gait?'

"'Divil a bit am I crazy,' sez I—I'm in me nathural sivin sinses; but, byes, Johnson's back.'

"'Nonsinse!' said Dennis.

"'No nonsinse about it!' sez I. 'He's come back in his coffin and he's sittin' up there on the flure in it a playin' 'Yankee Doodle,' 'Patrick's Day in the Mornin',' and the divil knows all the tunes else! It's jist a parfect Donnybrook fair he's got up there wid him!'

"'He's clane daft, poor divil!' sez one of the byes. 'That comes of his always sittin' alone and frettin' about poor Johnson,' sez another. 'Poor, poor fellow!' sez all hands, 'he's clean daft!'

"'Divil a daft!' sez I. 'Come wid me an' if I don't show you Johnson sittin' up there in his coffin playin' 'Yankee Doodle,' ye can put me in the crazy house!'

"'To satisfy the poor man, we'll all go and see what he is ravin' about,' sez one of the men, and they got up from their beds and sthruck a light.

"Givin' me a pair of ould shoes and wrappin' a blanket about me, they all wint wid me to me cabin. The door stood open and all was dark inside and still as death.

"'Where is all the music and the Donnybrook fair ye've been tellin' us about?' sez the byes. 'Ye've been dhramin', so ye have.'

"'Go inside wid the lanthern,' sez I, an' if the coffin is not there I'm a howlin' lunatic!'

"In we all wint. 'Here in the corner,' sez I. The light was turned

329

intil the corner and not a thing could be seen. We looked the cabin over, and there was nothing there.

"'What do ye think of yerself now?' sez Pat Donovan.

"'All I have to say,' sez I 'is that I don't understand it at all. Sure as we stand here there was the divil's own time in the cabin whin I left. Johnson sittin' in his coffin an' playin' the fiddle, an' two big divils wid tails a yard long a dancin' a jig. There was a cat as big as a cow that was—'

"'Oh, murdther! What is that now?' sez one of the byes. 'They're comin' agin!'

"Sure enough, outside somewhere we heard the music playin' 'Yankee Doodle.' Around the house it came and stopped at the door. Then the door began to open. Slow and creakin' it swung round toward where I stood. I could not see what was behind it pushin' it open. My hair began to rise. Not a man moved or said a word. My eyes were froze on that door. All at once a coffin began to crawl into the house, and wid its appearance 'St. Patrick's Day in the Mornin'' struck up.

"Everything whirled 'round wid me, and the last I remember was seein' Johnson jump out of the coffin, all nothing but bones, and come afther me wid his arms held out.

"Whin I got my sinses I found meself in me bunk and one of the byes holdin' a bottle of whisky to me mouth.

"A good big sup or two from the bottle put some heart in me, and I began to remember what had happened. 'Where is he—where is Johnson?' sez I.

"'No Johnson has bin here,' sez the byes.

"'I tell you, byes, he was here in his coffin and played "Yankee Doodle" at me till I thought he'd schplinter the cabin to pieces,' sez I.

"Wid this they all began to laugh till they could hardly spake.

"'It's the best joke of the saison,' sez Pat Donovan. 'Come in fellers,' sez he, and Mike Rooney, and three or four other byes from the creek came into the cabin wid a coffin.

"'There is Johnson's coffin!' sez I.

"'And here is Johnson,' sez Mike, takin' out of the coffin a bit of a box I could lug away under me arm.

"'What is that?' sez I.

"'Did you niver see a music box?' sez Mike.

"'A music box, is it? What the divil is a music box?' sez I, for thrue as I live I had niver in my life seen or heard of a music box. You see they didn't have music boxes knockin' about the cabins in the ould counthry—nather in the parts of America I'd then bin in.

"Thin the byes wint on to tell how that whin they were up in the town they found a raffle going on at Charley Young's jewelry store for a music box that played eight tunes, beginnin' wid 'Yankee Doodle' and 'Patrick's Day'—Ireland and America—so they bought a lot of tickets and had the luck to win the box.

"In drinkin' to their good luck they all got pretty full, and when they started home they concluded to play a thrick on me wid the box. As they came along the trail, talkin' it over, they fell in wid Mike Rooney and some more boys wid a coffin they were taking home for a man that was killed in a fight above on the creek.

"As soon as Pat Donovan and the others saw the byes wid the coffin they took them into their plot, and they all came to my cabin together, softly opened me door, slid in the coffin wid the music box in it, when they wound it up and slipped out.

"The byes of the cabin below then ran home and got into bed wid their clothes on, expectin' me to soon come tearin' in, while the byes from up the creek hid behind me cabin to watch the fun and to take out the coffin when I ran away, so they could play the thrick on me the second time.

"Even afther they tould me all this I could hardly belave the box made the music I'd heard. So the byes wound it up, and whin it began playin' I looked into the thing. There I saw a brass rowlin' pin wid teats on it, creepin' round and round, pickin' 'Yankee Doodle' out of the teeth of a big iron comb.

"Afther that, ould an' young so bothered me wid callin' out afther me, 'I say, Barney, how is the music box, and the two divils that danced the jigs?' that I sould me claim for a thrifle, left the place, and wint up to Omaga to live."

Nevada Nuggets

A Search for Solitude

The Wonderful "Liver Spring" of the High Sierras.

The shadowy desert, unfrequented woods,
I better brook than flourishing peopled towns;
There I can sit alone, unseen of any,
And to the nightingale's complaining notes
Turn my distresses, and record my woes.
—*Two Gentlemen of Verona*

*A*h, yes, that is what I need!" cried I, as I quoted the above lines.

"What?" asked my other half sharply, thinking I had suddenly resolved to make trial of some new medicine.

"Why, solitude," said I. Then, inspired by thoughts of wild and waste places, I cried: "Oh! Solitude! Sweet Solitude! Solitude, my dear—the solitude of the mighty mountains—is what I require. The solitude and the silence of the High Sierras. Shakespeare above all poets best knew how to touch the string of the human heart."

"You mean Lord Bacon, my dear," said my critical half— "William Shakespeare, you know, never wrote the plays attributed to him."

De Quille weaves Shakespeare into his yarn of the wonderful Liver Spring of the high Sierra. From the Salt Lake *Tribune,* August 22, 1891.

"Rather than again argue that point, my dear, I'll compromise with you. We'll just say that the plays were written by another fellow whose name was William Shakespeare. That matter being settled, let us talk of my going to the mountains."

"To the mountains!"

"Yes, to the mountains—to where the peaks of the High Sierras rise from a silent sea of pines! I must get away from the noise and worry of towns. I need the solitude of mountains—

> Where friends, the thieves of time, let us alone
> Whole days, and a man's hours are all his own.

"Nonsense!" cried my wife. "The doctor says it is owing more to want of exercise and a torpid liver than anything else that you are so nervous and irritable and snappish, and take such gloomy view of life."

"The doctor be blowed! I want rest—rest, both mental and physical. I hunger for the solitudes of the mountains—for the mountain fastnesses!"

"But you are not going to the mountains alone?"

"What a woman's question! How in blazes is there to be solitude unless I go alone?"

"Then I am not to go with you?"

"Not on this particular occasion, when the objects are solitude and silence."

"Were a grizzly bear to catch and swallow you, it would serve you right."

Not heeding this but slightly concealed wish, I said: "I've already hired my rig. I've got a little covered wagon—a craft that Mr. Camera, the photographer, uses on his landscape trips. Also I've got his horse. The wagon is a perfect little home on wheels—just the thing. Inspired by the odor of art lingering in the vehicle, I may sketch a little—yes, my dear, I'll bring you home some sketches."

"More likely the odor of chemicals is all the odor you'll find lingering about your cart."

"Well, the mountains will surely inspire me. Byron hits my case exactly when he says:

> I live not in myself, but become
> Portion of that around me; and to me,

336

High mountains are a feeling, but the hum
Of human cities torture."

I quoted this beautiful passage with much feeling and force, as I thought, but to my astonishment, my wife arose and flounced out of the room.

Three days later and I have left far behind me the noisy streets of Virginia City—am miles and miles beyond the reach of the scores of ear-piercing steam whistles of the mining works of the Comstock lode. I am high up amid the towering giants of the forest where "Wind, that grand old harper, smites his thunder-harp of pines."

I am still going—still traveling onward and upward. My eyes are fixed upon the topmost of many towering peaks and my cry is— "Excelsior!"

On, on I go. The one great desire of my heart is to ascend above the habitations of base and groveling man—to reach some high mountain dell, virgin to human foot, where God and silence reign. I have turned from all the broad and beaten roads, at each turn taking that showing least the traces of travel and that most steeply rearing itself upward toward the topmost height. I am determined to reach some solitude where I shall hear no other voice than that of nature, as sighed through the leaves of the pines.

Alas! the vanity of human wishes, and mere human endeavor! The last track of the solitary wagon I was following as a guide that would point out to me an open way to the upper solitudes ended before a newly erected cabin in the heart of the wilderness. In vain I looked for some continuation of the track. It ended squarely at the cabin.

So exasperated was I at seeing all my dearest hopes at once dashed to earth and shattered at my feet that I for a time seriously contemplated taking my wagon to pieces, packing it on my horse and so traveling on up the mountain. However, seeing only one man about the cabin, I concluded not to make any reckless experiments upon the strength of the spinal column of the old horse. I thought I would try and stand the one fellow off.

Upon making a critical survey, the amount of civilization visibly present did not seem to be very large, and I concluded I would try to endure it. So I pitched my tent under a mighty pine, and strove to imagine myself alone in God's wilderness.

337

While I was thus striving to imagine myself alone with nature, the man who lived in the cabin came out to me and said, probably smelling in me a squatter in search of a tract of timberland: "Ah, stranger, good evening! Glad to see you. Yes, sir, that is right; just let your tent stand where it is under my big pine tree; gather and burn as much wood as you like; I own everything around here; but make yourself at home—you are quite welcome!" Then the man smiled upon me the smile of a hyena, and rolled his eyes over my small worldly belongings.

I again began to meditate loading my wagon upon my horse and taking to a trail. I felt so sour that I did not reply to the fellow's welcome. Smiling again his hyena smile, he said: "Everything around here is mine"—waving his hand so abroad as to take in the whole country—"and I welcome you!"

I answered only with a sigh. I had started out in search of solitude—of a place where I would be alone, save the presence of silence and nature's God—and here I was, halted upon the possessions of some greedy and suspicious wretch. Worst of all was to have the man tell me that all was his property and bid me enjoy it.

"I welcome you!" repeated the man.

"Yes," said I bitterly, "I hear you say so!"

The fellow did not appear to notice the unwholesome tone in which I spoke. As he turned to depart he said: "Should you feel the want of a comb, a piece of soap, a towel, or any other little luxury while you are camped here on my ranch, call on me at my cabin and all will be as free as the air you breathe," and again smiling upon me, upon the old horse, the little wagon, and all the other traps, the fellow wended his way to his cabin.

I camped under the squatter's tree that night, and as I lay in my tent watching the flickering fire before it, tried to imagine myself alone away up among the bare peaks in some deep and solitary dell, but I couldn't do it worth a cent with that fellow in his cabin only five rods away.

"Blast him!" cried I, when I found I could not get him out of my head—"what business has he up here anyway? I ought to murder him and burn his cabin. All his land, all his trees and rocks, and I suppose all the air that comes upon his land is his while it remains inside of his lines!"

All night I fumed, fretted, and sighed for the solitude I could not find—solitude and the bounteous freedom of nature in her wilds. Here I was burning the squatter's wood and reposing upon his ground under his tree. Even when the fire went out, and there was only the light of the moon playing among the swaying boughs, I could take no comfort, for, I said: "It's that confounded fellow's moonshine—it is on his land!"

In the morning the fellow came again, smiled on me, hoped I had rested well, and again spoke of the wood, the comb, soap and towel. I was quite welcome and he should look upon me as his guest while I remained upon his ranch.

I finally took up my gun and was about to level it upon the fellow and end him, but thought better of it and laid the weapon down. I made up my mind that I would leave the spot at once—that I would turn and go down the mountain. So I told the fellow I was sick—that my liver was out of order—was as big as six ordinary livers.

"How fortunate!" cried the man. "Here you are right at a spring that works altogether on the liver. The great Liver Spring, sir. God must have guided you to it, sir!"

As I really had a very restless, uncomfortable liver, I now began to take some interest in what the fellow said. So I asked the distance to the spring.

"It's only a little way—a short mile, just up that way," and he pointed to a trail that went up the face of a steep mountain.

"I fear the spring is too distant," said I. "Even a short half-mile is a long road in this hot June weather."

"But, sir, if you have a bad liver you should not think of the distance. The Liver Spring never fails, sir. It at once cures all who try it. The day is not distant when hundreds will visit it—yes, thousands. And soon, sir, the water of the Liver Spring will be on sale in every drugstore."

"One drink of the water is not likely to do me much good, and as I have no way of bringing down a supply of the water it would hardly pay me to go up the mountain," said I.

"Oh, but I'll fix that for you," said the man. "Come with me."

He took me to his cabin and gave me a huge demijohn—not a regulation demijohn, but a big carboy of the kind used for holding acids. To my surprise I saw that the man had about forty of these carboys at his cabin. I took one that he handed me and started up the mountain. I thought I'd get the wonderful liver regulator and then

339

put out down the mountain and hunt up some little second-hand solitude. In that I'd repose myself, study the works of the Creator, and drink my liver water.

"A short mile!" cried I, as I seated myself upon a rock beside the trail and mopped the perspiration off my skating rink. "If I hain't traveled two miles already, I'm a bigger liar than Tom Pepper!"

After a rest I resumed the ascent of the mountain. On and on I went. The face of the mountain was becoming bare of timber, and there was no shade. Several times I was on the point of turning back; then I would reason that I must be near to the wonderful spring and would resume the march. I had become really anxious to see what effect the water would have on my refractory old liver. I wanted to give the great natural remedy a chance to work on a liver that would give it something to do—that would make it hump itself, so to speak.

At last I came to the spring—the great Liver Spring! It was simply a little hole in the ground, with no outlet or inlet that I could see. The Liver Spring was a hole inclosed in a little square box sunk in a patch of oozy ground.

I smelled of the water and found it to stink most dismally. I tasted it and the flavor was abominable. I was delighted. "Good!" cried I; "it has the flavor and the odor of those panaceas that are truly potent and sovereign! It was hard to reach, but now that it is at last found I am persuaded it is admirable. Nothing could so energetically evolve a stench so abominable unless charged and overcharged with medicinal virtue. I dare swear it's just the stuff to astonish and spur up an indolent and procrastinating liver!"

So I filled my stomach and then filled the carboy with the precious fluid.

To get that heavy carboy and the five gallons of water it contained down the mountain was a terrible task. However, after many halts by the way, and after the loss of nearly five gallons of perspiration, the feat was accomplished.

"Thank God!" cried I when at last I reached the foot of that awful mountain. "Ten dollars—no, twenty-five dollars wouldn't hire me to make another such trip."

Just at this moment a tall, rough-looking man came out from somewhere among the rocks and bushes, and sauntered along up to where I stood beside the carboy, mopping the top of my perspiration-pouring head.

"Been up to the Liver Spring?" asked the man in a sort of careless way.

"Yes, and the climate is a holy terror," said I. "It is enough to make a grizzly bear shed his hair!"

The man stooped and hefted the carboy. "About five gallons, eh?" said he.

"All of that," said I. "Probably nearer six."

"Oh, well, as you've had a pretty rough time of it getting it down, we'll call it five gallons; we won't have a fuss about what little there may be over that amount." At this I opened my eyes and stared at the fellow. "Why should we fuss about it?" I finally asked.

"True enough," said the man. "We don't want any fuss. It's rather precious stuff, the spring being so small, but we won't quarrel about the measure."

"Why should we?" I again asked, wondering why the fellow should care whether I had carried down even five gallons or six and over.

"That is right," said the man. "The price is not high; it is only $3 for five gallons, and that is a thousand times cheaper than doctors' stuff. It works powerfully on the liver—powerfully. Why, what you've got there is enough to straighten out forty livers—yes, fifty of the worst and rustiest old livers on the Pacific Coast!"

"You don't mean that I am to pay you $3 for this water?"

"Don't I!"

"But the man at the cabin gave me the demijohn and told me to go and get the water—insisted upon my getting the water and giving it a trial on my liver! He welcomed me to everything in the country— wood, water, and everything!"

"But the spring is outside of his lines. I own the spring. He forgot to tell you that. I have watched that spring for years—have camped and slept by it year in and year out. My fortune is in that spring. I discovered it years ago by accident, when I had only an ounce of liquor left, and it gave me a whole liver in three weeks. I wish I could show you my liver!"

"I think," said I, enraged at the fellow's impudence, "this is an infernal swindle, and I would very much like to see your confounded liver—would just like to flop it over with the point of my bowie (and I pulled my knife) and take a look at your abominable gall!"

"Oh! War, is it?" cried the fellow with an ugly smile. "I'll just see your old rusty toothpick and go you about five better!" and he pulled a six-shooter that looked to be a yard long. With a nasty coyote kind of smile, he then said:

"I guess, after all, a dose of my pills is what your liver is languishing for. I've got some pills here that beat all the patent pills in creation; and besides, they work more rapidly and at longer range than the old bowie scarifier. A man never wants more than one dose when I administer one of Dr. Colt's magic pellets!"

I put up my knife and said: "This savors of highway robbery. It looks like it. To sell a demijohn of nasty, stinking water for three dollars with a six-shooter held on a customer does not show up as the clean thing!"

"Do you intend to pay me, you confounded sneak?" cried the fellow with a flourish of his six-shooter.

"I pay under protest—I deliver up to a highway robber!" said I, throwing three silver dollars upon the ground and taking up the carboy.

As soon as I reached my camp at the big pine I harnessed up and prepared to take the back track. I stowed the carboy carefully away in the rear of my wagon. "After all," said I, "there may be the worth of the coin and trouble in the water. If it should bring my liver out all right I would not think it dear at fifty dollars."

Mounting my wagon I turned it about and began to descend the mountain. I had hardly passed the cabin before I heard a loud yelling of: "Hold on! Hold on there, you man in the wagon!"

Craning my neck and looking back round the cover of my vehicle, I saw the man of the cabin running after me. When the fellow came up I said: "Well, what is the matter of you?"

"Matter of me!" exclaimed the man. "Well, that is cool, and you running away without paying me for that demijohn!"

"The demijohn! Do you mean to say you want pay for your blasted old carboy?"

"Pay! Of course I want pay! I want a dollar and a half. What am I here for? Am I up here in these solitudes wasting my life for nothing?"

Looking back toward the cabin I saw the big bushy head of the fellow who had halted me at the foot of the mountain peering round a corner. I saw that I was in for it, so I said; "This is an infernal imposition—a trap, a put-up job! However, I'll pay rather than be murdered. Take your money and be hanged to you!" and I flung three half dollars into the road, whipped up and rattled off down the rough mountain road.

I hated myself for having come out second best in my intercourse with the two men of the mountains; still I felt somewhat consoled when I thought of the five-gallon carboy of water from the Liver Spring. "There," said I, "I have what will make forty pint bottles of the liver medicine. No liver regulator that is worth anything at all sells for less than fifty cents a pint, so at the least calculation I have here twenty dollars' worth of the stuff."

I was driving furiously in order to put distance between me and the thieves of the mountains. Just as I had figured up as above, I started full tilt down a steep, rocky hill. Suddenly the hind wheels of the wagon struck a big rock. Like a cannonball the carboy came bounding forward, pitched out over the front end of the vehicle and went rolling down the mountain. Soon it struck a big boulder. There was a jingle of glass, a gush of water that splashed over the face of the rock, and all that was left of $4.50 worth of the great liver-searcher was an abominable and widespread stench.

Hereafter I shall steadfastly dwell in crowded marts. No more will I seek solitudes and wilderness places in the hope of being allowed there to commune in quiet with nature, for vile man is in possession of all the mountain fastnesses—yea, of all the forests, streams, and springs thereof. While there remains to me even so much as the fragment of a liver, I will make my home—and be robbed—in the more congenial solitude of cities.

The Big Nevada Nugget

The Story of a Twenty-Four-Pound Lump of Gold. Tribulations of the Man Who Found and Stole the Golden Mass—In the Hands of "Birds of a Feather"—A Terrorized and Penitent Thief—The Restitution and a New Start in Life.

In the spring of 1872 was found at the Osceola placer mine, White Pine County, the largest single lump of gold ever discovered in the state of Nevada. The Osceola mine, whence the big nugget came, is situated on the western slope of Mount Wheeler (formerly Jeff Davis Peak) a mountain 12,309 feet in height, and the culminating point of the Snake River. The placer at Osceola is the only deposit of au-riferous gravel in Nevada approaching in depth and magnitude the great hydraulic mines of California. However, unlike the California digging, it is not a deposit formed by an ancient river, now dead, nor beneath the rolling waves of the ocean in the ages of the past, but is of local origin, being an accumulation of debris washed down from the slopes of Mount Wheeler. On the sides of this mountain are many large veins of auriferous quartz, more or less decomposed, and from these doubtless came the gold now found in the Osceola placer mine.

In the early days of its discovery this placer was worked by men of small means and with an inadequate supply of water. Though there was an abundance of water twenty-five miles off, to bring it to the mine would involve the expenditure of over $130,000, owing to the

---

Judge Goodwin indulged Dan's lengthy tale of theft and double-crossings. From the Salt Lake *Tribune,* January 1, 1891.

engineering difficulties to be overcome. The owners of the mine being men of moderate means, they were obliged to content themselves with the amount of water resulting from the melting snowbanks on the summit of the peak and obtainable at small cost. Thus they were able to sluice the gravel of their mine during a period of three or four months in spring and summer. In this way there was taken from the mine by the old owners in about fifteen years a total of $50,000, and very little impression was made upon the main mass of the deposit.

Now this mine at Osceola is owned by men in the East, principally of New York. Professor Maynard is, I believe, the directing spirit of the new company. This year a great ditch has been completed, and this season they have been able for the first time to work the placer after the manner of the great mines of California. They are equipped with monitors, have an abundant supply of water, and by means of electric lights are able to run day and night.

How the Wonderful Nugget Was Found and Stolen

At the time the big nugget was found, a Mr. Verzan was superintendent and principal owner of the mine. He had a small ditch which brought in sufficient water to run the sluices during the spring and summer months, and employed a small force of miners. One of these miners, whose name has never been made public, found the golden mass and stole it. With his find the thief found no end of trouble and distress of mind, and but for his final repentance it would never have been known that Nevada had produced so large a nugget.

The nugget as found weighed twenty-four pounds avoirdupois, and as it contained but a small amount of quartz, its actual coin value is supposed to have been at least $4,000. Such a lump of almost pure gold was a glittering ball of old Plutus that sent out a hundred rays to pierce the heart of its finder. The sight of the mass of gold almost took away the poor man's breath, and trembling in every joint he yielded to the suggestions of the special bit of Satan implanted in his brain.

A quick glance showed him that no one was near enough to see the shining mass. Lifting it along with a large fragment of rock that covered and hid it from sight, he bore it to the waste dump above the sluices, unobserved by Verzan or any of his fellow workers. Having succeeded in hiding the gold on the waste dump beneath the flat stone carried out with it, the thief felt a brief glow of satisfaction, and then his troubles began.

After a time the man who had thus stolen the lump of gold left the employ of Mr. Verzan, saying he was going out into the mountains to prospect on his own account. He was honestly paid his wages and sent away with a "Godspeed."

Though it came out after a time that such a mass of gold had been stolen by a miner from the Osceola diggings, and afterward given up by the conscience-stricken thief, who had received a full pardon, little more than bare mention of the fact has ever been published. The man who was tempted by old Satan and Plutus to steal the gold was an old friend of Mr. Verzan, and a man who had always before led a strictly honest and honorable life, though poor as the god of poverty could make him. Therefore Verzan, seeing him at his feet, bathed in the tears of a true penitent, promised that his name should never be made known in connection with the affair. Though the whole story of the thief was known to Mr. Verzan and his partners, it was not made public for the reason that various circumstances would have pointed out the guilty man had all come out at any time within a year or two, as the movements of individuals are closely followed and long remembered in thinly settled places.

It is only at this late date—about eighteen years after the event— that the story of the penitent thief and the true history of the big Nevada nugget has been told. I have the story from a man who was one of Mr. Verzan's partners at the time the theft occurred. In a confession made to Verzan, the thief gave a full history of his troubles from the time he first laid eyes on the lump of gold until he restored to the rightful owners that part of it which still remained in his possession. In giving back to his partners their share of the gold, it of course became necessary for Mr. Verzan to make some explanation. After pledging them to secrecy, he thereupon told them the whole story. Though the name of the man who stole the nugget is still withheld, the story of his adventures with the precious lump can no longer harm anyone. Also, the story contains a good lesson, as it shows how quickly a theft leads a man into the clutches of desperate characters almost in spite of himself. He does not find the new path into which he has turned destitute of travelers.

Verzan's Interview with the Nugget Thief

About two months after the time when the nugget was stolen, Mr. Verzan went to Ward, Nye County, on some business connected with mining. In Ward he met the man who had left the Osceola mine ostensibly to go on a prospecting trip. Now, the finder of the nugget was a man who had in times past been under great obligations to Mr. Verzan. We are always more pleased to meet those we have befriended than those who have befriended us, therefore Verzan greeted his old employee most cordially.

Perceiving that the man looked sad and troubled, Verzan suspected that he had prospected himself out of funds—that he was dead broke. He therefore offered to assist him in any way he might wish. At this the nugget thief looked more troubled than ever. The more Mr. Verzan urged the fellow to accept from him any money he might need, the more pale and haggard he became. At last, when Mr. Verzan tried to thrust a handful of gold into the man's pocket, he burst into tears and took to his heels.

Verzan stood gazing after his old friend in astonishment. He was pained to see the man in such a state of mind. He believed him to be utterly destitute, yet too proud to accept assistance. The next morning the man came to Verzan on the street. He was still haggard, but quite composed. He asked Verzan to go with him to some room where they could converse undisturbed.

When they were alone, the man told Verzan that he had a confession to make. He said he had long enough passed restless days and sleepless nights. He would now confess everything. Verzan began to suspect that his old friend was suffering from mental derangement of some kind, but soothingly requested him to state his troubles, pledging himself to secrecy.

At last the man turned to his old employer, and gulped out: "I am a thief—a robber. I have robbed you!"

"Crazy, luny—mad as a March hare," thought Verzan. "Nonsense!" cried he, bursting into a hearty laugh. "If that is your only trouble, make yourself easy. If you had ever robbed me, I most assuredly must have been aware of the fact. Ha! Ha! Robbed me; that is a good joke. You are heartily welcome to all that you ever robbed me of."

"Oh, but you do not know; you could not know, for you never saw the gold; still I robbed you. I stole out of your mine a lump of gold that weighed twenty-four pounds!"

"Poor devil," thought Verzan, "he is as crazy as a loon"; then turning to his old employee, he cried: "Twenty-four devils! Why,

347

there was never a nugget found in the mine that weighed one pound, not to speak of twenty-four!"

"That was just what it weighed as it came out of the ground," said the thief, "but of course some quartz came out of the mass when it was cut up and run into small bars. I have brought you all the bars I have left, and I want you to take them; I want to eat one meal that is not bought with stolen gold."

So saying, the penitent thief began to empty the pockets of his coat. He dropped bar after bar of solid gold into the hands of Verzan, who sat staring at the cubes of bright yellow metal in speechless astonishment. Bars to the value of $2,500 were laid in his hands and piled on his knees.

"What are you doing?" at last cried Mr. Verzan, as he saw his old friend thus emptying his pockets of the golden bars. "I don't understand this at all!"

"No," said the man who was ridding himself of the bars as though they were red hot. "No, but you will understand it perfectly well when I have told you my story."

"We shall see; we shall see," said Mr. Verzan; "let me hear the story of your wonderful nugget."

"You shall hear everything. I have come to you to make a clean breast of the business. You shall be told all; that is, all but the names of parties who assisted me in making the bars. I have solemnly sworn never to reveal their names."

"That is all right," said Verzan; "let the names go."

The man then proceeded to tell how he found the nugget, his sudden temptation, and the hiding of the gold as already related. What follows is the fellow's story of his tribulations and adventures as told to Verzan.

The Confession of the Man Who Stole the Big Nugget

"Almost as soon as I had hidden the lump of gold by placing on top of it the big flat rock, my troubles began. I feared that some one of the men would remove the rock, that the gold would be seen, and that I would be accused of having stolen and secreted it. I dreaded seeing anyone go to throw an armful of rocks on the waste dump. I felt almost sure that the stone would be knocked off before night. I was in

348

agony during the remainder of the day. Out of the corners of my eyes I watched every man that went near the dump. So it went on until we knocked off work in the evening, and my gold was still safe.

"I lingered a little behind as the men left the diggings in order to mark well the spot where the nugget lay, for that night I must get it away. I feared that if I left it on the dump it would be covered up and lost.

"About midnight that night, I crept out of my cabin with a sack in my pocket and hastened to the mine. I started at every sound and at times I trembled violently. However, quaking and bathed in perspiration, I secured the nugget in my sack and fled from the spot as rapidly as possible, for on a sudden it occurred to me that secretly a man might be employed at the mine of nights to guard against the sluice boxes being robbed.

"As soon as I was well away from the mine arose the question of where to hide the nugget. I could think of no good hiding place, and so, still walking on, I came almost to my cabin. My mind was in such a whirl that I could not think of any prominent or peculiar landmark, and at last, when near to my cabin, I went a few steps from the trail, and, scratching a hole with my hands beneath a big sagebush, there buried sack and all. I could not sleep till near morning for thinking of my gold, and as soon as I was up I took a walk past the sagebrush to see if the ground at its roots had been disturbed. No sooner had I done this, however, than I began to scold myself for having made so many tracks about the spot where the treasure lay.

"While at work that day, it came into my head that there had been bacon in the sack in which I had buried the gold. The sack being greasy, a coyote or a hungry dog might dig it up and drag into sight the big nugget. This thought worried me all day.

"That night I took the gold out of the sack and buried it beside a big rock, but no sooner had I got into bed than it occurred to me that I was a great fool. People always buried treasure at the side of some big rock, therefore it was about such rocks that persons would go prowling in search of valuables and money. I arose, dressed, and moved the gold to the root of a small cedar tree. During the three weeks that I remained at the mine after the gold came into my possession, I for one reason and another almost nightly carried it to a new hiding place, until at last I thought of burying it in front of my

349

cabin and covering the spot with a bucket of ashes. This done, I could see at a glance each morning and evening that my treasure was safe.

"When I had bought my donkey and was packing him to start out on my pretended prospecting expedition, I had the nugget in a sack and hid it in a big roll of blankets, well bound round at each end with cords. I suspected everyone that came near of knowing that I had stolen the nugget, and had several frights when neighbors put their hands on the blankets in assisting me to pack the donkey, a business at which I was awkward.

"I felt much relieved when I at last got away and was all alone on the road. Soon, however, I began to think of robbers and thieving Indians. Of nights I feared to lodge in houses, and when camping out was constantly uneasy, though I hid the lump of gold in the ground while leveling off a place for my bed. Even to myself I made a pretense of leveling the ground on which to spread my blankets, as an excuse for taking into my hands a shovel with which to fashion a secret sleeping place for my nugget.

"When I reached Ward, a place I had never before been in, I still had trouble, and thought everyone in the camp watching me, but as soon as I had bought a cabin well out in the suburbs of the little town I buried the gold in front of it, and covered the spot with ashes taken hot from my stove. I thought this safer than anyplace in the cabin or beneath its floor; besides, I could see at a glance in passing in and out of my home whether the ashes were disturbed.

"My greatest trouble, however, came when my ready money was all gone and I had to think of disposing of a portion of the stolen nugget. I could not cut off and sell pieces of it without exciting curiosity and perhaps suspicion. It would therefore be necessary to melt it down and mold it into small bars. In order to get the gold into the shape of bars I would require the use of a blacksmith's forge; also would need a crucible and proper mold.

"I spent some days in prowling about the camp in search of a blacksmith shop near some unworked mine in an out-of-the-way place. At last I found what I wanted. Half a mile from any house I discovered a forge, charcoal, and a lot of tools, in a blacksmith shop near a small mine in which work had been discontinued. The shop was a small frame shanty, the door of which was fastened with a padlock. While peering into the place through various chinks I saw what looked like a small plumbago crucible. In order to make sure that I had discovered such a treasure, after looking about to see if the coast was clear, I pried up a window at one end of the shop, and managed to clamber inside.

Caught in a Trap

"I found that the crucible was just what I wanted. With it in my hands I went about the shop looking for cold chisels with which to cut up the nugget. I was planning to visit the shop at night to melt my gold and mold my bars, pouring the metal into molds cut out in firebrick. I thought that in two or three nights I could work up the whole mass of gold.

"While going about busy with my plans, my head down, picking up and looking at tools in search of a good chisel, I was startled by a gruff voice crying: 'So, my fine fellow, I've caught you at last! You're the duck that's been stealing tools out of my shop!'

"Lifting my head, I saw a rough-looking fellow, bearded almost to the eyes, staring in at the window. I told the fellow that I had no intention of carrying anything out of the shop.

"'All very fine, but I see that you have a crucible under your arm and both hands full of tools at this very moment.'

"I said I was only looking at the things and had no thought of carrying them away. Then I told the fellow I did not believe he was any more owner of the shop than myself.

"The man gave a snort of wrath at this, and ran round to the door. 'That I have a key to the shop and can open the door shows that I have some right to it, doesn't it?' and in a moment he unlocked the door and stepped inside.

"The instant the fellow was inside he leveled a six-shooter at my head and said I would have to march to town with him; that he had been robbed long enough; more than fifty dollars' worth of mining and other tools had been stolen out of the shop; he'd been laying for the thief for three months; I must 'walk chalk.'

"Again I declared that I had no intention of carrying away a single tool; that the only thing that had induced me to enter the shop as I did was the sight of the crucible.

"'Ha, the crucible!' cried the fellow, eyeing me sharply. 'And what did you intend to do with the crucible?' 'Melt something in it, perhaps,' said I; 'make an assay of some ore.' 'Not likely. You've been in the mountains long enough to know that assays are not melted in a blacklead crucible. You know well enough that such a crucible is used for melting metals. Ha, you change color! I can guess what you wanted that crucible for—I can see it in your eye. It was to make something like this,' and the fellow held up a silver dollar.

"'Nothing of the kind,' said I. 'It was gold that—' Then I stopped short, for I had spoken without thinking, in my anxiety to deny that I was a counterfeiter.

"'Ah! Oho! Gold, eh? Better yet,' cried the man, his face lighting up. 'Come now, own up, pard—own up that you intended to do a little work in the queer line. Own up, pard, and I'll let you off.'

"'No, I know nothing of such business. I'm an honest—' Here I stuck again, for I remembered that I was the worst kind of a thief, having robbed my benefactor.

"'Ah, ha! Why don't you finish and say thief? Yes, good; you are like myself an honest thief. Come now, are you not a thief?'

"'I don't recognize your right to question me in that way,' said I.

"'No, not when I catch you making free with my property. But honor among thieves, say I, so I'll not march you into town. However, you must be friendly. Now, you've as good as told me why you were hooking onto that crucible, so I don't mind telling you that I'm pretty good at this stuff (showing a handful of silver), but if you can tackle the yellow boys you are ahead of me—you're an artist. I must take some lessons from you. You shall be as much at home in this shop as I am, night or day. Come, shake hands, pard.'

"I dare not refuse to take his hand; and as soon as we had shaken hands, he cried: 'Good! Now we understand each other. The new firm can now begin to think of business. You just tell me what you want; I'll get all the stuff if you'll agree to let me see you work.'

"This was getting along too fast, I was being adopted as a brother counterfeiter almost without a word of consent on my part. It was a condition of affairs in which I could not silently acquiesce; yet in declining the honor I must be careful not to arouse the ire of the man into whose clutches I had fallen. He was a powerful, broad-chested six-footer, with long, muscular arms and fists like those of a prizefighter at the ends of his great hairy wrists.

"It was with infinite trouble that I at last convinced this hairy giant that I knew nothing about the useful art of manufacturing false coin; but he finally gave up the point, though only to besiege me more closely than ever as to my intended use of the crucible. I had said I was

THE BIG NEVADA NUGGET

going to melt gold in it. Surely that meant something rather aside from the quiet routine of business pursued by men engaged in the ordinary pursuits of life. Was I thinking of making a few neat little bars?

"At this I started, but the fellow went on to say that if such were my intentions he could give me a few useful points. I gave up and let the man talk on, which he did quite enthusiastically, it appearing that counterfeiting and imitating the precious metals was his hobby. Indeed, he believed he was almost on the point of finding the philosopher's stone, therefore thought the business he was engaged in as honest as any other.

"At last we left the shop and started toward the town. On the way the man who had on so short an acquaintance adopted me as his full partner renewed his efforts to gain possession of my secret, and so insisted upon knowing the business I had in hand, and made so many promises to deal on the 'dead square' with me that I told him to come to my cabin that evening, when we would have further talk and might come to such an understanding as to do a little work together.

"'You're a cautious one, but I like you all the better for that,' said the giant as we parted. 'I feel too much confidence in my strength to beat much about the bush; I want to push all out of my way and go straight to my mark. That is my great fault. You are just the other way, so we will make the right kind of a team to work together.'

"I did not at all relish this kind of talk. It was evident that because I had shaken hands with the fellow, he considered all settled between us and a partnership fully agreed upon. However, I thought that I would be able easily to escape the fellow when done with him.

The Counterfeiter's Visit—The Big Nugget Dug Up

"That night my man was promptly on hand, with a hearty 'Good evening, pard!'

"After some preliminary skirmishing, in which the fellow renewed his promises of secrecy and good faith, I said to him: 'Suppose, now, for instance, that a friend of yours should happen to have in his possession a considerable number of pounds of gold—not bogus gold, but as good gold as ever was dug out of the ground—which he desired to smelt and mold into small bars, could you assist him in the work?'

"'Could I! Yes; and wouldn't I? No matter where or how he got it.

353

If you have anything like that to do, I'm the very man you want. The good God above, who does all things for the best, must have sent you to me. Why, do you know that we are this moment fully prepared for the work? Yes; we have everything that will be required. I once did a little in bogus gold bricks, and I had made some molds of various small sizes, mostly for bricks of the value of $25, $50 and $100. These are the kinds that small miners—those working with arastras and hand mortars—generally have to sell. I have punches with letters and figures on them to stamp weight, fineness, value, and all else if we need that work. But, after all, I never did a great deal in that line, for in towns assay offices are too handy. The trick can only be worked on the small ranchers and station keepers on the stage and wagon roads in out-of-the-way places in the mountains of California or other such regions. Even then you must be all the time traveling, and to make it pay you must once in a while trouble a stage driver to stop and hold up his hands. Ah! now it pops into my head why you were looking at the cold chisels. You have a big bar to cut up. By the holy poker! I begin to understand. You have done a good stroke of business up in Idaho or Montana, where the stages carry gold bricks, one of which is a small fortune?"

"Here I stopped the fellow, who was in such high feather that he rattled on incessantly from one thing to another. I told him that he was wrong; that the gold I had was a lump just as it came out of the bowels of the earth—a mass of gold that the eyes of no living being except myself had ever seen.

"The fellow's jaw dropped. Placing his elbow on my table and resting his chin in his hand, he gazed at me with a most puzzled expression of countenance, gruffly grunting 'Um, um!' At last, after sharply studying my face for full three minutes the coiner said: 'Ah, well! Now, how big is this lump of gold you tell of?' Said I, 'It weighs twenty-four pounds.'

"'Pard,' said the giant, rising, drawing himself to his full height and fixing his keen gray eyes upon me, 'Pard, I hope that you are in your right senses and on the square, but d——n me if you don't pile it on pretty thick—a little too thick. Now, I don't just exactly know whether you are a little luny on gold and the big nugget business or whether you are one of those infernal sneaks calling themselves detectives, who go about the country prying into the business of people

354

much more honest than themselves. If you are on the detective lay I've told you a little too much for your future welfare, and I'd as well settle with you at once, seeing that I'll never have a better opportunity.'

"Before I could open my mouth to reply a cocked revolver was at my head. 'You are either the one thing or the other,' cried the desperado; 'you either have something you believe to be gold or you are a sort of bungling detective. Now, show me that lump of gold at once or out go your brains!'

"I felt that I was caught again. 'If I show it to you you'll rob me of it,' stammered I; 'you'll kill me and take it.'

"'No,' said the rogue, reseating himself; 'No: I'll not harm a hair of your head. I am ready to swear to that. I'll only take what you agree to give me for my assistance, but I hope you'll be liberal. What, now, will you give me to mold your big lump of gold into bars?'

"'It is a thing in which you run no risk at all, but still I'll give you $300,' said I.

"'Make it $500, pard, and it goes,' cried the fellow.

"'Well, then, $500,' said I.

"'Now show me your gold,' cried my man, rising to his feet and again assuming a hostile look,'or I'll have to put a bullet through your head. You see I've got to be serious with you. You've wormed so much out of me with making me believe you a counterfeiter, a stage robber, or some such person as would be sure to do business on the square, that I feel a good deal ashamed and affronted, I assure you, at finding you nothing of the kind, but merely a sort of I don't know what—a fellow of no reputation.'

"During this long, threatening harangue I had regained control of my nerves and wits. I reminded the fellow that as he had not yet sworn to neither rob nor harm me, he could not expect me to produce the nugget.

"'That is true,' said the fellow, cooling down at once. He then took a solemn oath which I dictated, and in turn I took the same myself, swearing never to name or betray him.

"'Ah, now, this is business!' cried the fellow. 'Shake, pard!' and he nearly crushed the bones of my hand in his viselike grasp.

"I then told him to remain quietly in the cabin for a few minutes and I would go out and bring in the lump of gold.

"'No, you don't!' cried the ruffian, his old suspicions again instant-

355

ly aroused. With the muzzle of his cocked pistol at my head, he hissed: 'No, my chicken, you don't go out of here to make your signals and bring your hellhounds to catch me like a rat in a trap!'

"'How, then, am I to get the gold?'

"'Where is it?'

"'Buried in the ground outside.'

"'Far from the cabin?'

"'Not two rods.'

"'Can you find it in the dark?'

"'With my eyes shut.'

"'With a pistol at the back of your head?'

"'Yes; but remember your oath.'

"'True, there is the oath. Are you sure you are bound by it?'

"'As much as by a thousand.'

"'May I go with you to get your lump of gold?'

"'Why, of course. If I trust you to see the gold, what is the empty hole left behind in the ground?'

"'Pard, after all, I believe you are on the square. Now I'm only afraid that you've all along been fooling yourself with some lump of base metal. Lead the way and I'll follow, only asking to take my pistol along for fear of accidents.'

"'Take it in welcome, but keep it away from my head.'

"'All right, pard, I'll hold it down so, and guard you against surprise while you dig.'

The Big Nugget by Lamplight

"Without further parley, I led the way out of my cabin, the hairy giant following with his cocked pistol. There was no moon, but all the stars were shining brightly. I went directly to the pile of ashes, and, scraping it aside with my feet, got down upon my knees and began delving in the ground with my hands.

"I was a long while at this work, for the gold had been buried in a hole dug with a pick and shovel, and was much deeper than I had thought it.

"Meanwhile my ruffian guard was on nettles. Every moment he was asking: 'Do you feel it?' or 'Have you got it?' stooping lower and lower in his anxiety. At last he got down on his knees beside me and tried to peep into the hole.

"'I see you don't find it! Could anyone have taken it?' he whispered.

"'No,' said I, 'it must be deeper. Let me get at the ground with my knife,' and I reached back to my hip for my sheath-knife. Instantly my man was on his feet and had his pistol leveled. 'You don't catch a weasel asleep!' said he. 'If you have anything in that hole, get it out and be quick about it, too. You don't slip any knife into me, my fine fellow!'

"'Ah! Now I feel it—it's all right!' cried I, paying no attention to the suspicious rascal.

"I had touched the nugget at almost the first thrust of my knife and soon I had it in my hands and hugged it in my arms.

"I ran at once to the cabin with my treasure, leaving the robber to follow or clear out, as he pleased. He was close at my heels, you may be sure, and by the time he entered the cabin I had the big nugget in a bucket of water and was washing away the soil that had clung to it.

"My man had now put up his pistol and was becoming near almost consumed with curiosity. In anticipation of the best and fear of the worst, he was speechless. Having washed the mass of gold till it glittered in every part, I placed it on my table without a word and turned up my lamp to full height.

"'The Great Eternal!' cried the desperado, as he dropped into a chair before the mighty nugget. Then, lifting the golden mass, holding it up to the lamp, and turning it about to catch the gleam of the metal from a dozen different points, he cried: 'Yes, by the Eternal! it is gold—good solid gold as ever was dug, and by the gods it is placer gold! It is gold from a grand mine.'

"'You are right,' said I.

"'Pard, I did you a great wrong to suspect you of being a sneak and playing false. Here is solid proof of your truthfulness and worth!' And again he held up and viewed the nugget with greedy and sparkling eyes. Then, dropping the gold and rushing upon me he cried: 'Pard, you're a jewel! D——n me I've got to hug you!' And in a moment I was in a clasp compared with which that of a grizzly bear would have been gentle.

"The fellow was almost beside himself with joy. He danced about the room and in spite of my protests tried to repeat his hateful hug, saying he loved me so well he could 'break every bone in my body.'

"I had hard work to bring him to talk of my business, the molding of the mass of gold into bars, but at last he said we would begin the work the very next night. So often did the fellow return to and lift and fondle the huge nugget that I began to fear that he would take my life in order to possess the whole of it; in one of his hugs he might slip a knife into my heart.

"Fortunately, he at last began to burn to learn where I got the big lump of gold. It could have come from no place in Nevada; therefore, I must have stolen it in California, Idaho, Montana, or some other place where were big placer mines. 'Where did you get it?' he at last squarely asked.

"'That is my secret,' said I.

"'Of course; but if you came by it honestly, why should you not openly sell it?'

"'Would not the offering of such a mass of gold excite great curiosity and make a great noise? Would not everyone ask as you have done, "Where did you get it?"'

"'Oh, I suppose so—yes, of course.'

"'Well, that is just what I am not ready to tell. Suppose that you were out in the wilds of the mountains prospecting and should stumble upon a gravel deposit, and while digging in it should not only find plenty of small gold, but in addition such an immense nugget as this, would you not wish to preserve your secret until you had examined the country thoroughly in order to find out how you could get water to your placer, and also to see if you could find the quartz vein that had shed such quantities of gold? Suppose you had been obliged to strike into the settlements for provisions after only two day's work in your wonderful placer; would you want to have the whole country dogging your steps day and night as would be the case were you to go openly and aboveboard and sell a mass of gold like that?'

"'You are right; it wouldn't do.'

"'Of course it wouldn't, and that is why I am willing to make almost any sacrifice to keep my secret till I can go back well supplied with provisions to make a long stay. Then I can make sure of water, the quartz vein, wood, and all I want.'

"'So you have made such a discovery?'

"'Of course. Where else would I get such a mass of gold? If I had stolen such a wonderful nugget, would there not long ago have been a great howl about it in all the papers? Have you heard such a howl anywhere on the Pacific Coast?'

358

"'No. I'll tell you what I'll do; I'll turn honest if you'll trust me and let me go with you to your mine. All I ask is the second chance. You shall take all your claims first. I will stand by you as a brother; I swear it. I will fight for your rights, and I'm a terror in a fight. I'll defend you and your rights with my life if you will but take me with you.'

"'I will consider the matter,' said I. 'I had sworn to myself before I met you to go back by myself; to let no living man into the secret. But by accident you surprised me in that infernal old shop when I went to look for the crucible. Curse the shop, and curse the rotten old crucible!'

"'Oh, my friend, my pard, do not take on in that way. It was the will of God that we should meet there and in that way. Yes, I feel that it was so; the good God above wished to reform me. It was for that He brought us together. I am already a changed man. That lump of gold is now as nothing in my sight—nothing at all. And only to think that a few minutes ago I was gloating over it; was even thinking—I may now freely confess it since I have become your sworn brother—was even thinking of sticking my knife into you in order to get possession of the valuable nugget. But now God has changed my heart. He means for me to go with you, my brother, to your big gold mine, there to stand up and fight for your rights.'

"'We shall see; we shall see,' said I; 'but the first thing to do is to get through the work nearest our hands. Even this lump of gold is not to be despised, as it will furnish the means to secure whole mule loads as good, if not as big. Yes, when I go again, I shall take at least five, and perhaps ten mules.'

"'Is it far, brother?'

"'Not so far, my man—less than three hundred miles—but it is wild; awful piles of rocks, gorges, mountain wastes, roaring waters, and dark and deep valleys.'

"'So much the better, brother. In all these things I delight. It will be a paradise; I always feel nearer my God when in such lonely wilds.'

"It was growing late, and having agreed to meet at my cabin the next evening to go to the old shop and begin our molding, my desperado was taking his departure. As he was on his way to the door, he turned back and, glancing at the nugget, said, 'By the way, what will you do with the nugget tonight? You can't leave it there, you know.'

"'Oh as to that,' said I, 'it don't much matter. I'll chuck it under the bed or dump it down under the floor.'

359

"'Would it be safe? You know, brother, that ten mules and an outfit will cost some money.'

"'True,' said I, picking up the gold, 'and if you think you can keep it more securely than I can, take it along and take care of it till tomorrow night,' and so saying I placed it in the hands of the cutthroat.

"'No, no, brother! Do not trust me. I fear God has not yet made me sufficiently strong,' then he dropped into a chair and, covering his face with his hands, sobbed aloud. 'Oh, my brother, such confidence goes to my heart. God is doing his work in me. He means to give you a strong and faithful defender when you go to your great gold mine. No, I will not touch the gold; hide it away yourself,' and so saying he bounded to his feet and rushed from the house.

"As soon as he was gone, I bolted and barred my cabin, got my pistol handy, put the nugget into my stove, and built a fire on it that would make it red hot, then went to bed. I feared that my friend might have made a wrong diagnosis of his case when he said God was working in him—it was more likely to be the ruler of the brimstone regions.

"It was a lucky thought flashed into my brain that caused me to invent the story of my great gold mine. It so excited the greed of the ruffian who had got me in his clutches that he looked upon the nugget as a trifle. It saved my life and would keep me safe as long as the fellow believed I could guide him to such an El Dorado as I had pictured. When, in view of immensely greater gain, the fellow decided not to murder me for the nugget, he doubtless did feel such a change of heart as to think God was working in him, and that at last he was one of the pure in heart. No more need to rob, steal, counterfeit, and murder when he would soon possess a mountain of gold.

Appearance of the Partner Levi

"The next night my saintly ruffian was promptly on hand. During the day he had been at the old blacksmith shop and put it in order for work. He had surrounded the forge with curtains made of old canvas, pieces of blankets, and an old tent—stuff that had been stowed in a corner of the shop and which had no doubt done duty before when a different kind of work was in progress. The object of thus curtaining the forge was to prevent the light of its fire from being seen through the old shell of a shop in case of anyone through some accident passing that way.

"That night we cut up the nugget and made one melt in the crucible, molding several small bars. One of these I gave to the brother who had adopted me. The others and the remains of the nugget we carried back to my cabin.

"All the night my ruffian was very kind and affectionate, and again and again assured me that through the change God had wrought in his heart he felt himself a new man; his sins had all been wiped away and he was beginning a new life, as innocent as in the days of his childhood. He assured me that he had made up his mind to make an offering to the Almighty [of] his $500—almost his first honest money. He said he would give five dollars to the poor preacher who came to Ward once a fortnight to hold service. Then, his heart warming as his mind was turned to matters of religion, he placed his huge right hand upon my shoulder, his face all aglow and looking like one inspired. 'Brother,' cried he, 'soon we shall be in possession of the millions of our golden mountains; then, by G—d, we'll buy this preacher and start a church of our own!'

"The great hairy giant was as earnest and honest in this charitable thought as a schoolboy meditating his first Christmas present to a loved teacher. The good fellow was continually making bids for my admiration.

"The next night we were again at our work and made rapid progress. My giant was in excellent spirits. He would have roared out a song if he had dared venture upon such an exhibition of the joy that filled his breast. While we were in the midst of our melting and molding, the tattered curtains surrounding the forge parted and a strange face peered in upon us. I gave the giant a gentle hint upon one of his shins with the toe of my boot. He turned and stared at the face, his countenance expressive of the most unbounded astonishment, but stood with open mouth without uttering a word.

"'Why, hello, old pard, what is all this?' cried the intruder, passing within the curtained space. 'What is all this?' continued he. 'Doing a stroke of business without me? I am cast aside, eh? Your education is completed, I suppose, and you have taken a new partner and set up in business on your own account? But, my dear old chum, you should have said a word to me before opening at the old stand; it, you know, is still our common property.'

"While the stranger was thus talking, my giant pretended to be terribly confused and nonplussed. But turning to me, he managed to stammer that the man before me was his pard and one of the best and sharpest fellows in the world. He had not let him into the affairs of the nugget because he thought it my secret and my own private business. He had no right to divulge a thing he had sworn to keep a secret. However, since his partner had stumbled in upon us, he would be answerable for his honesty and good faith. He would explain to his partner, who would be sworn and all would then be well.

"The newcomer was a man about thirty years of age, was of slender build, had hands as small and white as those [of] a lady, sported a carefully trimmed and trained moustache, and was neatly dressed. He presented the appearance of a mining-camp sport. After my giant had made a full explanation of the business in which we were then engaged, and had dilated upon the piles of golden nuggets to be had in the El Dorado I had discovered, Arthur, as I shall call the new man, refused to take the oath of secrecy unless he received the same sum as his partner. As there were now to be three in the firm, all should start out on an equal footing. He squarely demanded $500.

"'Oh, brother,' said my giant, 'I was wrong not to tell you of this pard of mine, a friend of my soul, and submit to you the question of taking him into the firm. There I was wrong, my brother; but since he has come to us by chance, let us give him the $500. What is such a trifle to us? Say the word and, like three brothers, we will proceed with the work now before us.'

"Arthur stood by, scowling as though he felt that he had been greatly slighted and wronged. He was determined to have $500 out of the nugget. He felt nothing of the change of heart that had tamed my shaggy giant.

"I saw plainly enough the trick of the pair, but could not help myself. I agreed to give Arthur the sum he demanded, but stipulated that no more members should be brought into the firm. If more men were brought in, I declared that I would not guide the party to my secret mine.

"The pair agreed to everything, and swore to do all I might require of them. As soon as Arthur was sure of his $500, he dropped his sullenness. He became another man. He was all smiles and activity. He pushed the giant aside and himself took charge of the crucible and the molding of the bars. It at once became evident that he was an old hand at the business of managing metals. He searched about the back of the forge and pretended to find some fluxes, which I was sure he took from his pocket, and did more work in one hour than the giant had been able to do in four. Indeed, he so expedited the business that two hours before daylight we left the shop. The big nugget had been transformed into bars, and a division of these had been made that was pronounced satisfactory.

"On the way back to town, Arthur gave us a glimpse of some molds for silver coin, as he said, and told a very smooth story about his going to the old shop to do a little work on his own account; his great astonishment at finding the shop occupied and the forge in full blast, with sparks pouring from the chimney. He then laughingly bandied us for our carelessness in not fastening the door on the inside, and so managing the fire as to prevent sparks. Indeed, he was very jolly and agreeable. At parting he announced that he and the giant would call on me some evening during the week to talk over plans for an expedition to my secret mine. I soon discovered that Arthur was the brain and the big man the muscle of the odd partnership.

A Bird that Can Sing, But Will Not, Must Be Made to Sing

"I need not relate what was said on the occasion of the visit of the two worthies to my cabin that week, and on several other occasions; suffice it to say that nothing was talked of but my pretended gold mine, which I was made to describe again and again. Soon my partners, as they persisted in styling themselves, had spent and gambled away the money I had given them. Then they became urgent in regard to the trip to the secret mine, giving me hardly a single night's rest. By a cunning trick (doubtless planned by the brain of the firm) the giant so planned that we one night caught Arthur at making false silver coin. This was made to appear to me as a great joke. Being asked to hold and to handle certain tools and other things while in the shop, it was soon after asserted that I had assisted in the work of counterfeiting; then this, and a dozen other things, was brought to bear upon me to induce me to lead the way to my supposed gold mine. But for the loads of gold they expected to get out of this mine, the pair would long ago have robbed and, perhaps, murdered me.

"I am at my wits' end for excuses for delay in leading them to my supposed mine. I am now constantly watched by the pair, as they fear that I intend to steal away from them. Recently they have become threatening. They have given me to understand that if I do not soon go with them of my own accord, they will force me at the muzzles of their pistols to lead them to my mine. I am bad enough, but I have fallen into the hands of rascals who are the bane of my life—men who will either murder me or land me in the state prison."

Here the purloiner of the big nugget ended his confession, and with many tears begged Mr. Verzan to assist him in making his escape from the desperados into whose clutches he had fallen. Feeling that his old friend had received a lesson that would last him to the end of his days, Mr. Verzan gave him $250 and planned his escape from his rascally partners.

By Verzan's advice the penitent went to Mexico, carrying with him a letter that procured him employment in a silver mine. From Mexico he went to South Africa. There, within two years, he found in diamonds almost as great wealth as he had pictured to exist in his pretended gold mine.

Now the man who was tempted to appropriate gold not his own is an esteemed and envied citizen of a beautiful town in a state east of the Mississippi. There he dwells in peace in the midst of his children and grandchildren. Doubtless he delights the latter with many wonderful stories of big diamonds, but it is not probable that he has much talent for tales of big nuggets of gold.

With Verzan and his old partners in the Osceola the case is different, for each wears a beautiful South African diamond that constantly reminds him of Nevada's twenty-four-pound nugget.

Elam Storm

The Man of the Mountains and His Millions.

$\mathcal{A}$ fortnight ago I found myself at Lake Tahoe. I had not been at the lake an hour before I had the good fortune to fall in with my old California friend, Ned Meredeth.

"Just in time," said Ned, after we had exchanged greetings. "I had planned a trip to Emerald Bay for tomorrow and was just casting about in my mind for a fellow voyager when you hove in sight. We will make the trip together and go prepared to have a regular old-fashioned lunch ashore. We are sure to have a good time."

"All right; count me in," said I.

We took an early start and had a glorious sail up the lake and across the bay. With a spoon hook trailing astern of our boat, we caught several fine trout during our sail. Landing in a little cove, we went ashore for the purpose of roasting a trout and having a good substantial lunch. The roast trout was a success and we made a hearty meal. Having appeased our hunger, we lighted our cigars and stretched ourselves upon the ground to smoke, to listen to the wind whispering

---

A tale of a wild mountain man and his naturally-buried millions. From the *Territorial Enterprise*, July 29, 1877.

in the tops of the pines and to gaze listlessly upon the waves dancing and flashing far out on the lake.

I might here say something about the grand scenery in the midst of which we found ourselves, but scores of both pen and pencil pictures, better than I could hope to paint, have already made most of those who are likely to read this little sketch familiar with the more prominent points of interest about the lake; beside, my present object is to tell the story of a curious character it was our good fortune to encounter.

We had almost finished our cigars when the crackling of a dry stick just at our backs caused us to start up and face about. Approaching was a tall, gaunt, middle-aged man. He wore heavy cowhide boots, into which were thrust about half the length of a pair of stout corduroy pantaloons, and in place of coat and vest appeared no less than three woolen shirts, the two outer ones very heavy and worn open at the breast. His beard was long and yellow, and a shock of yellow hair thatched his head, almost rendering superfluous the tattered, slouched hat he wore. On his right shoulder he carried a long Kentucky rifle and an "Arkansaw toothpick" hung from his leathern waist belt.

Striding up to where we were standing, our visitor said: "Good day, boys," and dropping to the ground even as he so greeted us, laid his rifle by his side and, crossing his legs a la Turk, looked out at us from beneath the wide brim of his hat for a moment, then abruptly said: "I am a man of the mountains."

"So I should judge," said Ned.

"The voice of the wind in the trees is more familiar to me than the voice of man."

"Been long in the mountains?" asked Ned.

"I am Elam Storm and I have been in the mountains a long time— so long that they seem to have worn down a good deal since I first began traveling over them."

"Every pebble kicked from the top of a ridge rolls toward the bottom," remarked Ned.

"And every drop of rain sends some grains of sand in the same direction," pursued Elam.

"And the winds spread the dust of the mountaintop over the valleys," said Ned.

"And the rills from the melting snow," suggested I.

"And the landslides and the avalanches," ventured Ned.

"They are a power," said I.

"Great God!" cried Elam, "they *are* a power!" and he drew the brim of his hat down over his eyes as though to shut out some troublesome vision.

"Do you live in this region?" asked Ned, arousing Elam from a fit of musing that had lasted some minutes.

"Sometimes. I am a man of the mountains. My home is wherever I make my camp. When winter comes I move down the mountains in advance of the snow, and with the return of warm weather ascend to the upper valleys and peaks with the deer."

"Is your present camp here on the lake?" I asked.

"I have some traps and provisions stowed away in a hole in the rocks—a sort of cavern—over behind yonder mountain," and Elam pointed in the direction of a high granite ridge to the southwest.

"You are a hunter, are you not?" queried Ned.

"Yes, I am a hunter of gold—a hunter of gold. Boys," and Elam spoke in a low and impressive tone, "there is gold in these mountains; yes, millions on millions of gold!"

"Doubtless," said I, "but the trouble is to find it."

"It was found once and I'll find it again. Yes, I'll find it. I've looked for it years and years, but at last I shall find it. I know the place and I have seen the gold. Too much snow up there—always too much snow!" And thus concluding, the wild glitter died out of Elam's eyes, he sighed deeply, and his thoughts seemed far away.

"As but little snow fell last winter, you should be able to find the gold this summer," suggested Ned.

"Yes; this summer I shall find it—this summer or never!" And Elam grasped his gun and unfolded his legs as though about to arise.

"You are sure it is there?" queried I.

"As sure as that I am here. Some hint that I am not right here," touching his forehead, "but they do not know my story. I may tell it now—may tell it here, but not everywhere. Listen, and you, too, will know that the gold is there.

"Many years ago a man who was out hunting lost his way in these mountains. In his wanderings he came to a small stream—a mere rill—and lay down at it to drink. While drinking he saw gold on the bedrock—beautiful nuggets of gold glittering under the water!

"He remained until he had gathered not less than five pounds of nuggets, then—being out of provisions and almost starved—he was obliged to renew his efforts to find his way out of the mountains. He traveled down the rill till it entered a brook, down the brook till it was lost in a large stream, then down this last to a still larger, and so on, marking as he descended the mouth of each creek as he left it behind.

"This man lived not far from the town of Genoa, and was my nearest neighbor. He was much excited when he first reached home, and showed me specimens of the gold, at the same time giving some account of the way in which he found it, but he soon after became so close-mouthed that he would tell me nothing more; he pretended that his first story was nothing but a joke, and invented a new story to account for his being in possession of the gold he had shown me.

"I was not deceived. I knew the first story was the true one, and was sure that he would soon go back to his mine for more gold, so I watched his cabin and shadowed him day and night. I hardly allowed myself time to eat or sleep, and had always on hand, near his cabin, a hidden store of provisions sufficient to last several days, for I did not know what day or night he might start for the mountains.

"At last, after I had watched nearly a week, I saw my man steal forth in the dusk of the evening with a blanket, tools, and provisions on his back. I hastily secured my outfit and cautiously followed him. All that night I was his shadow, and all the next day I kept him in view. When night came, he camped, and after cooking his supper, rolled himself in his blankets and stretched out on the ground by his fire.

"I was cold and my teeth chattered, but I was afraid to make a fire. I did not once close my eyes that night, for there was gold ahead—thousands on thousands of gold!

"In the morning, after breakfast, my man again moved on, and I stealthily followed. He toiled up a deep, rocky ravine, and I skulked behind from rock to rock and from bend to bend. About noon he stopped and lunched, then went on two or three miles, till well up toward the summit of the main range, when he halted and, stowing away his blankets and other traps, soon began the work of picking up and panning out gold. He was at work on the south side of a deep ravine, at the foot of a great mountain, the face of which was covered with snow—all one sheet of snow—God knows how deep!

"Having discovered the golden secret, and being greatly in need of rest and sleep, I crept out of the ravine and made my way across the first ridge to the northward, where I might safely make a camp and build a fire. As I lay by my fire that night and thought that we two were the only human beings among all the great silent peaks standing about, and then considered the business we were on, there seemed something awful in it—the deep silence was absolutely painful. At last, however, I slept, and slept well till morning; indeed, till after sunrise.

"Leaving my traps in camp, I recrossed the ridge and, crawling from rock to rock and tree to tree, at last gained a position about fifty yards above the bottom of the ravine and just opposite where my man was at work. Peering round the end of a block of granite behind which I lay, I could see him picking the nuggets out from among the finer gold after he had washed a pan of dirt. How I longed for the day of his departure in order that I might take his place and dig my share of those golden nuggets! Thinking of this, I determined to put myself on a short allowance of provisions in order that I might remain in the mountains as long as possible. It then occurred to me that he would be likely to hit upon the same plan for prolonging his stay, and that I should be starved out by the time he left the spot.

"At one time I thought of boldly discovering myself and claiming a partnership in the mine; then it came into my head to steal upon my man at night as he lay by his fire, kill him, and take both his mine and the gold he had gathered, but I said: 'Git thee behind me, Satan!' Yet it was torture to see him heaping up gold that I could not touch. The conclusion I finally arrived at, however, was to husband my provisions and bide my time.

"I had kept my position and watch until nearly noon, and was thinking of making my way over the ridge to my camp, when a faint murmuring sound attracted my attention. I glanced rapidly about but could see nothing to which I could trace the strange noise. It seemed to fill the air overhead and on all sides, and was not unlike the hum of a large swarm of bees in full flight. Soon what began as a mere murmur became a decided roar, and, looking across the ravine, I saw a huge avalanche descending the face of the opposite mountain. All that was on the vast slope before me was in motion. Trees were uprooted and swept along with the descending masses of snow, and great rocks were torn from their beds. The roar of the avalanche, combined with the crashing and grinding together of rocks and the splintering of trees, produced a noise the like of which I never heard before nor since. It could only be compared to prolonged and deafening peals of thunder, rising through and heard above the steady roar of a tremendous waterfall.

"Dropping my eyes to my neighbor in the ravine, I saw him running, pan in hand, toward the place where he had deposited the gold he had taken out. He had proceeded but a few steps, however, before a great boulder came bounding down the mountain and, hopping into the ravine, landed full upon him. Almost instantly there followed a rushing hill of snow that filled the ravine and pushed its way nearly up to where I was standing; then all was silent as the grave. It was as though nothing had occurred, for in a moment the old calm and hush of centuries was again on the mountains and in the air. It was only when I looked at the denuded face of the mountain before me and the blockaded ravine at my feet that I could fully realize what had happened. The ravine was filled to the height of nearly one hundred feet with snow and rubbish, and at the bottom of this lay the crushed remains of the man I had so envied scarce two minutes before— under it also lay all the gold I so coveted!

"For many minutes I stood gazing on the scene before me, utterly astounded and stupefied. All was so unexpected, so terrific and overwhelming, that it appeared to be the sudden interposition of some supernatural power, either of heaven or the regions below.

"Months of labor could not now reach the gold. I must wait until the sun and rains had worn away the mighty mass of snow that filled the ravine. This I saw at a glance, yet for an hour or more I lingered about the place, then turned sadly away and took my course across the ridge to my camp, where I stretched myself upon the ground and seriously considered the situation.

"As my neighbor and myself disappeared from the settlement at the same time, it would be thought that we went away together, and should I return alone, it would be looked upon as a suspicious circumstance and in all probability I should be arrested as his murderer. True, I might conduct the officers of the law to the spot where the avalanche descended and there explain the whole affair; but then the gold—I could not give up the gold!

"After duly considering the strange affair in all its aspects, I crossed over to California, pitched my camp in the foothills and taking the name I now bear became a man of the mountains—a wanderer. In California I accidentally learned that the sudden disappearance of myself and neighbor was accounted for in the settlement on the supposition that we had been mixed up in some of the cattle-stealing affairs then of such common occurrence on that side of the mountains. This, though not very complimentary, was very satisfactory.

"Every summer and fall I have visited the spot where my fortune lies buried, but have always found the snow lying deep above it—ever too much snow. Heretofore I have always seen the remains of that old avalanche—so much new snow has fallen every year—but this summer it is almost gone. I have been on the ground, and in less than a month shall reap the reward of my long years of watching. Nearly all the rocks and broken trees lie well up on the north bank of the ravine, therefore I shall easily reach the gold—the great shining nuggets that I have so often seen in my dreams, by day and by night. Millions lie there, high up in the silent mountains, and they are all my own. No man can ever find the spot—no man who is not wandering, lost, and half crazed would ever go there. To find my gold you must first be lost.

"Now that you have heard my story, I'll thank you for a little smoking tobacco."

Ned passed his pouch.

"I presume you have a pipe?" said Elam.

Ned handed over his pipe.

Elam filled the pipe and then said: "All I now lack is a match."

Having received a whole bunch of matches, Elam used one, pocketed the others, and then settled himself for a good, square smoke. He sat in silence, often blowing the smoke out through his nostrils like a Mexican or an Indian.

When he had finished the pipe, he picked up his gun, arose to his feet, and gravely and earnestly said: "You two have heard what I have never before breathed to living man, and what I would not tell everywhere, but my reward is now near, and I felt that I could afford to tell you my story—that after so many years of silence it would be a relief to tell it. I don't ask you to believe it."

"We hope your most sanguine expectations may be realized," said Ned.

"Thank you," said Elam. "And now," continued he, "now that I am going, I'll just take two or three of those trout and what remains of your lunch, that is, if it is all the same to you. I am a man of the mountains, and I stand on no ceremony with those I meet in the mountains."

371

We both apologized for not thinking to ask Elam to partake of our lunch, saying that the interest we had taken in his strange story must be our excuse for our apparent lack of hospitality. He replied that he had lunched just before sighting our camp, or he should have asked for food.

Having received all he asked for, Elam muttered: "I am now begging broken victuals, but soon I shall have millions, millions!"

Without any leave-taking and still muttering something about gold, he strode away in the direction of the mountain he had pointed out as that behind which lay his camp.

Looking after Elam, Ned said: "He seems to talk straight enough once he is fairly under way, but do you think he is right up here?" tapping his forehead.

"I hardly know what to make of him. Did I not now see him marching away with those trout dangling from the barrel of his gun I should be in doubt as to whether any such man had been here. Let us up sail and away before some other man of the mountains comes this way and finds us."

California Reminiscences

Big Bill Scuffles

Or, the Fight at Foster's Bar.

---

*A*crowd of miners and men of all trades, and of no trade, had collected for the evening at a popular North C Street saloon. The bar was well lined with persons engaged in imbibing their favorite stimulants, while most of the seats along the walls of the place were occupied by men who had taken their drinks and were sufficiently exhilarated to find a fair degree of comfort in hearing themselves talk.

Into this saloon presently trotted rather an odd-looking little old man. His left eye was lacking, but his right was remarkably vivacious and aggressively piercing. This was probably because it was required to do double duty, just as the remaining hand of a one-armed man acquires strength exceeding that of most men who retain both hands. The man's hair was somewhat sprinkled with gray, his visage was thin, and his general complexion rather sallow and cadaverous, but the tips of his cheekbones and other protuberances of his face were quite roseate, presenting the appearance of sun-tipped peaks and hilltops rising above the dusky level of a plain. His nose was Roman and

---

Dan's story of the fight at Foster's Bar never gets told in this, one of his four tales published by the short-lived *Nevada Monthly,* 1 (March 1880), pp. 89–92, 95–99.

thin, with nostrils that were never at rest and which frequently expanded until the surrounding integument seemed a mere film.

Although sufficiently shabby, the little old fellow did not have the sullen and vicious look that generally marks the face of the confirmed tramp. He seemed a stranger in the town, but not a person desirous of remaining such. He was evidently as dry as a powder house, a lime-kiln, or anything else in which is found no moisture. His hope was that the purse of another would do for him that which his own was powerless to accomplish. This being the case, it was necessary for him to scrape acquaintance in some quarter.

Thirst made him startlingly alert. His one eye flashed now to the right and now to the left; his nostrils expanded, contracted, and quivered as he faced this way and that in the hope of finding an opening in some one of the conversations surging hither and thither and ebbing and flowing about him wherein he could start an entering wedge that would lead up to some sort of fellowship. He was desirous of being considered a member of some one of the little parties distributed about the room. He had chipped in several times in various quarters, but his manner being regarded as a little too forward and obtrusive—he was indiscreetly anxious—frowns were his only encouragement.

At length he found a seat near two men who were talking over some of the exploits of Fighting Sam Brown on the Comstock in the early days, and how he was finally hunted down and killed by Van Sickle at Genoa.

The little old man now changed his tactics. He listened splendidly—flattering both speakers with eye, nostril, and smile—and verily he had his reward. One of the men asked the other up to drink, and as he did so our little old fellow said: "Excuse me, gentlemen, but did you ever hear of the fight at Foster's Bar?"

They could not say, as there had probably been a thousand fights at Foster's Bar, as at all other noted California mining camps in the early days.

"The fight I mean," said the little old fellow, "was that between Grizzly Jim and Big Bill Scuffles."

The two men had never heard of the unpleasantness mentioned, but would the "stranger join in a drink"?

Wouldn't he and didn't he! The barkeeper looked very hard at him, he seemed unconscious of any special scrutiny from that quarter and got away with half a tumbler of very satisfying whisky.

The little old fellow stated to his newfound friends that he was not a drinking man—in fact, hardly ever drank a drop of anything—but being in a strange place and a little lonesome, anything like a show of friendship opened his heart at once and disposed him to fall in with the customs of the country.

The drinks disposed of, the three men reseated themselves, when the stranger said: "Well, as I was goin' to tell you, regardin' the fight at Foster's Bar, Big Bill Scuffles—"

"Ah!" cried one of the Comstockers, "speaking of Foster's Bar reminds me of a little adventure I once had a mile or two further up the river."

Trapped in a Shaft

"It was to some extent mirackelous. I fell into a shaft and got out without climbin' up the sides or even touchin' them, and all without the assistance of any human bein'. I'd been up a big gulch all day prospecting fur the blue lead, or some sich propersition, till late, and it come on dark soon after I left the mouth of the gulch. But I thought I knowed the road and struck my course across the flats. At that time all them flats was covered with timber, and it was devilish dark under the big pines and spruces.

"Somehow I lost my reckonin' and the first I knowed I went plump into a prospect hole. I landed in about two feet of mud and water and wasn't hurt a particle, but it was late in the season and the water was pretty devilish cold. I couldn't tell from the time I was about it whether I fell ten feet or a hundred. All I knowed was that it was all shaft as high up as I could reach on every side. If the stars had been shinin' I might have been able to give some kind of guess at the depth of the hole, but it was cloudy and as black at the top as at the bottom.

"I did some good strong yelling for an hour or two, then concluded it was a waste of breath, as it was not likely anybody would come along there in the night. After I had sloshed about in the water and mud a long time, I clawed out a lot of dirt and rocks on one side of the shaft and built up a dry bank to stand on.

"When daylight came I found that the shaft was only about fifteen feet deep; but it looked about as bad for me as if it had been fifty feet. I tried diggin' hand and footholds in the side of the shaft, but they were of no use—they tore out under my weight. All the time I was tryin' these experiments I took spells of yellin', but no one came. It was still cloudy, and once in a while there was a little sprinkle of rain.

"Along in the afternoon, though it seemed to me that I'd been there in the shaft a month, there came on about the worst storm I ever saw. The wind blowed a reg'lar hurricane and the rain poured down by bucketsful. Water began to pour in at the top of the shaft and sluice down big lumps of dirt and rocks. I began to be afraid I'd either be drowned or caved on and buried alive. All at once there was a fearful roarin' of the wind and then came the infernalist rippin' and crashin' and thunderin' that I ever heard. For a minute all was dark. Piles of dirt fell upon me and I seemed knocked about in all directions; still, I wasn't hurt.

"My first thought was that there'd been an earthquake. As soon as I got my senses a little, I felt that there was a lot of brush hangin' about my head. In three seconds I understood it all. The wind had blowed a big tree across the shaft and one of the limbs was hangin' down almost to the bottom. The trunk of the tree left a hole at the top of the shaft that let in light enough for me to see that I had a good ladder all the way up, and in about half a minute I was out and streakin' it down the river for my cabin and for a fire and grub."

"Blamed ef you didn't get out without touchin' the shaft and without the help of man!" cried Comstocker No. 2. "Now let's all take a drink on the miracle."

This suited the stranger, and he had soon hoisted in another half-tumbler of his favorite stimulant.

As soon as the men were again seated, the stranger said: "As I was goin' on to tell you regardin' the fight at Foster's Bar, you see, Big Bill Scuffles—"

Another Shaft Adventure

"Beg pardon," said Comstocker No. 2, "but strange as it may seem that two men should have experienced the same thing, I once fell into a prospect hole about twelve feet deep and got out without the help of a human person. It was above Downieville, at a place called Charcoal Flat. I was out hunting a mustang that I had turned out to pasture, and had a lasso along with me. I was scoutin' around among the bushes when all at once a rip snortin' big cinnamon bear jumped up and made after me. I broke and ran like a quarter hoss. As I was runnin', I turned my head to look back and went slap into an old shaft. It was about twelve feet deep, and I got to the bottom with no hurts but a few scratches on my left shoulder where I struck against the further side of the shaft.

"The bear—an old she devil with cubs in the thicket—was soon at the top of the shaft lookin' down at me and growlin' like the mischief. I was afraid at first that the ground at the edge of the shaft would give way and she would come down on top of me, but I soon seed there was no danger of that and began to wonder how I was to get out of the hole, even supposin' there was no bear at the top.

"Finally an idea struck me. I uncoiled my lasso and began throwing it at the bear. The third pass I made fastened it about her neck and, giving a heavy jerk, I drawed the noose so tight it must have cut into her flesh half an inch. She began backing out at a rapid rate, and, holding fast to my end of the lasso, I was out of the shaft and stretched full length on the ground in about three seconds. At first the bear seemed astonished at seein' me comin' after her in that style, but I was hardly on my feet before she made for me. I thought if I could hang on to the lasso and keep it stretched tight I might choke her down.

For a time she dodged about after me at sich a lively rate that I did not do much at stretchin' the lasso. Comin' to a small tree that forked about four feet from the ground, I pushed the end of the lasso down into the crotch in such a way that the knot on the end would hold it in place, then ran on with the bear close at my heels, but she soon brought up with a surge that took her off her feet. The knot held in the crotch and I saw that I had her. But she was game, and soon got up and tried to come for me.

"I then started and walked round and round the tree in such a way that in trying to follow me the bear was wound up. We made the circuit of that tree about fifty times and finally the bear was wound up to such an extent that she could only move her head about six inches. When I got her in that fix I took my knife and cut her throat. Then I went and got the cubs and, fastening the lasso to a forepaw of each, led them into Downieville and sold them to Cut-eye Foster, the butcher, for ten ounces, and for the old bear I got five ounces."

"Wonderful!" cried Comstocker No. 1. "Do you know if anybody

379

but you had told me that story I wouldn't have believed it? Let's all take a drink on the bear."

The stranger got another half-tumbler dose, and as soon as they were again seated, cleared his throat and said: "Regarding the fight at Foster's Bar and Big Bill Scuffles——"

Betting on a Dead Thing

"By the way," said Comstocker No. 1, "your speakin' of Cut-eye Foster reminds me of a trick he once played me. I was up at Sierra City at the Italian store, when Barney Sullivan who lived down at Downieville came in. He had got a big tomcat of somebody and was going to take it home to his cabin. He had it in a sack, and when he came into the store, which had a bar and was half saloon, he took the sack and cat into a back shed used as a sort of storeroom, then came back and set down to play a game of seven-up for the drinks. I went out into the shed and seen the sack, when it came into my head to play a trick on Barney.

"Out in the backyard of the place I'd seen a big white rabbit in a sort of cage or pen, so I got the rabbit, put it into the sack and put the cat into the pen out back. I then went on down to Downieville and kept watch for Barney. When he got into town, he went to a saloon to get a nip, putting his sack into a corner.

"'What have you in the sack, Barney?' says I.

"'A cat,' says Barney, 'and a devilish fine fella he is, too.'

"'Bet you \$10 you have no cat in the sack,' says I.

"'Take the bet!' says Barney.

"'Bet you \$50 you have no cat in the sack,' says I.

"'Bet you \$150 that Barney has a cat in his sack,' said Cut-eye Foster, who had been listening to the game.

"'I'll bet you \$250,' said I, 'that he has a white rabbit in his sack and no cat.'

"'I'll take the bet and go you \$50 better that he has a cat and no rabbit,' said Cut-eye.

"The money was put up with the barkeeper, the sack was opened and sure enough there was the d—— old tomcat.

"That cured me of bettin' on a dead thing. About three years after, I found that Cut-eye Foster, bein' in Sierra City pokin' about, seed me change the rabbit for the cat, and mistrustin' that something was up, went and changed them back as soon as I left, so he had a devilish sight deader thing than I had, and from fust to last Barney never knowed that his cat had been out of the sack at all. While I was a-layin' for Barney, Cut-eye was layin' for me, and with a better thing than four aces."

"Let's all take a drink on the cat," said Comstocker No. 2, and the stranger got another half-tumbler dose. He was getting to be tolerably thin in the knees and thick in the tongue by this time.

As the party returned to their seats he said: "As regardin' the fight at Foster's Bar 'n Bill Big Schuffle-z, yer see, Big Bill Schuffles he war—"

The Boot on the Other Foot

"That air transaction," said Comstocker No. 2, "reminds me of how I once put up a job and got sing'larly fooled.

"It was down to Columbia in 1858. There was a devilish fine young feller named Ned Ferris minin' not fur from my claim. Ned came to the camp without a splitter, and takin' a likin' to the feller, I showed him a piece of ground where I knowed he could make fair wages; also I pinted out to him an old cabin that had been vacant fur years and that he could make his own by movin' in an' takin' possession.

"Well, after Ned had been my neighbor for a year or two, what does he do but fall dead in love with a gal down in town named Nellie Martin, and the prettiest gal in the camp. Old man Martin and his wife were dead down on the business, though they couldn't find any fault with Ned, except that he was poor and likely to stay so for a time, unless he got a better streak in his claim. The old folks wanted Nellie to marry some rich old rooster that had a store down in Sonora, but she was all for Ned and wouldn't even treat the Sonora chap decent. Things was at a deadlock in the matrimonial line. Nell wanted Ned and wouldn't look at the Sonora feller, and the old folks had their eyes on the Sonora feller's spelter and wouldn't hear of Ned.

"Things bein' at this pass, I fixed up a job to help Ned out. He wouldn't hear of it at first. Finally I told him to tell the gal about it an' if she was in for it he needn't hang back. She said it was just the thing and that settled it with Ned. The plan was all easy enough—only a little lyin' to be done by me. I took a airly opportunity of telling old

Martin that Ned Ferris had struck it mighty rich in his claim—just how rich I couldn't say, but I was sure he was makin' bushels of money.

"'Very few people see any of it,' said old Martin, lookin' like he thought the story rather thin.

"'That's so,' says I, 'he's devilish close about it; but mistrustin' something, I've watched him. I just dropped on his style by accident, happened to get a glimpse of a thing one night when I was goin' to see him at his cabin, and since then I've watched him a little. No harm in that; I don't want to rob him, and I'm devilish glad of his good luck, for a better boy never lived.'

"'What did you see?' said old Martin, gettin' interested.

"'What you may see him do tonight if you like, or any night when he's been at work in his claim, for the matter o' that. I've seen him stowin' away gold—whole heaps of gold. He's got whole pickle jars and fruit cans full of it—all buried under his hearth.'

"The long and short of it was that after some talk old man Martin agreed to go with me that night and take a peep at Ned while at his work of stowing away gold. We were to peep in through a crack in the cabin and Ned was to be seen stowin' away his cans and things. In order that Ned might know when to be at this work, I was to be a little in advance of Martin and pull a string which would drag a small stone from a bench to the floor.

"All this was perfectly understood, and at night old Martin and myself were on hand, but the cabin was all dark and not a sign of Ned could we see or hear. We went round to the door and knocked, but no Ned answered. The next morning I was at Ned's cabin bright and early, but it was fastened up and Ned was not to be seen. I went to his claim, but he had not been there. I was a little hot, for old Martin had accused me of lying to him and trying to humbug him. This was bad because quite true.

"I did not see Ned for over a week and then he was dressed up to kill. He was walking arm and arm with old Martin. Both were jolly and smiling. My eyes bugged out when I saw this wonder, but I had no chance to ask questions. In less than an hour I was told that Ned had bought one of the finest ranches in the San Joaquin Valley; had whole herds of cattle and horses and sheep, and I don't know what all—the first stories being a little above the mark, of course.

"In a day or two Ned and Nellie were married and went off to the

Bay, Sacramento, or someplace, and all this time I was the most puzzled man on the coast. I couldn't figger out head nor tail of it. When Ned and wife came back from their weddin' trip I finally got a chance to talk with Ned alone.

"'Old feller,' said he, as soon as we were by ourselves, 'put it thar!' and we shook hands.

"'Old boy,' says he, 'I owe it all to you, and I'll never forget you, come what may.'

"'How did I do anything?' says I, 'you wasn't on hand at the cabin to carry out the plan and you got me into a nice scrape with old man Martin, now your blessed daddy-in-law.'

"'You did it all, though, for all that. It was all owin' to you. You see, when I took my pick and went to diggin' up my hearth to make a hole to put my dummy jars and cans in I came upon a lot of real ones, all filled with gold—a powder keg filled with gold—yeast powder boxes and pickle jars full of gold—gold everywhere. I had all I could do to sack it up and pack it away to a new hiding place before the time for you and the old man to come. You bet I did some heavy and lively work, and I played it fine to get it away to the Bay and turn it into coin without letting anybody know about it. Some poor devil who once lived in that cabin hoarded all that gold and then got killed, carrying to the grave the secret. Let us keep this to ourselves,' and Ned handed me a purse so full of twenties that it nearly jerked my arm off when he let go of it."

"Good boy!" cried Comstocker No. 1. "Now let us drink a health to Ned and Nellie," and the little old man got another goodly dose, though he was now so far gone from the effects of the mighty draughts he had previously quaffed that he was only dimly conscious of the business in hand.

Seeing him in this condition the two Comstockers, who had been taking moderate doses, slipped away while his tumbler was still fumbling about his mouth.

When he had finished his drink, the little old man zigzagged his way to the row of chairs against the wall and planted himself alongside of two newcomers seated there, under the impression that they were his late genial companions.

"Regardin' the fight at Boster's Far an' Bigbillscuffles," said he, slapping one of the men familiarly on the shoulder, "it's about time that I had my put in."

"Give us a rest, old man!" cried the person he had grappled, throwing the stranger's hand off his shoulder.

"I've been givin' you things your way all evenin'," said the stranger, "and now it's my put in. I'm goin' to tell you about the fight at Fosser's Bar'n Big Bill Scuffles. I'm no pilgrim, I ain't. I'm a roarin' lion when I get started."

"Go off and die!" cried the man addressed, giving the little old man a shove that tumbled him over upon the floor.

The barkeeper hereupon came to the front and hauled the little old man to his feet. The latter saw something familiar in his face and cried:

"Ha! you're the man—you're one of 'em. Now, damme, you've got to hear it. You've staved me off all night, now, damme, I'll tell you 'bout the fight at Foster's Bar!"

By the time he had finished thus declaring himself, the little old fellow found himself sprawling on the sidewalk, and the next minute he was under the wing of a policeman.

"What's the matter now?" said he.

"Nothing," said the officer, "except that you fell down and I picked you up."

"Oh, then you're my friend. Damme, you're my friend—then I'll tell you 'bout the fight at Fosser's Bar'n Big Billscuffles."

"You'll tell that tomorrow to Judge Knox. He is very fond of old forty-nine stories—he's one of the Old Boys himself."

"I'm an old boy an' a stubborn cuss, an' when I want to do a thing I want to do it all over, and I'm bound to do it. I've been staved off tonight an' made to listen to trash 'bout shafts an' bears an' tomcats, when I had a story that's his-histor'-cle—his-histor'cle, sir. The fight at Fostder's Bar, sir's, histor'cle. I'll tell it to you, sir, seein' you're my friend."

Thus muttering, the little old man was landed at the station house and tumbled into a cell along with a Chinaman. In about half an hour there was a terrible commotion in that cell. The Chinaman was yelling: "P'licee! P'licee!" at the top of his voice, and hammering wildly on the door. When Jailer Birdsall came to see what the row was all about, he found that the little old stranger had the Chinaman by the tail and was pouring into his unwilling ear the story of the fight at Foster's Bar and the terrible doings of Big Bill Scuffles.

"Me no likee one man clazy," cried John. "Too muchee Bill Scuf-
fle—too muchee fightee—me no sabe!"

Having suffered much in the same way himself, and being too
kindhearted to see a Chinaman tortured when the severest punishment the law could inflict would be nothing worse than hanging,
Jailer Birdsall removed the Chinaman and left the little old man to
turn his sting upon himself, scorpionlike, and die.

Luck:
A Prospector Strikes a Queer Streak

es," said Lucky Bill, quoting an old saw by way of comment upon a story of a lucky find in the old golden days, just told by a white-haired Argonaut, "Yes, 'Give a man luck, and you may throw him into the sea.'"

"There is only one noted and authentic instance of the kind of luck you speak of," said Grizzly Ben, "and that constitutes the telling point in the story of Jonah."

"And what then," triumphantly asked Lucky Bill, "what then becomes of the equally well-founded story of Arion, the Greek musician, who when cast into the sea by robber mariners was safely carried to land by a song-loving dolphin?"

"Oh, that is merely a fable of profane history," said Grizzly Ben. "I take my stand on holy writ—the Book of books."

"I have read several accounts of sailors being carried on the backs of whales," said Daddy Bob.

"Yes," said Grizzly Ben, "there's a notable instance of that kind in Baron Munchausen's book."

"To come ashore again upon the good old stamping ground of the

---

An intricately plotted tale of highwaymen, set in the Mother Lode of 1857. From the *Overland Monthly*, 17 (February 1891), pp. 165–76.

Golden State," said Dick Davis, "I'll tell you a story of a double dose of luck that I once experienced."

"Another story of a big find, I fear," growled Lucky Bill.

"Well, it's about one kind of a find," said Dick. "A man sometimes looks for what he does not want to find, and again finds what he is not looking for. My story is not one of the days of '49; it goes back no farther than 1857."

"Good boy!" grunted Lucky Bill.

"Even that will almost be ancient history in this year of our Lord 1890," remarked Daddy Bob.

"Where was I?" asked Dick Davis, looking inquiringly upon the faces of the half-dozen old boys seated about the table, within easy reach of the bean pot and pickles.

"Where were you?" cried Lucky Bill. "Why, you muggins, you have not yet begun your story! You've had your nose in your beer mug."

"True enough!" cried Dick, looking quite surprised. "Well, now I'm off.

"Well, as I was saying when I was interrupted, in the summer of 1857 I was footing it from the headwaters of the San Joaquin, where I had been prospecting, toward the northern camps. I was headed for Downieville, Sierra County, intending thence to go up the Yuba to Mooney's Flat or Lady's Cañon. I had prospected myself flat broke. I had tramped it through Hornitos, Coulterville, Big Oak Flat, Sonora, Columbia, and San Andreas without a splitter. However, I wanted for nothing. In those days the present race of tramps was unknown. A prospecting miner was then heartily welcomed in every cabin from Kern to Siskiyou. He had only to lay his course along the Sierras about the snowline, where he would always be among the mining towns and brethren of his guild. In every miner's cabin he found room to spread his blankets for the night, and in every cabin, day or night, he was invited to 'sit up' when the table was spread. In those times the latchstring was always out at the cabin of the miner. The wandering prospector, with his budget of news from a dozen differ-ent camps, was always welcome to the best the cabin afforded. Not unfrequently the broken miner who took to the trails in search of new diggings found himself the guest of an angel he had aforetime himself entertained unaware.

"As I have said, I had traveled as far north as San Andreas, through which town I had passed, and was trudging along the dusty highway feeling rather blue on account of having lost nearly three months' work on my wild-goose chase. I had nothing in the world except my revolver, a big Arkansaw toothpick, and a watch. At a time when I was flush and Mistress Fortune stood smiling at my very elbows as I swung my pick, I had bought the finest gold watch that $300 in gold would purchase. This watch was to give me consequence in the eyes of *the girl who was waiting* back in the States, and to sear the eyeballs of parents who stubbornly refused to recognize merit when not backed by wealth."

Just here Lucky Bill heaved a great sigh.

"Why do you sigh like that?" asked Dick Davis, stopping the thread of his story to stare at Bill.

"Alas!" said Bill, "the poor girl that was waiting!"

"As I plodded along the dusty road, I felt that I was a regular out-and-outer. I was out at the elbows, out at the knees, and the toes of my old boots were on the broad grin. The fact that I was ragged as an Indian did not much trouble me, however, as ragged men were then the fashion in the mountains. But the sand that entered at the open mouths of my boots did trouble me. My toes on the underside were not only worn to the quick, but also holes had in several places been worn through the skin, and these were kept raw and bleeding by the sharp quartz sand that was constantly lodging in them and drilling them deeper, just as boulders drill a pothole in the bedrock of a river.

"This being my dolorous case, you can imagine my delight when my limping steps brought me in sight of a pair of boots. The boots were lying in the center of the road, just as though placed there for my special benefit. 'Providence, who tempers the wind to the shorn lamb,' thought I, 'has had compassion on the poor old buck.' The boots were of stout cowhide, and sound as a dollar. As they were tied together at the tops I conjectured that they had fallen off the back of a pack animal or off the roof of a stagecoach. I was not long in discarding my old boots and installing my bleeding feet in the better ones that luck had lent me. The boots were just a fit, but I found them rather heavy, having been newly half-soled. Stamping to settle my heels fairly in my new footgear, I said:

> Matters at worst are sure to mend,
> The Devil's wife was but a fiend!

"'Yes, here my luck takes a turn!'

"However, while exulting in my good fortune, I was not unmindful of the fact that all mankind is concerned in charity. The recluse who ate a handful of plantains as he walked, believing that in his pious humility he had made himself the poorest being in the world, was surprised at seeing that a wretch that followed was eagerly devouring the husks he threw away.

"With thoughts like these in my mind, I tied together the straps of my old boots and left them in the middle of the highway. The turned up toes gaped hungrily, but the poor man following me might be so forlorn as to interpret this as a pleasant grin, or he might be a wretch cursed with bunions.

"However, there is no pleasure without some pain, and in all our joys is found some alloy. As I trudged on toward the town of Jackson, in Amador County, I began to find myself leg-weary. My newly acquired boots, with their thick half-soles, were too heavy for much walking. They were only fit to be worn in a mine. On a long tramp they were a great weight to carry. Still they saved my blistered, bleeding toes, and, promising myself to trade them for a lighter pair at some miner's cabin, I toiled on.

"I had traveled about five miles, after picking up the boots, when I came to a small creek bordered with willows and occasional clumps of alder, and with a thick growth of young pines on the slopes of the hills on either side. Leaving the stage road, I went up this creek several hundred yards till I found a pool big enough to afford room for a comfortable bath. Seating myself in the shade of a thick clump of willows in order to cool off before going into the water, I observed on looking at my boots that the under soles appeared to be quite thick enough for walking—that apparently they were little worn when the new ones were put over them.

"With my Arkansaw toothpick I soon pried the half-sole off one of the boots, when to my astonishment out dropped three twenty-dollar gold pieces. I was not long in prospecting the other boot, concealed in which I found the same number of double eagles as had tumbled out of the first. As I sat jingling the six big gold coins in my hand, I said aloud in my joy: 'Ah, ha! Did I not say that the Lord cares as much for the old buck as for the lambs?'

"'He does indeed seem to take them into his special keeping,' said a hearty and sonorous voice behind me.

"I turned my head and found myself looking into the muzzle of a six-shooter that was not two feet from my eyes. The man who was holding a pistol thus dangerously near my head had a fierce look and blazing black eyes, yet he spoke calmly and softly as he said: 'I am very sorry, my friend, to dash from your lips your cup of joy, but I must trouble you to hand over those six twenties.'

"'Do you mean that?' said I.

"'I mean just what I said,' cried the stranger, somewhat elevating his voice. Then he added in a milder tone, 'Do I look like a joker?'

"It grieved me to the very core of my heart to part with the gold, which had not even so much as been warmed in my pocket; yet I poured the pieces into the outstretched left hand of the fellow without delay; for his right hand still presented the cocked revolver. As I did so I could not help saying, 'There's many a slip 'twixt the cup and the lip!'

"'Old, but true,' said the fellow. 'Now hand over your knife and pistol; they might tempt you to a rash act that would cost you your life.'

"'It appears, then,' said I, 'that I am in the hands of a regular road agent.'

"'I am trying to proceed regularly,' was the answer. 'And now that I have your weapons, I must ask you to stand up. I dislike to be stooping; it does not seem regular. Ah, now I see that you have a watch; pass it out to me.'

"I handed out my cherished gold watch, but it was the worst blow of all—it seemed to draw after it my very heartstrings as I handed it over to the robber. The fellow uttered a cry of surprise at sight of the watch. 'By Jove!' cried he, 'this is no common ticker. Why, my man, you are either rich or foolishly extravagant!'

"I modestly said: 'Sir, I have seen better days,' then added, 'and even better times than at the present moment,' at which the fellow smiled.

"Encouraged by this indication that I was in the presence of a human animal, I allowed the sadness of my soul to become visible in my face. 'Sir,' said I, 'I could endure the loss of my money without a pang, but that watch was the last gift of a dying mother to her only son.'

"'Does your good father still live?'

"'No, sir; the good man has gone to his reward.'

"'Then I am in the presence of one of God's orphans?'

"'You are, sir—a full orphan.'

"'How long may I ask, my poor boy, have you been in this forlorn condition?'

"'Twenty years!' cried I with much enthusiasm; for I thought I was making the desired impression. Then pretending to brush away a tear with the sleeve of my shirt, I added, 'The good man, my father, died before my mother, who passed away to the angels in giving me birth.'

"'Sad, indeed,' said the robber; 'your little story is so pathetic that I must beg to keep this watch in remembrance of your excellent mother.'

"'Then, sir, you do not, in your business, respect the gift and last wishes of a dying parent?'

"'My dear fellow, you touch me now. I swear to restore to you all your property! I am only taking it for safekeeping; borrowing it for a short time. Now, my friend, turn all your pockets inside out; I do not wish to make any mistakes in the bit of business you and I have in hand; we must proceed regularly.'

"There being no coin among the traps that fell to the ground when I obeyed this order, the robber smiled and said: 'Ah, now I see! You were just making a draft upon your bank—you were replenishing?'

"At first I deigned no reply, for my heart was sore; but seeing that the robber, though a daredevil looking man, had nothing brutal or ferocious in his countenance, I told him about finding the boots in the road and what an agreeable surprise it was to me—I being dead broke—to see the gold tumble out of them.

"'Yes, damn me, and it was an agreeable surprise to me also, as I stood looking over your shoulders to see what you were about. My friend, we were both surprised—we shared in the surprise.'

"'I wish,' said I sadly, 'that we had also shared in the cause of it.'

"'I could not think of doing anything of the kind. I shall insist upon you keeping the whole—when I return it to you. Why will you persist in looking at this bit of business in the worst possible light? Don't I tell you that I am only borrowing your valuables?—yet you seem desirous of viewing it in no other light than downright robbery. You will think better of me when we become better acquainted.'

"'I—'

"'What was the remark you thought of favoring me with?'

"'Well, if you must have it,' said I, a good deal annoyed, 'I am quite content with the degree of ripeness to which our acquaintance has already attained.'

"'You are generous, my friend. I, on the contrary, am so well pleased with you that it is my desire and intention to further cultivate your acquaintance. Thus you see, my friend, that I am ready to give you full credit for any degree of merit to which you may be entitled. I am more generous than you have shown yourself.'

"'It is always safe to suspect some trick when the Devil turns preacher,' said I snappishly, for having nothing more to be robbed of I felt rather independent.

"'A very true saying, my friend, and in order not to give the lie to it, I commend you to roll up your blankets and take a little walk up the creek with me. We have spent too much time here already at cracking our little jokes. It is time to get to business.'

"'I beg your pardon, sir, but until now I had been under the impression that our business—mine, at least—was thoroughly completed.'

"'Never in your life were you guilty of falling into a more grievous error. My friend, take up your blankets and march. I will follow behind and guide you with my pistol. We are going up the creek to have a chat. You look sour now, but at our parting you'll drop a tear.'

"'Sir,' said I, with a great sigh sticking in my throat, 'if it's all the same to you, I'll drop it here, and not go up the creek.'

"'What a bothersome fellow you are!' cried the robber, scowling at me. 'I'd shoot you here in your tracks, were it not that your freaks and fears are rather amusing. Now, damn you, march! It pains me to speak harshly, but by God, you've got to go!'

"One look at the blazing black eyes, and I was enthusiastic to set out on the expedition up the creek. I did not stand marking time; I marched at once. The footpad marched me half a mile up the creek and then turned me aside and marched me to a dense thicket of evergreens about ten rods away. When we had penetrated the thicket a short distance I was halted. I instinctively looked about to see if my grave were ready dug and yawning for me.

"'Ha, ha!' laughed the robber. 'Ha, ha! Damn me if you aren't frightened at last.'

"I said nothing, but gazed heavenward through an opening at a small patch of blue sky, thinking of my sainted mother—who was then still alive and quite spry for a woman of her weight of years.

"'Come, my friend, you look worst just when I am going to do best by you. Do I look like a robber?'

"'Pretty is as pretty does,' sighed I.

"'Bah! You are as full of old saws as a second-hand lumber mill. Shall we ever get to business!'

"'My wish at present,' said I, 'is to retire from business, and from such a place of business as you have brought me to.'

"'In due time, my friend; but I have a great favor to ask of you. I hope soon to find myself under great obligations to you. Now, I do not want to be hard on a poor devil of a prospector—a broken one at that—into whose hands the fickle goddess has thrown a crumb or two to keep him in heart; therefore I again tell you that you will get back every cent of your gold, your watch, your pistol, and all else.'

"'What! You will give back all my property?'

"'All. I merely took your valuables to hold as security.'

"'Oh, that is what Vasquez always says,' said I, my heart sinking to zero.

"'Damn Vasquez! I am not one of his kind. I have plenty of money of my own right here in this forest. I have only taken your valuables to hold them as a pledge from you that you will do me a kindness and not betray me. You will get back your gold and twice as much more, if you do what I shall ask you to do for me.'

"'If it is nothing dishonest,' I answered, 'I will consider your proposition.'

"'Dishonest! Look in my face and tell me if you see a dishonest line in it.'

"'Pretty is as pretty does!'

"'Back again to the old sawmill!' said the man bitterly; then continuing, said: 'I see that I must place myself in your hands and make a clean breast of my troubles. I was going to try to send you into Jackson to buy me a horse and some traps on some slighter excuse, but I see I must throw myself upon your compassion—must appeal to your generosity. My friend, I have killed a man. I am in trouble and in hiding. If I am found by the friends of the man I shot and killed, I shall be hanged to the nearest tree.' All this was said in a sad tone, and the stranger at once seemed quite another man.

"'Did you kill the man in fair fight?'

"'No. No, sir, it was not in a fair fight. It was a very *unfair* fight. It was at Georgetown, where still linger some members of that vicious old clan of Georgians of the early days. The fellows I had trouble with came to drive me from a claim I had long worked in peace, capping up some sort of old title to it. They thought I had too good a thing. In the fight into which I was forced in the defense of my property, I killed one man and wounded two others, causing the attacking party to beat a retreat. That was two weeks ago, and I have been in hiding ever since.

"'I would have given myself up to the officers of the law, but I feared being taken from their custody by a mob of the clannish Georgians. Friends who concealed me for a day or two advised me to get out of the country for a time, as my enemies were scouring the whole neighborhood, armed to the teeth and swearing vengeance against me.

"'Such being the situation, I dug up my hoard of coin, packed it on the back of a donkey, and got out of the camp in the night. Now here I am. I have worked myself so far with my donkey, traveling of nights and hiding during daylight. I know the devils are on my track, for but two nights ago, when I ventured into Jackson to get something to keep me from starving, two of them came into the livery stable where I had lodged my donkey, and had a talk about me while I was crouched in a stall not five feet away. They were going down about Merced to look for me, therefore I shall strike for the valleys and go to Los Angeles, then to my old home in Sonora, Mexico, for a few months.

"'Now that I have trusted my life in your hands, will you try to assist me?'

"'I will do what I can for you,' said I, 'but I must say that I don't like the way in which I have been treated by you.'

"'No doubt I did wrong, but you see I had to have you.'

"'You frightened me out of a year's growth.'

"'That was doing you a favor. You are now a six-footer; do you want to grow to be a giant? But to tell you the truth, I was awfully frightened while holding you up. How did I do it? Was I regular, think you?'

"'Damnably like an old hand, to say what I thought at the time.'

"'Thank you—but I thought you the cool one. I was infernally afraid at one time that I had stumbled upon a professional—had caught a Tartar. See now how such affairs look to the two engaged in them, when both are quaking in every joint. Each thinks the other a man with the heart of a lion.' And the stranger laughed merrily.

"'Yes, but you still hold onto my valuables all the same,' said I dryly.

"'Yes, my friend, and I intend to hold onto them till I am ready to part with you. You do not yet more than half trust me, but when we part it will be with your best wishes for my safety; aye, with your blessing. Now go to Jackson and buy for me a good stout horse, with saddle, bridle, and all else belonging to a good rig; also, bring some hard biscuits and bacon, and some tobacco for cigaritos. Can I trust you away from me with as much as $300?'

"'With any amount, sir. I must have back my watch.'

"'Ah, yes; the last gift of a dying mother to her only son. I did well to secure an article about which cling such tender recollections, and which you must have possessed ever since the moment of your birth.'

"'You make very merry, sir, over a slip of the tongue when I was in fear of my life and greatly confused; just at the moment, too, of asking of me a great favor.'

"'Come, come, my friend. I touch no tender chord, as you well know. I saw through your little story as soon as you began it. Why, man, the cases of your watch are of California gold—gold not dug ten years ago. Forgive me if I am too merry, for your promise to get me a horse gives me great happiness. Let him be a good traveler; a horse such as you would choose for yourself if about to flee, as I am, from enemies thirsting for your blood.'

"'Where shall I find you, sir, on my return?' said I, as the stranger handed me a handful of gold.

"'Come to the little bluff of rocks opposite here on the creek, and whistle three times as near like a quail as you know how.'

"'Like this?' I asked, and you would have thought an old cock quail perched above my head.

"'Beautiful! Get me a Spanish saddle and rig; big spurs and all. I have trusted you with $350.'

"'Every cent shall be accounted for, sir, and I'll be back about sunset. That will be about the hour real quail will be whistling, therefore I'd better whistle four times.'

"'A delicate way of boasting of your skill; but four times let it be.'

"I was off to Jackson a moment later. The distance was less than two miles, and before the sun was down I was safely back on the creek with a splendid and powerful Spanish horse and a beautiful rig. No matter what lies I told in the town, I passed for an honest miner who had made a good find, and every word I uttered was believed. I bought every article I was sent for and had a few dollars left. I tried the paces of the horse on my way back to the creek. I found him swift and strong. On arriving at the rocks on the creek I stopped and gave the signal agreed upon.

"In a few moments thereafter a tall man wearing a stylish Peruvian hat and carrying a double-barreled shotgun on his shoulder made his appearance. I wished him in purgatory. He seemed a high-toned greaser. Halting as he came up to me, and resting his gun on the ground, he said: 'Buenas tardes, caballero.'

"'Buenas tardes, señor, Je me port sehr wohl,' said I, trying to be decently sociable.

"'Habla Español, señor?' asked he.

"'Sehr wenig, monsieur; nicht poco mas, a great deal,' said I. 'Parlez vous nicht Americano?'

"'Muy poco, señor,' said the stranger. 'Lo entiendo un poco, pero no lo hablo.'

"'Are you hunting, señor?'

"'Si, señor. Me think a me hear quail. You see some 'bout this place?'

"'No, señor, not here; but down the creek I just saw a big flock. Go at once and you'll find them.'

"'Fine horse you got. How much you sell?'

"'Not for sale. Plenty, mucho quail down creek.'

"'All very good. Me catch him poco tiempo. You see 'bout this place one tall Americano caballero?'

"'No, señor, I have seen no man. But I saw many quail—'

"'Nonsense! Let me talk of something besides quail. I am glad to see that you have no intention of giving me away.'

"I stared at the fellow, a tall, dark man with a black moustache fiercely waxed out, and said: 'So, I find you can speak English very well when it suits you?'

"'My friend, I am glad to find my disguise so perfect, and you so true to me. You have brought me a fine horse.'

"'Not that I am aware of,' I answered, still gazing at the fellow sharply, for I began to suspect that he was either a detective or a Georgian in disguise.

"'Here, my friend,' cried the man stepping to my side, 'you ought to know this,' and he showed me my watch.

"'Yes, I know that is my watch.'

"'Well, I am the man who took it from you, but I have disguised myself somewhat since you left me: shaved my chin, stained my face and hands, and made some alterations in my dress. Had any one come with you from town—you see I was not perfectly sure of you—you would not have seen your man in the Mexican quail hunter. Ha, ha! The Georgians will not know me in this shape!'

"I was now satisfied. 'Well, I am here with what you sent for— what next?' I asked.

"'Follow me,' and my man started up the creek I followed without a word.

"Going a short distance above the rocks the mysterious stranger left the creek on the side opposite that to which he had before escorted me at the muzzle of his pistol. He now led the way into the heart of a thicket so dense that in following him I was obliged to dismount and lead the horse. To my surprise we presently came to a camp—a brush shanty, lying about in which were cooking utensils and other traps.

"'You are now in the hole of the fox,' said my captor. 'Go now to the glade that lies a rod or two away straight before you, as you stand, and bring in a burro that you'll see feeding there. It will be best to get him in before dark.'

"I went as directed, and found a donkey that was as big as a medium-sized mule—the biggest I have ever seen. When I returned I found the stranger packing up such articles as he would require on a camping trip.

"'Put that packsaddle on the burro,' ordered my boss. 'You under-stand packing?'

"'Perfectly well,' I muttered.

"'I have one pair of blankets rolled up here to go on the horse; also

397

the other things that lie with the blankets go on the horse, but put your blankets and all else you see in the camp upon the burro. Throw the small tent you see there over the top of your load, and then rope on the whole firmly.'

"I did as directed, the stranger sitting by, rolling and smoking cigarettes while I worked. Occasionally he consulted my watch—out of pure deviltry, as I thought.

"'Now for a lunch,' said my man, 'and make it a hearty one, as I shall, for both you and I, my friend, must do some good traveling tonight.'

"'And must I do mine on foot?'

"'Yes, my friend; your boots are now light.'

"I sighed. Lunch over, and it growing dark, the stranger began packing his horse. His roll of blankets was strongly corded at both ends. While he was trying to strap it behind his saddle, it slipped to my side of the horse. In lifting it to push it back to its place I involuntarily gave a cry of surprise at its great weight.

"'My little hoard of money,' said the man; 'but also a considerable weight of ammunition and other such stuff.'

"All being packed, my man, who had been thoughtful and anxious for some time, struck a match and again consulted my watch. Taking his horse by the bridle, he then moved out into the thicket, calling sharply to me: 'Take the burro by the halter and follow!'

"'What! Am I to go with you?'

"'You heard what I said?'

"'Yes, sir.'

"'Then come along.'

"I followed, sad at heart. We traveled slowly down the creek, for the dense forest darkened the rocky path. Soon after we had reached more open ground, where there was some light from the stars, the stranger halted, 'Here,' said he, 'we first met, and here we part.'

"I looked, and saw the clump of willows whence my captor had pounced out upon me.

"'Seat yourself; we have plenty of time.'

"We seated ourselves side by side on the ground. The Georgetowner then took out a book, and asking my name and address, wrote them down, saying, 'You will often think of me as your good friend, and as you will wish to know whether I escaped the Georgians, I will send you a letter when I find myself out of their reach.'

"I thanked him.

"'Now,' said he, 'now, as I took your property, and also took possession of your person, to your great distress of mind, I am going to do what is right by you. I am about to show you that I am not the bad, heartless fellow you have all along thought me. Here in this purse are your six twenties, with six double eagles on top of them to keep them warm in their nest; here is your watch, also your pistol and knife. Now, besides, I give you my best friend, my faithful burro. Take good care of him. He understands camp life as well as an Indian. I also give and bequeath unto you all the plunder now packed upon the burro's back, and turn over to you this fair fowling piece, with which to defend yourself and belongings. That gun is another old friend; use it well.'

"As may be imagined, such a happy turn in my affairs quite overwhelmed me. It was an unlooked-for display of generosity on the part of my captor, for which I could hardly find words to express my thanks.

"'Never mind, never mind!' cried my eccentric companion. 'However, on second thought, if you can spare a thing so precious, you may drop on my hand the tear I spoke of a while ago'; and he laughed right merrily.

"'Also,' said I, 'you said I would send you forth with my blessing. Tears do not come at my bidding, but I can now honestly and heartily say to you, God bless and preserve you, my friend, wherever you go!'

"'Thank you, my man. My blessing may be of little use to anyone; but, such as it is, you have it. Now for my last instructions to you. Wait here an hour or two until the people in Jackson are housed, then skirt the town and do not halt till daylight. It is best not to be seen on foot with a burro by anyone who saw you buy this horse. It might start inquiries as to what you had done with the horse. It is always best not to be obliged to answer questions. After tomorrow morning, travel as you please—take your own way to Downieville.

"'Now I am off, for I know you'll not feel yourself perfectly safe while I remain.'

"He then mounted his horse, and in starting said: 'Tengo que marcharme. Adios, señor! Henceforward I am a Spaniard!' and away he cantered down the creek toward the main stage road.

"I obeyed instructions so well that I did not travel openly by daylight until I was beyond Volcano, well on my way to Shingle

Springs; I wanted no more trouble through the affairs of the Georgetown man. In a day or two all my fears were left behind. Gaily as a second Sancho Panza, I jogged along. In due time I arrived at Georgetown. I made it my first business to inquire about the great claim fight and the killing of a Georgian. All told me that no such affray had occurred in the town or vicinity, and some laughed at me when I asked about the fight. 'Someone,' said they, 'has been hoaxing you; or you have run against a blowhard.'

"There was no mistake about it: the mysterious stranger had lied to me. I was quite nonplussed—confounded. What was the object of the man in telling me such a yarn? Above all, what was his object in remaining in hiding?

"At last a ray of light was flashed into my mind that seemed to illumine the mystery. I had caught some talk all along the road of the stage having been robbed within a mile of the town of Jackson. It was said that over $10,000 in gold had been taken, coin which was being sent from San Francisco to a banker and dealer in gold dust in Jackson. Everywhere I had seen bills stuck up headed '$2,000 Reward,' but I gave no special attention to a thing so very common at that time. I did not feel that I was interested one way or another in a stage robbery.

"Now—my suspicions being aroused—I began to inquire about the robbery. The story was that the stage was stopped by three masked men, two of whom stood guard while the third, who was very tall and evidently an American, did all the talking and business. Wells, Fargo & Company's treasure box having been found in a vacant house in the outskirts of the town, it was pretty evident that the robbers were men belonging in the place, who had been studying and timing the shipments of dust to San Francisco and of coin to Jackson.

"Putting together what I had heard and what I had myself seen and experienced, I became well satisfied that I had helped in the escape of the chief of the party that had robbed the Jackson stage. Also, on comparing dates, I found that the stage had been robbed just three nights before I was captured and made use of. I was now heartily glad that I had told no one the story of the rather singular and improbable looking transactions that had taken place between myself and the stranger.

"Everywhere my big burro was admired, and daily a dozen men asked me where I found him. I had at first merely answered, 'Down in the lower country'; now, however, I boldly asserted that he came from Sonora, Mexico. I also was rather nervous when my fine fowling piece attracted notice.

"In fact, I now looked upon myself as the prize ass of all Christendom for having been so completely taken in and used by a stage robber, whom I might have captured had I been really bright. Besides all this, I did not know what trouble I might get into were it known that I had assisted in the escape of the criminal.

"That I would be taken back to Jackson, were my story known, was a sure thing. My account of my connection with the robber would look very gauzy, and the money, shotgun, burro, and other traps would tell against me. I was sick of myself when I thought how nicely the fellow had bamboozled me when asking if he appeared to do his work something after the 'regular' style, while he was operating on me.

"It may be imagined that when I reached Downieville and old friends, I kept to myself the most interesting episode of my journey. I was obliged to tell a thousand lies about my big burro and fine gun; even the tent and other traps attracted the notice of my old mining chums.

"About three months after my return to my old camp at Mooney's Flat, Ike Mooney one day brought me from Downieville a letter bearing the postmark of the City of Mexico. I opened the envelope and found a long letter, beginning, 'Richard Davis, Esq., Downieville, Sierra County, Cal.' Then it started off with a familiar and friendly 'Dear Dick.'

"Although I destroyed that letter as soon as I had read it, yet to this day I remember almost every word it contained. It was a cunningly worded document. It started off with: 'According to promise, I write to inform you that I escaped to this country safe and sound with the swag, thanks to your kind and valuable assistance. As I was not in the humor to give you the whole racket while we were together hiding in the woods, I now make amends for what, at the time when we were "working" together, may have seemed a lack of confidence in you— you, who have proved as true as steel to me. I will now tell you just how I worked the trick—what occurred during our hiding in the woods and at the secret camp being well known to you.'

"That is about the style of the first part of the letter. I saw at a glance that if it fell into other hands, it would be very likely to land me in San Quentin, and you may be sure that I took the first opportunity to put it into the fire. It almost made my hair stand on end. The fellow had evidently purposely so worded the letter that I would be compelled, in self-defense, to destroy it at once. That letter would have been an awful thing to have been found among my effects had I met with a sudden death in my mine. It was one of my robber friend's neat little jokes. I cannot begin to tell you how smoothly it was worded or how often he called me 'dear friend,' and his 'true and trusty friend.' He also took special pains to ask about the health of 'our noble burro,' and to speak of the shotgun, tent, and all the other 'traps.'

"That part of the letter alone would have caught me in ten thousand lies. No doubt the fellow heartily enjoyed writing all these seemingly innocent and natural inquiries. It was just his style of joke. Yet, to give the devil his due, he had some heart and a generous streak or two. He ventured into a minute account of the robbing of the stage. He had worked all alone. Twice before, at points down near the valleys, he had stopped the same stage, but had missed obtaining the large booty he anticipated. Then, in various disguises, he had hung about Jackson in order to more closely study the dust and coin shipments. He said that he was all alone when he secured the big prize he had so long coveted; that the two men supposed to have stood guard were the cheapest of dummies—only old shirts, pantaloons, and hats, stuck up on sticks.

"When the treasure box was thrown out by the driver, under the persuading influence of a leveled shotgun, and he had ordered the coach forward, he quietly gathered up his dummies (which were not even stuffed), piled the old clothes on top of the treasure box, and took all to a spot near at hand where 'our noble burro' was tied. The old clothes were arranged on the packsaddle; on these was placed the treasure box, then over all the 'tent we wot of' was spread and securely roped with a long lariat. Then, with his gun on his shoulder and the burro before him, he boldly took the road and followed the robbed stage into town.

"However, before he reached the town the alarm had been given. He met a posse of armed and mounted men, who halted and asked if he had seen three men anywhere down the road. He had seen no men. The posse dashed forward, and he (stripped of an over frock and dressed as an honest miner) quietly jogged on. It was only about nine o'clock at night when he entered Jackson. All was excitement and the streets full of people. He went whistling along, and when he came near the first groups of people, began talking to his donkey, saying to him: 'Courage, old fellow, your journey is about over now, and you shall have a big feed of barley!'

"Several among the men in the street approached the supposed belated prospector, to ask if he had seen a gang of robbers down the road. He said he was a stranger in that camp and didn't know the robbers from the honest men, but he had met half a dozen armed men just outside of town, riding down the road as if the Devil was after them.

"Of course the people knew about those men, and they left the fool prospector, and went in search of later news. Being thus deserted, the robber turned into a lonely cross street, and made his way to an old vacant house in the outskirts of the town. He had there secreted the tools he would need, and at his leisure he opened the box and secured the bags of coin, which he placed in the ends of a big grain sack, and slung across the back of his burro.

"Leaving the door of the old house ajar, in order that the rifled treasure box might be found early next morning, my robber friend then made his way to his secret camp in the evergreen thicket. His coin was soon buried and the burro turned out to graze in 'our beautiful glade,' when he sought his couch and enjoyed that sound sleep which is the reward of honest toil.

"He said he had at first thought of packing out of the country with the burro; but after getting the prize he sought he found himself anxious to reach a place as quickly as possible where he could safely enjoy it. 'But then,' said he, 'while I was watching by the creek to see if any officers were scouting out from the town, you, my friend, turned from the highroad and came to my assistance, rejoicing mine eyes as though you had been an angel sent from heaven. The wonders we did when we united our wits and worked together as two brothers, you well know.'

"Thus he grappled me with hooks of steel, until the very last word was written. The letter was signed, 'Your old friend and pard, Ketchum Jackson.' It would hardly have been made much plainer had he said, 'Me ketch um, Jackson.'

403

"Well, boys, you may be sure that after reading this letter I was not long in going down to the valleys in order to so dispose of my burro, gun, and other traps that I would never again see or hear of them."

"Thank God!" cried Daddy Bob, "a mystery is now solved that has worried me for thirty-two years."

"What is that?" asked Grizzly Ben.

"Why, I've a thousand times wondered who found those boots of mine, and whether the finder wore 'em out without discovering the six twenties. Now that I know that they fell into honest hands, I am sure of getting all back. But no interest—I'll take no interest. All I ask is that Dick call for another measure of beer."

"Yes, Daddy Bob," said Dick, "you're always ready to furnish the hook if someone else will find the bacon."

"Peace, brawler!" cried Lucky Bill. "Daddy Bob, you are wrong. 'The abbot must eat that sings for his meat.' Dick has kept us all wandering so long in the greenwood that I've just ordered Fred to bring on ham sandwiches and another half gallon of his best brew, for,

> 'Tis merry in hall,
> Where beards wag all!

Gunning for Market

Life Amid Lakes and Tule Swamps. An Expedition in Pioneer Days. A Winter's Sport on the Borders of the Sacramento River.

---

*I*n the old days of hydraulic mining in California, winter was a dreary season forty years ago, particularly, high above the snowline amid the black pine forests, mighty spurs, and tremendous cañons of the main range of the Sierra Nevada mountains. In many of the higher places among the mountain towns, snow frequently fell to the depth of from ten to twenty feet. In such places no work could be done at mining in winter except in the drift diggings. Many winters the majority of the houses in the high mountain towns were buried in snow. Then tunnels were run from house to house and across the streets. The people led a sort of semi-subterranean life. Like the bear, the badgers, and the dormouse, they hibernated, creeping about in their burrows and only coming to the surface occasionally on a bright day for a sunbath.

The winter life in these snow-buried towns was one of mental as well as physical dormancy. If mails came at all, it was at rare intervals and then by snowshoe carrier. All the old, tattered novels in a town

---

Dan reminisces about a winter's sport in the delta of the Sacramento River. From the San Francisco *Chronicle,* September 2, 1893. This and "Hunting Amid Tules," CH, September 9, 1893, should be compared with the pieces in Rawls, "Hunting for Market" and "Lost in the Tule Marshes."

went the rounds from cabin to cabin until worn out. When by chance the mail carrier slipped in between storms with his pack on his back, the newspapers he brought were devoured, even to the driest and least nutritious advertisements.

One or two winters of this kind of hibernating, or *"winterschlafen,"* as the Germans call it, was quite enough for one. To me, to remain housed up in the mountains when no work could be done seemed useless punishment. My mining neighbors said one could do nothing down in the valleys—that it was cheaper to hole up and remain in the mountains. They said the *winterschlafen* was a grand protracted rest that brought them out in the spring in fine trim to do a big summer's work. I thought some use of the muscles during the winter would in no degree lessen their strength for summer use; besides I wished to be in someplace where I could travel about and enjoy life. Instead of holing up, I determined to take a winter outing.

This was the winter of 1857–58, and my camp was Omega, Nevada County, eighteen miles above Nevada City. With me was a younger brother who was quite of my way of thinking as regarded the hibernation business. He said he was "not enough of a groundhog to enjoy it."

So down to the valleys we went. We headed for Sacramento, then went down to Sutterville, where we had a friend—Sam Corwin by name. Sam was running the Golden Eagle Hotel, having tired of mining. Both my brother and I were fond of hunting, and our intention was to spend the winter in warring upon the waterfowl of the lakes and tule swamps bordering the Sacramento River. Our idea was to combine business with pleasure by hunting for the game market. In this way we hoped not only to have a jolly good time, but also to come out even on the fun by "clearing our teeth."

So we broached the business to our friend Sam Corwin, who had been in the valleys for some years. Sam approved of our scheme. He said we could not only have a good time and "live on the fat of the land," but also make good wages. He told us that many men made hunting ducks, geese, and other waterfowl a regular business, and not a few made big wages.

"Can you shoot a bird on the wing?" asked Sam.

We told him that we could catch a prairie chicken or wild turkey on the wing with a rifle, therefore we were of the opinion that we could make it warm for a duck or goose with a shotgun.

We had got down to the valleys too early. Though it was November there had been no heavy rains or big storms to drive the game down from the north. We waited at Sutterville a week and then determined to take the field against the few ducks and geese to be found. We thirsted to begin the sport——to be banging away at the birds. So we went up to Sacramento and bought two splendid double-barreled shotguns, the steel-wire barrels of which rang like bells. My brother Hank selected a No. 12, but I went after a big No. 9, a gun with which I imagined I could sweep both sky and water. Then we bought all the powder flasks, shotbags and everything else the man of the gunshop told us we would require, and it was not a little. He was the most thoughtful man I ever saw. He could think of some new and necessary thing as long as there was a twenty-dollar piece in sight. When we tore ourselves away from him, we were covered and loaded down with his traps. Had we marched up into the mountains looking as we did when we marched out of that gun shop with our guns, revolvers, knives, and munitions of war, every stage driver we met would have halted and thrown out his treasure box without a word.

When we returned to Sutterville equipped as above related, our friend, Sam Corwin, was greatly impressed. He immediately conceived a high opinion of the amount of execution we would do when we turned ourselves loose among the gabbling and quacking flocks. "Now you must have a boat," said Sam. On his recommendation, we hired the biggest boat to be had at Sutterville—some kind of ocean craft. She was about thirty feet long and had a single mast with a huge sail. In this boat we would carry our game to market —in it we were to gaily sail up and down the river. It was romantic! We seemed to be entering upon a seafaring life—might yet become pirates!

We loaded our craft with kegs of powder, bags of shot, piles of boxes of waterproof caps and other munitions of war, but took aboard only a small stock of provisions. We had one sack of flour, some sugar, tea and coffee, and a few beans, with a small slab of bacon. As for other things, we were going to live off the country.

We had a vessel almost as large as that in which Columbus sailed over the ocean blue, but it seemed to us in our then excited state of mind none too big for the immense loads of game we would soon be shipping. Seeing our grand preparations, two men who were lounging about Sutterville made application for berths aboard our craft as partners. One of these was Bill Rounds, an Iowa friend of Sam Corwin, and the other Bill Johnson, a fisherman who had been working the Sacramento River and bordering lakes. We took the pair, as Rounds said he was a great cook—a regular Soyer—and as Johnson said he knew the whole country, with all its lakes, ponds, and marshes, and could sail the boat—was a second Sinbad. The great thing was to get a sailor, for, as we came from an inland region, we knew no more of sailing a boat than of navigating a balloon.

Bright and early one morning we went aboard our ship. The mast was up, but no "blue Peter" was flying from its head. Johnson said he did not think the Peter necessary, as the wind was square up the river, and we wanted to go down. He said we would be obliged to take down the mast and put out the oars. Johnson at once fell forty degrees in my estimation when he said we could not sail with the wind "dead ahead," as he expressed it. "Mr. Johnson," said I severely, "if you are right about this matter, what becomes of all this we read in 'Peter, the Whaler,' 'Peter Simple,' 'The Red Rover' and other piratical works about 'sailing in the wind's eye'?"

"I never heard of such a thing," said Johnson. "It is impossible. How could they do it?"

"You never heard of such a thing? Then, sir, you are here under false pretenses. You are no sailor, sir! I shipped you as a sailor, but it seems you don't know the first principles of sailing, for you can't even sail in the wind's eye, a thing all the old sea dogs do with the greatest ease. It is the simplest thing in navigation. All you have to do is to flatten your sail and haul hard on your windward lanyards."

"Ah, yes, I see!" said Johnson, "but for that work more than one sail is required. We would require sails on our jibboom, blowing out in such a way as to give the mainsail a purchase on the wind and hold it up to its work. As it is, we must ship the oars and give way, my hearties!"

This last expression renewed my confidence in Johnson to some extent. In a less severe tone than I had been using I said: "Mr. Johnson, you can go forward and take the wheel. It is your first dog watch at the oars." As Johnson seated himself at the forward pair of oars and Rounds at the rear ones I became still more affable, for I did not wish to be obliged to shed blood in quelling a mutiny before leaving port. Said I: "Mr. Johnson" (touching my sombrero), "you are now in command of the Wanderer; sail her as you like. All I ask is that you keep her on an even keel."

Mr. Johnson said: "Aye, aye, sir." He seemed rather surprised at my knowledge of navigation. Then, with four oars in action, we sailed away with an outflowing tide.

It was something to be afloat. That we could not hoist our sail was, of course, a disappointment, but that would come later—"at the next reach, perhaps," Johnson said. But at the next reach it was the same—wind dead ahead. We had the Wanderer for over five months, and always sailed her with the oars—wind always ahead.

Bounding over the yellow waters at the rate of two knots an hour we went down the river about sixteen miles, when Johnson said we were nearing a place where, on the east side, were many small lakes, ponds, and tule swamps—a place where we ought to find plenty of game. It was a place he called the Willows, not the place known as Willow Point.

When opposite the Willows, we found a small creek up which we hauled our boat till it was hidden in a thicket of willows and alders above the first bend. The place selected for our camp was half a mile inland near some small lakes, with a chain of larger lakes to the northwest extending out into the plains. No game was in sight, but Rounds said such flocks as would darken the air might any day come whirling and shrieking from the north, "provided there came a big storm up coast."

After packing our traps from the boat to the place selected for our camp in the edge of a beautiful grove, we lighted our fire and prepared our first meal. The next day we set about building a tule house. The frame was of willow poles and the sides and roof of tule thatch. The house was commodious, warm, and dry. We were about a week in building it, for, the rush of game not coming, we not only gave the structure great length, but also put on several fancy touches—as a porch in front under which to cook and a large movable side screen to keep the wind from the fire. Then at the rear we partitioned off a powder magazine.

Our house completed, we were ready for business, but no game came to our lakes. We could not kill as many ducks and geese as we could eat. When ducks could not be found we were obliged to live on mud hens—coots. By skinning these birds and parboiling them, they became eatable, as most of the strong and muddy flavor lies in the fat which sticks to and comes off with the skin.

Finally even these mud hens became scarce. They were driven

away from their principal haunt by a big gang of Chinamen who came down from Sacramento to dig tule potatoes. These so-called potatoes were found on the borders of ponds and were apparently the bulbs of water lilies. The provisions brought down in the boat were soon about exhausted and we were threatened with starvation if we remained at that place. The weather was still dry and very cold of nights. Of mornings, borders of ice from one to five rods in width were frequently to be seen around the lakes and ponds, ice that was nearly an inch thick at the shores.

One evening we had only one mud hen and a thin old hen mallard for supper, hardly a mouthful for four hungry hunters. The flour was low and we were on an allowance of two slapjacks each. All the bacon had disappeared except a single thick slice kept for a griddle-greaser in baking the slapjacks. Still we held on, being ashamed to go back up the river empty-handed.

The next morning after our light supper, we were up at break of day, and each man took a different route in the hope that some kind of game would be found. I came upon a solitary mud hen in a small circular lake, and turning loose on it with my No. 9, I broke one of its wings. It managed to paddle out into the center of the pond, about two hundred yards from shore, and there it remained—out of the reach of my gun. I was like the boy who was after the groundhog. I was hungry and had got to have that bit of poor meat. Though about the lake was a border of ice that extended thirty or forty feet from the shore, I stripped to the buff and went after that mud hen. With a club I broke a path through the ice and thought I would be able to wade out to my game. But I soon found myself compelled to swim. When I reached the middle of the lake and neared my game there was a regular circus. The mud hen tried diving and all manner of dodges, but its broken wing was against it, and at last I nabbed it. Taking a wing in my teeth I struck out for shore, but not the shore from which I started. The chase had led me across the lake, and in order to reach the land I was obliged to break ice from half an inch to an inch in thickness with my naked hands. When I got ashore both hands and feet were bleeding, but I had got my game. As I was hobbling back around the lake to where I had left my clothes and gun I said to myself: "What is the *winterschlafen* of the men of the mountains to the life of the bold hunter in the valleys?"

The other fellows had poor luck, though one of them brought in a sick-looking old jackrabbit. As the little game found on our arrival had been frightened away by our firing, and as no new flocks came, we tried fishing, but even Johnson, a fisherman by trade, could catch nothing in the river. About all the lakes, the beavers had subterranean passages, some of which extended inland beneath the shore a hundred yards or more. There were little underground canals leading to the lakes. As many holes had been broken into these beaver canals by cattle running over the ground we were able to see that the little channels swarmed with fish—minnows from half an inch to two inches in length. Placing a net made of the leg of a pair of knitted drawers at the mouth of one of the beaver canals at the edge of the lake, then going above and chasing the minnows down with long willow rods thrust into the many holes made by the cattle, we were able to make some great hauls. In this way we caught the minnows by the peck.

At first we tried scaling and cleaning them, but we soon gave that up. Instead we mashed them all into a kind of batter, all alive and kicking as they came from the water, then mixed a little flour with them and made pancakes of them. This is the Digger Indian way of utilizing minnows of diminutive size, plus the flour, and we found it very fine. All the boys said it beat a grasshopper diet. Bill Johnson said the only better thing was acorn bread with angleworm shortening.

While half starving on a diet of minnow pancakes and mud hen, we all hungered for something more substantial in the meat line. The only bit of bacon left was the slice used in greasing the griddle. As we could not bake slapjacks without something to grease the frying pan, this was precious. An old bummer of a yellow dog had in some way found his way to our camp and taken up his residence with us. He was half starved when he came, and a short stay with us rendered him perfectly wolfish. In order to keep the griddle greaser out of the way of the big hungry brute, it was always taken after use and placed on a log, the upper end of which rested in the crotch of a tree, about ten feet above the ground. This griddle grease had become the most precious thing about the camp. Nothing that remained to us was nearer to the heart of each man, as without it no slapjacks could be baked. We never left camp without someone asking, "Has the griddle grease been put up out of the reach of the dog?" for the dog, being worse than useless out in the field, was always left at camp in the hopes that he might develop into a watchdog.

One day I returned to the camp unsuccessful and ravenously hungry. None of the others had yet got in. I found a cold slapjack and began eating it, when thoughts of the griddle-greaser came into my head. I tried to drive the greaser from my mind, but in vain. The savor of it as it had often assailed my nostrils when Rounds was using it on a hot pan seemed to be in the air. I tried to resist, but while trying found myself, pancake in hand, walking up the log that led to the sacred deposit in the crotch of the tree.

Arrived within reach of the treasure, I surveyed the country far and near, and finding no one in sight grasped the precious morsel and sat down in the forks of the tree to enjoy it. From frequent contact with the hot frying pan the slice of bacon was well cooked, rather too much cooked, for little fat was kept in it. The old yellow dog well knew where the savory greaser was left. Often he had watched it being carried to its place of deposit with hungry eyes and watering mouth. Seeing me up in the tree crotch when no one was around the dog seemed to understand that I was about to do what he had often wished himself capable of doing. He came and sat below me, looking wistfully up, whimpering and thumping the ground with his tail. When he saw me begin to eat, the old fellow became absolutely frantic, got up on his hind legs and howled. In all my life I have never tasted a sweeter morsel than was that bit of shriveled bacon.

I had no more than got down from my perch in the tree and started a fire than my partners arrived. The trio brought a lean rabbit and one or two mud hens. Soon all were busy about the dinner, for our breakfast had been a sort of "Barmecide feast." Presently Rounds, chief cook, wanted the griddle-greaser. Out of the corner of one eye I saw him walk up the steep slant of the log until he had reached the crotch of the tree. Then he stooped and looked about. Soon he rose up and roared like a bull of Bushan: "Say, fellers, the griddle-greaser's gone!"

"What! The greaser gone?" cried all hands, bounding up from where they had thrown themselves about the camp. "It may be on the ground at the foot of the tree!" and two or three ran to look. It is needless to say that the precious bit of bacon was not found, and the pan had to be greased with the fat of a piece of the skin of a mud hen.

While all were speculating about the disappearance of the greaser, the old dog came and stood wagging his tail and snuffing the steam from the dinner pot.

"Here's the chap that ate the greaser!" cried someone. "He must have gone up that log and gobbled it; confound him!"

"That's so," said another, and charging upon the poor old dog, he gave him a kick that lifted him a foot from the ground, crying, "Get out, you old thief of Hades." No sooner had the starved old dog crept back than some other fellow got up and kicked him, and at last he was clubbed out of camp. However, when we were all seated at dinner the old fellow came creeping back in the hope of finding a few bones. "Here you are again, you old thief," cried Rounds. "By the Lord, I'll fix you this time. I'll learn you how to steal a griddle-greaser," and lifting his dinner pan from his lap he caught up his gun and made for the dog. "Don't shoot," cried I, but Rounds did shoot, after waiting until the dog had got off such a distance that he was merely slightly peppered with small shot. I said no more, fearing our enraged chief cook might give me the other barrel. Not one of that party ever found out what became of the griddle-greaser.

Some weeks later we took in as partners a party of hunters from an upriver camp. The old yellow dog, skulking and unwillingly following, came with them. No sooner had Rounds set eyes upon him than he cried: "By the Lord, there's the dog that stole the griddle-greaser!" and made for his gun. "That's our dog," said our new pards, and Rounds was obliged to subside. However, he gave the dog a bad character to his newcomers, and in support of what he said of the dog's infernal cunning, he pointed out to them the pole he had climbed.

A day or two after we lost the griddle-greaser we suffered another loss almost as great. While we were all out trying to find something to eat, our tule house took fire. Johnson, who was nearest, soon saw the smoke and flames. He reached the shanty in time to haul out our blankets and some of our other traps, when Rounds put in an appearance, yelling: "The powder! The powder! Snatch out the powder!"

Both men then turned to, tore out the rear of the structure and hauled the powder kegs out of the magazine. By the time the powder was carried to a safe place the whole shanty was in flames and, there being no water near, nothing could be done to save it. I and my brother had seen the great column of smoke shoot up and, guessing what had occurred, were soon on hand.

Although we had sworn not to go up to Sutterville until we could take with us a boatload of game, we were now obliged to knock under, as we had lost the little dab of flour, sugar, coffee, salt, and other eatables on which we had been holding out. Our council of war was brief. It was nearly sunset. In an hour or two the tide would be running up, when the boat must be got off. By the time we had carried the traps left us to the boat, it was dark. Johnson and Hank were sent up the river with the boat, while Rounds and I struck out for Sutterville by land.

We got lost in the swamps and did not reach Sutterville until three o'clock in the morning. Rounds having been a man-of-all-work about the Golden Eagle Hotel, we were able to get in by a rear door and find beds without arousing the house.

About sunrise Johnson and my brother arrived with the boat and we all met at breakfast. Our friend, Sam Corwin, and all his boarders roared and howled when they heard our story. We were the modern Nimrods, the "mighty hunters from the mountains," the men who were to "glut Sacramento with game," in short, we were the laughingstock of the whole town.

However, after a while Sam Corwin said: "Never mind. I knew you could do nothing as the weather held, and expected your return sooner. In a few days there will be swarms of game everywhere, even in the camp you have just left. The storms cannot hold off much longer up north."

Sure enough, game came at last. In about three days the heavens were black with flocks of ducks and geese coming down from the north. Then we prepared for a new start in great glee. The air was full of game. The *winterschlafen* up the mountains be blowed! Hurrah for the lakes!

Maroney's Last Shot

Romance of a Sierra County Miner. Nearly Two Years Blasting a Bowlder. Only One Big Nugget Found, but It Made the Prospector's Future.

---

*S*lug Cañon, Sierra County, has always been famous for the number and size of its golden nuggets. The cañon heads among the huge skyward-towering mountains that rise on the south side of the North Yuba, into which river it empties its waters just below the lower end of the famous old mining town of Downieville. In 1852, a son of Erin named Mike Maroney had a placer claim on this cañon of nests of golden eggs which, in his opinion, was nothing less than the secret storehouse of the Goblins of the Golden Mountains.

Mike's claim was not in the present or modern channel of the cañon, but upon a bench above it, where was a channel that had been formed by the stream in ancient times. In this old upper channel stood a boulder of enormous size—a granite rock as big as a cathedral. Mike was undoubtedly attracted to the particular piece of bench ground on which he staked out his claim by the immense size of the boulder lodged upon it—a rock so large it seemed to be a pinnacle broken from the top of one of the overhanging mountains. He in some way got it into his head that in the old channel, at the point

---

Dan brings Mike back to spend two years blasting a boulder. From the San Francisco *Chronicle*, January 13, 1895.

where he had staked out his claim, was gold proportionate to the size of the rock and in keeping with the difficulties to be overcome.

The boulder stood in the lower end of the old channel, which it blocked completely from wall to wall. To blast it out and get into and work the channel seemed a herculean task. Many a miner had looked the ground over and departed with a sigh—after a careful survey of the rock—before Mike Maroney set his stakes on the ancient channel. All thought well of the ground, but feared to attack the giant that stood in the way.

Mike built a small cabin on a bench of the cañon above high-water mark and settled down in full sight of the enemy he had determined to conquer. Alone and single-handed, he mounted the great granite rock and began drilling and blasting it. The rock was hard and the work went on slowly, but he was always to be seen hammering and banging away at the task he had undertaken. All the miners passing up and down the cañon halted for a word with Mike. They admired his pluck and cheered him on by telling him that under the boulder and behind it he would find enough gold to load a train of half a dozen mules.

Mike was a small man as to height, standing less than five feet in his boots, but he was immensely broad across the shoulders and in strength was a little Samson. Altogether he was a curiously constructed creature. He had a head big enough for a six-footer. His mouth seemed the result of a slash of a cleaver and he wore it with one corner drawn up toward his left ear in a very knowing way. On his broad, flat face was stuck a short stump of a nose with vast cavernous nostril. Add to these features a pair of enormous ears, little black eyes that twinkle beneath an overhanging crag of brow, then top out the whole with a thatch of coal-black hair the size of a haycock and you see Mike Maroney as he appeared mounted upon his big rock with drill and hammer in hand. Seen thus, he might well have passed for the king of the gnomes, just popped up from the chambers of his golden caverns for a mouthful of sunshine and a peep at the upper world.

Mike was nearly two years in blasting out his great boulder. When he first began, such was his enthusiasm that he thought he would make short work of it. But after he had been engaged upon it about three months, he began to understand more clearly the nature of the task he had undertaken. His stock of provisions was exhausted and he lacked money with which to procure a new supply. Also, he could no longer obtain powder, fuse, and other supplies on credit. It became evident that he must have money or he would be obliged to stop work on the boulder.

In this strait he went up into the town of Downieville and explained the situation to a number of friends. All knew Mike's claim and all had faith in it, for the old channel with the big rock in its mouth had been the talk of all the Slug Cañon miners long before Mike set his stakes there. Therefore, he found it a less difficult business than he had anticipated to raise money with which to proceed. Half a dozen friends became his backers, telling him to go ahead and call upon them as often as he needed money. They would take the chances of his finding enough gold to make them all right, once the big boulder had been conquered.

Again Mike set to work in high spirits. He told his backers that in two or three months more he would have utterly demolished the big rock, but when that time had passed the work seemed only fairly begun. After Mike had been at work for about a year and a half the men who were putting up for him began to grow tired of the whole business and did not come out with their coin so cheerfully as at first; and they asked rather anxiously in regard to the progress being made.

In order to cheer them up, Mike would say: "Byes, I do be knockin the ould rock to smithereens! I've got her so wakened now that she shakes wid ivery blasht!"

Finally the men tired of hearing this story when Mike came round to collect money, and he then began to say: "One more blasht, byes, and I've got her!" This went on so long that it became a byword in Downieville. Everywhere it was: "One more blasht, byes, and I've got her!" Mike's backers laughed with the others, and put up the money he asked for.

All things have an end, however, and when Mike's "lasht blasht" shattered the huge slab constituting the sole remnant of the once enormous boulder, he went to the base of the mass and began working under it with his pick. On a sudden the big block began to topple over. Mike dropped his pick and retreated with the rock following him on a steep downgrade. The situation was such that in order to escape being crushed to death Mike was obliged to leap into the cañon.

Owing to a spring freshet, the cañon was at the time a roaring torrent; therefore his leap was almost as that proverbial one from the frying pan. He was swept down the canyon about two hundred yards till almost at the verge of a vertical fall of some thirty feet, when he had the good fortune to grasp the top of an overhanging bush and drag himself ashore.

Mike escaped with a few slight cuts and bruises and the loss of his hat. These, however, were matters that did not trouble him. All his thoughts were of the spot whence had just tumbled down the steep the last fragment of the big boulder. Thither his mind ran faster than his legs were able to travel, though the latter soon landed him at the spot where he had so long and faithfully labored.

Looking down into the bed of that last huge slab of granite which had seemed to leap forth and chase him into the canyon, Mike beheld a large disk of pure and glittering gold. It was a piece of the precious metal about the size and shape of a dinner plate. He waited to see no more. Leaping down into the hole he grasped the golden prize, which looked to him as big as the face of the full moon, and then at once made a break for Downieville to find his backers, show them the gold, and tell them the great news of the final annihilation of the big rock.

Mike was wild as a hawk. In his hands he held a mass of gold that weighed nearly twenty pounds, and as he dashed down Slug Cañon with his prize, he shouted at every jump: "That lasht blasht fetched her! That lasht blasht fetched her!" Thus shouting, as he tore down the cañon, he passed several claims where miners were at work, but he halted at none of these for a single moment.

"Mike Maroney has gone crazy about his boulder!" cried the miners, on seeing him running bareheaded down the cañon trail. At some of the claims he passed, men threw down their tools, and scrambling up the bank of the stream to the trail, called out after him, but the only answer they received was: "That lasht blasht fetched her!"

When Mike reached Downieville and started up the middle of the town, hatless, dripping wet, shouting, and carrying before him his golden prize, he soon had a crowd at his heels. He paid no attention to the crowd, but when he saw on either side of the street miners of his acquaintance, he shouted to them in passing: "Byes, that lasht blasht fetched her! There's a whole bushel of goold undther the bottom of her!"

Strangers in the town thought they saw before them a crazy man, but every resident of the place knew Mike, and soon along the street was raised the cry: "Mike Mahoney has struck it at last! He's knocked the devil out of his boulder and got a chunk of gold bigger'n a fryin' pan!"

Hearing this news, others shouted: "Hurrah for Maroney and his 'lasht blasht!'"

"Yis, hurrah, byes," cried Mike, who felt himself in the seventh heaven of glory, "hurrah, for this minit I'm the pride of the wurruld!"

By the time Mike had found some of the friends who had for so long backed him with their coin, and had displayed his big nugget, there was a grand excitement in the camp. Some said he had found an old channel paved with nuggets as big as cobblestones, and others that great slabs of gold covered the bedrock.

Mike told his friends that though he had only stopped long enough to catch up the first big nugget he saw, he was sure there was a whole bushel of gold in the nest of the big boulder. With the sample brought in by Mike lying before them, all were ready to believe that he had made the strike of the age. Every man who heard of Mike's find said he always felt sure that there were mule loads of gold under the big boulder of Slug Cañon.

As soon as Mike's backers had collected their wits —scattered by the sight of the big nugget and his wild story of bushels of gold in sight— they dropped everything and prepared to go at once to the scene of the strike. With the elated Maroney in the lead, they set out, taking with them a pack mule that happened to be at hand. They were joined by a number of idlers as they passed through the town, and in going up Slug Cañon the crowd was increased by the miners at the several claims who desired to feast their eyes upon what by this time had grown to be "Mike Maroney's mound of gold."

Seeing the miners thus flocking after him, Mike cried: "Cheer for me, byes; the lasht blasht fetched her!"

During the absence of the party, the excitement in the town was at fever heat. Some new wonder was constantly being added to the story of the big find. Then occasionally there were false alarms. One of these that sent a crowd rushing down toward the river was to the effect that Mike and his friends were on their way back to town and were "just crossing the bridge at Jersey Flat with a muleload of gold."

At last, when the sun was just sinking behind the western mountains, the party came straggling back to town. They were a dejected-looking crowd, and gave short and surly answers to the questions fired at them on all sides. The backers were particularly gloomy and snappish. As for Mike himself, he was nowhere to be seen.

Finally the tongues of some of the disinterested idlers who had gone out with the party were loosened through the administration of copious doses of stimulants. They then said squarely and frankly that they had found nothing at all. The nest of Mike's big boulder was empty. In the smooth and soft bed of the rock they found the spot where Mike's "golden moon" had lain and saw his tracks beside it, but not a single nugget was in sight. Then they had dug into the edge of the old channel and found it barren and smooth as the bottom of an iron kettle.

"What has become of Mike?" asked someone.

"Ah, poor Mike! Well, we are afraid he is in a bad way. As soon as he found that there were no nuggets in sight, and was told that he had merely imagined them, he took on the color of a corpse. He reeled about, pawed the air, and then with a howl such as I never want to hear again, ran off to his cabin and locked himself up in it. As he couldn't be induced to come out, two men were left to watch him, for he is evidently upset in the upper story. No one can get anything out of him but mutterings about his last blast."

The next day Mike was brought into the town for medical examination. The doctors said his mental derangement was of a nature so mild and harmless that he might safely be allowed to remain in his cabin. Indeed, at times he seemed for a moment or two to get back his senses. One of his friends, happening to speak of his mother and his people in Ireland, he at once broke out with: "Byes, I don't care so much meself for the trouble and whorlin in me haid, but I do be thinking of the poor ould mother back across the wather. What will become of her, and of them all, widout the money I promised to sind?"

It was in vain they spoke of the big nugget he had found, telling him he should have it and do with it what he pleased. He would hear of nothing of the kind. That belonged to the men who had put up their money for him. His gold was still under the big boulder where he had fired his last blast. He had seen it once and he would see it again and get it.

The men who had backed Mike—half a dozen in number—ascertained the address of his widowed mother from men who had known him at home, and, selling the big nugget, which proved to be worth $3,600, sent her a check for the amount.

Mike shut himself up in his cabin and was seldom seen outside of it during the daylight hours. Men mining on the cañon, however, reported that he was in the habit of prowling about of nights. They said they had frequently seen a light up at his claim very late at night just at the spot where he had demolished the big boulder. Upon investigation by a friend, it was found that Mike had got it into his head that the pile of gold he had seen had been sunk deep into the ground by an evil spirit. However, he would yet get it, as one night each month at midnight—he did not know what night—all the big nuggets came up to their old nest under the boulder. All he had to do to beat the goblin that had lived under the big rock was to be on the watch and shout when the gold appeared, "Mine, in the name of the Blessed Virgin!"

Though he wanted nothing to do with anyone, yet he was always peering out at the chinks of his cabin, watching those who passed by. When anyone came along the trail, he would pop his head out at his door and utter his new war cry of "Mine, in the name of the Blessed Virgin!" Seeing that the life he was leading was making him worse, his friends on the cañon tried to get him out of his cabin, offering him big wages to work in their claims. All was useless, however, until one day a man happened to say he had a big boulder in his diggings he wanted blasted out. Instantly Mike pricked up his ears and was all attention. He was ready to set to work upon the boulder at once.

Being given a trial, it was found that he was able to work as well and intelligently as ever at drilling and blasting. While engaged in that work he seemed quite sane, but he could not be induced to do anything in the mines except blast boulders. For that business he seemed to have a perfect mania, and could accomplish nearly as much in a day as two ordinary men. Battling with the boulders was seen to brighten him up wonderfully, and he was given all the work he could do in his favorite line by the friendly miners up and down Slug Cañon.

One day after Mike had been for some months waging a war of extermination against the boulders of Slug Cañon, his friends up in Downieville had a big surprise. All unheralded and unexpected, the Widdy Maroney, with a raft of tall and buxom daughters, landed in their midst, fresh from the "Ould Sod." They had come to make their home in America, "and look afther poor Moik." Marriageable girls being at that time in great demand, the family were heartily welcomed and well provided for at once. It was then so contrived that Mike was suddenly brought into the midst of the whole crowd without a hint being given him beforehand that his mother and sisters were in the country. The surprise so shook him up mentally that the balance wheel in his head at once started up and moved along as smoothly and regularly as ever.

Soon the family were comfortably settled at Downieville, and Mike with them. His last blast had not been so very disastrous after all. It had not only fetched the big boulder, but had also fetched all his people out to America to a good home; and the raft of bouncing girls to where they all soon captured good husbands, three among whom had been Mike's backers, and helped pay for the powder exploded in firing his "lasht blasht."

The Reverend Olympus Jump

The Mountain Howitzer of God.

---

*D*o you know," said that weather-beaten miner, old Gurnsey Bob, as he thumped his glass on the table before him to call for another half-gallon of beer—"do you know it jist makes me sick to hear all the talk and furse they make about the fashionable, high-ferlutin' preachers of these times. I tell yer, boys, they ain't deuce high 'longside the preachers of the airly days."

"In course not!" "Don't begin!" "Hain't got the sand, nor the gift!" chorused old Bob's table companions—for he was putting up for the beer, therefore his opinion on this or any other matter was entitled to much consideration.

"I tell yer, fellers," said old Gurnsey, squaring himself for a big talk, once he found that he was going to have things all his own way; "I tell yer, fellers, I us'ter know a preacher what us'ter ride on what they call a circle, over in Caleforny, in '52, as was named Olympus Jump, an' he was a roarer, you kin jist bet!

"He wasn't one of yer stuck-up, kid-gloved kind, as would be afraid they'd dirty their hands by givin' the flipper of a miner a grip! No; he'd take hold of yer paw like a wolf trap.

The Mountain Howitzer of God is one of Dan's liveliest characters. From the *Territorial Enterprise,* August 26, 1877.

"He wasn't one of them kind as goes a prospectin' about, with noses in the air, a-smellin' roast chicken an' hot biskits afar off! Not at all! He was a God-fearin' man, an' pork an' beans was the highest ambition of his meek and lowly bowels.

"Olympus wasn't one of yer kyoters in sheep's clothin' what goes a sneekin' about among the ewes of the flock, makin' more Beecher scandals in one week than yer could wash out in six months by pipin' inter 'em with the biggest hydraulic in the mountains! No; that wasn't his style. He walked uprightly before the Lord, and was happy as the day was long with his own comely little wife and half a dozen little Jumps.

"He wasn't one of yer high eddicated, rose-water, butter-mouthed sort—Olympus wasn't. He had the gift nateral—right from the Lord—and when he onbuttoned his shirt collar an' began to talk in dead earnest, it made a feller think of a string of boulders thunderin' down a ground sluice under a big head of water.

"Olympus Jump wasn't one of these newfangled sort of preachers what stand up before yer Sunday after Sunday, never showin' up the color of the word o' God nor givin' you a single mouthful of the bread of life. Not a bit of it! He'd drifted and creviced all through the Bible, pannin' out bushels of chispas and scores and scores of great nuggets of gold. With these he was loaded clean up to the muzzle, an' when he turned loose an' began to fire scriptur' into an aujence, he might'er been called the mountain howitzer of God!

"He was full of the spirit, an' when he went forth to labor in the lord's diggin's he allurs meant business. He wasn't one of them kind o' prayers whose prayin' is jist a little sneakin' drizzle that only wets the earth here an' there, washing' away none of the dust of iniquity—never causin' a single seed of good to sprout or raisin' up the droopin' head of a single wilted plant! No. The prayer of Olympus was like a cloudbust on a mountain; it swept down through all the dark cañons of sin and sent all the miners therein end over end down the tail-flumes of the devil till they was glad to grab the fust branch of the tree of life that hung in reach and haul theirselves ashore, high an' dry on the rock of ages.

"Olympus wasn't one of yer stuck-up kind of laborers in the vineyard as couldn't preach without a morocco-bound, gold-clasped Scriptur' and a pulpit as grand as the gates of the New Jerusalem. Not a bit of it! Why, fellers, he'd jist haul his little old greasy pack of loose leaves of Bible out'n his pocket, shuffle it up, give it a cut, deal out a text, and then jist hammer h——l's bells outn' all the sinners on Sucker Flat!

"That was a preacher for yer, an' we shall never look on his like again! Fill up yer glasses, fellers; let's all drink to him, though he's now safe on the other side of Jordan."

Sources

WHAT FOLLOWS IS A LIST of the periodical sources cited in the introduction, the selections, and the references, together with the symbols used in referring to them.

Alta	San Francisco *Alta California*	K	New York *Knickerbocker Magazine*
Argo	*Argonaut*	MSP	*Mining & Scientific Press*
CFG	Cedar Falls *Gazette*	NM	*Nevada Monthly*
CFL	Carson City *Free Lance*	NYS	New York *Sun*
CH	San Francisco *Chronicle*	OM	*Overland Monthly*
CIM	*Californian Illustrated Magazine*	SFC	San Francisco *Call*
		SFP	San Francisco *Post*
EMJ	*Engineering and Mining Journal*	SLT	Salt Lake City *Tribune*
		TE	Virginia City *Territorial Enterprise*
EX	San Francisco *Examiner*		
GE	*Golden Era*	VDU	*Virginia Daily Union*
GHN	Gold Hill *News*		

ADDITIONAL REFERENCES

"Among the Old Boys," San Jose *Pioneer,* January 12, 1878.

Angel, Myron, ed. *History of Nevada.* Oakland: Thompson and West, 1881.

Armstrong, Robert D. *Nevada Printing History: A Bibliography of Imprints and Publications 1858–1880.* Reno: University of Nevada Press, 1981.

Beebe, Lucius. *Comstock Commotion: The Story of the Territorial Enterprise.* Stanford: Stanford University Press, 1954.

Benson, Ivan. *Mark Twain's Western Years.* Stanford: Stanford University Press, 1938.

Berkove, Lawrence I. "Dan De Quille and 'Old Times on the Mississippi.'" *Mark Twain Journal,* 24: 2 (Fall 1986), pp. 28–35.

———. "Free Silver and Jews: The Change in Dan De Quille." *American Jewish Archives.* In press.

———. "The Literary Journalism of Dan De Quille." *Nevada Historical Society Quarterly,* 28 (1985), pp. 249–61.

Branch, Edgar M. *The Literary Apprenticeship of Mark Twain.* Urbana: University of Illinois Press, 1950.

Browne, J. Ross. "A Peep at Washoe." *Harper's,* 22 (December 1860–February 1861), pp. 1–17, 145–62, 289–305.

Chesterman, E. E. "Wright, William" in *The Dictionary of American Biography, Supplement v. 1.* New York: Scribner's, 1944.

Clemens, Cyril. *Mark Twain and Dan De Quille: An Unpublished Incident.* San Francisco: T. P. Brown, 1942.

Clemens, Samuel L. *Mark Twain of the Enterprise: Newspaper Articles and other Documents 1862–64.* Ed. H. N. Smith. Berkeley: University of California Press, 1957.

———. *Mark Twain's Letters to his Publishers.* Ed. Hamlin Hill. Berkeley: University of California Press, 1967.

———. "Mental Telepathy." *Harper's,* 84 (December 1891), pp. 95–104.

———. *Roughing It.* Hartford: American Publishing Company, 1872.

———. *The Washoe Giant in San Francisco.* Ed. Franklin Walker. San Francisco: George Fields, 1938.

———. *The Works of Mark Twain: Early Tales & Sketches. Vol. I, 1851–1864.* Ed. E. M. Branch and R. H. Hirst. Berkeley: University of California Press, 1979.

Cummins, Ella S. *The Story of the Files.* San Francisco: Cooperative Printing, 1893.

"Dan De Quille." CFL, January 25, 1886.

"Dan De Quille." Fredericktown, Ohio, *Free Press,* September 11, 1875.

"Dan De Quille: Master of the Written Word." *Apple Tree,* September 19, 1976.

"Dan's Book." TE, February 23, August 11, 1876.

Davis, Samuel P., ed. *The History of Nevada.* 2 vols. Reno and Los Angeles: Elms, 1913.

[———] "Mark Twain and Dan De Quille." Argo, January 31, 1880. From Carson City *Appeal.* Reprinted as *The Typographical Howitzer.* Sacramento: Meteorite Press, 1944; also reprinted in *Butterfield Express,* 4 (December 1965), pp. 1, 6.

De Groot, Henry. *Recollections of California Mining Life.* San Francisco: Dewey, 1884.

Delmore, Edith. "Journalism in Nevada." Master's thesis. University of Nevada, 1938.

Doten, Alfred R. *The Journals of Alfred R. Doten, 1849–1903*. Ed. Walter Van Tilburg Clark. 3 vols. Reno: University of Nevada Press, 1973.

——. "Early Journalism in Nevada." *Nevada Magazine* (September–November 1899), pp. 45–58, 181–90, 253–63.

Drury, Wells. *An Editor on the Comstock Lode*. New York: Farrar & Rinehart, 1936.

Dwyer, Richard A. and Richard E. Lingenfelter. *Lying on the Eastern Slope: James Townsend's Comic Journalism on the Mining Frontier*. Miami: University Presses of Florida, 1984.

Emrich, Duncan, ed. *Comstock Bonanza*. New York: Vanguard, 1950.

Fatout, Paul. *Mark Twain in Virginia City*. Bloomington: Indiana University Press, 1964.

——. *Meadow Lake, Gold Town*. Bloomington: Indiana University Press, 1969.

Fender, Stephen. *Plotting the Golden West*. New York: Cambridge University Press, 1981.

Ferguson, De Lancey. "The Petrified Truth." *Colophon*, 2 (Winter 1937), pp. 189–96.

Fitch, Thomas. *Western Carpetbagger: The Extraordinary Memoirs of "Senator" Thomas Fitch*. Ed. Eric N. Moody. Reno: University of Nevada Press, 1978.

Goodman, Joseph T. *Heroes, Badmen and Honest Miners: Joe Goodman's Tales of the Comstock Lode*. Ed. Phillip I. Earl. Reno: Great Basin Press, 1977.

Goodwin, Charles C. *As I Remember Them*. Salt Lake City: Commercial Club, 1913.

[——]. "Dan and His Quills." TE, February 3, 1876.

Gorham, Harry M. *My Memories of the Comstock*. Los Angeles: Sutton House, 1939.

Graham, Jared B. *Handset Reminiscences*. Salt Lake City: Century Publishing, 1915.

Lauber, John *The Making of Mark Twain. A Biography*. New York: American Heritage, 1985.

Leland, Charles G. "The Editor's Table." K, 59 (January 1862), p. 109.

Lewis, Oscar, ed. *The Life and Times of the Virginia City Territorial Enterprise*. Ashland: Lewis Osborne, 1971.

Lillard, Richard G. "Dan De Quille, Comstock Reporter and Humorist." *Pacific Historical Review*, 13 (1944), pp. 251–59.

——. "Studies in Washoe Journalism and Humor." Ph.D. dissertation. Pt. 2. State University of Iowa, 1943.

Lingenfelter, Richard E., and Karen Rix Gash. *The Newspapers of Nevada: A History and Bibliography 1854–1979*. Reno: University of Nevada Press, 1984.

Loomis, C. Grant. "Dan De Quille's Mark Twain." *Pacific Historical Review*, 15 (1946), pp. 336–47.

————. "The Tall Tales of Dan De Quille." *California Folklore Quarterly,* 5 (1946), pp. 26–71.

Mack, Effie Mona. "Dan De Quille (William Wright), 1829–1898." *Nevada Magazine* (September 1946), pp. 6–9, 33–34; (October 1946), pp. 6–9, 33; (November 1946), pp. 6–11, 35.

Moss, George. "Silver Frolic: Popular Entertainment in Virginia City, Nevada, 1859–1863." *Journal of Popular Culture,* 22 (1988), pp. 1–31.

Mott, Frank L. "Facetious News Writing, 1833–1883." *Mississippi Valley Historical Revue,* 29 (1942–43), pp. 35–54.

Paine, Albert B. *Mark Twain: A Biography.* 4 vols. New York: Harper, 1912.

Putnam, C. A. V. "Dan De Quille and Mark Twain." SLT, April 25, 1898.

Rogers, Franklin. "Washoe's First Literary Journal." *California Historical Society Quarterly,* 36 (1957), pp. 365–70.

[Stephens, Louise G. Wright.] *Letters from an Oregon Ranch by "Katharine."* Chicago: A. C. McClurg, 1905.

Tilton, Cecil G. "Dan De Quille, a Sketch of his Career." Book Club of California. *Quarterly Newsletter,* 21 (Winter 1955), pp. 5–13.

Walker, Franklin. *San Francisco's Literary Frontier.* Revised ed. Seattle: University of Washington Press, 1969.

Watson, Margaret G. *Silver Theatre: Amusements of the Mining Frontier in Early Nevada, 1850 to 1864.* Glendale: Arthur H. Clark, 1964.

A Checklist of the Writings of Dan De Quille

Published works are presented chronologically. Excluding his daily mining reports, this list attempts to include all of Dan De Quille's imaginative writing and significant journalism. Those reworked by De Quille are followed by a cross-reference in square brackets. Items reprinted in this century are cross-referenced in parentheses. Any anonymous work attributed to De Quille is followed by an asterisk. Some items identified only by clippings in the William Wright Papers (WWP) are listed without other provenance.

MANUSCRIPTS

Berkeley, California. Bancroft Library, University of California. William Wright Papers. P–G 246.

Box 1: Correspondence, 1860–1897

Letters written by William Wright: one to his brother-in-law, Dr. J. M. Benjamin from Omega, California, 1860, and eighteen to his sister Lou (Mrs. Benjamin), 1874–85; one by his daughter Mell, 1878; and thirty-seven letters received, 1875–97.

Box 1: Manuscripts of Sketches, arranged by title

"About the Precious Opal." Incomplete, ca. 1894.
"Adventures of Brother Bob: His Battle with the Decoits of the Himalayas." 24 pp., ca. 1897 plus an additional typed copy.
"The Boy Miners." 87 pp. Incomplete.

"Bret Harte as a Delineator of Western Character and Scenery." 14 pp. Not in his hand.

"Courtship's Perils." 11 pp. [GE, June 15, 1862. Also reprinted in other periodicals].

"A Dead Man's Dust." 160 pp.

"The Demon Coroner of the Comstock." 15 pp. typed and copyedited (cf. ed. Rawls, 1980, pp. 45–66).

"The Demon Hand." 39 pp. [Louisville *Courier-Journal,* June 1, 1891].

"Dives and Lazarus: Their Wanderings and Adventures in the Infernal Regions." 227 pp. (ed. Berkove, 1988).

Box 2: Manuscripts of Sketches, arranged by title

"Description of System of Timbering Mines." 11 pp.

"The Earth Never Dies." 6 pp. [TE, April 18, 1878].

"Earthquakes in Owens Valley." 22 pp. plus another version of 11 pp.

"Fighting Horse." 36 pp. [cf. TE, June 28, 1874].

"The Ingenuity of Mrs. Smiley." 13 pp. typed [cf. TE, December 6, 1874].

"Josephus." 37 pp., missing pp. 1–14.

"The Lead Miner and His Cave." 78 pp.

"Life in the Dark—The Crusoe of the Caverns." 16 pp. typed.

"The Living Dead Ones: A Legend of California." 77 pp.

"Mineral Veins, Walls and Dikes." 11 pp.

Notebook. 1885–1886.

"A Piute Legend: Pahnenit, Prince of the Land of Lakes." 86 pp., ca. 1891.

"The Salt Deposits of Nevada." 27 pp., incomplete.

"The Sorceress of Attu." 57 pp. plus letter to editors of OM, November 22, 1894.

"Stuttering Tom: A Christmas Story." 23 pp.

"Su-ee Sin Faa, the Chinese Lily." 18 pp.

"Sunday Frivolities: A Mormon Novel; Comstock Turks." 4 pp. Not in his hand [TE, September 30, 1877].

"That Wonderful Lake." 12 pp.

"Uncle Pete and Little Benny: A Christmas Sketch." 16 pp.

"The Vouivre: The Witch of the Vosges." 101 pp., incomplete.

Box 3: Notes of Ideas for Stories and Articles; Notebook; Maps; Papers of other members of the Wright family

Cartons 1 and 2: Clippings of Wright's Own Writings and other clippings collected by him

Berkeley, California. Bancroft Library. University of California. C. Grant Loomis Papers. C–B 911. Seven folders in Carton 2: Transcriptions from TE and GE.

Reno, Nevada. Special Collections, University of Nevada. Library. NC 55:

William Wright Correspondence. Nine items 1884–87: letters to him (four from James G. Fair), and a manuscript of "Tom Collette's Bath," [TE, December 2, 1877].

San Francisco, California. California Historical Society. Library. Manuscript 15: William Wright file of twelve folders.

Folder 1: "The Indian Messiah." 32 pp. January 7, 1891 (ed. Rawls, 1980, pp. 109–21).

Folder 2: Two letters to Dan.

Folder 3: "The Haunted Cabin of Jim Crow Canyon." 49 pp., ca. 1893 (ed. Rawls, 1980, pp. 68–89).

Folder 4: Nine sketches, 78 pp.: "The Corn Shucking"; "The Wonderful Bee Tree"; "The Trained Swine"; "The Reckless Ride, a la Mazeppa"; "Wonderful Sagacity of the Buffalo"; "A Whole Band of Indians Exterminated"; "A Great Howl of Wild Turkeys"; "A Herculean Blow of the Fist"; "The Transformed Indian" (ed. Rawls, 1980, pp. 20–33) [TE, April 21, 1867, except for sketches 7 and 9] (ed. Loomis, 1946, nos. 16–22).

Folder 5: "Superstitions of Miners." 12 pp.

Folder 6: Notebook (ca. 20 pp.) of story ideas, prices, and dates of submission. ca. 1890s.

Folder 7: "Marier's Room." 23 pp. [TE, December 6, 1874].

Folder 8: "Bookkeeper of the Bouncer." 19 pp. plus clipping.

Folder 9: "Lost in the Tule Marshes." 18 pp. (ed. Rawls, 1980, pp. 99–106) [cf. related stories CH, September 9, 1893].

Folder 10: "Hunting for Market." 19 pp. (ed. Rawls, 1980, pp. 92–99) [CH, September 2, 1893].

Folder 11: "John Boyle's Experiment." (ed. Rawls, 1980, pp. 36–38); "The Perilous Conundrum." (ed. Rawls, 1980, pp. 39–40); "The Old French Doctor." (ed. Rawls, 1980, pp. 41–42); three humorous sketches in dialect.

Folder 12: "Rigdon Tandler, the Demon Coroner of Tunneltown." 59 pp. (ed. Rawls, 1980, pp. 45–66).

EDITIONS

De Quille, Dan. *History of the Big Bonanza.* Hartford: American Publishing Company; San Francisco: A. L. Bancroft, 1876, 1877; reissued as *The Big Bonanza.* Introduction by Oscar Lewis. New York: A. A. Knopf, 1947; Apollo paperback, 1969; Nevada Publications, 1983. Cited as BB.

[————]. *The Wonders of Nevada. Where They Are and How to Get to Them.* Virginia City: Enterprise Printing House, 1878; reprinted Glendale: La Siesta Press, 1966.

————. *A History of the Comstock Silver Lode and Mines.* Virginia City: F. Boegle, 1889; reprinted New York: Arno Press, 1973; Promontory Press, 1974.

————. *The Local Editor, His Duties and Delights.* Los Angeles: Ward Ritchie Press, 1953.

————. *Snowshoe Thompson.* Preface by Carrol D. Hall. Los Angeles: Glen Dawson, 1954.

————. *Washoe Rambles.* Ed. Richard E. Lingenfelter. Los Angeles: Westernlore Press, 1963.

————. *Dan De Quille of the Big Bonanza.* Ed. James J. Rawls. San Francisco: Book Club of California, 1980.

————. *Silver Walled Palace.* Ed. Dave Basso. Sparks: Falcon Hill Press, 1981 [twenty-two items from GE, December 1860–January 1865].

————. *Little Lucy's Papa: A Story of Silverland.* Sparks: Falcon Hill Press, 1987 [reprinted from GE, July 1864].

————. *Dives and Lazarus, Their Wanderings and Adventures in the Infernal Regions.* Ed. Lawrence I. Berkove. Ann Arbor: Ardis, 1988.

PERIODICAL ARTICLES

1860

"California Correspondence." CFG, June 15; July 13.

"Letter from Washoe." GE, November 18; December 16, 30.

"Ye Hydraulic." GE, November 25.

"From Our Utah Correspondent." CFG, November 30.

"Steamboat Springs." CFG, December 28.

"California." GE, December 30 [GE, July 10, 1864].

1861

"Mammoth Trees of California." CFG, January 4, 11.

"Ye California Miner." GE, January 6.

"Letter from Washoe." GE, January 6, 13; May 5.

"Ye Chinaman." GE, January 13.

"The Great Cave of Calaveras County, California." CFG, January 18.

"Spudder on the 'Pewterinktum.'" GE, January 20.

"The Little Frenchman's Luck and Lead." GE, January 27.

"Ye Bummer." GE, February 3.

"Our Washoe Correspondence." GE, February 3, 24; March 3.

"Utah Correspondence." CFG, February 8; from this "An Arkansaw's Nest," reprinted in GE, September 15.

"The Wife's Dream Visit." * N.p., February 14; WWP clipping of poem addressed to Mrs. Caroline W. of Iowa.

"Ye Office Seeker." GE, February 17.

"From Our Utah Correspondent." CFG, March 8; April 5, 12, 19; May 3.

"Adventures in Utah: Prospecting Trip to the Washoe Mines." CFG, March 15, 22, 29 [BB, 1876].

"Washoe Pictures. A Meeting of Our Company." GE, March 17.

"Washoe Pictures. Another Strike." GE, March 24.

"The Wealth of Washoe. A Day in the Silver Mines." GE, March 31.

"Washoe Pictures. 'No Wife Nor Mother's Care.'" GE, April 14 [SLT, July 12, 1885].

"Adventures in California. Bill Ryder and the Grizzly." CFG, April 26.

"Country and Scenery between the Yo-Semite Falls and Mono Lake." GE, April 28.

"Letter from Washoe." GE, April 28.

"Story of the $6,000 Chunk." CFG, May 3.

"The Young Inventors." GE, May 5.

"Washoe Rambles. A Week in Palmyra." GE, May 12.

"Our Utah Correspondent." CFG, May 17.

"Washoe Rambles. A Visit to Steamboat Springs." GE, May 26.

"Washoe Rambles. Steamboat and Washoe Valleys and the Ophir Works." GE, June 2.

"Washoe Rambles. Wisconsin District and Prospecting in the Sierras." GE, June 16.

"Downeaster and the Bull; or Peleg on the Prairies." GE, July 7.

"Letter from Dan De Quille." CFG, July 26; August 2; September 13; October 4, 11; November 8; December 13, 20, 27.

"Washoe Rambles. A Trip Among the Mountains, Lakes and Deserts to the Eastward." GE, July 28–December 1; California Magazine and Mountaineer, 6, September–December (ed. Lingenfelter, 1963).

"Ye Secesher." GE, September 1.

"The 'Old Diamond Hunter' of the Sierras." GE, September 29.

"The Way of Love in the Wilderness." GE, October 20.

"About Snakes." GE, November 17.

"Virginia City." TE, November 17.

"Our Soldiers." GE, November 24; from TE.

"Weelyum and La Belle Fanny." GE, December 15.

"California Gander Pulling." GE, December 29 [CH, September 16, 1893].

1862

"Knick and Mace in Washoe." K, 59 (January); repr. GE, March 9.

"My Exertions During the Flood." GE, January 12.

"Letter from Dan De Quille." CFG, January 17, 31; February 7; March 14; July 4; September 12.

"The Feller What Aint Runnin' for No Office." GE, January 26.

"Of Spending Money." GE, February 9.

"Tom Bently; or Love, Art and Gold." GE, February 16–March 30.

"The Festival of the Tombs." GE, March 30.

"Uncle Bob an Expert in the Black Art. How He Found His Fiddle." GE, April 6.

"We Gave Our Willie." GE, April 6.

"Waifs from Washoe." GE, April 13; June 8.

"How Uncle Bob 'Got' his 'First Injun.'" GE, April 20.

"Little Johnny." GE, May 4.

"How Uncle Bob 'Got' His 'Second Injun.'" GE, May 11.

"Courtship's Perils." GE, June 15; from TE [cf. "The Goblin of the Gate,"
  CFG, August 14, 1863].
"How to See Washoe." * GE, July 27.
"Orthon, the Familiar Spirit; or The Invisible Bride." GE, August 17, 24.
"Lectures on the Five Great Questions by Dr. Gratumdictis, the Wild Phi-
  losopher." GE, December 21, 28.

1863

"From Dan De Quille." CFG, January 9.
"Letter from Dan De Quille." CFG, January 30; April 3; May 29.
"Night Imps." CFG, July 10.
"A Highly 'Colored' Lecture." CFG, July 17.
"Meditations of a Loafer." CFG, July 24.
"A Carniverous Sermon." CFG, July 31.
"War Widows' Tete-a-tete." CFG, August 7.
"The Goblin of the Gate: or The Misadventures of a Night." CFG, August
  14 [cf. GE, June 15, 1862, from TE].
"Strange, Odd and Funny." CFG, August 21.
"Petrified! or the Stewed Chicken Monster." GE, August 30.
"An Ocean Letter. On Board the North Star Sunday Aug 9." CFG, Sep-
  tember 4.
"Let Us be Charitable." CFG, September 18.
"Our Washoe Correspondence." GE, September 20, 27; October 4, 11.
"Is It Tracts We Want?" CFG, September 25.
"A Few Chips." CFG, October 2.
"Don't Put on 'Frills.'" CFG, October 9 [GE, November 29].
"No Head Nor Tail." GE, December 6 (Loomis, Pacific Historical Review).
"Onto the Deep." GE, December 13.

1864

"The Women of the West." GE, January 10; from TE.
"Amung the Seelestials." GE, January 17.
"Lost in the Sierras." GE, March 27; from The Occidental [CFG, July 15; TE,
  August 19, 1877; Alta, October 2, 1877].
"A Promising Mine and a Model Superintendant." GE, April 3; from The
  Occidental.
"Mark Twain and Dan De Quille, Hors de Combat." Co-authored with
  Mark Twain. GE, May 1 (Clemens, 1979) from TE.
"California." GE, July 10 [GE, December 30, 1860].
"Little Lucy's Papa. A Story of Silver-land." GE, July 17 (reprinted 1987).
"How My Quaker Uncle Fixed a Fighting Ram." GE, July 31.
"A Chapter on Cats." GE, September 4; from TE.
"Courting an Emigrant Female." GE, October 2.
"Eloping with a Quakeress." GE, November 6.

1865

"The Baby Crop." GE, January 1; from TE.
"Dan De Quille at the Fair." GE, January 22; from TE.
"A Villainous Outrage." GE, January 29; from TE.
"The Wonder of the Age. A Silver Man." GE, February 5 (ed. Emrich, 1950).
"A Shocking Mistake." GE, February 19; from TE.
"Comfort in Affliction." GE, April 9; from TE.
"The Legend of Pyramid Lake." GE, April 9; from TE.
"Information Given." GE, May 14; from TE.
"Said Smith and Said Jones." GE, June 11; from TE.
"Advice to Sea-Sick Passengers." GE, June 25.
"A Pi-ute Legend." GE, July 9; from TE.
"Great Expectations." GE, July 30.
"Summit City." GE, August 20; from TE.
"Dan De Quille Meets Half-and-Half." GE, October 15; from TE.

1866

"A Trip Among the Mountains." TE, August 12, 14.
"Letter from Excelsior." TE, August 18, 28.
"Letter from Dan De Quille." TE, December 4, 25.

1867

"Letter from Dan De Quille." TE, January 1.
"The Washoe Zephyr." * TE, February 21 [TE, August 12, 1871, November 24, 1874, BB, chap. 35] (ed. Loomis, 1946, no. 24).
"A Bug Mine." * TE, March 26 (ed. Loomis, 1946, no. 4).
"Ever Prospecting—Always Behind." * TE, April 14.
"Our Angels and Our Imps." TE, April 14.
"Munchausen the Second." TE, April 21 (ed. Loomis, 1946, nos. 16–22) (ed. Rawls, 1980, pp. 20–23).
"A Boy's Traveling Experience, or a Night with a Crazy Woman." TE, May 26.
"Traveling Stones." * TE, October 26 [MSP, November 16, 1867; *Antioch Ledger,* July 16, 1870; TE, March 31, 1872, November 11, 1879; BB, ch. 3] (*cf.* ed. Loomis, 1946, no. 1).

1868

"A Singular Kind of Fish." * TE, May 31 (ed. Loomis, 1946, no. 6).
"A Ghost in Ophir." * TE, June 5 (ed. Loomis, 1946, no. 39).
"The Snorer." * TE, June 7.
"The Local Editor—His Duties and Delights." TE, June 28 [TE, January 2, April 9, 1878] (reprinted 1953).
"Trip to Carson." TE, November 28.
"The Washoe Behemoth." * TE, November 29 (ed. Loomis, 1946, no. 23; ed. Emrich, 1950).

1869

"Letter from Donner Lake." TE, July 14.

1870

"Another Joke Pulled Off on Mark Twain." * TE, February 17.
"Mule Gives Birth!" * TE, May 24.
"A Big Injun 'Takes De Gas.'" * TE, May 31.
"A Wonderful Spring." * TE, July 12 (ed. Loomis, 1946, no. 7).
"Mark Twain Should be Here." * TE, August 5.
"The Logsons in Town." * TE, August 5, 9.
"The 'Coming Man' Marries the 'Coming Woman.'" * TE, August 20.
"The Washoe 'Shoe Fly.'" TE, October 14, 28 (ed. Loomis, 1946, no. 8).
"A Haunted House—Ghost with a Waterfall." * TE, December 16 (ed. Loomis, 1946, no. 40).

1871

"An Impromptu Excursion." * TE, January 12.
"In Regard to the Catawba Duck." * TE, June 7.
"Perkins' Ghost Appears to a Bootblack." * TE, July 21 (ed. Loomis, 1946, no. 41).
"Strange Manifestations in Washoe Valley." * TE, July 22 [sequel, TE, July 26, August 11].
"Manufacturing a Giant." * TE, July 30 (ed. Loomis, 1946, no. 9).
"A Melon-Choly Affair." * TE, August 11.
"A Railroad Conductor as a Detective." * TE, August 12.
"Washoe Zephyr." * TE, August 12 [TE, February 21, 1867; November 24, 1874; BB, chap. 35].
"Last of the Great Expeditions. The Mighty Hunters All Dead." * TE, September 6.
"Ringing Rocks and Singing Stones." * TE, October 19 [*Reese River Reveille,* October 23, 1871] (ed. Loomis, 1946, no. 11).
"Description of an Old Mine." * TE, December 10.
"A Window Pane Ghost." * TE, December 15.

1872

"The Old Prospector." * TE, January 23.
"Those Famous Rolling Stones." * TE, March 31 [TE, October 26, 1867, November 11, 1879.]
"Supernatural Occurrences." * TE, November 13.

1873

"The Ghost of the Bell." * TE, March 29 (ed. Loomis, 1946, no. 42).
"Water Excitement." * TE, June 13.
"Tabaskine." * TE, August 10 (ed. Loomis, 1946, no. 12).
"The Old Maid and Her Last Fly. A Case of 'Notional' Insanity." * TE, September 14.

"The Craniometer." * TE, November 2.
"The Ghost of Lower Gold Hill." * TE, November 19.
"Frozen Fish Restored." * TE, December 14 (ed. Loomis, 1946, no. 25).

1874

"Hiring a Fighter." * TE, May 20 [BB].
"The Big Shadow." * TE, May 23 [BB].
"Washoe Zephyr." * TE, June 17 [BB, ch. 35].
"Wanted to be an Actor." * TE, June 23.
"The Fighting Horse of the Stanislaus." * TE, June 28.
"Sad Fate of an Inventor." * ("Solar Armor") TE, July 2 [EX, July 7; "A Mystery Explained." TE, August 30; EX, September 4; *Scientific American,* vol. 31 (July 25, 1874), p. 51] (ed. Loomis, 1946, no. 2; ed. Emrich, 1950).
"The Troubles of John Smith." * TE, July 8 [CFP, February 8, 1886].
"An Unknown Visitor." * TE, July 16 (ed. Loomis, 1946, no. 43).
"Tricks of Washoe Undertakers." * TE, July 16 [BB].
"New Fishing Apparatus." * TE, July 19 (ed. Loomis, 1946, no. 13).
"A Cave of Oblivion." * TE, July 28 [BB].
"How Dat Was?" * TE, July 30.
"A Bit of Babel." * TE, August 7 [BB].
"A Caged Starling." * TE, August 11.
"Uncle Pete on the 'Great Sorrow.'" TE, August 19.
"Wrong Boots." * TE, September 3.
"The Crematorium." * TE, September 5 (ed. Loomis, 1946, no. 14).
"A Strange Monomania." * TE, September 13.
"'Blazer' Finds a Paradise." * TE, September 27 [BB ch. 49]
"What Became of the Bottom of the Well." * TE, October 2 [BB ch. 49].
"Down in a Silver Mine." TE, October 10.
"A Beggar in Luck." * TE, October 11.
"How Old Taggart Died." TE, November 1 [La Porte, Iowa, *Progress*; BB, ch. 49].
"Butter-Mouth Bill." TE, November 8 [TE, September 10, 1882; NYS, July 7, 1886].
"A Hash Fiend." * TE, November 10.
"Has No More Trouble with His Hair." * TE, November 15.
"State Mineralogist. The Duties of the Office Defined." * TE, November 15 [BB].
"Some Washoe Men Have a Baby Adventure." * TE, November 19.
"Terrible Indian Fight." * TE, November 20.
"The New Rock of Horeb or the Physician's Miracle." TE, November 22.
"Amusing Scene." * TE, November 24.
"The Decay of San Francisco. A Horrible Dream." TE, November 26.
"The Eucalyptus." * TE, December 1 (ed. Loomis, 1946, no. 15).
"Marier's Room." TE, December 6.
"Got Out by a Scratch." * TE, December 13.

"The Red Wing, or the Lucky Cruise of a Prairie Schooner." TE, December 20 [American Press Association, 1893].

1875

"McGreggor's New Year." * TE, January 5.
"A Comical Stampede for the Hills." * TE, January 7.
"Pilot Wylie: Life on the Old Massasipp." TE, January 24 (ed. Loomis, *Pacific Historical Review;* Berkove, 1986).
"Diffey's Dog 'Duplex.'" * TE, January 26.
"The Grasshopper and the Bonanza Meet and Telescope." * TE, January 29.
"A Tough Horse Yarn." * TE, January 29 (ed. Loomis, 1946, no. 28).
"Old Sol Winters Makes Himself Known." * TE, February 3 [BB, chap. 49].
"Jim Riddley's Shoes." * TE, February 4 [CFP, February 15, 1886].
"Bonanza Vernacular. 'Ingomar' and 'Jacob Little.' " * TE, February 9.
"The Legend of the Golden Slipper." * TE, February 23.
"Old 'Tuck' Benoit in a Tight Place." * TE, April 18.
"Our Shattered Idols. * TE, April 25.
"A Sketch of Early Times." * TE, June 6, 13, 20 [BB].
"Letter from Dan." TE, June 30; August 6; September 3, 5, 8.
"A City of Steps." * TE, November 16.
"Frightening a 'Snoozer.'" * TE, December 4.
"Piute Jim Gets Mad." * TE, December 4.
"The Lone Honey Lake Boy." * TE, December 5.
"A Female Jumper." * TE, December 11.
"The Blood Bath. A New Cure for Paralysis." * TE, December 19.
"Another Columbus." * TE, December 19.
"Spoaker's Serenade." * TE, December 26 [EX, March 25, 1888].

1876

"The Boss Snorer." * TE, January 1.
"How McDugan was Surprised." * TE, January 2.
"Out of the Wilderness." TE, January 9.
"Mary Jane Simpson." * TE, January 23.
"The Goblin Frog." TE, January 30 [McClure Syndicate, November 1885; EX, April 22, 1888].
"One of the Lost." * TE, February 6.
"Didn't Want Work." * TE, February 9.
"Snowshoe Thompson." TE, February 13 [Alta, February 20, 1876; Sacramento *Record-Union,* November 1885; OM, October 1886].
"The 'Peep-Stone.'" TE, February 16.
"The Wreck of a Stern Endeavor." * TE, February 18.
"Ah Ki." TE, February 20 [NYS, February 28, 1886].
"Chispa." TE, February 27.
"Old Jack Meets with a Mishap." * TE, March 9.
"Stillwater Poker." * TE, March 12.

"The Frenchman and His Fiddle." * TE, April 20.
"'Sorry' and 'Grieve.'" TE, May 16 [sequel, June 24].

1877

"The Legend of Donner Lake." * TE, February 4.
"An Untold Tale." * TE, March 17.
"The Nameless." * TE, April 1.
"A Strange Story." * TE, April 12 [BB, 1876].
"Shearing a Camel." * TE, June 17.
"A Little Tough." * TE, June 28 (ed. Loomis, 1946, no. 29).
"Bob and His Squaw." * TE, July 7.
"The Fiend Gymnasticus." * TE, July 7.
"A Robber Story." * TE, July 8.
"Under Difficulties. The Ways of Jerry and Jonas." * TE, July 8.
"Stealing from Himself." * TE, July 13.
"Norah McKee." * TE, July 14.
"In the Midst of a Cave." * TE, July 22.
"The Cat and the Bees." * TE, July 28.
"Flam Storm." TE, July 29 [Lorborn Syndicate, April 1887].
"New Mown Hay." * TE, August 3.
"Moosic! A Carnival of Chinese Dead." TE, August 5 [Alta, August 17, 1877].
"He Kissed Her." * TE, August 7.
"A Sazeracist." * TE, August 7 (ed. Loomis, 1946, no. 30).
"Mrs. Walkinshaw's Baby." * TE, August 9.
"A Shea Tartar." * TE, August 11.
"Duck in the Box." * TE, August 11.
"Hunted Down and Lifted Up." * TE, August 16.
"Out of the Frying Pan Into the Fire." * TE, August 19.
"Lost in the Sierras. The Gold-Hunter's Fate." TE, August 19 [GE, March 27, 1864; CFG, July 15, 1864; Alta, October 2, 1877].
"The Joss House." * TE, August 22.
"Sh-h-h-h." * TE, August 26.
"Rev. Olympus Jump. The Mountain Howitzer of God." TE, August 26 [Argo, September 8; EX, April 1, 1888].
"Baddy Fooled." * TE, August 31.
"The Child and the Star." TE, September 2.
"Twenty Years After." * TE, September 5.
"Sunday Frivolities: Tough; 'Woolwich' on Moons; War on the Zodiac; etc." TE, September 16.
"Thrilling Wildcat Adventure." * TE, September 22.
"Sunday Frivolities: Ruined by a Ghost; An Ex-Granger; A Thriving Place; Our Old Settlers (ed. Loomis, 1946, no. 32); An Unsatisfactory Experiment (ed. Loomis, 1946, no. 33)." TE, September 23.
"A Musical Mountain." * TE, September 26.
"A Ghostly Lecture." * TE, September 28.

"Sunday Frivolities: A Mormon Novel; Comstock Turks; A Bit of Volatility; etc." TE, September 30.

"The Village of 'Lo.'" * TE, October 6.

"Sunday Frivolities: Fried Onions ["Driven from the Field" NYS, 1885]; Burial of A Sazerac (ed. Loomis, 1946, no. 31); etc." TE, October 7.

"Sunday Whims and Frivolities: Torture Unutterable." TE, October 14.

"Sunday Whims and Frivolities: The Wolf and the Wild Hogs; The Repentant Passenger; Not a Judge." TE, October 21.

"Sunday Whims and Frivolities: The Flowery Ghost; Arizona Steaks (ed. Loomis, 1946, no. 34)." TE, October 28.

"The Two Goats—an Allegory." * TE, October 31.

"Sunday Whims and Frivolities: The Musical Coffin [SLT clipping 1889]; A Hot 'Cold Deck' [NYS clipping, May 1885]." TE, November 4.

"Sunday Whims and Frivolities: The Telephone; Ruined by an Explosion; Neuralgia [CFL, November 9, 1885] etc." TE, November 11.

"Sunday Whims and Frivolities: Old Johnny Ranchero; Among the 'Old Boys'; An Accommodating Witness. etc." TE, November 18.

"Sunday Whims and Frivolities: Pere Barometre and Mons. Rosbiff [NYS, September 12, 1886]; Self-Examination; A Miner's Welcome; An Amazed Piute; Mines That Have Never Been Found." TE, November 25.

"Sam Davis's Pumpkin." * TE, November 28.

"Sunday Whims and Frivolities: The Lost Diamond; Josh and His Friends; A Persistent Scribe; Lost His Turkey. etc." TE, December 2 [TE, December 8].

"Tom Colette's Bath." * TE, December 2.

"A Christmas Story: Under the Ice." TE, December 25 [SLT, February 14, 1886] (ed. Loomis, 1946, no. 35).

"A Startling Experience." * TE, December 30.

1878

"Uncle Pete on His Last Legs." TE, January 1.

"About Jones' Great Toe." * TE, January 2 [TE, June 28, 1868].

"The Daft Watchman." * TE, January 9.

"A Chinese Wedding." * TE, January 12.

"He Didn't Cough." * TE, January 13.

"A Piute Penitent." * TE, February 13.

"Old Time Winter Evenings." * TE, February 15.

"Sook Tine Kishwund. A Wonderful Nevada Cave." TE, February 24.

"Queer Bonanzas." * TE, March 8.

"Goat Plaster." * TE, March 21.

"Cured of It." * TE, March 29.

"What Fun a 'Local' Has." * TE, April 9 [TE, June 28, 1868].

"Angry Wives of Virginia." TE, April 11 ["A Red Hair." SLT, April 18, 1886].

"The Earth Never Dies." TE, April 18.

"The Pelicans of San Diego." Argo, April 20 [SLT, March 28, 1886].
"Mark Twin's Cabin At Aurora." TE, April 24 [CFL, December 21, 1885].
"Sleepy Pete. He Communes with Big Horn Smith." * TE, June 6.
"Dem Boots." * TE, June 7.
"How Oysters Talk." Argo, June 15.
"Our Bearded Indian." * TE, June 18.
"Prospecting for Rural Beauties." * TE, June 18.
"A Ghost in a Tenement House." * TE, June 29.
"A Book Agent Who Never Bothers." * TE, June 30.
"Old Tunneling Pete." * TE, September 29.
"Mrs. Bower's Peep Stone." * TE, October 6.
"Stocks Did It." * TE, October 11.
"Waking Dreams and Sleeping Portents." * TE, December 4.
"The Doings of the Hayseed Family." * TE, December 31.

1879

"Those 'Traveling Stones'—We Throw Up the Sponge." TE, November 11
   [TE, October 26, 1867, March 31, 1872; BB, chap. 3] (ed. Loomis, 1946,
   no. 1).

1880

"Was It Cold in Como?" TE, January 2 (ed. Loomis, 1946, no. 44).
"A Dantziger's Revenge." NM, February.
"Big Bill Scuffles." NM, March (ed. Emrich, 1950).
"The Monarch of the Cliffs." NM, May.
"Bob Kemble's Sisters." NM, June.
"A Legend of the Sierras: The Gnomes of the Dead Rivers." NM, August,
   "To be continued."
"A Smart Boy." * TE, December 26.

1881

"Journalists Roughing It." In Myron Angel, ed. History of Nevada, pp. 319–
   21.

1882

"Out to the Front. The Carson and Colorado Railroad." TE, September 3.
"Foot-loose. Random Jottings of Men and Things." TE, September 5.
"Jim Townsend's Brooms." TE, September 8.
"Butter-mouth Bill. His Torture in a Dream." TE, September 10 [TE,
   November 8, 1874; NYS, July 7, 1886].

1883

"We Had the First Shave." Truckee Republican, April 18 [Reno Gazette,
   April 18].
"A Mountain Cayman." TE, August 30.
"Phantom Fleas. The Shadows on a Wall." TE, October 7.

1884

"Nevada." In *Encyclopedia Britannica*, 10th ed.

"Old Owley and Little Geese." *San Franciscan*, March 22.

1885

"An Olla Podrida." SLT, February 22.

"Old Time Gold Delvers. Mark Twain's Experience as a Pocket Miner." Alta, March 22.

"Staging in the Early Days." Alta, April WWP clipping.

"Die Gruene Ganse." SLT, April 5—weekly through December.

"The Comstock Vein." Alta, May 30.

"A Hot Cold Deck." NYS, May WWP clipping [TE, November 4, 1877].

"The Scholarly Tramp." NYS, June 21.

"John Levining's Vision." SLT, July 12 [GE, April 14, 1861].

"The Old Sierra Nevada 'Boom.'" CFL, August 24.

"Bumble and Rumble; The Bat." CFL, September 7.

"About Cats." CFL, September 14.

"Death in Masses." SLT, September 20.

"A Shaft Adventure." CFL, September 21.

"Amoor Gold Mines." SLT, October 4.

"Escape of the Canary Bird." CFL, October 5.

"The Boss Butler." SLT, October 11.

"Blood on the Mountains." CFL, October 12 (*Nevada Historical Society Quarterly,* Fall, 1984).

"Piute Astronomy." SLT, October 18.

"The Comstock." SLT, October 25.

"Comstock Spice." SLT, November 1.

"Tales of Timber." CFL, November 2.

"Quille Drops: Di Wrong Suit, Boss." CFL, November 2.

"Prosperity Anew." SLT, November 8.

"The Home 'Under the Star.'" NYS, November 9.

"A Tough Pair. The Miner and the Pill Peddler." CFL, November 9.

"Neuralgia. A Diagonal Diagnosis." CFL, November 9 [TE, November 11, 1877].

"Done Cotch Him!" *Wasp*, November 14.

"Comstock Kinks." SLT, November 15, 25.

"Quille Drops: a Table Leg Worth $1,000." CFL, November 16.

"Mark Twain's Old Partner Writes of the Queer Things on the Comstock." Cincinnati *Enquirer*, November 22.

"Vive la Crinoline." CFL, November 23.

"The Frenchman's Ghost. The Story of a Lost Mine." SFP, November 28.

"Quille Drops: The World Too Much Improved." CFL, November 30.

"Snowshoe Thompson." Sacramento *Record-Union*, November [TE, February 13, 1876; OM, October 1886].

"The Amateur Horse-Tamers." *Maverick,* November WWP clipping.

"Button Family." NYS, November.

"The Goblin Frog." McClure Syndicate, November [TE, January 30, 1876; EX, April 22, 1888].

"The Bad Man of the Hills; Uncle Billy Forgets Himself." CFL, December 7.

"Quille Drops: Mark Twain's Cabin at Aurora." CFL, December 21.

"Bendix Briaro [sic] and His Three Sisters." Sacramento Bee, December 24.

"In the High Sierras." Cincinnati Enquirer, December 27.

"Quille Drops: a Turkey Raffle." CFL, December 28.

"He Had to Stay." NYS, December 30.

"A Marital Lesson." New York Weekly(?), WWP clipping, n.d.

"Menagerie." Cincinnati Enquirer, December [Maverick January 23, 1886].

"Driven From the Field." NYS, WWP clipping, n.d. ["Fried Onions" TE, October 7, 1877].

"Chispa Charley." WWP clipping dated 1885 [cf. NM, March 1880].

1886

"Comstock Jottings." SLT, January 2.

"Comstock Kinks." SLT, January 3, 10.

"About Horns." CFL, January 4.

"Quille Drops." CFL, January 4, 11.

"Little Hello." New York Weekly, January 9 [SFC, October 6, 1895].

"Uncle Jeff and Aunt Dinah." SLT, January 17.

"Quille Drops: Pilgarlic's Dream." CFL, January 18.

"The Menagerie." Maverick, January 23 [Cincinnati Enquirer, December 1885].

"Comstock Christmas Croppings." NYS, January 24.

"Queer Comstock Kinks." SLT, January 24.

"Quille Drops: a Malachite." CFL, January 25.

"Jim Sparks 'of Plumas.'" Maverick, January [from New York Weekly].

"Nigger Sermon." SFP, January.

"Retailing a House." SFP, January.

"Quille Drops: the Last Man gets Mad." CFL, February 1.

"A Family Mine." West Liberty, Iowa Enterprise, February 4 [from TE].

"Quille Drops: Tribulations of John Smith." CFL, February 8 [TE, July 8, 1874].

"The Mountains." West Liberty, Iowa Enterprise, February 11.

"Under the Ice." SLT, February 14 [TE, December 25, 1877].

"Dem Alligator Shoes." CFL, February 15 [TE, February 4, 1875].

"How John McCullough Put an Army to Flight." CFL, February 22.

"A Remarkable Chinaman." NYS, February 28 ["Ah Ki" in TE, February 20, 1876].

"Poisons Old and New." SLT, February 28.

"Quille Drops: The Gold Bugs." CFL, March 1.

"An American Lord." SLT, March 7.

"Quille Drops: on Travel." CFL, March 8.

"Some Comstock Kinks." SLT, March 14.

"Quille Drops: Beeswax and Candles." CFL, March 15.

"The Obeah-Man." SLT, March 21.

"Quille Drops: The Man with the Tail; The Mountains." CFL, March 22.

"San Diego Pelicans." SLT, March 28 [Argo, April 20, 1878].

"Quille Drops: Aboriginal Cremationists." CFL, March 29.

"Quille Drops: Liverpool Bill." CFL, April 12 [SFP].

"A Red Hair." SLT, April 18 [TE, April 11, 1878].

"Quille Drops: The Old Forty-Niner." CFL, April 19.

"Holy Easter Day." SLT, April 25.

"Quille Drops; Drivelings of an Amateur Idiot." CFL, April 26.

"Dreamland Excursions." SLT, May 2.

"Some Random Dashes." SLT, May 9.

"More Random Dashes." SLT, June 13.

"Quille Drops: the Coming Barnum." CFL, June 14.

"Quille's Random Dashes." SLT, June 20; July 4, 11.

"The Fall of Aerolites." SLT, July 6.

"Buttermouth Bill." NYS, July 7 [TE, November 8, 1874, September 10, 1882; CH, November 1886].

"A Frontier Bishop." SFP, July 17.

"New Zealand's Terror." SLT, July 25.

"Irrigation Works." SLT, August 8.

"A Shot at the Cats." NYS, September 12 [TE, November 25, 1877].

"Other Random Notes." SLT, September 19.

"Buckeye Memories." SLT, September 26.

"Snowshoe Thompson." OM, 8 (October), pp. 419–35 [TE, February 13, 1876; Sacramento *Record-Union,* November 1885] (*Sierra Club Bulletin* [February 1935] pp. 8–19; edition with preface by C. D. Hall, 1954; ed. Emrich, 1950).

"Notes From Nevada." SLT, October 3.

"Dan De Quillisms." SLT, October 6.

"Ancient Signal Fires." SLT, October 17.

"Blood on the Moon." CFL, November 1.

"Earth's Mad Monarchs." SLT, November 7.

"About Human Noses." SLT, November 14.

"Islamism on the Comstock." SLT, November 21.

"More Comstock Notes." SLT, November 28.   ·

"Tongue-Oil Timothy Dead." CH(?), November WWP clipping [TE, November 8, 1874, September 10, 1882; NYS, July 7, 1886].

"Dan De Quillets." SLT, December 5.

"Comstock Matters." SLT, December 12.

"Random Dashes." SLT, December 19.

"Uncle Pete and Little Benny, A Christmas Story." *New York Weekly*(?), WWP clipping, n.d.

1887

"More Random Jottings." SLT, January 9.
"Comstock Memories." SLT, January 16.
"Freaks of the Earth." SLT, February 27.
"The Green Dragon of the Plains." NYS, February 27.
"Wildcat Joe." TE, March 6.
"The Perils of the High Sierras." OM, 9 (March), pp. 311–22.
"Comstock Jottings." SLT, March 13.
"Elam Storm." Lorborn Syndicate, April [TE, July 29, 1877].
"The Haunted City of the Sierra Madre." Lorborn Syndicate, June, WWP clipping.
"A Hoosier's Love Story. Elicited by the Mysterious Miss Dwyer." NYS, June 30.
"A Haunted Mine." EX, November 27.
"Los Angeles Railroad." SLT, December 4.
"A Brave Knocked Out." EX, December 18.

1888

"The Seven Nimrods of the Sierras." OM, 11 (January) pp. 60–72.
"Death Valley. The Strange Region Known as the American Thirstland." EX, January 29.
"Pony Express." Lorborn Syndicate, January [from TE].
"Isthmian Sports." EX, February 5.
"Artemus Ward: His Great Definition of Genius as Confided to Mark Twain." EX, February 26.
"Wind Puddings." EX, March 11.
"A Female World-Ranger." EX, March 11.
"Notes from Silverland." SLT, March 18; July 26; August 12; November 18; December 16, 23.
"Spoaker's Serenade." EX, March 25 [TE, December 26, 1875].
"Hair-Breadth Escapes." McClure Syndicate, March.
"Rev. Olympus Jump. The Mountain Howitzer of God and His Good Works." EX, April 1 [TE, August 26, 1877; Argo, September 8, 1877].
"A Goblin Frog." EX, April 22 [TE, January 30, 1876; McClure Syndicate, November 1885].
"Saga of Comstock." SLT, May 13.
"Our Land and Peoples." SLT, September 9.
"Urging Water Storage." SLT, September 23.
"Our Big Arid Region." SLT, September 30.
"Old Eden Luders." EX, September WWP clipping.
"He Had to Call." NYS, December 3.

1889

"The Flute Player of the Plains." SLT, January 1.
"The Sun's Total Eclipse." SLT, January 13.

"How I Write My Novels." SLT, January WWP clipping.

"Ships of the Desert." SLT, February WWP clipping.

"The Great Arid Zone." SLT, February.

"A Land Worth Capture." SLT, March 3.

"Some Shots on the Wing." SLT, March 10.

"Odd Sticks of Ohio." Fredericktown, Ohio, *Free Press* April 18, 25 [from SLT].

"Fisher Folk." SLT, April 21.

"Our Isthmian Games." SLT, May 5.

"Sage of the Comstock." SLT, May 13.

"Notes on Going Events." SLT, June 9.

"Gravitation, Weight." SLT, June 16.

"Some Random Jottings." SLT, June 23.

"The Stone Elephant of Inyo." OM, 14 (August), pp. 113–17.

"In the Great Basin." SLT, August WWP clipping.

"The Island of Navassa." SLT, October 21.

"Nevada Water Storage." SLT, November 3.

"Free Coinage and Mines." SLT, December 15.

"Long-Haired Sam." CH, WWP clipping, n.d.

"The Musical Coffin." SLT, WWP clipping [TE, November 4, 1877].

1890

"An American Miner in Mexico." OM, 15 (January), pp. 34–45, (February), pp. 145–56.

"Nevada 1889–90." SLT, January 12.

"Mining Aphorisms." Hood River, Oregon, *Times,* February 10.

"Let the People Awake." SLT, February 16.

"Money of the People." SLT, February 23.

"Notes from Nevada." SLT, March 2, May 11.

"A Home Metallic Currency." SLT, March 9.

"Looking Backward." SLT, March 30.

"The Industries of America." SLT, March WWP clipping.

"America's Greedy Miners." SLT, April 27.

"The Real Party in Power." SLT, May 4.

"Highly Protected Gold." SLT, July 2.

"Mysterious Diablery." SLT, August 24.

"Jottings from Silverland: The Indian Messiah." SLT, September 13, December WWP clipping.

"Nevada Wonders." CH, November 30.

"Lady Franklin in Washoe." EX(?), November WWP clipping.

1891

"The Big Nevada Nugget." SLT, January 1.

"Luck: a Prospector Strikes a Queer Streak." OM, 17 (February), pp. 165–76.

"The Eagle's Nest." OM, 17 (May), pp. 535–45.

"The Demon Hand." Louisville *Courier-Journal,* June 1.

"A Cat-Haunted Frenchman." SLT, June 14.

"A Search for Solitude." SLT, August 22.

"Indian Rain Maker." SLT, September 27.

"An Indian Trick." CH, October 18.

"The Prospector." EMJ, 52 (November 7) p. 528.

"The Old California Prospector." EMJ, 52 (November 14) pp. 567–68.

"Natural and Supernatural." SLT, November 15.

"The Epoch of Silver." EMJ, 52 (November 28) pp. 615–16.

"Great Bear of the North." SLT, November 29.

"Land of Sage and Silver." SLT, November WWP clipping.

"The Discovery of the Comstock Lode." EMJ, 52 (December 5) pp. 637–38.

"Comstock as a Mining Superintendant." EMJ, 52 (December 19) pp. 700–701.

1892

"The Silver Miner of the Comstock." EMJ, 53 (January 9) pp. 84–85.

"The Story of a Lost Child." SLT, January 14.

"Discoverers of the Comstock Lode." EMJ, 53 (January 16) p. 112.

"Old Times on the Prairies." SLT, January 24.

"An Aerial Vortex." *Inyo Index,* February 10.

"About Aerial Navigation." SLT, February 14.

"The Grosh Brothers—a Mysterious Pair." EMJ, 53 (February 27) pp. 254–55 [BB, chap. 3].

"Undesirable Thriftiness." SLT, March 6.

"The Boss Rain-Maker." CH, April 10.

"Secret Process for Working Comstock Ore." EMJ, 53 (May 21) pp. 544–45.

"Old Boys Looking Back." SLT, May WWP clipping.

"The Tricks of Miners." EMJ, 53 (June 11) pp. 618–19.

"Do Brutes and Birds Talk?" SLT, June 12.

"The Sheep of the Incas." SLT, August 7.

"Early Mining Operations on the Comstock." EMJ, 54 (August 13) p. 152.

"Some Topics of the Times." SLT, August 21.

"Within the Silver State." SLT, August 28.

"A Thief's Punishment." CH, September 4.

"The Rats of the 'Lower Levels'." EMJ, 54 (September 24) p. 300 [BB, chap. 45].

"On Infectious Diseases." SLT, September 25.

"Camels in the Mines." *Mining Industry & Tradesman* vol. 11 (October 6), p. 16; (*New Mexico Historical Review*, vol. 24 [January 1949], pp. 54–61).

"Superstitions on Birds." SLT, October 20.

"Curiosities of Memory." SLT, October 26.

"Promising Prospecting Enterprise on the Comstock." EMJ, 54 (November 12) pp. 463–64.

"Superstitions About Cats." SLT, November 20.

"Nevada Mines and Product." SLT, November 27.

"The 'Minx.' The Romance of a Typewriter." SLT, December 25.

"Bill Lowden's Ride." SFP, WWP clipping, n.d.

"The Black Mountaineer." American Press Association [Huntington, Indiana *Evening Herald,* February 7–8, 1893].

"Three Natives of Pike." American Press Association, n.d.

1893

"The Passing of a Pioneer." EX, January 22 (ed. Lewis, 1971).

"The Old 'Gold Lake' Story." SLT, January 29.

"The Black Mountaineer." Huntington, Indiana *Evening Herald,* February 7–8 [American Press Association, 1892].

"An Old Comstock Dodge." EMJ, 55 (February 11) p. 126.

"Lorenzo Dow's Miracle." EX, February 12.

"A Brief Golden Dream." EMJ, 55 (February 18) p. 150.

"Salad Days of Mark Twain." EX, March 19 (ed. Lewis, 1971).

"Peter Crow Among the Witches." CIM, 3 (April) pp. 643–49.

"Silverland Lamentations." SLT, May 7.

"Springtime in Nevada." SLT, May 28.

"'Big Jim' Cartter is Dead." EX, May 30 [BB, chap. 50].

"The Death Blow to Silver." SLT, July 9.

"The Rule of the Wreckers." SLT, July 16.

"Reporting with Mark Twain." CIM, 4 (July), pp. 170–78.

"Spirit of the Rock." CH, July 30.

"Free Coinage, Free Money." SLT, August 13.

"Bricks Without Straw." SLT, August 20.

"The Masses a Commodity." SLT, August 27.

"Artemus Ward in Nevada." CIM, 4 (August) pp. 403–6.

"Gunning for Market." CH, September 2.

"Hunting Amid Tules." CH, September 9.

"A Gander Pulling." CH, September 16 [GE, December 29, 1861].

"We're On the Ragged Edge." SLT, September 17.

"Copper Mines of Nevada." SLT, October WWP clipping.

"Points for Miners." CH, November 5.

"Under Wall Street's Rule." SLT, November 12.

"The Rich to be Made Richer." SLT, November 25.

"The Credit of the Nation." SLT, December 3.

"The Shylock Curse of the World." SLT, December 24.

"Importing an Ancestor." American Press Association clipping, n.d.

"The Red Wing." American Press Association [TE, December 20, 1874].

1894

"The Repeal of the Sherman Law." SLT, January 7.

"A False Set of Values." SLT, January 13.

"As to Honest Money." SLT, January 20.

"The Promised Shylock Prosperity." SLT, February 10.

"To Restore Old Prosperity." SLT, February 11.

"Wall Street Comes Up Groggy." SLT, February 17.
"Money That Robs the Many." SLT, March 5.
"The Suffering Unemployed Workers." SLT, March WWP clipping.
"The Proposed New Departure." SLT, April 27.
"The Great Commercial Depression." SLT, May 6.
"About the Divining Rod." SLT, June 17.
"Paradise for Nimrods." SLT, September 9.
"The Lost Seal Island." SLT, October WWP clipping.
"Ben Kent of Kern." SFC, November 25.
"Spooks of the High Trails." SFC, December 23.

1895

"Maroney's Last Shot." CH, January 13.
"The Black Dog of the Bend." SFC, May 19.
"An Indian Story of the Sierra Madre." *Cosmopolitan,* 19 (June) pp. 180–95.
"The Gold Belts of Nevada." EMJ, 59 (June 8) pp. 532–33.
"Death Valley." *Mining Industry & Tradesman,* June 13.
"The New Comstock Enterprise." EMJ, 60 (July 6) p. 3.
"Mineral-Bearing Veins." SLT, August 5.
"Little Tum Tum of Barton's Bar." SFC, October 6 [*New York Weekly,* January 9, 1886, WWP clipping].
"Millions in Gold Beneath the Lava Flows." EMJ, 60 (December 7) pp. 537 38.

1896

"World on the Warpath." SLT, January 17.
"The World's Greatest Goldfield." MSP, 72 (January 25) p. 66.
"The Opening Up of Our Big Goldfield." EMJ, 61 (June 6) p. 541.
"The Geological Age of Gold." EMJ, 62 (July 18) p. 54.
"A Gold-Paved Valley." MSP, 73 (August 8) p. 108.
"Meteorites and Meteoric Showers." SLT, August 13.

1897

"The Copper Mines of Nevada." MSP, 74 (January 23) p. 70.
"A Combat with Tigers." SFC, May 16.
"The Divining Rod." *Mining Industry & Tradesman.*
"Tricks and Humors of Miners." *Mining Industry & Tradesman.* September 15.
"The Typical Prospector." *Mining Industry & Tradesman.*

UNDATED CLIPPINGS

"Billy Clist and the Cook." *
"A Call. The Man Who Never Bores One." * TE.
"The Dogs of War Turn Themselves Loose." SLT.
"The Durndest Knowingest Dog That Ever Wore Hair." * TE.

"He Kissed the Blackberry Girl." NYS.

"The Nevada Camels." CH.

"Poor Bob." WWP clipping. *

"Quille Drops: Fishing for Suckers; The Old Forty-Niner; The Chinese at Home; The Rara Avis & The Acrobat." CFL.

"A Ring-Tailed Robber." CFL.

"Uncle Abe Praeter's Hunting Cat." NYS.